BRITAIN WITHIN THE EUROPEAN COMMUNITY

Also by Ali M. El-Agraa

THE ECONOMICS OF THE EUROPEAN COMMUNITY
(*editor*)
THEORY OF CUSTOMS UNIONS (*with A. J. Jones*)
INTERNATIONAL ECONOMIC INTEGRATION (*editor*)
THE THEORY OF INTERNATIONAL TRADE
TRADE THEORY AND POLICY: Some Topical Issues

BRITAIN WITHIN THE EUROPEAN COMMUNITY
The Way Forward

Edited by

Ali M. El-Agraa
University of Leeds

90222

First published 1983 by
THE MACMILLAN PRESS LTD
London and Basingstoke
Companies and representatives
throughout the world

ISBN 0 333 34523 1 (hardcover)
ISBN 0 333 35841 4 (paperback)

Printed in Great Britain by
Camelot Press
Southampton

To Frances, Mark and Diana

Contents

Preface and Acknowledgements

The aims of this book are : to explain the major areas in
which the European Community (EC) plays a role in decision-
making or where it will be expected to play an active part
when the integrative process is further advanced; to
identify the costs and benefits of each policy,
particularly for the United Kingdom; and to propose
feasible ways in which the policies could be adapted to
suit British conditions without imposing undue constraints
on the rest of the EC. It is therefore implicit that the
contributors see the EC as an evolving institution,
irrevocable membership of which confers the ability to play
an active role in its development. Hence the emphasis in
the book is on the way forward. Of course, it is intended
that the book should be seen as a positive contribution to
the current debate on whether or not Britain should remain
within the EC; that is why all the contributors are British
and are, therefore, personally involved.

The book contains sixteen chapters which are grouped in
four basic parts. Part I is general and consists of two
chapters : chapter 2, by John Pinder, director of the
Policy Studies Institute, on the history, politics and
institutions of the EC; and chapter 3, by Stephen Holt,
professor of European Studies at the University of Kent, on
membership of the EC and its alternatives. Part II, which
comprises three chapters, is devoted to the theoretical
dimensions of the 'common market' aspects of the EC :
chapter 4, written by myself, gives a broad review of the
theory of customs unions; chapter 5, by Anthony Jones,
lecturer in economics at the University of Leeds, uses a
macroeconomic framework to analyse the implications for the
UK of withdrawal from the EC; and chapter 6, by Dr. David
Mayes, chief statistician at the National Economic
Development Office and ex-editor of NIESR Review, discusses
the empirical data relating to trade and factor mobility.
Part III, consisting of 5 chapters, is devoted to the
microeconomic policies of the EC : chapter 7 by

Dr. Alan Butt Philip, lecturer in the politics of the EC at the Centre for European Industrial Studies, University of Bath, is on EC competition and industrial policies; chapter 8, by myself, looks at the true cost of the Common Agricultural Policy;   chapter 9, by Kenneth Gwilliam, professor of transport economics at the University of Leeds, examines the future of EC transport policy; chapter 10, by professor David Pearce and Richard Westoby of the department of political economy at the University of Aberdeen, deals with EC energy policy; and chapter 11, by Dr. Doreen Collins, senior lecturer in social policy and administration at the University of Leeds, is on EC social policy. The macroeconomic policies of the EC are discussed in four chapters in Part IV : EC fiscal policy is tackled in chapter 12 by myself; Britain's options within EC monetary arrangements in chapter 13 by professor David Llewellyn of Loughborough University; the assignment of regional policy powers in chapter 14 by Harvey Armstrong, lecturer in economics at the University of Lancaster; and an EC defence policy in chapter 15 by Dr. Keith Hartley, reader in economics, University of York. The book contains an Introduction with an appendix on basic statistics and a concluding chapter which brings together information directly relevant to discussion of whether or not UK membership of the Community has been an 'unmitigated disaster'.

Of course, this book could not have taken its present form without the co-operation of my distinguished contributors who are all outstanding authorities in their specialist area. I wish to record my appreciation to all of them for making the book possible.

Finally, I should like to thank Mrs. Christine Loker of Harrogate for her excellent typing of the final manuscript and Mrs. Margaret Mann, my secretary, for her typing assistance with earlier drafts of the book.

Leeds   Ali M. El-Agraa

Notes on the Contributors

Harvey W. Armstrong is Lecturer in Economics at the University of Lancaster. He was previously Lecturer in Economics at the University of Loughborough (1970-73) and Visiting Associate Professor at the University of British Columbia (1969-70). He has published articles in the fields of European Community regional policy, regional unemployment, and transport economics. His publications also include (as co-author with J. Taylor) Regional Economic Policy and Its Analysis (1978).

Alan Butt Philip lectures at the Centre for European Industrial Studies, Bath University, specialising in the politics of the European Community. He is the author of The Welsh Question (1975) and co-author of Capital Markets and Industrial Investment in Germany and France (1980). He has published articles in academic books and journals on regionalism, EC harmonisation, EC pressure groups and European financial integration. Since 1980 he has been special adviser on regional policy to the House of Lords Select Committee on the European Communities.

Dr. C. Doreen E. Collins is Senior Lecturer in the Department of Social Policy and Administration, University of Leeds. She is chiefly concerned with studies of the European Community and of social policy in Western European states. She is the author of The European Communities: The Social Policy of the First Phase (1975) and numerous recent articles on the social policy of the EC. She is currently working on a comparative study of social policy in selected industrial nations.

Ali M. El-Agraa is Senior Lecturer in Economics, School of Economic Studies, University of Leeds. He was Senior Research Officer (1964-7) and Lecturer in Economics (1967-71), Faculty of Economic and Social Studies, University of Khartoum, and was also Economic Adviser to the Ministry of

xv

Finance and Economics, Khartoum, between 1967 and 1968. He
has published several journal articles and numerous
discussion papers. He is editor of The Economics of the
European Community (1980), co-author (with A.J. Jones) of
Theory of Customs Unions (1981); editor of International
Economic Integration (1982); author of Theory of
International Trade (forthcoming, 1983); and author of
Trade Theory and Policy : Some Topical Issues (forthcoming,
1983).

Kenneth M. Gwilliam is Professor of Transport Economics at
the University of Leeds. He has previously held posts at
the Universities of Nottingham and East Anglia. He is joint
editor of the Journal of Transport Economics and Policy and
is author of: Transport and Public Policy (1964); The
Economics of Transport Policy (1975) (with P.J. Mackie);
and A Comparative Study of European Rail Performance (1979)
(with C.A. Nash et al). He has been an expert advisor to
the Transport Directorate of the EC and has recently
completed a study for them on transport research needs for
the Community. He is presently a Director of the National
Bus Company.

Keith Hartley is Reader in Economics and Director of IESR
and IRISS, University of York. He was Visiting Associate
Professor, University of Illinois, USA (1974); a NATO
Research Fellow (1977) and in 1980 he received a Duke
University-Rand award for developing case study materials
(on joint aerospace projects) for US postgraduate policy
study courses. He has been a consultant to various
government agencies in Eire, EC, UK and the USA. In
addition to numerous articles in academic journals, his
books include NATO Arms Co-operation (1983), The
Collaboration of Nations (with D. Dosser and D. Gowland,
1982), Micro-economic Policy (with C. Tisdell, 1981),
Problems of Economic Policy (1977) and Export Performance
and the Pressure of Demand (with R. Cooper and C. Harvey,
1970).

Stephen C. Holt is Professor of European Studies at the
University of Kent at Canterbury and held the same position
at the University of Bradford from 1970 to 1980. He was
Chairman of the University Association for Contemporary
European Studies (1980-83) and is a member of the Editorial
Board of the Journal of Common Market Studies. His
publications include: The Common Market: the conflict of
theory and practice (1967); Six European States: the
countries of the European Community and their political

systems (1970); and co-author (with J.E. Farquharson) of Europe from Below: an assessment of Franco-German popular contacts (1975). He has more recently been working on the problems of the British contribution to the EC Budget and made two submissions to the House of Lords Select Committee on the European Communities in 1979.

Anthony J. Jones is Lecturer in Economics, School of Economic Studies, University of Leeds. He is author of a number of articles on theoretical aspects of regional economic integration and co-author (with A.M. El-Agraa) of Theory of Customs Unions (1981).

David T. Llewellyn is Professor of Money and Banking and Head of the Economics department at Loughborough University. He was previously an economist at the International Monetary Fund and at H.M. Treasury. He is the author of International Financial Integration (1980), and co-author of The Framework of UK Monetary Policy (1982).

David G. Mayes is the Chief Statistician at the National Economic Development Office and Honorary Research Fellow at the University of Exeter. He was previously Editor of the National Institute Economic Review, and Senior Lecturer in Economics and Social Statistics at the University of Exeter. He has also held a visiting chair in the Netherlands and is an editor of the Economic Journal. He has publications in many journals, and is author of The Property Boom: The Effects of Building Society Behaviour on House Prices (1979); Introductory Economic Statistics (with A.C. Mayes, 1976); Projects in Economic and Social Statistics (editor, 1976, 1978) 2 vols.; Applications of Econometrics (1981); and Modern Portfolio Theory and Financial Institutions (with D.C. Corner, 1982).

David W. Pearce is Professor of Political Economy at the University of Aberdeen. He has taught at the Universities of Lancaster, Southampton, Leicester in the UK and at Adelaide and Flinders Universities in Australia. He is the author of more than a dozen books, including Cost Benefit Analysis '(1971), Environmental Economics (1976), Social Projects Appraisal (with C.A. Nash, 1981) and is currently completing a monograph for the International Labour Organisation on the impact of rising energy prices on the Egyptian economy. He has been a consultant to the Environment Directorate of OECD (Paris), the International Labour Organisation, the Economic Commission for Europe (Geneva), the Commission of the European Communities, the

World Bank, the Egyptian Government and a number of UK Ministries. He is a member of the National Radiological Protection Board and is on the advisory boards of a number of major economics, energy and environmental journals.

John Pinder (OBE), is the Director of the Policy Studies Institute. He was formerly the Director of PEP, which in 1978 merged with the Centre for Studies in Social Policy to become PSI. He was also for a number of years head of the economics department at the College of Europe, Bruges. His publications include Britain and the Common Market (1961), Europe against de Gaulle (1963), The European Community's Policy towards Eastern Europe (with Pauline Pinder, 1975) and Policies for a Constrained Economy (with Charles Carter, 1982).

Richard Westoby is a doctoral student in the Department of Political Economy, University of Aberdeen. He was previously a research assistant at Birmingham University. He has written several papers on energy policy and production function approaches to energy and non-energy substitution.

1 General Introduction

Ali M. El-Agraa

<u>INTERNATIONAL ECONOMIC INTEGRATION</u>

A worthwhile discussion of Britain's role within the European Community (EC) can be attempted only if the EC is understood in its proper context of 'international economic integration'. International economic integration is one aspect of 'international economics' which has been growing in importance in the past two decades or so. The term itself has a rather short history; indeed, Machlup (1977) was unable to find a single instance of its use prior to 1942. Since then the term has been used at various times to refer to practically any area of international economic relations. By 1950, however, the term had been given a specific definition by economists specialising in international trade to denote a state of affairs or a process which involves the amalgamation of separate economies into larger regions, and it is in this more limited sense that the term is used today. More specifically, international economic integration is concerned with the discriminatory removal of all trade impediments between the participating nations and with the establishment of certain elements of co-operation and co-ordination among them. The latter depends entirely on the actual form that integration takes. Different forms of international integration can be envisaged and some have actually been implemented:
   (i) <u>free trade areas</u>, where the member nations remove all trade impediments among themselves but retain their freedom with regard to the determination of their policies <u>vis-a-vis</u> the outside world (the non-participants) - for example, the European Free Trade Association (EFTA) and the Latin American Free Trade Area (LAFTA);
   (ii) <u>customs unions</u>, which are very similar to free trade areas except that member nations must conduct and pursue common external commercial relations - for instance, they must adopt common external tariffs on imports from the non-participants as is the case in

1

the EC; the EC is in this particular sense a customs
union, but, as we shall presently see, it is more
than that;

(iii) common markets, which are customs unions that also
allow for free factor mobility across national member
frontiers, i.e. capital, labour, enterprise should
move unhindered between the participating countries -
for example, the East African Community (EAC), the EC
(but again it is more complex);

(iv) complete economic unions, which are common markets
that ask for complete unification of monetary and
fiscal policies, i.e. a central authority is
introduced to exercise control over these matters so
that existing member nations effectively become
regions of one nation;

(v) complete political integration, where the
participants become literally one nation, i.e. the
central authority needed in (iv) not only controls
monetary and fiscal policies but is also responsible
to a central parliament with the sovereignty of a
nation's government.

It should be stressed that each of these forms of
economic integration can be introduced in its own right:
they should not be confused with stages in a process which
eventually leads to complete political integration. It
should also be noted that within each scheme there may be
'sectoral' integration, as distinct from general across-
the-board integration, in particular areas of the economy,
for example in agriculture as is the case in the EC - hence
the Common Agricultural Policy. Of course, sectoral
integration can be introduced as an aim in itself as was
the case in the European Coal and Steel Community (ECSC),
but sectoral integration is a form of 'co-operation' since
it is not consistent with the accepted definition of
international economic integration.

In concluding this section one should point out that
international economic integration can be positive or
negative. The term 'negative integration' was coined by
Tinbergen (1954) to refer to the removal of impediments on
trade between the participating nations or to the
elimination of any restrictions on the process of trade
liberalisation. The term 'positive integration' relates to
the modification of existing instruments and institutions
and, more importantly, to the creation of new ones so as to
enable the market of the integrated area to function
properly and effectively and also to promote other broader
policy aims of the union. Hence, at the risk of
oversimplification, it can be stated that sectoral

integration and free trade areas are forms of international economic integration which require only 'negative integration', while the remaining types require 'positive integration' since, as a minimum, they all require the positive act of adopting common external relations. However, in reality, this distinction is unfair since practically all existing types of international economic integration have found it necessary to introduce some elements of 'positive integration'.

NATURE AND AIMS OF THE COMMUNITY

The EC consists of six original member states, namely, Belgium, France, West Germany, Italy, Luxembourg and the Netherlands, and three members who joined in 1973: Denmark, Ireland and the United Kingdom. Greece joined the EC as a full member in January 1981 and Portugal, Spain and Turkey have already submitted applications for full membership.

The EC is in reality an amalgamation of three separate communities: the European Coal and Steel Community (ECSC), established by the Treaty of Paris in 1951 and valid for fifty years; the European Economic Community (EEC), created under the Treaty of Rome in 1957 for an unlimited period; and the European Atomic Energy Community (Euratom), formed by another Treaty of Rome in 1957 and also of unlimited duration. Subsequently, other texts have added to, or have amended, these three basic documents and any significant changes are incorporated in treaties which must be ratified by each member state in accordance with its own legal processes. Hence for example, changes in the budget procedures and the agreements to admit Denmark, Ireland and the UK to the EC constitute the subject of special treaty instruments and the totality of these documents, together with the legislative acts to which they give rise and the case law of the Court of Justice (see below), can be considered as the constitution of the EC - see Collins (1980).

It follows that the aims of the EC extend beyond those stated in this constitution to include other objectives which the EC may deem necessary in the future. Moreover, uppermost in the minds of the original instigators of the EC was the eventual political union of its member nations (see chapter 2) and recent developments seem to indicate a revival of this notion. Therefore, it can be stated that the EC has an evolving (dynamic) set of aims and aspirations, hence it is far from static in nature.

The initial objectives of the EC can be summarised as:

(i) The establishment of free trade between the member nations such that <u>all</u> impediments on intra-EC trade are eliminated. The Treaty does not simply ask for the elimination of tariffs, import quota restrictions and export subsidies, but of all measures which have an equivalent or similar effect (non-tariff trade distortions). Moreover, the Treaty calls for the establishment of <u>genuine</u> free trade and therefore specifies rudiments of common competition and industrial policies;

(ii) The creation of an intra-EC free market for all factors of production by providing the necessary pre-requisites for ensuring perfect factor mobility. These include taxes on, and subsidies to, capital, labour, enterprise, etc;

(iii) The formation of common policies with regard to particular industries which the EC deemed it necessary to single out for special treatment, namely, agriculture (hence the Common Agricultural Policy - CAP) and transport (hence the Common Transport Policy - CTP);

(iv) The establishment of a common commercial policy <u>vis-a-vis</u> the outside world, i.e. the creation and <u>management</u> of the common external tariff rates (CETs), the adoption of a common stance in multinational and multilateral trade negotiations and a common attitude towards the association of other countries and the consideration of new membership.

These initial aims should be supplemented by those pertaining to (v) a common market for, and equitable access to, steel and coal as expressed in the treaty establishing the ECSC and (vi) a common approach to energy as expressed in the treaty creating Euratom. One must also add the aim of achieving (vii) monetary integration as expressed in the Werner Report (1970), with the European Monetary System (EMS), established in 1979, being its latest manifestation - see Sumner and Zis (1982) and chapter 13.

It is obvious that these aims cannot be achieved without the provision of some institutional arrangements to facilitate them. On the administrative side (see Shanks, 1977 and Collins, 1980), the main executive body is the <u>Commission</u> whose work is harmonised and increasingly directed by the <u>Council</u> which is a body of ministerial representatives. The Commission is ultimately responsible to the <u>European Parliament</u> which hopes eventually to become the main legislative body but, at this stage, even though it has the power of sacking the Commission in its totality, it is a platform for public comment and is therefore

largely advisory in nature, although it possesses certain
budgetary powers some of which it has actually used - see
chapter 2. The Court of Justice is responsible for the
settling of all legal matters concerning the EC regulations
and procedures. However, the administrative structure is
not as rigid as is suggested by this brief, and inevitably
generalised description, since it includes regular
consultations between the governments of member nations at
both the ministerial and head of state levels and also
allows for representations by various lobbying groups,
particularly farmers. On the financial side, the
arrangements include the creation of a European Social
Fund (ESF), with the aim of improving employment prospects
and raising living standards, and the European Investment
Bank (EIB), with the object of exploring new avenues for
the promotion of economic expansion within the EC.

In the light of this general discussion it can therefore
be categorically stated that the EC is a common market with
definite aspirations for complete economic and political
unity.

BASIC ECONOMIC INDICATORS

The self-explanatory statistical tables appended to this
chapter provide the reader with the basic economic
indicators essential for a proper understanding of the
discussion in the following chapters. The data are not
meant to provide a comprehensive coverage : they are
intended to give some idea of the general economic
structure of the member nations of the EC, of their
immediate potential partners and, for a general sense of
perspective, of Canada, Japan and the USA. Hence the choice
of the years 1975, 1977, and 1980 is, in a sense, purely
arbitrary; more relevant and consistent comparative
information is given in the specialist chapters. Also,
summary tables of some very basic comparative indicators
are given and discussed in the concluding chapter.

ABOUT THE BOOK

The aim of this book is threefold : to explain the major
areas in which the EC plays a role in decision-making or
where the EC will be expected to play an active part when
the integration process is further advanced; to identify
the costs and benefits of each policy, particularly for the
UK; and to propose feasible ways in which the policies
could be adapted to suit British conditions.

The chapters are grouped in four basic parts. Part I is
general and consists of two chapters : chapter 2, by John
Pinder, on the history, politics and institutions of the
EC; and chapter 3, by Stephen Holt, on membership of the EC
and its 'alternatives'. Part II, which comprises three
chapters, is devoted to the theoretical dimensions of the
'common market' aspects of the EC : chapter 4, written by
myself, gives a broad review of the general-equilibrium
theory of customs unions, albeit expressed in partial-
equilibrium terms; chapter 5, by Tony Jones, uses a
macroeconomic framework to analyse the implications for the
UK if it withdraws from the EC; and chapter 6, by David
Mayes, discusses the empirical data relating to trade and
factor mobility. Part III, consisting of 5 chapters, is
devoted to the micro policies of the EC : chapter 7, by
Alan Butt Philip, is a new look at EC Competition and
Industrial Policies; chapter 8, by myself, is on the true
cost of the CAP; chapter 9, by Ken Gwilliam examines the
Transport Policy; chapter 10, by David Pearce and Richard
Westoby deals with the Energy Policy; and chapter 11, by
Doreen Collins, is on the Social Policy. The macro policies
of the EC are discussed in 4 chapters in Part IV: the EC
Fiscal Policy is discussed in chapter 12 by myself; the
European Monetary Union and the European Monetary System in
chapter 13 by David Llewellyn; the Regional Policy in
chapter 14 by Harvey Armstrong; and an EC Defence Policy in
chapter 15 by Keith Hartley. The book contains a concluding
chapter which brings together information directly relevant
to discussion of whether the UK's membership of the EC has
been an 'unmitigated disaster'.
Four further points should be made regarding the book.
The first is that all the contributors are British
specialists. The fact that they are British is not meant
to suggest that non-UK specialists have nothing worthwhile
to contribute or that their contribution would be biased in
any direction. The contributors are British simply because
I felt that, given the nature of the subject, analysis
should be undertaken by people who are personally involved.
The second point is that the contributors, who are all
outstanding authorities in their specialist area, see the
EC as an evolving institution, irrevocable membership of
which confers the ability to play an active role in its
development. That is why the book covers aspects usually
neglected in books on 'Britain in Europe'. Thirdly, given
that the book has many contributors, I have endeavoured to
ensure, as far as is feasible, that it has the necessary
continuity. Finally, I have not written a separate chapter
summarising the conclusions reached in the different
chapters simply because there are no apparent mutual
contradictions in them.

STATISTICAL APPENDIX

TABLE 1.1: AREA AND POPULATION

	Area ('000 sq.km)	Year	Agricultural Area ('000 sq.km)	Tillage ('000 sq.km)	Population ('000)	Population Density (inhabitants per sq.km)	Crude Birth rate (per '000)
Belgium	30.5	1975	15.3	8.1	9801	321	12.1
		1977	15.2	8.1	9830	322	12.4
		1980	14.5	7.8	9857	323	12.7
Denmark	43.1	1975	29.4	26.6	5060	117	14.2
		1977	29.3	26.5	5089	118	12.2
		1980	29.1	26.5	5125	119	11.1
France	549.1	1975	324.2	189.2	52,743	96	14.1
		1977	322.3	190.9	53,084	97	14.0
		1980	319.1	190.1	53,713	98	14.9
West Germany	248.6	1975	133.0	80.6	61,829	249	9.7
		1977	132.3	80.1	61,400	247	9.5
		1980	128.1	77.6	61,566	248	10.1
Greece	132.0	1974	88.2	38.9	9,046	69	15.7c
		1977	88.2	39.0	9,268	70	15.5
		1980	88.6	39.3	9,599	73	15.9
Ireland	70.3	1973	48.4	12.4	3,127	44	21.6
		1977	48.5	12.5	3,180	45	21.4
		1980	48.5	12.5	3,401	48	21.9
Italy	301.2	1974	175.0	122.9	55,812	185	15.1
		1977	175.3	123.2	56,446	187	13.4
		1980	175.9	124.6	57,042	189	11.5
Luxembourg	2.6	1975	1.3	0.6	359	138	11.1
		1977	1.3	0.6	355	137	11.4
		1980	1.3	0.6	365	140	11.4
Netherlands	40.8	1975	20.9	8.5	13,654	335	13.0
		1977	20.8	8.5	13,853	340	12.5
	41.2	1980	20.2	8.6	14,144	343	12.8
United Kingdom	244.0	1975	185.8	69.6	56,042	230	12.5
		1977	185.7	69.8	55,919	229	11.7
		1980	184.8	70.1	56,010	230	13.5
Portugal	92.0	1975	42.0	36.7	9,449	103	19.3
		1977	41.3	36.0	9,773	106	18.6
	92.1	1980	42.0	36.7	9,966	108	16.4
Spain	504.8	1975	280.6	208.3	35,219	70	18.8
		1977	275.8	206.6	36,672	73	18.0
		1980	272.9b	205.3b	37,381	74	15.1
Canada	9,976.1	1975	635.6	392.6	22,831	2	15.7
		1977	640.6	401.6	23,316	2	15.5
		1980	647.9a	413.9a	23,959	2	15.4
Japan	372.3	1974	58.6	56.2	110,990	298	17.2
		1977	57.8	55.4	113,860	306	15.5
		1980	57.0	54.6	116,782	314	13.6
USA	9,363.4	1974	4301.6	1882.2	213,540	23	14.7
	9,363.1	1977	4303.3d	1865.5d	216,817	23	15.3
		1980	4281.6	1906.2	227,658	24	15.8

a = 1978
b = 1979
c = 1974
d = 1976

Sources (for all the tables except 1.12): Eurostat, Basic Statistics of the Community, The OECD Observer and OECD various statistical publications.

TABLE 1.2: GROSS DOMESTIC PRODUCT

	Year	GDP (in million US $)	GDP per capita	Years	Annual rate of growth of GDP
Belgium	1975	62245	6352	1958–64	4.7
	1977	79210	8060	1965–75	3.8
	1980	116480	11820	1975–80	2.85
Denmark	1975	35451	7006	1958–64	5.9
	1977	46020	9040	1965–75	2.7
	1980	66380	12950	1975–80	4.6
France	1975	335744	6360	1958–64	5.3
	1977	380660	7170	1965–75	4.0
	1980	651880	12140	1975–80	3.3
West Germany	1975	424835	6871	1958–64	5.8
	1977	516200	8410	1965–75	3.8
	1980	819120	13310	1975–80	3.35
Greece	1975	20980	2320	1958–64	5.0
	1977	26210	2830	1965–75	5.25
	1980	40410	4210	1975–80	4.35
Ireland	1975	7800	2492	1958–64	–
	1977	9380	2940	1965–75	4.0
	1980	17800	5190	1975–80	3.95
Italy	1975	172104	3084	1958–64	6.1
	1977	196050	3470	1965–75	4.0
	1980	393950	6910	1975–80	3.85
Luxembourg	1975	2197	6102	1958–64	–
	1977	2750	7700	1965–75	1.3
	1980	4580	12570	1975–80	2.35
Netherlands	1975	81202	5949	1958–64	5.4
	1977	106390	7680	1965–75	4.1
	1980	167630	11850	1975–80	2.55
United Kingdom	1975	228820	4089	1958–64	3.9
	1977	244340	4370	1965–75	2.3
	1980	522860	9340	1975–80	1.6
Portugal	1975	14620	1550	1958–64	4.7
	1977	16300	1670	1965–75	–
	1980	24080	2430	1975–80	5.2
Spain	1975	101040	2870	1958–64	5.5
	1977	115590	3150	1965–75	2.0
	1980	211110	5650	1975–80	2.15
Canada	1975	159707	6995	1958–64	4.3
	1977	200250	8590	1965–75	1.6
	1980	253340	10580	1975–80	3.05
Japan	1975	490634	4437	1958–64	–
	1977	694360	6100	1965–75	7.3
	1980	1039980	8910	1975–80	5.1
USA	1975	1513828	7087	1958–64	4.3
	1977	1878840	8670	1965–75	0.9
	1980	2587100	11360	1975–80	3.9

TABLE 1.3: CONSUMER PRICE INDEX (1975=100)

	1973	1974	1976	1977	1978	1979	1980	Average Annual Increase 1976-81 (% p.a.)
Belgium	79	89	109	117	122	128	136	6.1
Denmark	79	91	109	121	133	146	164	11.0
France	79	90	110	120	131	145	165	11.2
West Germany	88	94	104	108	111	116	122	4.4
Greece	70	88	113	127	143	170	213	18.5
Ireland	71	83	118	134	144	163	193	14.5
Italy	72	86	117	137	153	176	213	17.2
Luxembourg	83	90	110	117	121	126	134	5.7
Netherlands	83	91	109	116	121	126	135	5.6
United Kingdom	69	81	117	135	146	166	196	13.4
Portugal	72	86	117	148	179	-	-	18.0
Spain	74	86	117	143	172	200	-	22.0
Canada	-	-	-	-	-	-	-	9.7
Japan	72	89	109	118	123	127	137	5.7
USA	83	92	106	113	121	135	153	9.8

TABLE 1.4: WHOLESALE PRICE INDEX (1975=100)

	1973	1974	1976	1977	1978	1979	1980
Belgium	85	99	107	110	108	114	121
Denmark	78	95	108	117	122	133	155
France	80	99	110	118	123	138	154
West Germany	86	99	106	108	107	114	123
Greece	70	92	114	130	143	173	222
Ireland	71	81	120	140	152	171	188
Italy	66	92	123	144	156	181	217
Luxembourg	-	-	-	-	-	-	-
Netherlands	85	94	107	113	-	-	-
United Kingdom	65	81	116	139	153	172	200
Japan	74	97	106	108	105	112	132
USA	77	92	105	111	123	135	154

TABLE 1.5: USE OF GROSS DOMESTIC PRODUCT (AT MARKET PRICES)

	Year	Private consumption	Collective consumption of general government	Gross fixed capital formation	Change in stocks	Balance of exports and imports of goods and services
			Use of GDP in %			
Belgium	1975	60.5	16.8	22.3	−0.6	+1.0
	1977	62.0	−	21.2	−	−
	1979	61.9	17.8	21.0	+0.4	−1.2
Denmark	1975	58.1	24.7	19.9	−1.7	−1.0
	1977	56.2	−	23.3	−	−
	1979	55.8	25.1	21.5	+0.6	−3.0
France	1975	62.3	14.5	23.4	−1.1	+0.9
	1977	62.0	−	22.6	−	−
	1979	62.3	14.9	21.3	+1.6	−0.1
West Germany	1975	60.9	14.7	21.5	−0.4	+3.3
	1977	58.8	−	20.9	−	−
	1979	59.7	13.7	22.7	+2.1	+1.8
Greece	1975	71.6	−	21.0	−	−
	1977	66.7	−	23.0	−	−
	1979	67.8	16.2	25.2	+3.4	−12.6
Ireland	1975	67.7	20.6	22.3	−4.3	−6.3
	1977	64.7	−	24.7	−	−
	1979	63.1	20.1	32.4	+0.7	−16.2
Italy	1975	67.8	13.6	21.1	−1.2	−1.3
	1977	63.9	−	19.8	−	−
	1979	62.8	16.2	18.7	+3.0	−0.7
Luxembourg	1975	59.9	15.0	29.2	+2.8	−6.9
	1977	61.8	−	25.8	−	−
	1979	58.7	15.5	26.2	−1.4	+1.0
Netherlands	1975	57.8	18.0	21.2	−0.7	+3.7
	1977	58.3	−	21.1	−	−
	1979	58.1	18.8	21.7	+0.4	+1.0
United Kingdom	1975	61.4	22.2	19.9	−1.3	−2.2
	1977	59.2	−	18.1	−	−
	1979	60.9	20.3	17.8	+1.5	−0.4
Portugal	1975	84.6	−	13.6	−	−
	1977	75.5	−	20.4	−	−
	1979	72.4	14.8	19.9	+2.2	−9.3
Spain	1975	69.3	−	23.2	−	−
	1977	69.0	−	21.5	−	−
	1979	71.6	10.9	19.0	+1.3	−2.8
Canada	1975	57.4	20.1	24.1	−0.2	−1.4
	1977	56.7	−	22.7	−	−
	1979	56.0	19.2	22.5	+1.7	+0.6
Japan	1975	56.6	11.1	30.9	+1.3	+0.1
	1977	58.0	−	30.0	−	−
	1979	58.8	9.7	31.7	+0.1	−0.8
USA	1975	64.3	19.4	16.2	−1.0	+1.1
	1977	64.6	−	17.5	−	−
	1979	64.2	18.0	18.1	+0.7	−1.1

TABLE 1.6: GENERAL INDICES OF INDUSTRIAL PRODUCTION (EXCLUDING CONSTRUCTION)

	1954	1955	1956	1957	1958 = 100 1959	1960	1961	1962	1963	1964	1972	1973	1974	1975 = 100 1976	1977	1978	1979	1980
Belgium	92	99	105	105	104	112	119	125	135	145	100	107	111	108	109	111	116	115
Denmark	87	89	90	96	112	121	128	139	-	-	104	107	106	109	110	113	117	117
France	-	82	89	96	101	110	116	122	128	138	99	105	108	109	111	113	118	117
West Germany	75	86	93	97	107	120	127	133	137	150	101	108	107	107	111	113	119	119
Greece	-	-	-	-	-	-	-	128	137	152	84	97	96	111	113	121	129	129
Ireland	-	-	-	-	-	-	-	-	-	-	94	104	107	109	119	129	136	134
Italy	77	84	90	96	111	128	142	156	169	170	96	106	110	112	112	114	122	128
Luxembourg	85	96	103	104	104	114	117	112	113	124	111	124	128	104	107	108	111	108
Netherlands	-	-	-	-	109	122	126	133	139	151	93	100	105	108	108	109	112	112
United Kingdom	-	-	-	-	105	113	113	114	119	127	100	108	105	103	108	111	115	107
Portugal	76	81	88	94	106	116	127	134	146	-	91	103	105	103	117	125	134	141
Spain	-	-	-	-	-	-	-	-	-	-	85	98	104	107	120	115	115	117
Canada	83	92	100	101	108	108	112	120	127	138	93	102	106	106	108	112	118	116
Japan	-	-	-	-	-	-	-	-	-	-	101	106	112	111	116	123	133	142
USA	92	103	107	107	113	116	117	126	133	141	102	110	110	111	117	124	130	125

TABLE 1.7: THE GOVERNMENT SECTOR

	Year	Current government expenditure & revenue as % of GDP		Net official development assistance to less developed countries and multilateral agents (% of GDP)	Gross domestic expenditure on R & D in natural sciences and engineering	Total official reserves (SDR millions)
		Expenditure	Revenue			
Belgium	1975	41.6	40.7	0.59	1.2	5206
	1977	43.5	41.8	0.46	-	4535
	1980	48.1	43.3	0.49	1.4a	5451c
Denmark	1975	43.0	45.0	0.58	1.1	915
	1976	42.8	46.5	0.60	-	2471
	1980	-	-	0.72	1.0a	2246
France	1975	38.9	40.6	0.62	1.8	9728
	1977	40.4	42.2	0.60	-	10692
	1980	43.1	45.4	0.62	1.8a	21991
West Germany	1975	41.7	40.9	0.4	2.1	34798
	1977	41.3	43.5	0.27	-	41353
	1980	41.2	42.8	0.43	2.4a	40886
Greece	1974	24.6	26.7	-	-	925
	1977	29.0	29.4	-	-	914
	1980	33.7	34.1	-	0.2a	722
Ireland	1973	34.8	35.0	-	0.7	1837
	1975	43.3	36.8	-	0.8	2064
	1980	42.4a	36.2a	-	0.8a	2290
Italy	1975	39.8	34.7	0.11	0.8	6654
	1977	42.5	37.4	0.10	0.9	11380
	1980	41.1	37.5	0.17	0.8a	19631

	Year					
Luxembourg	1975	42.1	50.6	--	--	5206
	1976	44.4	52.8	--	--	4535
	1980	44.9b	53.6			5451c
Netherlands	1975	50.5	53.6	0.75	1.9	7387
	1977	52.3	54.0	0.85	1.9	5822
	1980	55.1a	55.8a	0.99	2.0a	9562
United Kingdom	1974	39.5	40.0	0.37	2.1	4230
	1976	41.5	40.6	0.37	--	13100
	1980	40.9	40.4	0.34	2.2a	13757
Portugal	1974	22.6	23.0	--	--	1302
	1976	31.1	28.3	--	0.2	1507
	1980	--	--	--	0.3d	1054
Spain	1974	22.0	23.1	--	0.3	5284
	1977	23.4	26.7	--	--	7963
	1980	28.9	28.5	--	--	9974
Canada	1975	37.1	37.4	0.58	1.0	5843
	1977	37.0	36.4	0.51	1.0	3507
	1980	36.1a	36.0a	0.44	1.2	3755
Japan	1975	20.8	23.5	0.24	1.8	16604
	1977	22.3	24.5	0.21	1.7	25714
	1980	24.7	27.6	0.32	2.0	25083
USA	1975	33.9	30.7	0.26	2.3	18319
	1977	32.6	32.0	0.22	2.3	15032
	1980	31.5a	32.5a	0.27	2.5a	25502

a = 1979
b = 1977
c = BLEU
d = 1978

TABLE 1.8: EMPLOYMENT

	Year	Total civilian employment ('000)	% of which in: Agriculture, forestry and fishing	Industry	Other	Unemployment rate as % of total labour force
Belgium	1975	3,748	3.6	39.9	56.5	4.2
	1977	3,711	3.3	37.9	58.8	6.3
	1980	3,751	3.0	34.8	62.2	9.0
Denmark	1975	2,332	9.8	31.5	58.7	4.9
	1977	2,414	9.1	30.4	60.5	5.1
	1980	2,470	8.1	28.6	63.3	6.9
France	1975	20,764	11.3	38.5	50.1	4.1
	1977	20,962	9.6	37.7	52.7	4.9
	1980	21,142	8.8	35.9	55.3	6.3
West Germany	1975	24,828	7.3	46.0	46.7	4.1
	1977	24,511	6.8	45.3	47.9	4.0
	1980	25,265	6.0	44.8	49.2	3.1
Greece	1975	3,190	35.4	28.2	36.4	3.0
	1977	3,167	33.2	29.2	37.6	1.1
	1980	3,356	30.3	30.2	39.5	2.2*
Ireland	1975	1,030	24.5	29.8	45.7	8.0
	1977	1,022	23.1	30.3	46.6	9.4
	1980	1,148	19.2	32.4	48.4	6.0
Italy	1975	18,818	15.8	44.1	40.1	3.3
	1977	19,847	15.9	38.6	45.5	7.1
	1980	20,572	14.2	37.8	48.0	7.4
Luxembourg	1975	150	6.2	47.3	46.5	0.1
	1977	147	5.9	45.1	49.0	0.5
	1980	159	5.7	38.4	55.9	0.7
Netherlands	1975	4,535	6.6	34.8	58.6	4.3
	1977	4,555	6.3	33.2	60.5	4.5
	1980	4,954	6.0	31.9	62.1	4.9
United Kingdom	1975	24,632	2.7	40.9	56.4	3.4
	1977	24,550	2.7	40.0	57.3	5.5
	1980	24,397	2.6	38.0	59.4	7.4
Portugal	1975	3,081	28.2	33.6	38.2	5.3
	1977	3,781	32.5	33.1	34.4	7.8
	1980	3,924	28.6	36.1	35.3	7.6
Spain	1975	12,576	21.9	38.5	39.6	4.7
	1977	12,462	20.7	37.4	41.9	6.3
	1980	11,254	18.8	36.1	43.1	11.2
Canada	1975	9,363	6.1	29.3	64.6	6.9
	1977	9,754	5.7	28.9	65.4	8.1
	1980	10,655	5.5	28.5	66.0	7.5
Japan	1975	52,230	12.7	35.8	51.5	1.9
	1977	53,420	11.9	35.4	52.7	2.0
	1980	55,360	10.4	35.3	54.3	2.0
USA	1975	84,783	4.1	30.7	65.2	8.3
	1977	90,546	3.7	30.9	65.4	6.9
	1980	97,270	3.6	30.6	65.8	7.0

* = estimate.
N.B. The unemployment data are not strictly comparable.

TABLE 1.9: THE FOREIGN TRADE SECTOR

	Year	Total imports as % of GDP	Total exports as % of GDP	Foreign Tourism (US $ million) Receipts	Expenditures
Belgium*	1975	49.3	46.3	864	1410
	1977	49.1	45.7	993	1635
	1980	59.2	53.3	1810.4	3271.7
Denmark	1975	29.1	24.6	746	642
	1977	28.8	21.9	940	942
	1980	29.1	25.2	1337.4	1560.2
France	1975	16.2	15.6	3470	3064
	1977	18.5	16.7	4377	3920
	1980	20.7	17.1	8235	6026.9
West Germany	1975	17.5	21.2	2848	8502
	1977	19.5	22.8	3804	10805
	1980	22.7	23.4	6639.5	20827.2
Greece	1975	25.3	10.9	644	92
	1977	25.9	10.4	981	89
	1980	26.3	12.8	1733.5	190.2
Ireland	1975	49.1	41.4	265	153
	1977	57.4	46.8	323	237
	1980	62.7	47.8	611.7	-
Italy	1975	22.3	20.2	2582	1051
	1977	24.3	23.0	4762	894
	1980	25.3	19.8	8913.9	1907.4
Luxembourg*	1975	49.3	46.3	864	1410
	1977	49.1	45.7	993	1635
	1980	59.2	53.3	1810.4	3271.7
Netherlands	1975	43.3	42.4	1106	1657
	1977	42.9	41.1	1110	2454
	1980	45.9	44.0	1640	4637
United Kingdom	1975	23.4	19.2	2442	1921
	1977	26.1	23.5	3805	1921
	1980	23.0	22.0	6932	6454
Portugal	1975	26.2	13.3	242	200
	1977	30.4	12.4	404	135
	1980	38.6	19.3	1145.9	289.4
Spain	1975	16.1	7.6	3404	385
	1977	15.4	8.8	4003	533
	1980	16.2	9.9	6967.7	1228.6
Canada	1975	21.3	20.2	1525	2065
	1977	19.7	20.8	1616	2829
	1980	23.3	25.6	2284	3121
Japan	1975	11.8	11.4	252	1367
	1977	10.2	11.6	424	2151
	1980	13.6	12.5	644	4593
USA	1975	6.4	7.1	4876	6417
	1977	7.9	6.4	6164	7451
	1980	9.3	8.5	10100	10385

* Belgium and Luxembourg are counted together as BLEU.

TABLE 1.10: IMPORTS FROM EC COUNTRIES (PERCENTAGE SHARE OF TOTAL IMPORTS OF IMPORTING COUNTRY)

	1957	1958	1959	1960	1961	1962	1963	1964	1974	1975	1976	1977	1978	1979	1980
Belgium) Luxembourg)	43.5	46.6	47.1	47.9	50.6	51.0	52.5	53.3	66.1	67.2	67.5	67.7	69.1	64.5	63.1
Denmark	31.2	35.6	36.7	38.5	39.4	37.8	35.9	35.4	45.5	45.8	47.2	47.7	49.7	50.4	49.2
France	21.4	21.9	26.8	29.4	31.5	33.6	35.8	37.4	47.6	48.8	50.0	49.4	51.4	52.5	46.3
West Germany	23.5	25.8	29.0	29.9	31.3	32.5	33.4	34.9	48.1	49.5	48.2	49.0	50.1	50.2	47.8
Greece	40.8	42.7	37.9	33.6	38.1	43.4	39.8	42.3	43.3	42.5	39.7	42.5	43.8	43.6	39.7
Ireland	-	-	-	-	-	-	15.4	15.6	68.3	69.2	69.4	68.2	70.2	71.9	74.5
Italy	21.4	21.4	26.7	27.7	29.5	31.2	33.0	32.7	42.4	43.0	43.6	43.1	44.7	44.9	44.3
Netherlands	41.1	41.9	44.4	45.8	49.2	50.2	51.6	52.0	57.4	56.9	55.2	54.8	57.4	56.8	53.7
United Kingdom	12.1	14.2	14.0	14.6	15.4	15.8	16.0	16.6	30.0	32.4	32.2	38.5	38.0	41.1	38.7
Portugal	37.1	39.2	39.0	38.2	38.1	36.6	34.7	33.1	43.5	40.2	41.7	43.6	45.8	40.8	42.1
Spain	21.3	23.8	22.3	25.2	26.1	29.7	33.6	35.9	35.8	33.6	33.1	34.2	34.7	36.0	31.0
Canada	4.2	4.7	5.3	5.3	5.5	5.5	5.2	5.4	9.6	9.8	8.5	-	9.3	8.9	8.1
Japan	-	4.9	5.0	4.7	5.4	6.1	5.9	5.6	6.4	5.8	5.6	5.9	7.6	6.8	5.6
USA	11.7	12.5	15.6	15.0	15.2	15.0	14.8	15.2	19.0	17.3	14.8	15.2	17.0	16.4	15.3

TABLE 1.11: EXPORTS TO EC COUNTRIES
(Percentage Share of Total Exports of Exporting Country)

	1957	1958	1959	1960	1961	1962	1963	1964	1974	1975	1976	1977	1978	1979	1980
Belgium) Luxembourg)	46.1	45.1	46.3	50.5	53.2	56.8	60.8	62.6	69.9	70.6	73.7	71.2	71.6	73.3	71.8
Denmark	31.2	31.2	31.7	29.5	29.1	28.4	28.8	28.1	43.1	45.0	45.7	42.3	47.9	49.6	50.5
France	25.1	22.2	27.2	29.8	33.5	36.8	38.2	38.8	53.2	49.2	50.6	50.4	52.5	53.8	51.9
West Germany	29.2	27.3	27.8	29.5	31.7	34.0	37.3	36.5	53.2	43.6	45.7	44.9	45.8	49.5	49.1
Greece	52.5	47.9	44.1	33.0	30.5	35.7	32.8	37.5	50.1	49.7	50.0	47.7	50.8	49.1	47.6
Ireland	-	-	-	-	-	-	7.5	11.5	74.1	79.4	75.8	76.5	77.7	77.9	74.9
Italy	24.9	23.6	27.2	29.6	31.3	34.8	35.5	38.0	45.4	45.1	47.8	46.5	48.0	51.0	49.0
Netherlands	41.6	41.6	44.3	45.9	47.6	49.2	53.3	55.7	70.8	71.1	72.1	70.4	70.9	73.2	72.2
United Kingdom	14.6	13.9	14.8	15.3	17.4	19.3	21.1	20.6	33.4	32.3	35.6	36.6	37.8	42.4	42.7
Portugal	22.2	24.6	22.8	21.8	21.8	23.2	21.8	20.7	48.2	50.3	51.5	51.8	55.5	56.4	57.8
Spain	29.8	28.2	27.8	38.5	37.7	38.0	37.9	38.9	47.4	44.7	46.4	46.3	46.3	48.0	50.1
Canada	8.3	8.6	6.2	8.3	8.4	7.3	7.0	6.8	12.6	12.5	11.9	-	9.3	10.8	12.9
Japan	-	4.3	3.9	4.3	5.0	5.6	6.1	5.5	10.7	10.2	10.8	10.9	11.3	12.3	12.8
USA	15.3	13.6	13.6	16.8	17.0	16.8	17.0	17.2	21.9	21.3	22.1	22.0	22.3	23.4	25.2

TABLE 1.12: AVERAGE TARIFFS (%) 1953

	Benelux	France	West Germany	Italy	EEC (Six)	Denmark	United Kingdom	Canada	USA
Instruments (86)	13	22	8	17	16	3	27	19	29
Footwear (851)	20	21	10	21	19	19	25	24	19
Clothing (84)	20	26	13	25	21	19	26	25	32½
Furniture (821)	13	23	8	21	17	11	20	25	24
Building parts and fittings (81)	15	19	8	25	17	8	15	16	20
Transport Equipment (73)	17	29	12	34	22	8	25	17	13
Electric machinery etc. (72)	11	19	6	21	15	8	23	18	20
Machinery other than electric (71)	8	18	5	20	13	6	17	9	12
Manufactures of metal (n.e.s. 699)	11	20	10	23	16	6	21	18	23
Ordnance (691)	9	14	17	17	11	1	22	13	26
Iron and steel (681)	5	13	7	17	10	1	14	12	13
Silver, platinum, gems, jewellery (67)	5	13	3	7	6	5	11	13	29
Non-metallic mineral manufrs. (66)	12	16	6	21	13	9	17	21	13
Textiles etc. except clothing (65)	14	19	11	20	16	9	23	21	26
Paper, paperboard etc. (64)	14	16	8	18	15	6	13	17	10½
Wood mfrs. etc. except furniture (63)	11	19	7	22	16	4	15	12	18
Rubber manufactures (62)	17	17	10	19	18	8	21	18	18
Leather etc. (61)	11	11	12	18	12	11	16	17	17
Chemicals (5)	7	16	8	17	12	4	15	11	24

The figures are subject to the reservations stated in the source.
The figures in brackets refer to SITC classification.

Source: PEP, Atlantic Tariffs and Trade, Allen and Unwin 1962.

Part I
General

2 History, Politics and Institutions of the EC

John Pinder

On 9 May 1950 Robert Schuman, the French Foreign Minister, in launching his plan for pooling coal and steel production which resulted in the first European Community, explained that this was intended to be 'the first concrete foundation of a European federation which is indispensable to the preservation of peace.'[1] Two years later, at the inaugural session of the High Authority of the European Coal and Steel Community of which he was the first President, Jean Monnet developed this theme: "According to the methods of the past, even when the European States have been convinced of the necessity of a common action, even when they have set up an international organisation, they have kept their full sovereignty. Thus the international organisation can neither decide, nor execute, but only address recommendations to the States ... Today, on the contrary, six Parliaments have decided, after mature deliberation and by massive majorities, to create the first European Community which merges a part of the national sovereignties and submits them to the common interest. Within the limits of competence conferred by the Treaty, the High Authority has received from the six States the mandate to take, in complete independence, decisions which are immediately in force on the whole of their territory. It is in a direct relationship with all firms. It obtains financial resources, not by contributions from States, but from levies imposed directly on production ... It is responsible, not to the States, but to a European Assembly. ... The members of the Assembly are not bound by any national mandate ... The Assembly controls our action. It has the power to withdraw its confidence from us. It is the first European Assembly endowed with sovereign powers. The acts of the High Authority are challengeable in the courts....not before national tribunals, but before a European tribunal, the Court of Justice."[2].

This speech of Monnet's has been quoted at some length because it shows in detail how explicitly this European Community was based on federal principles: legislature,

21

judiciary and executive all independent of the member
states, with the executive responsible to the federal
legislature and its acts challengeable in the federal
court; relationships with the citizens (in this case
economic agents) of the territory, including the raising of
taxes from them, direct instead of through the institutions
of the member states. Why did the Community's institutions
constitute, as Monnet underlined, such a radical departure?
The answer is one of the keys to understanding the history
and institutions of the European Community, and may still
be germane to its future development.

THE COMMUNITY, FEDERALISM AND NATIONAL SOVEREIGNTY

The current of federalist ideas was flowing strongly in the
early postwar period in the six countries that were to
establish the ECSC. The way in which these ideas spread
through the resistance movements during the war and were
embodied after the liberation in organisations and
political programmes has been thoroughly documented by
Professor Lipgens.[3] In his view the outstanding body of
literature developing European federalist ideas was
produced in 1939–41, ironically enough in Britain where so
little sympathy was shown after the war for the
Community's federalist aspirations. During this period a
brilliant group of academics and politicians, including Sir
William Beveridge, Ivor Jennings, Lord Lothian,
R.W.G.Mackay, Lionel Robbins, K.C.Wheare, Harold Wilson and
Barbara Wootton, wrote a stream of books, pamphlets and
papers[4] advocating the creation of a European federation
after the war as a basis for lasting peace. Seized of the
impending catastrophe, they sought, through Federal Union
and the Federal Union Research Institute of which Beveridge
was the Chairman, to analyse the breakdown of the
international order and work out the means of establishing
a better order after the war. This body of literature
contained a powerful critique of national sovereignty as
the cause of the downfall of the League of Nations and of
efforts to maintain the peace; insisted that a democratic
federal government had to be given powers over defence and
some economic matters; and assumed that the member states
must include as a minimum Britain, France and a democratic
postwar Germany to ensure that war would not break out
again among the principal powers in Western Europe. The
underlying cause of this need to transcend national
sovereignty was identified as the 'progress of science and
invention', which had 'sped ahead of our moral and

political ideas, which are still rooted in a past that science has made obsolete' (Currie 1939). But whereas these authors were crystal clear about the reasons why they believed a federation to be essential and the principles on which it should be constructed, most of them paid little attention to the politics of bringing a federation about. The implicit assumption seemed to be that public opinion would be persuaded of the necessity and the European democracies would then deliver the goods.

The work of these federalist authors, and that of many others on the Continent, did indeed fall on fertile ground in the public opinion of the founder members of the ECSC, where people were looking for a way to ensure that war among their countries would never recur and to rebuild their economies together.   The federal principle was accepted by leading statesmen: not only Schuman, but also Adenauer, de Gasperi and Spaak, for example. The structure and self-confidence of each of these states had been undermined by defeat in war. Fear of Stalin, encouragement from the United States and the common effort to rebuild the economy provided a peculiarly favourable context. Yet the political realism of Jean Monnet, who inspired the Schuman Plan, led him to avoid a head-on confrontation with national sovereignty on a broad front, as the federalists of the time wanted. Instead, he selected for the first federalist venture one particular narrow front: the production of coal and steel. This embodied a vital issue, the containment of resurgent German economic power, without threatening such citadels of the nation-state as the currency or the armed forces. Weak though the nation-state then was, Monnet thought it prudent to steer clear of these, at least at first.

The wisdom of this was demonstrated only two years later when the French Parliament voted to shelve the project for a European Defence Community (EDC) of the six founder-members of the ECSC. The motive for the EDC proposal was not very different from that for the ECSC. After the shocks of the Berlin blockade and the Korean war, the Americans were demanding the rearmament of Germany in order to strengthen NATO. Just as the reviving German coal and steel industries looked safer to France within a Community in which the two countries, together with the other members, would be equal partners, so German troops would be safer within a common European army. For the federalist opinion that was so widespread at the time, moreover, the EDC would be the decisive assault on the citadel of national sovereignty, the key to full federation; and the point was hammered home by the six countries' parallel project for

a European Political Community to provide the political
framework. The point was, indeed, only too clear to the
Gaullists and Communists who, with assorted Deputies from
other parties, together comprised a majority in the French
Parliament that refused to vote for ratification, although
the EDC treaty had been signed by France and ratified by
the Parliaments of the other five countries. Despite the
knocks it had taken during the war, the nation-state was
stronger in France than in the other five, and this was
reflected in the strength of the opposition to so explicit
a renunciation of state sovereignty.

ESTABLISHMENT OF THE EUROPEAN ECONOMIC COMMUNITY

The fate of this Community-that-never-was taught a lesson
that was later overlaid by the success of the next
Communities to be established: the European Economic
Community (EEC) and Euratom. The lesson was that the
nation-state, even within ten years of a war that had done
so much to discredit it, retained such a tough political
structure that the ground on which federalists might plan
any encroachment on it had to be very carefully considered.
Nobody could have forgotten that lesson by 1955, however,
when the Messina conference set in train the negotiations
that were to lead to the creation of the two new
Communities, leaving defence aside altogether and avoiding
such politically sensitive economic issues as monetary
integration.

This time the motive that was powerful enough to extend
the Community's method to a broad economic field was twofold: the determination of a generation of postwar
statesmen, supported by public opinion, to continue the
political unification that had started with the ECSC; and
the need for a wide market to accommodate the great postwar
industries, of which consumer durables such as cars were
typical, and in which the outstanding leader was then the
United States - though the French were at that time keener
on joint action with regard to atomic energy than on a
commitment to completely free trade with the other members
(see Camps 1964, p.31). Consonant with the need for a wide
common market, the backbone of the EEC Treaty was a hard
and detailed commitment to eliminate progressively tariffs
and quotas on trade among the member states and to erect a
common tariff on imports from other countries. Since the
French, then less confident about their growing industries,
were hesitant about industrial free trade but were eager to
secure markets for their agriculture, the other strong

commitment was to the Common Agricultural Policy. For the rest, the Community had the scope to be involved in a wide range of policies relating to areas such as money, transport, energy, industry, regions and social affairs, but few policy instruments assigned to it. Pursuing the liberal theme of internal free trade, the competition policy was provided in the EEC Treaty with a basis of law, to be enforced by the Commission and the Court of Justice. On the side of the economic and welfare interventions there were the Investment Bank (EIB) and the Social Fund (ESF) as minor concessions to the Italians, who, with the weakest of the six economies, wanted Community instruments to help their economic and social development. But otherwise the EEC was left, for the most part, to work through the member states' policy instruments or to secure subsequent decisions to transfer instruments to the Community; and as we shall see, the former turned out, as the early federal unionists would have predicted, to be a slow, weak and uncertain way of proceeding, while the prospects for transferring instruments waned as the nation-states recovered their strength.

The institutions in which the business of the Community was to be conducted looked similar to those of the ECSC; but there was a significant dilution of the federalist principle, particularly in the relationship between the executive, in the form of the Commission, and the member governments, represented in the ministerial Council. This stemmed from the rebuff inflicted on federalism by the failure of the EDC, which caused the leaders of the 'relance européenne', as the effort to establish the EEC and Euratom was called, to be cautious in promoting supranational institutions - see Camps (1964, p.41). The position of the Court and the Parliament remained much as in the ECSC. The Court is the final arbiter on questions of Community law; although it has no means to enforce its decisions other than the enforcement agencies of the member states, almost all of its decisions have in fact been executed. The Parliament's powers were confined to its right to dismiss the Commission by a two-thirds majority. But the existing members of the Commission, who are appointed by unanimous agreement among the member governments, would remain in place until a new set of Commissioners had been unanimously appointed. Thus a single government could veto the Parliament's decision to replace the Commission. The Parliament has subsequently gained new powers over the Community budget and has become directly elected, as foreseen in both ECSC and EEC Treaties. But it has been reluctant to try using its power to dismiss the

Commission, partly because its decision could so easily be frustrated by one government, and partly because the Commission has been seen as the European body that needs support in its relations with the governments.

With its functions of initiating new policy proposals and of executing the policies decided by the ministerial Council, as well as other functions in ensuring that the provisions of the Community Treaties are fulfilled, the Commission is a great deal more powerful than the secretariats of other international organisations. It has been seen, in a federalist perspective, as the embryo government of a European federation in which the Council would become a Senate. But the position of the Commission in relation to the Council under the EEC Treaty was somewhat weaker than that of the High Authority under the ECSC Treaty; and the reassertion of the nation state, led by General de Gaulle, was to exploit these weaknesses and to confine the Commission to a more humble role.

THE RISE AND DECLINE OF NEO-FUNCTIONALISM

For some time it was possible to see the EEC as a great leap forward on a straight road to federation; and many people did view it like that. It is hard to realise, a quarter of a century later when the Commmunity already has some of the attributes of middle age, what an immense achievement the Treaties of Rome represented and how exciting the Community was to many who were involved or closely observing it. In the early years of the EEC, the Community had an extraordinary run of success. The internal tariff disarmament ran ahead of timetable and trade among the members grew very fast; the common external tariff and the Common Agricultural Policy were put in place; in 1961 the British started to negotiate with a view to membership; in July 1962 President Kennedy stressed the need for an 'equal partnership' between the United States and 'a strong and united Europe'. Evidently, the common market was the idea to suit the time, in the middle of two decades of economic expansion when European industries found, in the Community's ample economy, the scope to catch up with the hitherto dominant industries of the United States. Big corporations, so vividly depicted in America by Galbraith, were the engine of affluence and the Community was on a scale that enabled them to develop and flourish in Europe.

It was in these understandably euphoric circumstances that the school of thought most prevalent at the time in the political science literature on the Community led to

the illusion that there was an automatic process of
'spillover', whereby one transfer of functions to Community
institutions would result in tensions with other functions
that remained in the hands of the member governments, which
would be resolved by the transfer of these other functions
to the Community, until a full integration had been
achieved. The founder of this school, Ernst Haas (1958),
developed the idea by observing the ECSC in its early
years; and the establishment of the EEC and Euratom
appeared as a triumphant vindication. The theme was
repeated in the early years of the EEC - see Lindberg
(1963). The idea that such spillover could be more-or-less
automatic was partly, no doubt, due to a vulgarisation of
neo-functionalist ideas among people who were not careful
scholars and who were over-impressed by the astonishing
progress of the Community in the earlier years. But the
leading neo-functionalist writers were partly to blame.
This was a pity because their analysis of the Community
institutions and of the ways in which social, economic and
political forces related to them was a useful contribution
to understanding the Community, provided that the erroneous
assumption of automatic spillover was not made. This error
was at least partly retracted in some of the neo-
functionalists' later works[5] for reasons that will quickly
become evident; but the damage to the reputation and
development of political scientists' work on the Community
took some time to repair.

General de Gaulle came to power after the Treaty of Rome
had been signed and, although he heartily disliked its
supranational features, he did not repudiate it because he
did not wish to renege on an engagement made by the French
government and, no doubt, because he judged that he could
use the Community for his own purposes and that, in any
trial of strength between himself and its supranationalism,
he would be the victor. This view proved justified in the
event. After freeing himself of the incubus of the Algerian
war, in January 1963 de Gaulle unilaterally announced his
veto on the British approach to membership, and having thus
shaken the Community partners who set much store by the
Community's collective procedures, he immediately concluded
the Franco-German Treaty, demonstrating that as far as he
was concerned traditional inter-state relations took first
place. The Community was subsidiary to the Franco-German
relationship in which France was intended to be the rider
and Germany the horse.

The stoutest defenders of the Community's method were the
Commission, whose President was then Walter Hallstein, and
the Dutch. In 1965 they chose the most favourable ground on

which to challenge de Gaulle, linking agreement to a
financial regulation for the Common Agricultural Policy,
dearly wanted by France, with budgetary control by the
European Parliament, which was anathema to the General. He
immediately withdrew his Ministers from any sessions of
the Council at which new decisions were to be taken and
kept them away, thus frustrating any further progress,
until 1966 when the other member governments accepted the
'Luxembourg compromise', whereby it was agreed that 'when
issues very important to one or more member countries are
at stake, the members of the Council will try, within a
reasonable time, to reach solutions which can be adopted by
all members of the Council ...'. But the French delegation
further insisted that 'discussion must be continued until
unanimous agreement is reached'; and although the other
five governments did not formally subscribe to this, the
procedure of unanimity, i.e. the power of any member
government to veto any decision, became the normal practice
for the following fifteen years.

Thus brutally de Gaulle taught those who harboured any
illusion that integration was an almost automatic process
the power of the nation state. The state has the armies and
the police, that is the power on which the enforcement of
laws and decisions depends; and, despite the transfer to
the Community of instruments of trade policy, agricultural
policy and one or two others, the state retains the bulk of
the instruments of economic policy. The Community cannot
pursue an effective policy on the basis of the member
states' instruments of economic policy and without
Community instruments. The member governments are usually
very slow to reach agreement on policies that involve the
use of their own instruments; and economic policy is so
complex and fluid that even when they have agreed,
generally on a weak compromise, differences in the
interpretation of how decisions are to be executed will
quickly arise and the supposed Community policy will
degenerate into the several national policies. The earlier
federalist writers were very clear about this. They wrote
more about armed forces and defence policy, and for
economic policy they were more concerned with the taxation
needed to finance defence policy and with the issues of
tariffs and currency than with the range of instruments
with which postwar economic policy has been conducted; but
even if the range of economic instruments that interested
them was limited, they insisted that no common policy which
depended entirely on national instruments for its execution
would be effective, and in this they were surely right.
Thus further policy integration requires the transfer of

further policy instruments to the Community; and this requires political decisions by the member states. That such decisions may be hard to secure should have been plain without the need for a brutal Gaullist lesson.

Instead of focussing so much attention as the neo-functionalists did on the Community's institutions, political scientists should have concentrated more upon the political decisions and battles in the member states concerning the handing over of powers and instruments to the Community. The decisions taken in 1950-51 to establish the ECSC; the political battles in 1952-54 over the EDC Treaty; the period 1955-57 when the EEC and Euratom Treaties were negotiated and ratified; the great debates in Britain in 1961-63 and 1970-72; and numerous efforts, some of them successful, most of them not, to add to the Community's stock of instruments: these are the proper material for research on the capacity of states to take decisions to transfer policy instruments.

Behind those decisions and struggles, moreover, lie the economic, social and strategic forces that provide the context for the political process within the states. The founder members of the EC were willing to transfer important powers and instruments not only because defeat had undermined their confidence in the nation state, but also because they were influenced, in contrasting ways, by the strategic might of the Soviet Union and of the United States, and because the development of the modern economy required a wider market. In the 1960s, on the contrary, détente took the heat out of the strategic issue and the Community-wide market was already set up. The umbrella of the Atlantic Alliance and further market-widening through GATT trade negotations seemed to many people to be enough; the impulse to undergo the difficult political process of transferring powers and isntruments was thereby weakened. Thus economic and strategic forces combined with the recovery of the nation state to hinder further developments in policy integration; and the two decades following 1963 showed that neo-functionalist optimism had therefore been misplaced.

TRANSNATIONAL DOLDRUMS

There were hopes, after de Gaulle's resignation in 1969, that the Community would start another dynamic phase of policy integration. There have been achievements in the subsequent years; but the balance sheet supports the view that one of de Gaulle's legacies was a consolidation of the nation state, which made it more difficult to transfer new instruments to the Community.

Soon after de Gaulle had gone, Pompidou and Brandt agreed at the Community's Hague Summit meeting in December 1969 to a 'triptych' of new developments: British entry, the financial regulation for agriculture, and steps towards monetary union. The accession of Britain, together with Denmark and Ireland, on 1 January 1973, was a vindication of the Community approach to economic integration, as against the free trade area approach without quasi-federal institutions and with much less cooperation in economic policy that had earlier been espoused by the British. British entry also brought a large widening and some deepening of the Community's association with francophone African states, into the relationship through the Lomé Convention with almost all African states and a number in the Caribbean and the Pacific; and it lead to the formation of the regional development fund (ERDF). But apart from these by-products of its entry, Britain's presence has not so far contributed to a strengthening of the Community's policy instruments. The Community's achievements in this direction have, indeed, been almost as meagre in the 1970s as they were in the second half of the 1960s, following de Gaulle's démarche that led to the 'Luxembourg compromise'. It would not be fair to attribute too much responsibility for this to the British, however: the doldrums predated our entry by nearly a decade, only the first half of which was under de Gaulle's long shadow. The experience of the attempt to launch an economic and monetary union (EMU), which took place between the departure of de Gaulle and the arrival of Britain, showed that neither economics nor politics were favourable to policy integration among the Community's founder members either.

The grand idea of EMU was to establish a common currency, which the 'Werner Report' to the ministerial Council and the Commission on the subject affirmed would require that 'the principal decisions of economic policy will be taken at the community level and therefore that the necessary powers will be transferred from the national plane to the Community plane', which implied the need for a Community centre of decision of economic policy that 'will be politically responsible to a European Parliament' (EC Commission, 1970). France refused to accept these institutional conditions, which the authors of the report believed to be necessary and which were backed not only by the Commission but also by Germany and other member countries. The grand proposal was therefore reduced in the event to a modest device for currency coordination, nicknamed 'the snake in the tunnel', with a vague commitment to the goal of a common currency; the forces favouring modesty were demonstrated when the German mark was floated in May 1971, only three months after the decisions to launch the economic and monetary union had been taken. The economic turbulence of the 1970s was already having an impact on minor measures of policy integration; and France after de Gaulle was still not ready to accept the federal implications of major measures. Launched in 1979, the European Monetary System (EMS) brought the currencies of all the members except Britain into a new exchange rate mechanism, which has reduced short-term fluctuations among them without preventing changes of parity, and laid plans for a second stage in which a fifth of the member countries' reserves would be placed in a common Reserve Fund. This could be a very substantial instrument of Community monetary and currency policy. But the governments have not yet agreed that the time is ripe to establish it; so the EMS remains another, though more successful, modest exchange rate mechanism, with some other fairly modest monetary instruments related to the European Currency Unit.

The times have been truly difficult since the early 1970s for measures of economic policy integration, even minor ones such as the exchange rate mechanism of the EMS, because the great stagflation has undermined confidence in the efficacy of economic policy instruments and has tended to turn countries in on themselves. But even if the institutional implications of major policy integration have been rejected, by Britain, France and Denmark at least, the 1970s have been a surprisingly innovative period in the field of institutions particularly if the accession of new members is included in this category, since the decade started with the entry of Britain, Denmark and Ireland and ended with negotiations for the entry of Greece, Portugal and Spain, which have already led to Greek accession in January 1981.

Two of the principal institutional developments have had a strongly intergovernmental character. The procedure for cooperation in foreign policy, which was started in 1970, takes place in a ministerial committee misleadingly called the Political Committee, which on French insistence was kept quite separate from the Community institutions. The separation from the Community has become less rigid, and will be removed if the Colombo-Genscher proposals, made in 1981 by the Italian and German Foreign Ministers, are adopted. But the federal element found in the Community institutions has been absent from the activity of this

Committee, whose achievements have been modest, though significant. More dramatic has been the development of summit meetings among the member states which started in 1969 and by a decision of the December 1974 summit were formalised into the European Council. This, too, was at first kept formally separate from the Community institutions, although Community problems and policies comprised the bulk of its business; but in 1977, Roy Jenkins secured agreement to participation in the meetings by the President of the Commission. The European Council has taken a number of important decisions for the Community, including the arrangements to conclude Britain's 'renegotiation' and the launching of direct elections to the European Parliament.

The first direct elections in 1979 and the other major innovation relating to the European Parliament, the Amending Treaty of 1975 which gave the Parliament powers over the Community budget, both had a distinctly federalist character. A directly elected parliament had been an essential feature of federalist plans, in order to secure democratic control over the common instruments of policy. But such control would not be secured unless the parliament had the necessary powers. Hitherto its only substantial power had been the right, probably largely illusory, to dismiss the Commission. In 1975, however, the Amending Treaty strengthened the Parliament's powers to amend and modify the budget, and gave it a power to reject the budget as a whole. While it still lacks power over Community legislation, and while most of the Community's expenditure, termed 'compulsory' in that it has been decided by the ministerial Council under its Treaty powers, effectively escapes the Parliament's control, the Parliament now has significant power over the budget.

These distinct advances in the position of the Parliament, however, do not negate the general impression that the Community has spent the 1970s in the doldrums. If asked what it had been doing during this period, the Community's best answer might be, like that of the French aristocrat after the revolution, that it had survived. The accession of new members is a kind of triumph; the European Council, the foreign policy cooperation and the EMS are achievements in their different ways; the rise of the Parliament has given hope to federalists. There have been few great quarrels and the habit of cooperation has become more entrenched. But the general impression has been that the Community is no longer a dynamic force, or at least that the early federalist impulse has been scotched by the revival of the nation state.

Political scientists have responded to this by applying theories of interdependence, intergovernmentalism and transnationalism to study of the Community.[6] These theories do not write off the nation state, as the neo-functionlists did, or assume, like the federalists, that its sovereignty must be limited by a federal constitution. On the other hand the new theories do, like neo-functionalism, tempt those who use them to extrapolate the existing trend in the Community: in this case a steady state, without radical breaks either towards federation or back to less fettered national sovereignty, in place of the bland accretion of power to the Community institutions that the neo-functionalists envisaged.

While the new theorists have removed one source of error that invalidated the neo-functionalist prognosis by allowing for the tough survival value of the nation state, they have like the neo-functionalists tended to neglect the economic and strategic forces that underlie the relationship between the member states and the Community. Yet if political scientists do not take account of the development of these forces, it is hard to see how they can do other than extrapolate the existing trends in institutions; and, given the changes of trend that have been experienced in the last thirty years, this does not seem to reflect the character of contemporary international relations and thus to be a good guide to the future. The neo-functionalists did not realise that the degree of integration embodied in the Rome Treaties was enough to satisfy the economic needs of the period, without further economic policy integration, and that the Community institutions were already strong enough to manage the required customs union. This ensured that when it encountered an obstacle, their process of spillover was checked. Could it be that, conversely, the rough strategic and economic forces of the 1980s will precipitate a radical break from the steady state that the Community and its institutions maintained through most of the 1970s?

FROM STRATEGIC AND ECONOMIC TURBULENCE TO RADICAL CHANGE IN THE COMMUNITY?

Of the roughness of the strategic and economic forces that prevail in the early 1980s there can be no doubt. The East-West balance of power is unstable, relations with the Soviet Union are bad, and the state of the western economies recalls the 1930s, in sharp contrast to the 1950s and 1960s.

The freezing of détente follows a long period of inexorable growth in Soviet military power, underlined by its use in Afghanistan and by the Soviet manoeuvres in and around Poland before the military takeover in 1981. Following a time of uncertainty after the Vietnam war and Watergate, the United States has an administration determined to rebuild American power and to react sharply to any Soviet behaviour seen as provocative. While West Europeans have been worried by the the Soviet military expansion and shaken by events in Poland, they in general wish to preserve what they can of détente. But this must depend on acceptable behaviour on the part of the Russians;and even if the Russians behave acceptably from the European point of view, détente also depends on the interaction between the Soviet Union and the United States. The political and strategic equilibrium is unstable and could be upset, not only by acts of policy but also by scarcely controllable events.

These strategic pressures could affect the Community in various ways. They could be an agent of disintegration, particularly if they became so acute that some countries were to run for cover under the American wing whilst others sought accommodation with the Russians. The pressures could on the contrary lead to more cooperation among Community members on defence; the inclusion of security cooperation with foreign policy cooperation in the Colombo-Genscher proposals, as well as signs that the French government may be becoming more open-minded on the issue, show that this is quite likely to happen, at least if the strategic pressures remain at their present level. Could it follow that stronger pressures would push the Community in the direction of military integration and hence towards a federal system such as was envisaged by the EDC? It seems unlikely. At times of crisis people tend, rather, to fall back on the more familiar institutions, which in this case are those of the nation state and of the Atlantic Alliance. Because military integration goes straight to the heart of national sovereignty, it is not likely to occur unless national sovereignty has ceased to be an issue. This could happen, as it almost did in the early postwar period, after the nation states have been shattered by war. It could also result from an experience of economic integration that was sufficiently far-reaching and satisfactory to the countries involved to allay doubts about this futher, apparently less revocable step.

Economic pressures might, like strategic pressures, have either integrative or disintegrative consequences for the Community. Unemployment and stagnation make the adjustments

caused by trade hard to take, and the danger of a rise of
protection among the member states has been only too
apparent. On the whole, the member governments' efforts to
grapple with the problem of stagflation have been inimical
to integration, whether through German resistance to
further monetary integration for fear of infection from
other member countries' inflation and of the cost of
supporting their currencies, or through the weaker
countries' industrial policies which may amount to
protection within the common market. If stagflation
continues or gets worse, will the national policies become
more and more disintegrative? This could happen. But the
chances of its doing so depend on the type of policies
pursued and on how well they deal with the stagflation.
For successful policies would not only counter the
disintegrative forces but would, it will be argued, imply a
further degree of integration.

If stagflation were caused by monetary disorder, it would
be cured by monetary control. With free movement of money
across frontiers, it might be supposed that the monetary
control should be exercised by institutions beyond the
nation state, such as the European Community or the
International Monetary Fund; and since the Community has a
stronger political capacity to exercise such control, this
would seem to imply a central bank and a common currency
for the Community, as envisaged by the Werner Report. But
those who assume the cause and cure of stagflation to be
monetary usually think in terms of national monetary
control, so that this type of policy has little integrative
potential. Nor, in this writer's view, can monetary control
alone cure stagnation in the modern economy, whose
structure contains market imperfections that give rise to
pay push and high adjustment costs and thus impede the
allocation of resources to the investment and development
on which employment as well as growth depend. Either the
monetary control is accompanied by other policies such as
are normally pursued in the mixed economies of Western
Europe, or stagnation will continue and the Community will
be likely to disintegrate.

A second view is that stagflation is inherent in the
capitalist system, so that the cure is to replace this by
another system, sometimes known as central planning. Here
again, logic might point towards central planning of a
market wider than the nation state. But its advocates in
practice envisage national planning, hence disintegration
of a common market. This view provides one of the motives
for the Labour Party's policy to take Britain out of the
Community. Although some of the intellectual support for

this has a Marxist slant,[7] Soviet writers on the Community
stress on the contrary that integration is a condition of
the scientific and technological development of the modern
economy, or in their words, an 'objective phenomenon',
providing a 'higher level of internationalisation of
production and of economic links' (Maximova, 1971, p.128,
my translation). Thus even in Marxist terms, a policy of
disintegration is seen to be inappropriate for the modern
economy. To those who, like the present writer, regard a
highly centralised form of economic management as equally
inappropriate, a policy of national central planning and
international disintegration is doubly condemned to
failure.

The mainstream of policy in Western Europe is, however,
running towards neither laisser-faire monetarism nor
directive central planning but a further evolution of the
mixed economy. This includes efforts to counter pay push
through various forms of incomes policy and to promote
investment and industrial development through industrial
and manpower as well as macroeconomic policies. The
manpower and the incomes policies are, corresponding to the
extent of the labour markets, largely a matter for national
governments. But the industrial and macroeconomic policies,
if they are to be effective, must be conceived in a wider
context. Investment and development in difficult
circumstances require a range of support from public
policy. Neither interest rates nor exchange rates should be
too high. Both are subject to powerful international
influences, particularly from the United States; and
whereas the single European countries are powerless to
resist these influences, the Community as a whole could do
so if it had adequate instruments of monetary intervention
such as a Reserve Fund with which to buy or sell dollars on
a sufficient scale and, if necessary, an exchange control
for the Community as a whole. Industrial development, with
the high cost of new investment and of adjustment away from
old capacity, also needs to be promoted by various means
such as subsidies for research and development, incentives
for investment, adjustment assistance and rationalisation
programmes, which are seen in their most advanced form in
Japan but are also practised to a greater or lesser degree
in all the Community countries. Since the costs of
adjustment and development are not only high but growing,
the scope of such industrial policy is likely to increase,
even if the emphasis is changing from propping up the
uncompetitive to easing them out and promoting more
promising activities. If the growing weight of national
industrial policy is not to disintegrate the Community, the

Community's own industrial policy will have to be strengthened, and this implies Community instruments such as funds for promoting adjustment and development and greater powers to promote rationalistation programmes, as well as a more effective and constructive use of existing powers with respect to state aids and competition policy.

If this line of reasoning is right, the member countries will be unable to bring stagflation under control and restore their economies to price stability with full employment and healthy growth unless they provide the Community with substantial instruments such as the proposed Reserve Fund and adequate funds for Community industrial policy, as well as ensuring that its institutions are decisive enough to deploy effectively both these new instruments and the existing ones; and this brings us back to the question whether states are likely to transfer any of their sovereign powers.

WILL THE MEMBER STATES TRANSFER SOVEREIGNTY?

Although the states in the Community are now much stronger than were the states that founded it after the war, which tells against the transfer of sovereignty, economic forces are propelling them towards a form of economic management for which a customs union combined with national macroeconomic policies is not enough. While one reaction is to seek to pull out of the free trade system, that is widely understood to be incompatible with the development of a modern economy for the small and medium-sized countries of Western Europe.   Conviction that common Community policies need to be developed is therefore likely to grow; and the intensity of discussion in the Community institutions on subjects such as steel, shipbuilding and textiles shows that this is accepted in principle. Realisation that without Community instruments such discussions do not lead to adequate action is also likely to spread. Yet even when it is understood that economic forces are pressing us towards policy integration, instruments will not be transferred or Community institutions strengthened without a powerful political impulse. One element in such an impulse must certainly be political leadership in one or more of the major member governments, with a sufficiently receptive response from the others.   Such a political conjuncture is not likely, however, without economic events that bring the general drift of economic forces sharply to the surface. Such an event could, for example, be an acute crisis of stagflation in the United States, which may occur in the next year or two and could induce the Community to defend itself collectively against disruption from the American monetary system. Such a crisis would also tend to deflate the Community economy and heighten the danger of protection among the member states, unless the Community responded with a common industrial policy to revive the member countries' industries without the disintegrative effect that purely national policies would have.

If any such events did impel the member countries to give the Community substantial instruments of monetary and industrial policy, the Community institutions with their present form and procedures would not be likely to use them effectively. Although such a heavily intergovernmental system has proved able to manage the customs union, its performance with respect to issues of industrial policy for sectors such as shipbuilding and steel has been poor. Industrial and monetary events are fast-moving; tough decisions are often required; and institutions unable to deliver tough decisions swiftly are therefore inadequate. If the economic pressures cause governments to shift instruments of policy to the Community, either those pressures will continue strong enough to induce changes in the institutions that ensure the effective use of the instruments, or the instruments will eventually be shifted back to the nation states.

The changes required in the institutions could appear modest, although they would necessarily imply a crucial shift in the locus of power. From an intergovernmental perspective, the practice of majority voting on important as well as minor matters could enable the Council to act swiftly and decisively. In this case the majority votes of May 1982 on farm prices, inconvenient though they may have been for Britain at the time, might lead to an effective Community which should be to the advantage of all. From a federalist perspective, it is not thought likely that the more powerful governments will in fact usually behave like that, even if the principle of majority voting is accepted; so more power has to be given to the Parliament where normal democratic procedures apply. Even here, however, the necessary reform could be quite simple: the Parliament could be given the power of co-decision with the Council for Community legislation and for the appointment of the Commission as well as for the budget, which it already has; and a limit of, say, six months could be set, beyond which time the Council could not delay the passage of bills except by a majority vote to amend or reject them. The watershed between the Community's existing institutions and an effectively federal system is as narrow as that.

Even if it is accepted that the underlying economic
forces favour such policy integration, scepticism will
doubtless suspend belief that the transfer of substantial
further instruments is possible, let alone the reform of
institutions to make their use effective. If that is so,
the trend of economic policy, with increasing need for
microeconomic intervention of the sort practised in Japan,
will probably lead to the disintegration of the Community,
not easily distinguished at first from a steady state since
the disintegration is more likely to take the form of a
creeping process than a big bang. But creeping or not,
contemporary economic forces and modern economic policy may
not leave the steady state of a customs union as an option
for the Community. If this is so, we will have to choose
between disintegration and a degree of policy integration
that could be defined as federation. Students of the
Community cannot foretell which the outcome will be. But
the purpose of this chapter is to show that, if the choice
is to be made in full knowledge of the implications, we
should focus our study on the essentials of our
contemporary economic problem and of the Community's role
in its solution. Thus we must take account of the economic
forces that make for policy integration and for changes in
the system of economic management; of the policy
instruments that the Community may require to make this
management effective; of the institutional requirements if
the instruments are to be used effectively; and of the
balance of political forces in the member states that will
determine decisions whether or not to give the Community
the instruments and accept the changes to its institutions.
The interaction between economic policy integration and the
Community's response to strategic developments also needs
to be considered. One result of such study might be a neo-
federalist theory which adapts the thinking of the
Community's founders and of the earlier British federal
unionists to contemporary needs.   But the main purpose
would be to help the citizens of the Community to make an
intelligent choice about its future development.

NOTES

1.   Statement made by M.Robert Schuman on 9 May 1950,
     cited in full in Pryce (1962).
2.   Speech of 10 August 1952, cited in Jean Monnet, Les
     Etats-Unis d'Europe ont Commencé (1955) pp. 56-7 (my
     translation).

3.   Walter Lipgens (1968 and 1982); the English edition
      (1982) includes contributions by Wilfred Loth and
      Alan Milward.
4.   For example, Sir William Beveridge (1940);
      W.Ivor Jennings (1940); Lord Lothian (1939), reprinted
      in Ransome P. (ed.) (1943); R.W.G. Mackay (1940);
      Lionel Robbins (1939 and 1940); K.C. Wheare (1941),
      reprinted in Ransome P. (ed.)(1943); J.H. Wilson
      (1940); and Barbara Wootton (1941).
5.   See for example Haas (1967); Haas's preface to the
      1968 edition of Haas (1958); and Lindberg and
      Scheingold (1970).
6.   The concepts are analysed in Webb (1977).
7.   See for example Holland (1980).

3 Membership of the EC and its Alternatives

Stephen C. Holt

<u>INTRODUCTION</u>

Whatever the verdict of History may ultimately be on the wisdom of Britain's decision to join the Community it will certainly not be easy to justify to our grandchildren or great-grandchildren the tortuous process by which the decision was made. Whether they have by then confirmed and consolidated British membership or have faced the upheaval of undoing it, they can hardly look back on the Rake's Progress of Britain's European policy since the war with any satisfaction. We have neither remained aloof with dignity and produced a tailor-made commercial policy of our own as did Sweden in the early post-war years nor did we secure entry on favourable terms that avoided repeated <u>de facto</u> re-negotiation. The untied ends of previous rounds of bargaining with our Community partners like the Budget and Fisheries issues, persist in alienating British public opinion and keeping alive the continued agonising about whether Britain should withdraw. The purpose of this chapter is not to criticise that agonising as such but to argue that if there is to be a further public debate on the issue, incorporated in a General Election campaign, then it needs to be on more constructive and coherent lines than it has ever been in the past. If not, Britain will continue to get the worst of both worlds i.e. neither pursuing an alternative strategy nor able to commit herself wholeheartedly to membership because of constant glances at the apparently greener grass in the next field.

The question of Britain's membership of the EC has been the plaything of party politics. Critics of our adversary style of politics will add it to their list of examples (alongside incomes policy, nationalisation and industrial relations) of how costly that system can be. Clearly it has not been treated by the political class with the degree of seriousness that earlier generations treated the great party splitting issues of Home Rule for Ireland and Free Trade versus Protectionism. It was not seen as an issue on which careers should be put on the line. While it has played a part in the Labour-SDP split, it would never have caused this split on its own. Yet is not Britain's

membership of the EC an issue of comparable importance to
Home Rule and Free Trade? If the Community manages to hold
together and if the main objectives of the Rome Treaties
are attained and joined by others in the political field,
then it could be argued that in terms of the balance of
power this is the most important development in Europe
since the French Revolution.

If the issue of Britain's continued membership is to be
publicly debated once again, then we need a clear map and a
compass. The purpose of this chapter is to provide an
outline map and a set of bearings concerning the relevant
choices that have to be made. But before looking at the
alternatives, and the consequential questions that may
arise, it is necessary very briefly to recapitulate some of
the turning points in the previous public debate. In doing
this we are, of course, enjoying the benefit of hindsight
and indeed successive Governments have sometimes adjusted
their policies accordingly, but in this writer's view,
enough lessons from hindsight have not yet been learned and
certain mistakes are likely to be repeated.

Even with our subsequent knowledge, it is not really hard
to understand why a Labour Government that had just
completed a considerable domestic programme of
nationalisation that included Coal and Steel did not want
to put these industries under international control by
joining the ECSC. Nor is it hard to appreciate how a large
Free Trade Area would have suited Britain better in the
fifties. But once we had failed to persuade the member
states of the EC to co-operate with such an arrangement and
the option of full EC membership for Britain had been
chosen, the failure publicly to face up to the full
implications of membership only stored up trouble for
later. The first round of negotiations of 1961-3
constituted a heavy overdose of British pragmatism – an
overconcentration on the short term practical problems
rather than looking first at the well-advertised
destination of the train we were about to board. The long
term political implications, the implications for national
sovereignty were determinedly played down.[1] This strategy
was resorted to because so many influential politicians in
the Government and the Opposition had so recently gone on
record as saying how inappropriate the aims and objectives
of the EC were for Britain. Within Britain this strategy
worked in holding off divisive and politically damaging
disputes within the major parties as the politically
easiest option was taken of "waiting for the terms".
Jo Grimond, the Liberal leader at the time, likened these
people to someone in the mid-sixteenth century who went

round saying that they could not decide whether they were
for or against the Reformation until they saw what price
the monasteries would fetch.[2] This stratagem worked so well
from the point of view of party managers that it was
resorted to again during the second attempt in 1967, during
the 1970-71 negotiations and even during the renegotiation
of 1974-5. The debate was largely kept on the level of
practicalities and away from basic doctrine. While anti-
marketeers criticised fundamentals, it was all too easy for
voters generally favourably disposed towards the
politicians advocating entry to regard such talk as wildly
exaggerated and accept the latter's low key, minimalist
approach. While it might be legitimate to dismiss the idea
that the Community will ever become a single Federal State,
it was surely unwise for promarketeers not to be more
frank, for example, about the far-reaching implications of
economic union. The evidence for this is the continued
shock and dismay amongst the media and public about many of
the fresh pieces of harmonisation that emanate from
Brussels under Article 100 of the EEC Treaty.

The 1961-63 negotiations became so bogged down in detail
and were consequently so dragged out that De Gaulle was
able to pronounce his veto with impunity. While lessons
were learnt from this in that in 1970-1 and 1974-5, British
negotiators tried to concentrate on the real essentials, a
heavier dose of Cartesian medicine was evidently required
on such issues as the Budget and Fisheries. But it was the
Referendum of 1975 which should have provided the best
opportunity for a fundamental national debate because on
this occasion the restraints of party unity could be
temporarily set aside. Furthermore, the principal advocate
of the Referendum, Mr. Tony Benn, had indicated before and
after the poll that the result should be accepted.[3]

Unfortunately, the Referendum lacked the coherence it
might have had for a number of reasons. While the main
justification for holding the first ever British national
referendum was that a putative transfer of sovereignty was
involved in membership, the campaign was by no means
confined to argument about the nature and extent of the
sovereignty transfer. It was about policy matters too and
voters were regaled with statistics as in a General
Election. On the other hand, the campaign was unlike a
General Election in one very important respect - there were
not two or more competing programmes each with at least
some internal consistency from which voters could choose.
The debate was again conducted as it had been since 1961 in
terms of whether membership of the EC was a good or bad
thing for Britain. While the National Referendum Campaign

in its leaflet 'Why you should vote NO' formally put
forward the alternative of industrial free trade, this was
a low key aspect of the campaign because there were
influential supporters within its ranks like Tony Benn who
favoured import controls. Enoch Powell has always favoured
the free trade option as, at that time, did Peter Shore
who, in a specially written Fabian pamphlet commended the
kind of industrial free trade agreement that our former
EFTA partners had made.[4] A Labour Research Department
pamphlet[5], again written for the Referendum, seemed to
imply that the EC might give us an industrial free trade
agreement and allow us to impose selective import controls
at the same time. Its authors also seemed unaware that an
industrial free trade agreement entails accepting the
essence of the Community's competition regulations[6].

The Referendum voters found the issues so complex, with
experts still divided as they had been before entry[7], that
they seem to have allowed the ordinary processes of
political leadership to work and followed the advice of the
leaders in whom they had come to have confidence on other
issues.[8] With these forces of polarisation at work, the two
to one majority vote in favour of continued membership had
no connection with the degree of enthusiasm for the
intended destination of the Community train. The result was
undoubtedly misread in the other Member States and this can
only have contributed to the worsening irritation over
continued British equivocation after all this time. Unlike
them, we had the advantage of watching the EC at work for
more than a decade before deciding to join.

Since the Referendum, one part of the picture has become
slightly more coherent, namely that the Labour Party has
adopted withdrawal as official party policy by a Conference
vote of 6,213,000 to 782,000. This vote was taken after
less than an hour's debate in which not a single overtly
pro-market supporter came to the rostrum.[9] It was only
afterwards that the Conference voted to set in train an
enquiry into the 'full economic and political consequences
and opportunities' involved in withdrawal.[10] Following this
enquiry the Labour Party will presumably endeavour to agree
and adopt a clear alternative strategy to membership of the
EC to put before the voters at the next election. It will
have to do this if it wants its policy of withdrawal to be
taken seriously. Pro-marketeers on the other hand, have to
realise that very large numbers of voters continue to
express their disappointment in opinion polls about the
results of membership, in such areas as the British Budget
contribution, import penetration and so on. Many are
prepared to contemplate withdrawal in principle and hence

will wish to discuss alternatives. What are these
alternatives and what are the questions concerning them
that have to be resolved?

The alternatives fall into three broad categories each
one containing certain sub-variations: (i) an industrial
free trade agreement with the EC; (ii) a policy of long
term import controls; or (iii) a policy of 'export led'
growth which eschews both (i) and (ii). We must look at
these in turn.

INDUSTRIAL FREE TRADE

We should first be clear exactly what is meant by this
option. It is not a realistic proposition simply to return
to EFTA. While this organisation still exists, it is now
even more clearly the 'staging post' that it always was. It
should be remembered that the other members of EFTA do more
trade with the EC than they do with each other and
following the separate Free Trade Agreements they
negotiated with the Community at the time of British entry,
their exports overall to the EC have increased, in the
cases of Norway and Portugal dramatically so[11]. In order to
obtain these Agreements, they had to accept a series of
conditions and obligations, which we will return to
presently, but at this stage we should note that crucial
among these were some rather stringent 'rules of origin'
that define the status of goods traded between themselves
and the EC. To incorporate too many foreign components in
certain manufactured goods risks that they will 'lose
origin' and the whole product be treated as not home-
produced and therefore subject to the EC's common external
tariff. If Britain therefore rejoined EFTA but did not also
secure a bilateral Free Trade Agreement with the EC she
would face the same handicaps on 'origin' as the Americans
and the Japanese. In any case, the reasons which made EFTA
inadequate in 1961, namely its insufficient size (giving us
access to an additional market of only 40 million) apply
just as much today.

If we are to think seriously about industrial free trade
as an alternative to full membership of the EC, it would
have to be in the context of a directly negotiated Free
Trade Agreement between the UK and the Community. The first
issue to be considered is, would we get such an agreement?
It should not be automatically assumed that we would. Only
a few people on the continent, within the circle that would
actually decide, have gone on record on the subject. One
who has is Leo Tindemans, leader of the European People's

Party, former Prime Minister of Belgium and President of
the Council of Ministers. His view is that it is far from
certain that Britain would be granted the status of a
preferential trading partner if she withdraws.[12] Off the
record opinion, in this writer's experience, seems to
conflict, with some saying definitely no and others
believing that after a couple of years continental
exporters would exercise sufficient pressure to re-open
trading links with Britain and it would be too inconvenient
to the Governments of these countries to resist any longer.
Undoubtedly, however, the diplomatic and psychological
atmosphere in which 'terms of withdrawal' were negotiated
would be frosty in the extreme, as we inflicted on our
former partners massive inconvenience and cost. It would be
hazardous, would it not, to count too positively on the
outcome of those 'terms of exit' being 'fair'
'satisfactory' or 'acceptable' in the way these words were
used so glibly in the years 1961-71?

However, for the sake of argument, let us assume that the
Community decides immediately to let us leave, while
continuing to enjoy industrial free trade. What questions
do the British have to resolve in deciding whether this
option now suits them?

The first and most obvious advantages involve the
shedding of the burden of our Budget contributions and the
closely linked Common Agricultural Policy. The advantage to
the balance of payments and to our standard of living of
being free to buy imported food in the cheapest market,
would, in some people's view, be so considerable as greatly
to outweigh the numerically larger list of disadvantages.
The British Parliament would fully recover its much prized
sovereignty. Any Community legislation which previously had
'direct effect' would now require further enactment in
Westminster if we chose to follow it. The decisions of the
European Court of Justice would not be automatically
binding and so on. The often vexing proposals for
harmonisation of various industrial standards under Article
100 that flow out of Brussels would be voluntary as far as
Britain was concerned - voluntary that is, unless we wished
to continue trading <u>inside</u> the EC. Once we wished to do
that, even as a non-member we would have either to comply
with these new standards or cease trading inside the
Community in that product. Having given up the British seat
in the Council of Ministers, we would not have been
consulted during the formulation of such proposals and, of
course, could not have used a veto, such as it is worth, to
stop something inconvenient to our traders being agreed.

During the long prelude to British accession in 1973,

there was always heated argument about the CAP, the effects of the Common External tariff on Commonwealth trade and so on.   But until the time of the referendum, there was a widespread belief within industry that in terms of industrial competition, British industry could hold its own and on balance the effects would be beneficial[13]. While it is now clear that the so-called 'dynamic industrial benefits', (that were going to compensate for the CAP), have in many cases been slow in coming and indeed may never come, no one can say that this side of the problem was not thoroughly investigated. At each round of our approach to the Community - in 1961-63, in 1971-2 and again in 1974-5, the most extensive surveys of British industry and/or reports were undertaken by such organisations as the CBI, the Chambers of Commerce and various Industrial Associations.[14] Independent publications like The Times and the Economist also undertook their own surveys.[15] The vast majority of these surveys produced majorities in favour of joining or staying in the EC.   Certain economists in universities, some of whom were taking a wider macro-economic view, and who came to opposite conclusions, had the difficulty of arguing their viewpoint without seeming to imply that they knew better that the people who actually had to sell the boots and shoes etc., whether these markets would be forthcoming. The fact is however, that these so-called 'dynamic industrial benefits' have been slow in coming. Undoubtedly the situation has been greatly complicated by the oil crisis which was not yet upon us when we decided to join and its long-term implications were not fully realised even at the time of the referendum. But this is not a very weighty excuse. All member states have had to grapple with the problems caused by the oil crisis and even though the Founder States have not had the burdens of adjusting to Community membership during this period as Britain has, they have not had North Sea oil either, which, it seems to them, should have been more than adequate compensation.

If a Free Trade Agreement between Britain and the Community could be negotiated, there are certain features of that arrangement that we know in advance would be inescapable. As indicated earlier, all the EFTA countries that have negotiated such agreements with the Community have had to accept the equivalent of the competition regulations of the full member states. Each Treaty has its equivalent of Article 85 (dealing with price fixing agreements), of Article 86 (concerning monopolies and monopoly practices) and Article 92 (concerning state aids to enterprises). It is inconceivable that a large developed country like Britain would be admitted to the existing free trade system in western Europe without promising to observe the same rules in these fields as everyone else. It would undermine fair competition in the entire grouping if an exception were made. The fact is that with or without a Free Trade Agreement, any trade we wished to conduct inside the Community would be subject to these competition regulations. With an Agreement, disputes between Governments would be discussed in a Joint Committee and there would be no right of access to an independent arbiter like a Court. If the dispute were not resolved amicably, there would be nothing to stop tariff concessions being withdrawn and the whole Agreement renounced with one year's notice.

As a substantial steel producer, like five of the EFTA countries, we would have to accept the alignment of steel prices without consultation (see Article 20 of the ECSC/Sweden Agreement). As a major oil producer, we would now certainly have to give assurances not to discriminate in our oil policy between Community countries and ourselves, otherwise this might be deemed unfair competition. An indication that this is likely to be so can be seen from the fact that Finland, Sweden and Norway were held to good conduct on both supply and price of paper and pulp.

Even if the other 'terms' which Britain might secure in a new Free Trade Agreement were favourable, the inescapable basic terms contain several of the same features that anti-marketeers, particularly on the Left, have found objectionable in full membership. They want to be free of all these shackles, because they believe that hemmed in by such restrictions, British industry will be unable to pull itself up by its bootstraps.

Much more research needs to be done about why expectations expressed before entry by many sections of British industry have not been fulfilled. (No Economics postgraduate interested in this area need be short of a thesis topic.) But until such research has been done, it is difficult to avoid the provisional conclusion that British industry was not in such good shape as it imagined. Views differ as to whether the situation is improving and can be relied upon to improve further. For example, the Commission's analysis of British-EC trade published in August 1981 highlighted a favourable movement of the import/export ratio in the non-oil sector under most headings, [16] but this is complicated by the undoubted effect of the recession on imports. But suppose, for the sake of argument, it were to be accepted that British

industry were poorly placed to compete with most of the
rest of the Community even in the long term, we are still
left with the question - what is to be done? In politics as
in so many other spheres of life you have to proceed from
where you are at the time.

IMPORT CONTROLS

The most widely canvassed alternative to Britain continuing
to trade freely with the Community (either as a full member
or under a Free Trade Agreement) is to adopt a policy of
general or selective import controls. Import controls in an
emergency are permissable even within the terms of
Community membership, although of course they require the
agreement of a qualified majority of the other member
states and must be limited in scope and duration .[17] Italy
made recourse to this emergency clause in 1974 and 1981.
However, most advocates of long term import controls in
Britain have in mind a long term programme of ten years or
more which would constitute an effective instrument of
economic planning.
   Not much space will be devoted to the merits and demerits
of long term import controls, because chapter 5 eludes to
it and an elaborate discussion of its fallacious nature can
be found in El-Agraa (1982). But the main considerations
can be summarised briefly.
   Undoubtedly, if British industry were to give even the
degree of protection involved in freezing imports at their
present levels, substantial inroads could be made in the
unemployment figures as all further growth in demand is met
by domestic production. In the short run, the benefits
might well be rapid, but in the longer term, serious
disadvantages can ensue which are difficult to reverse. For
example, an increasingly high cost structure is allowed to
develop which makes it likely that when the time comes that
we wish to acquire further growth by increasing exports,
our goods would no longer be competitive in world markets.
Furthermore, if the degree of protection offered by general
or selective import controls were to be effective, the
levels of tariff imposed would have to be high. Where these
tariffs did not stop imports completely, the internal
effects could be highly inflationary. Similarly, the
formerly favoured strategy of a depreciation of sterling,
because it increased the cost of all imports, was also
inflationary and did nothing per se to improve
competitiveness. Unless the breathing space provided is
properly used, long term inflation is simply stoked up

further. Quotas, however, where they are feasible are undoubtedly less inflationary than tariffs.

THE EXPORT-LED GROWTH ALTERNATIVE

A leading exponent of export promotion as a remedy for Britain's economic difficulties is Professor A.P. Thirwall of the University of Kent. His ideas are set out in a series of important papers written alone and with others since 1975.[18] Taking the period 1970-79 over 17 Industrial Orders, Thirlwall has demonstrated that, apart from Coal and Petroleum products and Mechanical Engineering, there is a strong rank correlation of 0.621 between the rate of employment decline and the rate of deterioration in the balance between imports and exports - see Thirlwell (1982, p.35). Because, in Britain, economic growth requires so much in the way of imports, unless exports have risen equally fast (and usually they have not), then a balance of payments crisis has ensued and internal demand has had to be damped down with all its consequences for investment. The worrying feature from Britain's point of view is that it has one of the lowest rates of increase in volume of exports in the western industrialised world and one of the lowest balance of payments equilibrium growth rates. It is not much more than one half of the rate of its major European neighbours (Thirwall and Dixon, 1979). If Britain is to escape the syndrome of slow growth and low productivity (or falling employment) it must raise the rate of growth of exports and/or lower the income elasticity of demand for imports (Thirlwall and Dixon, 1979). The fundamental point at the aggregate level is that no country can grow faster than that rate consistent with balance of payments equilibrium on current account unless it can finance ever growing deficits. The balance of payments equilibrium growth rate itself is determined by the rate of growth of export volume, divided by the income elasticity of demand for imports, if relative prices in international trade remain relatively unchanged in the long run. Attempts to grow faster by expanding demand are doomed to failure in the long run, unless the rate of growth of exports rises or the income elasticity of demand for imports is reduced.

Import penetration can also be of an 'autonomous' nature (i.e. not induced by income growth), and if exports do not rise to match, there will be a loss of employment. As indicated earlier, there are considerable long term difficulties about doing anything very significant to restrain imports.

While economists may continue to disagree about whether there is any other way of resolving Britain's economic problems than by bringing about a steep increase in exports, it would be fair to say that few, if any, would disagree that if this could be brought about, in the visible but non-oil sector, then rapid results in reducing unemployment would appear. Here is not the place to attempt to evaluate the evidence pointing to the view that export-led growth is <u>the only</u> solution to Britain's economic problems. We ought, however, to set out what steps might have to be taken to pursue this strategy and consider the obstacles that could stand in the way inside or outside the EC.

Once the industries with good export growth potential have been identified (either because of price elasiticity or by their ability to trade up-market), how best can they be backed? Exporting usually requires more effort than selling at home, so it has to be made demonstrably worthwhile.

The most straightforward way is to encourage the companies concerned with a series of export profits tax reliefs (EPTR). A cross country comparison of what has been done here appears in an article by G.C. Hufbauer in the <u>National Tax Journal</u> (March 1975). Spain, for example, allowed half the tax liability on exports profits to be placed in a special reserve fund for export related investment; and in the USA, after 1972, it became possible to establish a Domestic International Sales Corporation enabling the taxation of export profits to be reduced from about 48 per cent to 36 per cent.[19] The only country to exempt export profits from taxation entirely, albeit at a reducing rate, has been the Irish Republic (after 1958) and this is now being phased out. No new exemptions were entered into after 1st January 1981 although some of the previous ones are to be allowed to run until 1990. The Irish Government was simply persuaded by the Commission and the other member states of the EC that such a tax was incompatible with Community membership. While the issue was never tested in the European Court of Justice, it is safe to assume in this case that the Commission had Community Law on its side. Since 1st January 1981, Ireland has a new 10 per cent corporation tax which is still the lowest in Europe. While this tax does not discriminate between exports and home production, it is, together with certain other incentives, a powerful magnet for foreign investment, which in turn creates jobs. But from Ireland's point of view, it is unfortunate that the tax exemptions on export sales had to be abolished. The results of one study suggest

a substantial policy effect for EPTR of the order of 30,000 manufacturing jobs between 1960 and 1974.[20]

Making the assumption (which is almost certainly correct) that an EPTR of the pre-1981 type is incompatible with Community membership, what would the position be if Britain were <u>outside</u> the EC? A number of Third World countries have resort to EPTR but they are in most cases not members of the GATT. Generally speaking in the GATT, tax relief which stimulates investment is in order but direct incentives to foreign trade are ruled out under Article XVI. Nevertheless, there are examples of countries who have successfully flouted the spirit of this agreement over a period of years. It is difficult to see, for example, how the Australian Government gets away with its Export Expansion Grants Scheme. Perhaps because the grants are on a regressive scale and are also taxable, other GATT members may not think a dispute worth the candle. Undoubtedly, Britain could sail even nearer to the wind than Australia, because her influence in GATT, having been a leading founder member, is much greater. For the reasons stated earlier (i.e. to avoid discriminatory tariff moves against her), Britain would almost certainly wish to remain in GATT even if she left the EC. She would accordingly have to remain within its practically tolerable if not its formal restraints.

Another tempting candidate for promoting exports is the device of greatly extending export credit guarantees. But in this area too our hands are tied, this time by the 'Consensus Rules' within the OECD which govern down payments, minimum interest rates and maximum periods of repayments. If anything significant were to be done here we would need to obtain a special derogation, assuming again that we wished to remain members of OECD.

A great deal of research needs to be done on precisely which forms of export promotion Britain could realistically use within the constraints of the international organisations to which she may wish to continue to belong. The <u>prima facie</u> evidence suggests that a large battery of small but sophisticated devices would have to be used if a really successful export drive were to be launched. There are all kinds of small 'loopholes' to be exploited where we could learn from other countries, like the Japanese freight subsidies and the way France has made such skilful use of export credits in trade with the developing countries of the Franc zone. There are ways of tying this in with Development Aid that technically comply with international rules.

If Britain were to decide to leave the EC, the Export-led

Growth alternative seems in many ways to be the most promising. It has the virtue of not requiring the consent of our Community partners to a Free Trade Agreement and not driving a coach and horses through the international trading system by imposing swingeing import controls. Nevertheless, it is fraught with difficulties and any future Government contemplating such a course would have to do the most careful homework beforehand and ensure adequate popular backing. The consequences if the strategy started to go wrong could be appalling. Moreover, a policy that relies heavily on the exploitation of 'loopholes' is far from being a panacea for British ills. In any case, a new trade policy would have to be combined with a matching industrial policy.

Speaking personally, this writer hopes that this research will be done for two reasons. First, because the Labour Party may enter the next election having painted itself and the country into a corner over EC withdrawal and they could be elected for reasons unconnected with the Community. If that happens, we shall need a more carefully thought out strategy for foreign trade than has so far been produced. But secondly, and most importantly, even those political parties committed to keeping Britain inside the Community may find some useful export promotion devices that are not incompatible with Community rules and then any Government could implement them within a Community-wide consensus. This will not undermine the policy's impact because although it is a game in which all the EC member nations may participate, we stand to gain more simply because we trade more with the outside world while the rest of the EC does not.

NOTES:
1. See in particular Harold Macmillan's speech in House of Commons, 26 November 1956, Hansard cols. 37-38, and speech by Harold Wilson, col. 57.
2. Closing speech at Liberal Assembly, 1962 (unpublished).
3. Extract from letter to Mr. Benn's constituents, 29 December 1974 and quoted in Facts, November/December 1981, European Movement (British Council), London. Also see this statement reported in The Times, 7 June 1975.
4. Europe: the way back. Fabian Tract 425, p.26.
5. The Common Market IN or OUT: 1975 Referendum. LRD Publications, London, 1975.
6. Ibid p. 30.

7. See for example the two letters simultaneously published in The Times on October 22, 1971, after the publication of the Government White Paper setting out the 'terms' of entry. They were signed by 142 university economists favouring acceptance of the terms and by 154 favouring rejection.

8. In this regard, the respective leaflets of both sides show an interesting contrast. The National Referendum Campaign's 'Why You Should Vote No' concentrates on the arguments, whereas the Britain in Europe leaflet 'Why You Should Vote Yes' gives prominence to quotations from respected political leaders in Britain and the Commonwealth (Roy Jenkins, William Whitelaw, Edward Heath, Jo Grimmond, Shirley Williams and the Prime Ministers of Canada, Australia and New Zealand).

9. The Guardian, 2 October 1981.

10. Ibid.

11. EFTA Trade 1979-80, Secretariat of the European Free Trade Association, Geneva, pp. 25 and 26.

12. Press Release by European People's Party, Brussels, 31 July 1981.

13. A number of well known Economists, however, did not take this view. For one detailed analysis of the problem see Nicholas Kaldor's article in the New Statesman, 12 March 1971, The Truth about the 'Dynamic Effects'.

14. See, for example, Britain and Europe Vol. 3: a programme for action, Confederation of British Industry, London 1967 (this volume includes a report on consultations with industry). The Europe Steering Committee of the CBI produced an updating of this report which was published by the CBI in January 1970 entitled Britain in Europe: a second industrial appraisal.
    A sample survey by the London Chamber of Commerce in mid 1974 among large, medium and small sized companies indicated 75 per cent in favour of Britain remaining a member of EC (reported in European Community, October 1974, published by Commission of the European Communities, London). Most of the main industrial associations or groups representing the service industries like the Food and Drink Industries Council and the British Tourist Authority produced their own surveys and reports.

15. The Times Survey on Britain and the EC (reported in The Times, 9 April 1975). Also, see The Economist, 17 May 1975.

16. British Trade in the Common Market (published by the

London Office of the Commission of the European Communities.

17. See Article 109 of the EEC Treaty.
18. See Thirwall (1978), Thirlwall and Dixon (1979) and Thirlwall (1979, 1980 and 1982).
19. Hufbauer, G.C. (1975), 'The taxation of export profits', National Tax Journal, March. Quoted in B. Moore and J. Rhodes (1975) Industrial and Regional Policy in the Republic of Ireland, Department of Applied Economics, University of Cambridge, unpublished manuscript.
20. op. cit. B. Moore and J. Rhodes, 1975.

Part II
Trade and Factor Mobility: Theory and Evidence

4 The Theory of Economic Integration: the Customs Union Aspects

Ali M. El-Agraa

INTRODUCTION

In reality, the EC was proposed for political reasons even though the arguments popularly put forward in its favour were expressed in terms of possible economic gains. However, no matter what the motives for EC integration are, it is still necessary to analyse the economic implications of such regional economic and political integration.

At the customs union level, the possible sources of economic gain can be attributed to:

(i) enhanced efficiency in production made possible by increased specialisation in accordance with the law of comparative advantage;

(ii) increased production levels due to better exploitation of economies of scale made possible by the increased size of the market;

(iii) an improved international bargaining position, made possible by the larger size, leading to better terms of trade;

(iv) enforced changes in economic efficiency brought about by enhanced competition; and

(v) changes affecting both the amount and quality of the factors of production due to technological advances.

Since the level of EC integration is to proceed beyond the customs union level, the economic union level and beyond, then further sources of gain become possible due to:

(vi) factor mobility across the borders of member nations:

(vii) the coordination of monetary and fiscal policies; and

(viii) the goals of near full employment, higher rates of economic growth and better income distribution becoming unified targets.

Let us discuss these considerations in some detail.

59

THE CUSTOMS UNION ASPECTS

(i) The Basic Concepts
Before the theory of second-best was developed, it used to
be the accepted tradition that customs union formation
should be encouraged. The rationale for this was that since
free trade maximised world welfare and since customs union
formation was a move towards free trade, customs unions
increased welfare even though they did not maximise it.
This rationale certainly lies behind the guidelines of the
GATT articles which permit the formation of customs unions
and free trade areas as the special exceptions to the rules
against international discrimination.
    Viner (1950) challenged this proposition by stressing the
point that customs union formation is by no means
equivalent to a move to free trade since it amounts to free
trade between the members and protection vis-à-vis the
outside world. This combination of free trade and
protectionism could result in 'trade creation' and/or
'trade diversion'. Trade creation is the replacement of
expensive domestic production by cheaper imports from a
partner and trade diversion is the replacement of cheaper
initial imports from the outside world by more expensive
imports from a partner. Viner stressed the point that trade
creation is beneficial since it does not affect the rest of
the world while trade diversion is harmful and it is
therefore the relative strength of these two effects which
determines whether or not customs union formation should be
advocated. It is therefore important to understand the
implications of these concepts.
    Assuming perfect competition in both the commodity and
factor markets, automatic full employment of all resources,
costless adjustment procedures, perfect factor mobility
nationally but perfect immobility across national
boundaries, prices determined by cost, three countries H
(the home country), P (the potential customs union partner)
and W (the outside world), plus all the traditional
assumptions employed in tariff theory, we can use a simple
diagram to illustrate these two concepts.
    In Figure 4.1 (I am using partial equilibrium diagrams
because it has been demonstrated that partial and general
equilibrium analyses are, under certain circumstances,
equivalent - see El-Agraa and Jones 1981) S_W is W's
perfectly elastic tariff-free supply curve for this
commodity; S_H is H's supply curve while S_{H+P} is the
joint H and P tariff-free supply curve. With a non-
discriminatory tariff imposition by H of AD (T_H), the

effective supply curve facing H is BREFQT, i.e. its own
supply curve up to E and W's, subject to the tariff $\left[S_W (1 + t_H)\right]$ after that. The domestic price is therefore OD
which gives domestic production of Oq_2, domestic
consumption of Oq_3 and imports of q_2q_3. H pays
q_2LMq_3 for these imports while the domestic consumer
pays q_2EFq_3 with the difference (LEFM) being the tariff
revenue which accrues to the H government. This government
revenue can be viewed as a transfer from the consumers to
the government with the implication that when the
government spends it, the marginal valuation of that
expenditure should be exactly equal to its valuation by the
private consumers so that no distortions should occur.

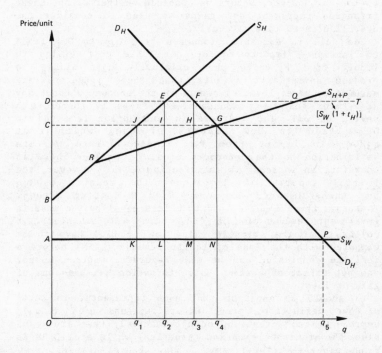

FIGURE 4.1

If H and W form a customs union, the free trade position will be restored so that Oq_5 will be consumed in H and this amount will be imported from W. Hence free trade is obviously the ideal situation. But if H and P form a customs union, the tariff imposition will still apply to W while it is removed from P. The effective supply curve in this case is BRGOT. The union price falls to OC resulting in a fall in domestic production to Oq_1, an increase in consumption to Oq_4 and an increase in imports to q_1q_4. These imports now come from P.

The welfare implications of these changes can be examined by employing the concepts of consumers' and producers' surpluses. As a result of increased consumption, consumers' surplus rises by CDFG. Part of this (CDEJ) is a fall in producers' surplus due to the decline in domestic production and another part (IEFH) is a portion of tariff revenue now transferred back to the consumer subject to the same condition of equal marginal valuation. This leaves the triangles JEI and HFG as gains from customs union formation. However, before we conclude whether or not these triangles represent net gains we need to consider the overall effects more carefully.

The fall in domestic producton from Oq_2 to Oq_1 leads to increased imports of q_1q_2. These cost q_1JIq_2 to import from P while they originally cost q_1JEq_2 to produce domestically. (Note that these resources are assumed to be employed elsewhere in the economy without any adjustment costs or redundancies!) There is therefore a saving of JEI. The increase in consumption from Oq_3 to Oq_4 leads to new imports of q_3q_4 which cost q_3HGq_4 to import from P. These give a welfare satisfaction to the consumers equal to q_3FGq_4. There is therefore an increase in satisfaction of HFG. However, the initial imports of q_2q_3 cost the country q_2LMq_3 but these imports now come from P costing q_2IHq_3. Therefore these imports lead to a loss equal to the loss in government revenue of LIHM (IEFH being a re-transfer). It follows that the triangle gains (JEI + HFG) have to be compared with the loss of tariff revenue (LIHM) before a definite conclusion can be made regarding whether or not the net effect of customs union formation has been one of gain or loss.

It should be apparent that q_2q_3 represents, in terms of our definition, trade diversion, and $q_1q_2 + q_3q_4$ represent trade creation, or alternatively that areas JEI plus HFG are trade creation (benefits) while area LIHM is trade diversion (loss). (The reader should note that I am using Johnson's 1974 definition so as to avoid the unnecessary literature relating to a trade-diverting welfare-improving customs union promoted by Lipsey, 1960, Gehrels, 1956-57 and Bhagwati, 1971.) It is then obvious that trade creation is economically desirable while trade diversion is undesirable. Hence Viner's conclusion that it is the relative strength of these two effects which should determine whether or not customs union formation is beneficial or harmful.

The reader should note that if the initial price is that given by the intersection of D_H and S_H (due to a higher tariff rate), the customs union would result in pure trade creation since the tariff rate is prohibitive. If the price is initially OC (due to a lower tariff rate), then customs union formation would result in pure trade diversion. It should also be apparent that the size of the gains and losses depends on the price elasticities of S_H, S_{H+} and D_H and on the divergence between S_W and S_{H+P}, i.e. cost differences.

(ii) The Cooper/Massell Criticism

Viner's conclusion was challenged by Cooper and Massell (1965a). They suggested that the reduction in price from OD to OC should be considered in two stages: firstly, reduce the tariff level indiscriminately (i.e. for both W and P) to AC which gives the same union price and production, consumption and import changes; secondly, introduce the customs union starting from the new price OC. The effect of these two steps is that the gains from trade creation (JEI + HFG) still accrue while the losses from trade diversion (LIHM) no longer apply since the new effective supply curve facing H is BJGU which ensures that imports continue to come from W at the cost of q_2LMq_3. In addition, the new imports due to trade creation (q_1q_2 + q_3q_4) now cost less leading to a further gain of AJIL plus MHGN. Cooper and Massell then conclude that <u>a policy of unilateral tariff reduction is superior to customs union formation.</u>

(iii) Further Contributions

Following the Cooper/Massell criticism have come two independent but somewhat similar contributions to the theory of customs unions. The first development is by Cooper and Massell (1965b) themselves, the essence of which is that two countries acting together can do better than each acting in isolation. The second is by Johnson (1965) which is a private plus social costs and benefits analysis expressed in political economy terms. Both contributions utilise a 'public good' argument with Cooper and Massell's

expressed in practical terms and Johnson's in theoretical
terms. However, since the Johnson approach is expressed in
familiar terms this section is devoted to it – space
limitations do not permit a consideration of both.

Johnson's method is based on four major assumptions:

    (i)   governments use tariffs to achieve certain non-
economic (political, etc.) objectives;

    (ii)   actions taken by governments are aimed at
offsetting differences between private and social
costs. They are, therefore, rational efforts;

    (iii)   government policy is a rational response to the
demands of the electorate;

    (iv)   countries have a preference for industrial
production.

In addition to these assumptions, Johnson makes a
distinction between private and public consumption goods,
real income (utility enjoyed from both private and public
consumption, where consumption is the sum of planned
consumption expenditure and planned investment expenditure)
and real product (defined as total production of privately
appropriable goods and services).

These assumptions have important implications. Firstly,
competition among political parties will make the
government adopt policies that will tend to maximise
consumer satisfaction from both 'private' and 'collective'
consumption goods. Satisfaction is obviously maximised
when the rate of satisfaction per unit of resources is the
same in both types of consumption goods. Secondly,
'collective preference' for industrial production implies
that consumers are willing to expand industrial production
(and industrial employment) beyond what it would be under
free international trade.

Tariffs are the main source of financing this policy
simply because GATT regulations rule out the use of export
subsidies and domestic political considerations make
tariffs, rather than the more efficient production
subsidies, the usual instruments of protection.
Protection will be carried to the point where the value of
the marginal utility derived from collective consumption of
domestic and industrial activity is just equal to the
marginal excess private cost of protected industrial
production.

The marginal excess cost of protected industrial
production consists of two parts: the marginal production
cost and the marginal private consumption cost. The
marginal production cost is equal to the proportion by
which domestic cost exceeds world market cost. In a very
simple model this is equal to the tariff rate. The marginal

private consumption cost is equal to the loss of consumer surplus due to the fall in consumption brought about by the tariff rate which is necessary to induce the marginal unit of domestic production. This depends on the tariff rate and the price elasticities of supply and demand.

In equilibrium, the proportional marginal excess private cost of protected production measures the marginal 'degree of preference' for industrial production. This is illustrated in Figure 4.2 where: S_W is the world supply curve at world market prices; D_H is the constant-utility demand curve (at free trade private utililty level); S_H is the domestic supply curve; S_{H+u} is the marginal private cost curve of protected industrial production, including the excess private consumption cost.

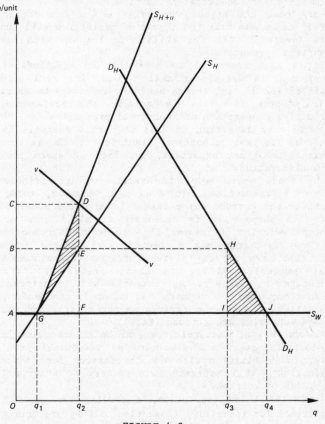

FIGURE 4.2

[FE is the first component of marginal excess cost –
determined by the excess marginal cost of domestic
production in relation to the free trade situation due to
the tariff imposition (AB) – and the area GEF (=1HJ) is the
second component which is the dead loss in consumer surplus
due to the tariff imposition]; the height of vv above S_W
represents the marginal value of industrial production in
collective consumption and vv represents the preference for
industrial production which is assumed to yield a
diminishing marginal rate of satisfaction.

The maximisation of real income is achieved at the
intersection of vv with S_{H+u} requiring the use of
tariff rate AB/OA to increase industrial production from
Oq_1 to Oq_2 and involving the marginal degree of
preference for industrial production v.

Note that the higher the value of v, the higher the
tariff rate, and that the degree of protection will tend to
vary inversely with the ability to compete with foreign
industrial producers.

It is also important to note that in equilibrium, the
government is maximising real income, not real product:
maximisation of real income makes it necessary to sacrifice
real product in order to gratify the preference for
collective consumption of industrial production.

It is also important to note that this analysis is not
confined to net importing countries. It is equally
applicable to net exporters, but lack of space prevents
such elaboration.

The above model helps to explain the significance of
Johnson's assumptions. It does not, however, throw any
light on the customs union issue. To make the model useful
for this purpose it is necessary to alter some of the
assumptions. Let us assume that industrial production is
not one aggregate but a variety of products in which
countries have varying degrees of comparative advantage;
that countries differ in their overall comparative
advantage in industry as compared with non-industrial
production; that no country has monopoly/monopsony power
(conditions for optimum tariffs do not exist); and that no
export subsidies are allowed (GATT).

The variety of industrial production allows countries to
be both importers and exporters of industrial products.
This, in combination with the 'preference for industrial
production', will motivate each country to practise some
degree of protection.

Given the third assumption, a country can gratify its
preference for industrial production only by protecting the
domestic producers of the commodities it imports (import-

competing industries). Hence the condition for equilibrium remains the same: $vv = S_{H+u}$. The condition must now be reckoned differently, however: S_{H+u} is slightly different because, firstly, the protection of import-competing industries will reduce exports of both industrial and non-industrial products (for balance of payments purposes!). Hence, in order to increase total industrial production by one unit it will be necessary to increase protected industrial production by more than one unit so as to compensate for the induced loss of industrial exports. Secondly, the protection of import-competing industries reduces industrial exports by raising their production costs (due to perfect factor mobility!). The stronger this effect, ceteris paribus, the higher the marginal excess cost of industrial production. These two components will be greater, the larger the industrial sector compared with the non-industrial sector and the larger the protected industrial sector relative to the exporting industrial sector.

If the world consists of two countries, one must be a net exporter and the other necessarily a net importer of industrial products and the balance of payments is settled in terms of the non-industrial sector. Hence both countries can expand industrial production at the expense of the non-industrial sector. Therefore for each country the prospective gain from reciprocal tariff reduction must lie in the expansion of exports of industrial products. The reduction of a country's own tariff rate is therefore a source of loss which can only be compensated for by a reduction of the other country's tariff rate (for an alternative, orthodox, explanation see El-Agraa 1979b and 1981).

What if there are more than two countries? If reciprocal tariff reductions are arrived at on a 'most-favoured nation' basis, then the reduction of a country's tariff rate will increase imports from all the other countries. If the tariff rate reduction is, however, discriminatory (starting from a position of non-discrimination), then there are two advantages: firstly, a country can offer its partner an increase in exports of industrial products without any loss of its own industrial production by diverting imports from third countries (trade diversion); secondly, when trade diversion is exhausted any increase in partner industrial exports to this country is exactly equal to the reduction in industrial production in the same country (trade creation), hence eliminating the gain to third countries.

Therefore, discriminatory reciprocal tariff reduction

costs each partner country less, in terms of the reduction
in domestic industrial production (if any) incurred per
unit increase in partner industrial production, than does
non-discriminatory reciprocal tariff reduction. On the
other hand, preferential tariff reduction imposes an
additional cost on the tariff reducing country: the excess
of the cost of imports from the partner country over their
cost in the world market.

The implications of this analysis are:

    (i)   both trade creation and trade diversion yield a
           gain to the customs union partners;

  (ii)   trade diversion is preferable to trade creation
           for the preference granting country since a
           sacrifice of domestic industrial production is
           not required;

 (iii)   both trade creation and trade diversion may lead
           to increased efficiency due to economies of
           scale.

Johnson's contribution has not achieved the popularity it
deserves because of the alleged nature of his assumptions.
However, a careful consideration of these assumptions
indicates that they are neither extreme nor unique: they
are the kind of assumptions that are adopted in any
analysis dealing with differences between social and
private costs and benefits! It can, of course, be claimed
that an

> "...economic rationale for customs unions on public
> goods grounds can ony be established if for political
> or some such reasons governments are denied the use of
> direct production subsidies - and while this may be
> the case in certain countries at certain periods in
> their economic evolution, there would appear to be no
> acceptable reason why this should generally be true.
> Johnson's analysis demonstrates that customs union and
> other acts of commercial policy may make economic
> sense under certain restricted conditions, but in no
> way does it establish or seek to establish a general
> argument for these acts" (Krauss, 1972).

While this is a legitimate criticism it is of no
relevance to the world we live in: subsidies are superior
to tariffs, yet all countries prefer the use of tariffs to
subsidies! It is a criticism related to a first-best view
of the world. Therefore, it seems unfair to criticise an
analysis on grounds which do not portray what actually
exists; it is what prevails in practice that matters. That
is what Johnson's approach is all about and that is what
the theory of second-best tries to tackle. In short, the
lack of belief in this approach is tantamount to a lack of

belief in the validity of the distinction between social and private costs and benefits.

(iv)   Dynamic Effects

The so-called dynamic effects (Balassa, 1962) relate to the numerous means by which economic integration may influence the rate of growth of GNP of the participating nations. These ways include the following:

 (i)   scale economies made possible by the increased size of the market for both firms and industries operating below optimum capacity before integration occurs;

 (ii)   economies external to the firm and industry which may have a downward influence on both specific and general cost structures;

 (iii) the polarisation effect, by which is meant the cumulative decline either in relative or absolute terms of the economic situation of a particular participating nation or of a specific region within it due either to the benefits of trade creation becoming concentrated in one region or to the fact that an area may develop a tendency to attract factors of production;

 (iv)   the influence on the location and volume of real investment; and

 (v)   the effect on economic efficiency and the smoothness with which trade transactions are carried out due to enhanced competition and changes in uncertainty.

Hence these dynamic effects include various and completely different phenomena. Apart from economies of scale, the possible gains are extremely long-term in nature and cannot be tackled in orthodox economic terms; for example, intensified competition leading to the adoption of best business practice and to an American type of attitude, etc. (Scitovsky, 1958) seems like a naive socio-psychological abstraction that has no solid foundation with regard to both the aspirations of those countries contemplating economic integration and to its actually materialising!

Economies of scale can, however, be analysed in orthodox economic terms. In a highly simplistic model, like that depicted in Figure 4.3 where scale economies are internal to the industry, their effects can easily be demonstrated. $D_{H,P}$ is the identical constant-utility demand curve for this commodity in both H and P and D_{H+P} is their joint demand curve; S_W is the world supply curve; AC_P and AC_H are the average cost curves for this commodity in

P and H respectively. Note that the diagram is drawn in such a manner that W has constant average costs and that it is the most efficient supplier of this commodity. Hence free trade is the best policy resulting in price OA with consumption which is satisfied entirely by imports of Oq_4 in each of H and P giving a total of Oq_6.

If H and P impose tariffs, the only justification for this is that uncorrected distortions exist between the privately and socially valued costs in these countries – see Jones (1979) and El-Agraa and Jones (1981). The best tariff rates to impose are Corden's (1972) made-to-measure tariffs which can be defined as those which encourage domestic production to a level that just satisfies domestic consumption without giving rise to monopoly profits. These tariffs are equal to AD and AC for H and P respectively, resulting in production of Oq_1 and Oq_2 in H and P respectively.

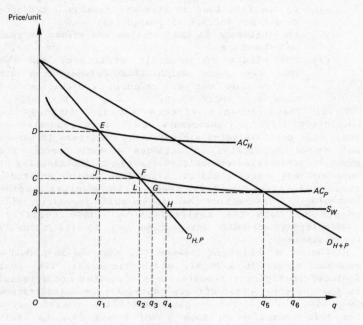

FIGURE 4.3

When H and P enter into a customs union, P, being the cheaper producer, will produce the entire union output - Oq_5 at a price OB. This gives rise to consumption in each of H and P of Oq_3 with gains of BDEG and BCFG for H and P respectively. Parts of these gains, BDEI for H and BCFL for P, are 'cost-reduction' effects. There also results a production gain for P and a production loss in H due to abandoning production altogether.

Whether customs union formation can be justified in terms of the existence of economies of scale will depend on whether the net effect is a gain or a loss, since in this example P gains and H loses, as the loss from abandoning production in H must outweigh the consumption gain in order for the tariff to have been imposed in the first place. If the overall result is net gain then the distribution of these gains becomes an important consideration. Alternatively, if economies of scale accrue to an integrated industry, then the locational distribution of the production units becomes an essential issue.

(v)   The Terms of Trade Effects

So far the analysis has been conducted on the assumption that customs union formation has no effect on the terms of trade. This implies that the countries concerned are too insignificant to have any appreciable influence on the international economy. Particularly in the context of the EC (and groupings of a similar size), this is a very unrealistic assumption.

The analysis of the effects of customs union formation on the terms of trade is extremely complicated - see Mundell (1964) and Arndt (1968). At this level of generality, however, it suffices to state that nations acting in consort or in unison are more likely to exert an influence than each acting alone. It could also be argued that the bigger the group the stronger its bargaining position vis-à-vis the outside world. Indeed, Petith (1977) found evidence of improved terms of trade for the EC.

It should be stressed, however, that possible gains from improved terms of trade can be achieved only if the outside world does not retaliate. Indeed, the gains found by Petith for the EC could be attributed entirely to this factor. Hence, larger groupings do not necessarily automatically guarantee favourable changes in the terms of trade since such groupings may also encourage joint action by those nations excluded from them.

ECONOMIC UNIONS

The analysis of customs unions needs drastic extension when applied to economic unions. Firstly, the introduction of free factor mobility may enhance efficiency through a more efficient allocation of resources but it may also lead to depressed areas and therefore create, or aggravate, regional problems and imbalances. Secondly, fiscal harmonisation may also improve efficiency by eliminating non-tariff trade distortions and by subjecting factors of production to equal treatment hence encouraging their mobility. Thirdly, the coordinaton of monetary and fiscal policies implied by monetary integration will ease unnecessarily severe imbalances hence promoting the right atmosphere for stability in the economies of member nations.

These 'economic union' elements must be considered simultaneously with trade creation and trade diversion and that is why separate chapters in this book deal with them in the context of British membership of the EC; those interesed in a general discussion of these matters should consult El-Agraa (1980a).

MACROECONOMICS OF INTEGRATION

We have seen that trade creation and trade diversion are the two concepts most widely used in international economic integration. We have also seen that their economic implications for resource reallocation are usually tackled in terms of particular commodities under conditions of global full employment. However, the economic consequences for the outside world and their repercussions on the integrated area are usually left to intuition. Moreover, their implications for employment are usually ruled out by assumption.

In an effort to rectify these serious shortcomings, I have used a macroeconomic model (see chapters 6-8 of El-Agraa and Jones, 1981) with the purpose of investigating these aspects. The model is still in its infancy and a sophisticated model is now being constructed. However, even the crude model so far published indicates that the advantages of using a macro model are that it clearly demonstrates the once-and-for-all nature of trade creation and trade diversion. It also shows the insignificance of their overall impact given realistic values of the relevant coefficients: marginal propensities to import; marginal propensities to consume; tariff rates, etc. The model also demonstrates that trade creation is beneficial for the partner gaining the new output and exports but is detrimental to the other partner and the outside world. Also that trade diversion is beneficial for the partner now exporting the commodity but is detrimental for the other partner and the outside world. Because of its importance, the next chapter by A.J. Jones is devoted to a refined version of this model and to utilising it for analysing the economic consequences of UK withdrawal from the EC.

CONCLUSIONS

The conclusions reached here are consistent with my (1979a) conclusions and to some extent with those of Jones in El-Agraa and Jones (1981) [the contributions by Dixit (1975), Berglas (1979), Collier (1979), Riezman (1979), Whalley (1979) and McMillan and McCann (1981) do not affect these conclusions substantially to merit separate consideration in the particular context of this chapter]. They are:

Firstly, that the rationale for regional economic integration rests upon the existence of constraints on the use of first-best policy instruments. Economic analysis (apart from Johnson's) has had little to say about the nature of these constraints. Hence, the evaluation of any regional scheme of economic integration should incorporate a consideration of the validity of the view that such constraints do exist to justify the pursuit of second- rather than first-best solutions; Johnson's approach provides a useful framework in this respect.

Secondly, that even when the existence of constraints on superior policy instruments is acknowledged, it is misleading, but only in orthodox terms, to identify the results of regional economic integration by comparing an arbitrarily chosen common policy with an arbitrarily chosen national policy. Ignorance and inertia may provide sufficient reasons why existing policies may be non-optimal but it is clearly wrong to attribute gains which would have been achieved by appropriate unilateral action to a policy of regional integration. Equally, although it is appropriate to use the optimal common policy as a point of reference, it must be recognised that this may overstate the gains to be achieved if, as seems highly likely, constraints and inefficiencies in the political processes by which policies are agreed prove to be greater among a group of countries than within any individual country. It should, however, be stressed that this applies to the orthodox approach only.

Thirdly, and most importantly, in principle at least, a strong general case for economic integration does exist :

in unions where economies of scale may be in part external
to national industries, the rationale for unions rests
essentially upon the recognition of the externalities and
market imperfections which extend beyond the boundaries of
national states; in such circumstances, unilateral national
action will not be optimal whilst integrated action offers
the scope for potential gain – see, in particular, chapters
1-3, 5, 15 and 16.

As with the solution to most problems of externalities
and market imperfections, however, customs union theory
frequently illustrates the proposition that a major
stumbling block to obtaining the gains from joint optimal
action lies in agreeing an acceptable distribution of such
gains. Thus the fourth conclusion is that the achievement
of the potential gains from economic integration will be
limited to countries able and willing to cooperate to
distribute the gains from integration so that all partners
may benefit compared to the results achieved by independent
action.

Regional economic integration is not easily achieved as
the present debate regarding the cost of the CAP for
Britain and about monetary integration in the EC
illustrates. However, if positive commitment to the EC by
participating nations is forthcoming and if direct efforts
by those concerned are constantly made, the equitable
distribution of such gains can be achieved. This is the
moral to stress in the context of Britain's membership of
the EC: direct involvement allows the UK to influence the
path taken by the EC from within.

5 Withdrawal from a Customs Union: a Macroeconomic Analysis

Anthony J. Jones

INTRODUCTION

With the example of the formation of the EC as a spur, economic analysis of the effects of economic integration has focussed on the issues raised by the formation and enlargement of a customs union and by the possibilities of monetary integration and economic union. Now that important political parties in both Greece and the UK are advocating withdrawal from the EC, however, it seems appropriate to change the focus of the analysis and to concentrate instead on the consequences of the regional economic disintegration associated with the withdrawal of one member country from an existing customs union.

This problem will be examined here mainly in general, theoretical terms and, although reference will occasionally be made to the specific issues of UK withdrawal from the EC as illustration of the general argument, there will be no attempt to construct an empirical model which purports to provide detailed quantitative estimates of this particular case[1]. Accordingly, as in the orthodox theory of economic integration, the theoretical framework will consist of a world of three separate economies which will be identified as the home country, the home country's (former) customs union partner, and the rest of the world and which will be indicated, wherever necessary, by the subscripts 1, 2 and 3 respectively. It will be assumed that initially the home country and partner impose a common external tariff t^* on trade with the rest of the world which, in order to keep the argument as simple as possible, will also be assumed to levy an identical tariff on trade with members of the customs union.

The orthodox approach to the problem would be to use the three-country version of the modern neo-classical theory of tariffs and trade which I have recently summarised elsewhere[2] and which can indeed provide at least some theoretical support for an empirical analysis to check whether or not net gains might accrue to a particular member country from a policy of withdrawal from a customs union.

75

It is now a clearly established result of the orthodox theory of economic integration that, in a tariff-ridden world, the potential level of welfare within a customs union is higher than the sum of the welfare levels available to countries following unilateral policies. It is possible, however, that, as whenever the gains from collusive action are contemplated, the political possibilities for redistribution of the gains may not prove sufficient to ensure that all participants believe that they have received a fair share of those gains or even to ensure that each single participant does in fact benefit compared to the possibilities available to that country via unilateral action. Similarly, although the theoretical potential superiority of customs union membership (and of the enlargement of existing customs unions) has been established, it may be the case that constraints on policy choice at the Community level cause actual policies within the union to fall further away from the theoretically optimal configuration than would be the case for purely national policies. It then follows that a second-best case could be made for withdrawal from a customs union on the empirical argument, which would have to be carefully evaluated in each case, that, within the existing constraints of policy-making, attainable unilateral action may be superior to the results achieved by continued membership of the union.

Such an argument, however, is firmly rooted in the orthodox neoclassical model and cannot be used consistently by those economists who reject that theory as irrelevant to their case for the use of national import controls.[3] Indeed, it must be noted that the first-best solution within such a framework is to improve joint-policy making within the union and to seek successful co-operation within countries outside the union. Given the heroic abstractions from reality made in the neoclassical theory of trade, however, such conclusions are vulnerable to charges of irrelevance particularly in so far as, in most standard presentations of the argument at least, full employment is assumed to exist at all times in all countries.

It is therefore proposed to tackle the problem here in the context of a 'Keynesian' approach to customs union theory which, contrary to the orthodox approach, is based on the assumption of the existence of unemployment within each economy. This theoretical framework was pioneered by my colleague, A.M. El-Agraa,[4] but it is my own recent extension and development of the approach (Jones, 1982) which provides the theoretical foundation for the subsequent argument here.

A Keynesian Framework

The basic simplifications of this approach include the assumptions that money wage rates are fixed within each economy for the period under consideration, that the marginal product of labour is everywhere constant and that monetary, fiscal and exchange-rate policies in each country are also fixed at levels which are regarded by the national governments as providing the best feasible configuration of such policies which they can achieve. It follows, without further loss of generality, that the various commodities produced within an economy can be grouped together, via the 'composite commodity' theorem, to form a single aggregate national product for which units of measurement can be chosen so that, for each economy, the factor cost price of a unit of its national product is one (measured in any currency). With the further simplifying assumptions that there are no internal sales or other indirect taxes, that transport costs are zero and that, within each country, the market prices of each national product differ from factor cost prices only by the amount of any import duty, it follows that the consequences of withdrawal from the customs union flow from the effects that this policy has on the market prices of each national product in each of the three separate economies identified in the model.

Of course, the great unknown in analysing the consequences of one country's withdrawal from a customs union is the reaction to this by other countries but, in order to keep the present argument within manageable proportions, the analysis will initially focus on the case in which withdrawal from the customs union is accomplished by the adoption by both the home country and its former partner of the existing common external tarff t* to apply to mutual trade flows as well as to trade with the rest of the world.

Given the assumptions of the model, such a policy change will have no (immediate) impact on the market prices of domestic output in any country or on any prices within the rest of the world. Accordingly the immediate consequences of the home country's withdrawal from the customs union can be summarised as working through the changes in the market prices within the former union members of intra-union imports, i.e.

$$\Delta P_{12}/P_{12} = \Delta P_{21}/P_{21} = + t^* > 0, \tag{1}$$

where P_{ij} is the market price of country j's product in country i.

Following the standard macroeconomic treatment of the commodity market, the consequential changes in national output can be evaluated by use of the equilibrium condition:

$$\Delta Y_i = \Delta C_i + \Delta I_i + \Delta G_i + \Delta M_{ki} - \Delta M_{ij} - \Delta M_{ik}, \qquad (2)$$

where Y_i, C_i, I_i and G_i are, respectively, national output, private consumption, private net investment and government expenditure on goods and services in country i, all measured at the constant factor prices of unity, and where M_{ij} is the factor cost measure of country i's imports from country j and hence, equally, of country j's exports to country i.

To simplify the argument as far as possible, it will be assumed that the import content of exports, investment and government expenditure is zero, that, initially at least, investment is unaffected by the price changes resulting from the change in trade barriers and that government expenditure is subject to the requirements of a balanced budget so that:

$$\Delta G_i = t_i \Delta Y_i + \Delta T^*_{ij} + \Delta T^*_{ik} , \qquad (3)$$

where $0 < t_i < 1$ is the (constant) marginal rate of direct taxation in country i and T^*_{ij} is the tariff revenue collected by country i on its imports from country j.

By adopting the argument in Jones 1982, it will also be assumed that:

$$\Delta C_i = c_i \Delta T^*_{ij} - \Delta T^*_{ik} \text{ where } 0 < c_i < 1, \qquad (4)$$

and hence that the change in real domestic expenditure $(\Delta E_i = \Delta I_i + \Delta I_i + \Delta G_i)$ is dependent solely on any changes in factor income which result from the formation of the union, i.e.

$$\Delta E_i = e_i \Delta Y_i, \qquad (4a)$$

where $0 < e_i = c_i + t_i < 1$ is the marginal propensity to spend in country i.

There are a number of possible ways of modelling expenditure on imports but, for the purposes of the present argument, it is helpful to use a two-stage share-of-expenditure import function which can be derived from the nested CES utility function originally suggested by Verdoorn and Schwartz (1972) following the work of Armington (1969), i.e.

$$M_{ij}* = u_i^{\sigma_i}(P_i^m/p_{ij})^{\sigma_i-1}M_i*, \qquad (5a)$$

with $\qquad M_i* = v_i^{\varepsilon_i}(P_i/P_i^m)^{\varepsilon_i-1}C_i*, \qquad (5b)$

where: $0 < u_i, v_i < 1$ are parameters reflecting the strength of preferences in country i between competing imports and beween all imports and domestic output respectively; $\sigma_i \gtrless \varepsilon_i > 1$ are the elasticities of substitution between competing imports and between domestic output and total imports respectively[5]; and P_i and P_i^m are domestic cost-of-living and import prices indices defined to be consistent with the aggregation of national products implied by the underlying utility function. Accordingly the market price changes resulting from the home country's withdrawal from the customs union, as summarised in (1), can also be represented as having the following effects on the domestic cost-of-living and import prices indices in both the home country and its former partner: (i.e. for i = 1,2)

$$\Delta P_i^m/P_i^m = \mu_{ij}t* > 0, \qquad (5c)$$

and

$$\Delta P_i/P_i = \lambda_{ij}t* > 0, \qquad (5d)$$

where: $0 < \mu_{ij} = M_{ij}*/M_i* < 1$ is the share of the total expenditure on imports in country i devoted to imports from its former partner j; and where $0 < \lambda_{ij} = M_{ij}*/C_i* < 1$ is similarly the share of total consumption at market prices in country i taken by the national product of its former partner j.

It then follows that total differentiation of (5a,b) when combined wih (5c,d) yields the following result for the change in expenditure in either of the former partners on imports from the rest of the world:

$$\Delta M_{i3}* = \lambda_{i3}\Delta C_i^* + C_i*\Delta\lambda_{i3}, \qquad (6a)$$

where $\qquad C_i*\Delta\lambda_{i3}*[(\sigma_i - \varepsilon_i)\mu_{ij} + (\varepsilon_i - 1)\lambda_{ij}] > 0. \qquad (6b)$

Since domestic expenditure on imports also includes the payment of tariff revenue, collected by the government of the importing country, the actual change in imports (at factor cost prices) to either former partner from the rest of the world can be identified as :

$$\Delta M_{i3} = m_{i3}\Delta Y_i + C_i*\Delta\lambda_{i3}/(1+t*), \qquad (6c)$$

where $0 < m_{i3} = \lambda_{i3}c_i/(1+t^*) < 1$ is the marginal propensity of country i to import from the rest of the world.

It can be seen from (6c) that the change in demand for imports from the rest of the world can be split into two major components. The first term on the RHS is dependent on the ultimate change in national income and may be viewed as a secondary effect induced by whatever changes in income result from the primary, price effects of the break-up of the union. In Jones 1982 the reverse price effects associated with the formation of a customs union are related to the Vinerian concept of trade diversion and in the context of the withdrawal by the home country from the customs union, it seems appropriate to define this as the 'trade diversion reversal effect' (d_i), i.e.

$$d_i = C_i^* \Delta\lambda_{i3}/(1+t^*) = t^* M_{i3}\lfloor(\sigma_i-\varepsilon_i)\mu_{ij}+(E_i-1)\lambda_{ij}\rfloor > 0. (7a)$$

Total differentiation of (5a,b) also enables the change in trade flows between the former partners to be identified as:

$$\Delta M_{ij} = \Delta M_{ij}^* - \Delta T_{ij}^* = \lambda_{ij}\Delta C_i^* - C_i^*\Delta\lambda_{ii} - C_i^*\Delta_{i3} - \Delta T_{ij}^*, (9a)$$

since, by definition, $\Delta\lambda_{ij} = -\Delta\lambda_{ii} -\Delta\lambda_{i3}$. As the change in tariff revenue on the trade between the former partners can be identified as:

$$\Delta T^*_{ij} = m_{ij}\Delta M_{ij} + t^* M_{ij}, \tag{10}$$

it follows that (9a) can be rewritten as :

$$\Delta M_{ij} = m_{ij}\Delta Y_i - r_i - d_i - t^* M_{ij}, \tag{9b}$$

where : $0 < m_{ij} = \lambda_{ij}c_i/(1+t^*)<1$ is the marginal propensity in country i to import from its former partner; and $t^* M_{ij}$ is the (notional) value of the tariff revenue which would be received by country i if the new tariff on trade with its former partner was levied on the volume of trade which existed prior to the home country's withdrawal from the union. In addition to the trade diversion reversal effect, d_i,(9b) also contains one further term,

$$r_i = C_i^* \Delta\lambda_{ii}/(1+t^*) = t^* M_{ij}(\varepsilon_i - 1)\lambda_{ii}, \tag{7b}$$

This will here be termed the 'trade reduction effect' since it measures, at factor cost prices, the effect on imports from the partner due to the increased share in domestic expenditure gained by domestic output at the expense of imports from the partner. As such, of course, it can also be viewed as a domestic output and employment creation effect and, indeed, such an increased share of the domestic market seems to lie at the heart of the protectionist case for import controls. In order to see whether this view is justified in this model, however, it is necessary both to complete the formal framework and to solve the model.

COMPLETING AND SOLVING THE MODEL

The first of these tasks is simply achieved by noting that since, by assumption, imports into the rest of the world are unaffected by any price effects, the changes in these trade flows depend solely on income changes, i.e.

$$\Delta M_{3i} = m_{3i} \Delta Y_3 \ , \tag{11}$$

where $0 < m_{3i} = \lambda_{3i} c_i /(1+t^*) < 1$ is the marginal propensity of the rest of the world to import from country i.

The solution of the model is then obtained by substitution of (3), (4), (6c), (7a), (9b), and (11) into (2) and can be summarised, as :

$$\Delta Y_1 = K_{1i}F_1 + K_{2i}F_2 + K_{3i}F_3 \ , \tag{12}$$

where K_{ij} are the multipliers of the primary effects (F_i) resulting from the home country's withdrawal from the union. For both the former members of the union these primary effects can be identified as :

$$F_i = - d_j - (r_j - r_i) - t^*(M_{ji} - M_{ij}), \tag{13a}$$

whilst, for the rest of the world,

$$F_3 = d_1 + d_2. \tag{13b}$$

The multipliers all involve complex combinations of the parameters but fortunately their signs can be evaluated, as in Jones (1982), from the general restrictions placed on the range of values taken by the parameters. Thus, by defining $0 < h_i = 1 - e_i < 1$ as the marginal propensity to hoard and $0 < b_i = h_i + m_{ij} + m_{ik} < 1$ as the marginal propensity not to spend on domestic output, it can be shown that all multipliers can be expressed in the form

$K_{ji} = \alpha_{ji}/D$ where

$D = h_i\alpha_{ii} + m_{ij}(\alpha_{ii} - \alpha_{ji}) + m_{ik}(\alpha_{ii} - \alpha_{ki})$, where

$\alpha_{ii} = b_k(h_j + m_{ji}) + m_{jk}(h_k + m_{ki})$ and where

$\alpha_{ji} = n_{ki}m_{jk} + m_{ji}b_k$. It then follows that

$\alpha_{ii} > \alpha_{ji} > 0$, that $D > 0$ and that accordingly the

multipliers K_{ii}, K_{ij} are unambiguously positive whilst, equally clearly, $K_{ii} > K_{ji}$.

By substitution of (13a,b) into (12), it is then possible to identify the effects of withdrawal from the customs union on output (and hence, by implication, employment) in the home country:

$$\Delta Y_i = - (K_{11} - K_{31})d_2 - (K_{21} - K_{31})d_1$$
$$- (K_{11} - K_{21})\left[t^*(M_{21} - M_{12}) + r_2 - r_1\right]. \qquad (12a)$$

From the restrictions so far placed on the value of both multipliers and multiplicands it can be seen that the first term in (12a), i.e. the 'trade diversion reversal effect' in the partner, is a certain source of loss for the home country. In order for the policy of withdrawal to make economic sense for the home country within the framework of this model, it is therefore necessary that the remaining two terms should be sufficient source of gain to outweigh these losses. Although it is theoretically possible that this could be the case, the general presumption here is that this is highly unlikely.

Consider first the second term in (12a), i.e. the consequential change in the income of the home country which results from the 'trade diversion reversal effect' in that country. It is intuitively improbable that this could have any significant effect in that country itself simply because its direct effects are felt only in the former partner (which suffers a decline in aggregate demand) and in the rest of the world (which benefits from a gain in aggregate demand). Thus the only effects in the home country depend on the relative strengths of the 'repercussion' effects for the the home country which stem from the direct changes in the other countries. Formally this is shown by the fact that the sign of $(K_{21} - K_{31})$ is the same as the sign of $[M_{21}(1 - e_3) - M_{31}(1 - e_2)]$. This will only be of a significant negative value (which is the requirement for d_1 to have a significant positive effect on home output) if the marginal propensity to import from the home country and the marginal propensity to spend are much lower in the former partner than in the rest of the world. Although this is a theoretical possibility which could be explored for any specific case, there is no reason to believe that this is likely to be of any general significance and, indeed, if El-Agraa's suggested basic set of 'hypothetical but representative values' for the parameters is employed[6] the multiplier $(K_{21} - K_{31})$ is zero.

With regard to the last term in (12a), since the multiplier, $- (K_{11} - K_{21})$ is unambiguously negative, the possibility of the home country gaining from the policy of withdrawal is seen to depend on whether the multiplicand $[t^*(M_{21} - M_{12}) + r_2 - r_1]$ is also negative. Proponents of UK withdrawal from the EC do in fact point to one component in the multiplicand which does have such a negative effect. This is $-r_1$, the (negative of) the 'trade reduction effect' in the home country which provides a stimulus to domestic output as domestic demand switches away from imports from the partner towards domestic output. A crucial feature of the present model, however, is to suggest that the 'trade reduction effect' in the partner must also be taken into account and that this directly offsets the 'trade reduction effect' in the home country. Indeed if the definition of the 'trade reduction effect' (7b) is employed, the final multiplicand in (12a) can be rewritten as

$$t^*\left[(M_{21} - M_{12}) + M_{21}\lambda_{22}(\varepsilon_2 - 1) - M_{12}\lambda_{11}(\varepsilon_1 - 1)\right]$$

which, in the neutral case of initial trade flows between the home and former partner country being balanced, simplifies further to:

$$t^*M_{12}\left[\lambda_{22}(\varepsilon_2 - 1) - \lambda_{11}(\varepsilon_1 - 1)\right].$$

Such an expression will be significantly negative only if the share of total expenditure devoted to domestic output and the elasticity of substitution between domestic output

and imports is far higher in the home country than in its
former partner. In the case of possible UK withdrawal from
the EC, I know of no empirical information which suggests
that this is likely and, when the home country has a trade
surplus with its customs union partner (as the UK had with
the rest of the EC in 1980 and 1981 – see chapter 6), the
possibility that the multiplicand in the last term of (12a)
could contribute significant benefit to the home country
becomes even more remote.

Even if the home country did gain, however, it is
important to recognise that the same multiplicand is
present but with signs reversed in determining the outcome
for the former partner. Thus, if the policy has any benefit
for the home country, it is only as the result of a beggar-
my-neighbour effect on the former partner.

Of course, if it is believed that the former partner will
not retaliate to the home country's withdrawal from the
customs union, and continues to offer free access to its
market whilst the home country raises tariff barriers on
imports, both r_2 and d_2 will be zero as will t^*M_{21}
and there would be a very good chance that the beneficial
effects for the home country of r_1 would outweigh any
adverse effects which might arise from the 'trade diversion
reversal effect' (d_1) in that country. The same applies
to any further unilateral increases in trade barriers
(which many advocates of UK withdrawal from the EC seem to
favour). Such increasing trade barriers will increase the
size of r_1 and the resultant gain to the home country
becomes larger. Any such gains, however, remain beggar-my-
neighbour effects and are dependent on the assumption of no
significant foreign retaliation. The validity of this
assumption (which clearly lies outside the bounds of
scientific economic analysis) is critical and, to the
author at least, seems generally extremely dubious.

WITHDRAWAL AND THE BALANCE OF PAYMENTS

This applies even when the assumption is combined with the
argument that the higher tariff barriers should be used to
remove the balance of payments constraint on expansionary
domestic policies so that foreign retaliation would be
unjustified as total imports would remain unaltered. Such
an argument implies rather more faith in the accuracy of
the timing and the estimation of the effects of different
kinds of policy and in the sympathetic understanding of
foreign governments than seems justified.[7] In addition it
fails to recognise the discriminatory change associated

with withdrawal from a customs union.

Thus consider the basic case analysed here in which the primary effects of the home country's withdrawal from the union on that country's balance of trade (at the pre-withdrawal level of income) can be identified as

$$\left[r_1 - r_2 + t*(M_{12} - M_{21}) - d_2\right].$$

It is impossible to identify the sign of this effect with complete generality but there is a presumption that it would be negative because, whereas the 'trade reduction' and tariff revenue effects tend to be offset directly by their counterparts in the partner, the loss to the home country of the 'trade discriminination reversal effect' in the partner has no offset. Thus, in general, the effect of withdrawal from a customs union could be expected to worsen rather than improve any balance of payments constraint. The same would be equally true for the former partner, whilst it is the rest of the world which could be expected to gain.

If, as is arguably the case for both the UK and the rest of the EC, domestic expansion to full employment is constrained for both members of the union by the balance of payments and the unwillingness or inability to use devaluation of the exchange rate, the model here clearly points to the superiority of continued membership of the union in which domestic expansion is combined with an expenditure-switching policy by the union as a whole. In the absence of the possibility of devaluation, perhaps the most obvious expenditure-switching policy of the union is the raising of its common external tariff.

Of course, at least two major problems arise with such a policy. The first is the possibility of retaliation by the rest of the world. This may indeed be a real danger which might effectively make such a policy option counter productive. If, however, the members of the union are genuinely constrained from reaching full employment by balance of payments considerations, then, unless the rest of the world is willing to countenance some form of expenditure-switching policy which the union members could adopt, the problem must be traced to this source and the solution to the global problem of payments adjustment should be sought on an appropriately wider-scale. Failing such a solution, however, continued membership of the customs union does still offer at least two potential advantages over withdrawal. The first concerns the relative bargaining strength (in a world where retaliatory action is common) of a customs union compared to individual members acting alone. The second concerns the fact that, with membership of the union, both the home country and the partner will have lower marginal propensities to import from the rest of the world than otherwise would be the case. Accordingly domestic expansionary policies within the union will have less adverse effects on such member's balance-of-payments vis-a-vis the rest of the world than would be the case for non-membership of the union.

This point, however, leads to the second major problem associated with the possibility of joint union action. As is correctly pointed out by Begg, Cripps and Ward (1981), the balance of payment constraint is unlikely to be equal for all members. Accordingly the general policy of combating unemployment within the customs union may be constrained once full employment is reached in one partner. The existence of such a problem, however, merely points to the need for the possibility of expenditure-switching policies between member states - at least until the time when factor mobility is sufficient to reduce the scale of the problem to be amenable to the kinds of 'regional' policies currently attempted within many countries. It is, however, not at all clear why devaluation should not be the obvious way of pursuing this or that, if constraints on the possibility or effectiveness of devaluation are introduced, why it would be that the unilateral use of barriers to trade offers scope for greater success.

CONCLUSION

Of course, all this argument does nothing to negate the general conclusion of the orthodox analysis. Real problems do exist in identifying and in agreeing on optimal policies and it may be that constraints on national policy choice within the union and/or distributive problems cause one member to be able to gain from withdrawal from the union in order to pursue less-constrained national policies. Equally, however, given the assumed existence of constraints on the use of domestic and exchange-rate policies to achieve full employment, the present model points to the general potential superiority of continued union membership to a policy of withdrawal.

NOTES

1. As such, the approach adopted here is in sharp contrast to a recent edition of the "Cambridge Economic Policy Review" (Dec. 1981, Vol 7, No. 2) in which a case for British withdrawal from the EC is

made with the aid of an econometric model of the Community. Unfortunately, despite the willingness of the authors to reach sweeping conclusions about the prospects for the UK of continued membership of the EC, they do not reveal either the extent to which they had to 'lean on' their model in order to generate their published results or even the basic form of the model itself.

2.   El-Agraa, A.M. and Jones, A.J. (1981), ch.2, 4 & 5.

3.   See, for example, Godley, W.(1981) and El-Agraa's discussion of this, El-Agraa, (1982a, b).

4.   El-Agraa A.M. and Jones A.J. (1981, ch. 7).

5.   The restriction that both elasticities exceed unity has been made to simplify the subsequent argument but, although the assumption appears empirically plausible, it should be noted that it is in fact critical to the validity of the general conclusions reached here and that it has a theoretical significance which can be compared with the results of McMillan and McCann (1981).

6.   pp. 108-9, El-Agraa and Jones (1981).

7.   For a fuller evaluation of this see El-Agraa (1982b).

6 EC Trade Effects and Factor Mobility

David G. Mayes

Perhaps because economists who work in the area of international economics feel they have a professional duty to exploit the theory of comparative advantage the subject has developed in a rather different way from many of the other areas of economic inquiry. Furthermore within international economics the study of economic integration has also followed a separate route. In particular the study of the effects of economic integration on trade has tended, in estimation, to take a very unstructured view of the way in which economies adapt upon the formation or enlargement of a complex arrangement like the EC.

There are two main reasons why such a view should be formed of the trade effects. The first is that the information which is readily available and the constraints that time and effort provide tend to dictate that only fairly simple forms of analysis are practicable - this point is developed in more detail in Mayes (1982). The second is that the initial analysis of the effects on trade was conducted within an entirely static framework and even when dynamic effects were included analysis tended to assume that the factors of production, labour and capital, were largely immobile. The economic treatment of economic integration has tended to pursue a different course from that of the behaviour of multinational corporations and the path of investment overseas. Some recent attempts at integration of parts of trade and overseas investment theory have made progress in reconciling the two approaches (see contributions to Black and Dunning, 1982, for example) but the ground has been only lightly covered.

With purely national companies foreign trade is the alternative to domestic consumption of domestic production. With multinational companies there is the further choice of production overseas. Changes in trading arrangements such as the enlargement of the EC will have complex effects on trade flows according to the joint decision of the siting of production and the increased trade arising from the removal of barriers.

Capital is not the only factor to be considered as in the

absence of factor price equalisation it will be
advantageous for some firms to move to areas of low labour
costs. In addition there are also movements of the labour
force from areas of low wages to areas of high wages. The
effects on trade patterns will differ according to whether
production is moved from one country to another or labour
moves or only the product moves.

As with the traditional treatment of changes in trade
flows, factors may be able to move more freely within the
EC than previously hence perhaps offsetting changes in
trade flows. However, if products can move more freely this
offsets the need for factors to move. Thus investment from
outside the EC may be encouraged to offset the losses from
a worsening of competitive position as tariffs are removed
on trade between members but retained against non-members.
Similarly direct investment by EC countries in non-members
may be encouraged if intra-EC demand can be met from
homebased production. Clearly the possibilities are
complex.

This chapter attempts to set out the way in which changes
in trade and factor flows can be expected to operate in the
EC and looks at such evidence as is available on movements
over the recent past to provide some indications of
movements in the future. The analysis is largely confined
to trade in manufactured goods, but the initial discussion
includes the whole range of goods and services.

THE EFFECTS ON TRADE FLOWS AND THEIR MEASUREMENT

It is convenient to divide total trade flows into four
categories when considering how they are affected by the
EC. First trade in manufactured goods (SITC 5-9) which is
the area to which the traditional theory of the effects of
the formation of customs unions can be most readily
applied. It is here that goods were subject to non-zero
tariffs which were abolished on trade between member
countries and adjusted to a common external level on trade
with other countries which were not party to either the
Free Trade Agreements with EFTA members or associated
countries. In the second category of agricultural products
(SITC 0-1) trade was also affected by restrictions and
subsidy under the Common Agricultural Policy, but because
prices were fixed in terms of EC currencies rather than in
direct relation to world prices the whole pattern of
effects could be expected to be different - in general this
category has been excluded from analysis as it is
considered in chapter 8. These two categories leave the

remainder of visible trade, mainly crude materials and fuels (SITC 2-4) which were, in the main, subject to either zero or very low tariffs (largely because of the lack of possible domestic supply). Here the changes due to the EC are totally swamped by the discovery and exploitation of North Sea oil and the change in the price of oil relative to other commodities in 1973 and thereafter. Finally, the current account is completed by invisible trade whose determinants are somewhat different from those of the foregoing categories and where prior restraints by EC countries took forms other than tariffs.

The relative magnitudes and shares in trade by value are set out in Table 6.1 for 1972 the last year before accession and 1980, the most recent year for which there are comprehensive data. These show the primary influences on trade patterns over the period, with a substantial decline in the importance of agricultural imports, primarily the effect of the CAP; a dramatic rise in exports of fuels, with the exploitation of North Sea oil and the change in relative prices (much of the change in the balance of interest, profits and dividends, lower down the table, is also due to the effects of the exploitation of North Sea oil with the repatriation of profits in 1980 when the earlier foreign investment in discovery and development was rewarded) and lastly the increase in the importance of imports of manufactured goods and the decline in the relative importance of their export. (It should, however, be borne in mind that 1980 was not in all respects typical of the previous few years owing to the rapid recession in the UK, both absolutely and relative to her main trading partners.)

The difficulty in proceeding further towards the analysis of the effects of the EC on trade flows is that it is not possible just to point to the relative changes which have taken place since 1972 and ascribe them to the effects of the EC. It is necessary to hypothesise what would have happened had the EC not been formed. This is difficult on two grounds. In the first place it is by no means clear what the most plausible alternative trade grouping would have been. It is possible that all the EFTA countries would have formed free trade areas with the EC in manufactures, thus entailing that with the exception of the movement to the Common External Tariff the tariff changes for manufactured goods would have been the same under both arrangements. However, it is also arguable that it was only the full membership of the UK and Denmark which provided the incentive for the FTA agreements. Another possibility might have been a further step down the road of

TABLE 6.1: COMMODITY DISTRIBUTION OF UK TRADE

	Exports(a) (%)		Imports(b) (%)		Balance (£ billion)	
	1972	1980	1972	1980	1972	1980
Food, beverages and tobacco (SITC 0,1)	6.8	6.8	21.0	12.2	-1.50	2.38
Basic materials (SITC 2,4)	3.4	3.1	11.1	7.4	-0.81	-1.95
Mineral fuels and lubricants (SITC 3)	2.6	13.5	9.3	14.3	-0.71	-0.17
Semi-manufactured goods (SITC 5,6)	32.4	29.9	25.5	27.1	+0.46	+1.63
Finished manufactures (SITC 7,8)	51.9	43.7	31.5	36.5	+1.69	+3.87
Other commodities (SITC 9)	3.0	2.9	1.6	2.6	+0.12	+0.18
Total Visible	100.0	100.0	100.0	100.0		
	(£ billion)		(£ billion)			
	9.44	47.39	10.19	46.21	+0.19	+1.18
Services	4.29	15.81	3.59	11.62	+0.71	+4.19
Interest profits and dividends	1.74	8.20	1.21	8.24	+0.54	-0.04
Transfers	0.26	1.75	0.51	3.87	-0.24	-2.12
Total Invisible	6.30	25.76	5.31	23.74	+1.00	+2.03
Total current account	15.74	73.15	15.49	69.95	+0.25	+3.21

(a) invisible credits, visible trade on a balance of payments basis.
(b) invisible debits, visible trade on a balance of payments basis.

Source: United Kingdom Balance of Payments, 1981 edition.

multilateral tariff reductions although the experience of
the Tokyo Round following the Kennedy Round suggests that
these possibilities were rather limited. Indeed as the work
of Page (1979) indicates the tendency over recent years has
been to increase not decrease the barriers to international
trade.

However, all these contentions can be no more than
speculation and hence in forming any judgement about the
effects of the EC the usual choice has been to assume that
trade patterns would have developed after 1972 in the same
sort of way that they did previously, modified in some
cases by an assessment of relative performance in third
country markets to take account of differences in the rate
of economic growth in member and non-member countries. This
choice seeks to avoid the second difficulty in finding a
plausible anti-monde, namely the need to explain what
actually determines trade flows. The normal procedure in
economic analysis would be to estimate a model explaining
how trade is determined, decide what exogenous variables
would have changed as a result of the enlargement of the EC
and then using the estimates of the parameters already
obtained to calculate the effects on trade flows. The
method of using extrapolated trends from the past, however
modified, avoids this and consequently may introduce
serious biases into the calculation.

On the one hand attributing all changes from previous
trends to the EC causes the standard problem of bias from
omission of changes in other variables which may have
affected trade, which in the period under consideration
with the oil crisis and the generally depressed level of
world activity could have been very considerable. On the
other, in any stochastic model of economic behaviour there
will be an unexplained random residual and if the effect of
the EC is calculated as the actual value less the
extrapolated trend value then all this residual is ascribed
to the effect of the EC. In the case of both biases the
effect cannot be signed without estimating a proper
structural model of behaviour. Yet the whole problem is
that available resources entail that it is not really
practicable to estimate such structural models, although
the 'Eurolink' and other models are trying to move in this
direction. Even if they were estimated there is no
guarantee that the level of efficiency associated with
these unbiased estimates would be such as to achieve a
marked improvement over the simple biased methods - a
fuller discussion of this argument is given in Mayes (1978
and 1981).

Even if we accept, however reluctantly, that this

approach of some form of trend extrapolation is the only
viable means of providing approximate estimates of the
effects of the EC on trade flows the results require
considerable care in interpretation. They are an amalgam of
several effects and cannot be interpreted in the
traditional theoretical framework of trade creation and
trade diversion. As is pointed out very clearly in Gremmen
et al. (1981) many authors have described any increase in
trade of the member countries above that expected in the
anti-monde as trade creation and any decrease in imports
from non-members below expectation as trade diversion.
However, trade creation is not just the change in trade
flows it is the static welfare gain from the change in
tariff levels (or rather from the consequent change in
prices). The welfare gain is the extent of the reduction in
resources which have to be used in the production of the
increased quantity traded over what would have been used
had the union not been formed. In the same way trade
diversion reflects the resource cost of switching imports
from the lower cost non-member country to the higher cost
partner. Just because the increase in total imports exceeds
the fall in imports from non-members, this does not entail
that the welfare effects are positive. They can be
positive, negative or zero according to the change in
resource costs of the two movements.

The total change in trade flows from those otherwise
expected, even if it correctly reflected only changes due
to the enlargement of the EC, would include far more than
the simple static effect just outlined. In the first place
it is unrealistic to assume that the formation of a
grouping as large as the EC(9) has no effect on world
prices. The change in tariffs and the eventual price
changes which these entail will not necessarily be the
same. We would expect such a union to change the terms of
trade and hence trade flows, creating further gains or
losses for the member (and non-member) countries.

Evidence on the size of the terms of trade effect is very
limited. The result depends upon the ratio of the
elasticity of substitution between imports from partner
countries and imports from third countries and the
elasticity of substitution between domestic products and
imports as a whole. Petith (1977) has made some suggestions
for the possible size of the effects which occurred after
the formation of Benelux, EFTA and the EC(6) for a
plausible range of values of the elasticity ratio (from 1.6
per cent to 8.9 per cent). This results in a spectrum of
effects ranging between 0.2 per cent and 1.5 per cent of
GNP.

Since the maximum size usually suggested for the static welfare effects is 1 per cent of GNP and most estimates lie considerably below that, the terms of trade effect is likely to be of considerable relative importance. Indeed Petith concludes (p.272) that the improvement in the terms of trade may be the principal economic effect of economic integration in Western Europe and moreover that this improvement was consciously one of the major goals of the integration of trade in manufactures. Movements in the terms of trade since 1972 are going to be much more difficult to dis-entangle with the substantial movements in the price of oil dominating other changes. Furthermore Petith's analysis is undertaken almost entirely under a regime of fixed exchange rates where the adjustment processes of import and export prices are likely to be different from those under the subsequent floating exchange rates.

A potentially more important part of the amalgam of effects captured by the estimation method is however that which stems from the dynamic behaviour of the economies concerned rather than from any simple analysis in comparative statics. Even a small increase in the rate of growth of GNP could lead to effects which easily outweighed the once and for all gains we have considered thus far. The emphasis of the potential gains to the UK from membership of the EC in the two white papers Cmnd 4289 and 4715 was very much in terms of being able to participate in the better economic performance of the EC countries, thus raising the UK's rate of growth in absolute terms and lowering the gap between it and the performance of the other member countries.

The 'stylised facts' on which this hope was based are clear from Table 6.2. The rate of economic growth in all the member countries increased in the period after the EC(6) was formed. However, this does not of itself tell us what proportion of that change was due to the formation of the EC or even if the change in the anti-monde would have been even greater or negative. Since, as the table shows, the growth rates of all the EFTA countries (except Austria) and the USA, Canada and Japan also increased during the same period it is clear that it is relative changes in growth rates which would be more appropriate to examine. Otherwise all the reduction in the rate of growth since 1972 would be attributable to the enlargement of the EC.

TABLE 6.2: GROWTH RATES OF REAL GNP/GDP (% p.a.)

	Change between 1958/9-64 and 1953-58/9	1962-72	1973-81*
Belgium	2.4	4.8	0.7
Denmark	2.9	4.6	0.4
France	0.9	5.7	1.9
Germany	0.2	4.5	1.7
Ireland		4.2	1.6
Italy	0.8	4.6	1.6
Netherlands	1.1	5.4	1.1
United Kingdom	1.4	2.7	0.2
Austria	-1.9	4.9	3.0a
Norway	2.4	4.7	4.4a
Sweden	1.2	3.6	1.4a
Switzerland	1.1	3.7	0.0

a 1974-80

* estimated values for 1981.

Source: OECD Economic Surveys and Main Economic Indicators

In order to be able to estimate the effect of the enlargement of the EC on economic growth, the contribution of trade flow changes to that and the consequences of growth for trade we need to be able to specify the mechanism by which the increase in growth takes place. There are several suggestions which have been made, the simplest of which is that the static effects provide an impulse to economic activity because real incomes are increased but more especially because demand in many exporting industries increases rapidly even though this may be matched by a decline in demand for import competing industries. The change in trade flows and increased competition leads to greater investment; productivity increases through the use of technologically more advanced capital equipment and through greater usage of existing equipment and hence this gives a further competitive advantage through the reduction in unit costs, leading to greater exports again and so on through the economic system. There are obviously other avenues of expansion, through increased employment and hence income and expenditure for example.

The debate remains over whether this is merely some form of simple 'multiplier' effect which will peter out at some

higher level of output, hence showing an increase in growth
rates for a limited period only or whether the rate of
economic growth is increased permanently. (Changes in
growth rates due to other subsequent major shocks to the
international system may obscure this 'permanent' effect
quite quickly.) From the point of view of assessing the
likely effects on trade in the future it is essential to
decide whether the change in growth is permanent.
Experience thus far is not necessarily a helpful guide as
the barriers to trade both from tariffs and from other
sources such as government purchasing agreements and
differing safety standards are not removed all at once but
progressively. Thus even with no permanent effect the
increase in the rate of growth could persist for over a
decade allowing for operation of lags. The dismantling of
non-tariff barriers is a continuing process within the EC
and hence no limit could be placed on the length of time it
takes to come into effect. Traditional macro-econometric
models of the UK economy, such as those of the National
Institute, the Treasury and the London Business School,
whose simulation properties have been published, indicate
that any growth rate effect from an export stimulus would
have virtually disappeared after four years (Laury, et al.,
1978). Even on this basis growth rate effects from the 1973
enlargement could persist into the 1980's.

Krause (1968) estimated the contribution to the rate of
economic growth of the EC countries from the increase in
the ratio of investment to GDP (using an average marginal
capital output ratio which ignores the composition of the
extra investment). However, while he found it possible to
obtain a positive effect for the member countries after the
formation of both EFTA and the EC(6), the same method can
be applied to the change in the investment GDP ratio of
non-members. When this is done for Canada, the USA and
Japan, positive results are also obtained (Mayes, 1976);
indeed in the case of Japan the effect is larger than
that for any of the individual members of the two
groupings. This further illustrates the danger in
attributing the whole observed change in a variable to a
single identified cause and ignoring any other possible
influences.

The reasons why such a step in the investment ratio
should occur are not always spelt out. The line of argument
is that the reduction in tariffs and the increased ease of
access to markets increases the competition that companies
face both at home and abroad and in the struggle to remain
competitive they will have to innovate at a much faster
rate than was necessary under tariff protection. Evidence

on actual behaviour is not clear cut and the way in which companies react to pressures on competitiveness might be expected to vary according to whether they were in an expanding or a contracting market. Experience in the recent recession in the UK suggests that in the face of severe cash flow pressures firms do cut back on investment postponing action until the immediate situation improves. Certainly evidence on productivity trends (Wenban-Smith, 1981, for example) does suggest a clear positive relation between growth of output and growth of productivity over the last 15 years. The discussion of the expected effects of both the formation and the enlargement of the EC envisaged an expansionary framework and not the depressed picture observed since 1973.

Perhaps the most fundamental of all the theoretical expectations is that the abolition of tariffs would result in increasing specialisation of production (through the exploitation of comparative advantage). Under such circumstances it should be possible to exploit the advantages of economies of scale and hence enjoy further welfare gains from the reduced unit cost of output. Here again quantification is difficult although comparisons with the USA (Prais, 1982, for example) suggest that there are considerable opportunities in many industries. Analysis of relatively aggregated trade flows has, however, tended to indicate that both exports and imports of commodity groups have increased. To a large extent this is purely a measurement problem and while specialisation has taken place on an intra-industry rather than an inter-industry basis, if a sufficiently fine classification were to be used the expected specialisation would be found. Partly, however, it reflects the sheer rate at which comparative advantage can be eroded in modern industries.

The importance of disaggregation if a clear disentangling of the causes of trade flow changes is required should not be underestimated. The aggregate flows on which much published discussion is based obscure changes in commodity composition. They also obscure the extent of structural change required in industrial production to meet the changes in competitive circumstances. Any study of the effects on trade flows which can be more than indicative therefore is a very substantial undertaking indeed and quite outside the scope of the present chapter.

The lack of detailed information has also led to concentration of much of the public discussion of trade effects on the size of balances rather than on their components and the welfare effects on those components. An understandable reason for this is that the welfare effects

on a static basis have generally been acknowledged to be
small whereas the adjustment cost of correcting substantial
imbalances both through inflation and structural change in
the case of deficits may have very important consequences
for the stance of short-run macro-economic policy.
Furthermore in the period immediately after the UK joined
the EC both the (non-oil) bilateral trade balance and the
UK's total current account balance worsened considerably,
making considerations of balance pre-eminent.

THE PATTERN OF CHANGES SINCE 1972

The search for some underlying trend in trading patterns in
the post-war period unadulterated by the effects of
economic integration is clearly doomed to failure. Trends
prior to the formation of the EC (and EFTA) are now so far
into the past that they cannot reasonably be extrapolated
into the 1980's. In any case the brief period after trading
patterns had become in some sense normal following the
Second World War and the Korean War was itself
characterised by multilateral tariff reductions so there is
no sense in which it is possible to determine trends which
isolate changes due to income effects and technological
development.

Trends from the period between 1960 and 1972 must also be
thought substantially misleading because the general trend
in world trade has behaved so differently since then. Prior
to the first oil crisis in 1974 trade has been
characterised by growth cycles, whereas in 1975 total world
trade fell by 4 per cent and trade in manufactures by 5 per
cent. Despite rapid recovery since then trade rose by only
33 per cent between 1973 and 1980 compared with 85 per cent
during the previous period of seven years.

These problems of trend extrapolation apply not just to
the growth of total trade or the ratios of trade to output
and consumption but also to the distribution of trade.
Product and country compositions of trade vary with the
rate of growth of the total. For example, the UK's share in
trade has tended to be inversely related to the rate of
growth of world trade.

In nearly a decade since the UK joined the EC it has been
very difficult to point to any years which show behaviour
clearly similar to that experienced during the previous two
decades. The first seven years following the UK's accession
to the EC were characterised by substantial deficits on the
balance of trade, after a period when the balance had been
much more favourable, as is illustrated in Table 6.3.

TABLE 6.3: UK VISIBLE TRADE WITH THE EC, 1970-80*

	UK Exports to EC (10)		UK Imports from EC		Balance with EC (10)	Balance all areas
	£m	as % of total exports	£m	as % of total imports	£m	£m
1970	2,416	29.7	2,325	28.4	+91	-34
1971	2,536	28.1	2,720	30.7	-184	+190
1972	2,849	30.2	3,441	33.8	-592	-748
1973	3,851	32.3	5,178	35.7	-1,327	-2,586
1974	5,546	33.8	7,680	35.3	-2,134	-5,351
1975	6,227	32.2	8,734	38.5	-2,507	-3,333
1976	8,936	35.5	11,194	38.4	-2,258	-3,929
1977	11,674	36.8	13,606	40.0	-1,932	-2,284
1978	13,348	38.1	15,863	43.3	-2,515	-1,542
1979	17,306	42.6	19,935	45.2	-2,629	-3,458
1980	20,422	43.1	19,713	42.7	+709	+1,178

*   1981 figures are not available, but in so far as they
    can be constructed from those of the other EC
    countries, they indicate a larger surplus for the UK
    with the EC(10) and even larger increase to £7-8
    billion for the total surplus on trade with all
    countries.

Source: United Kingdom Balance of Payments, 1981 edition

In 1974 the deficit was as much as 6 per cent of GDP and it
was not until 1980 that the balance moved back into
surplus. The rapid increase in the surplus on services and
the continuing surpluses on net payments of interest,
profits and dividends prevented the final impact on the
current balance from being so substantial although its
cumulative value in purely nominal terms alone was £6½
billion by 1979, equal to some 15 per cent of exports of
goods and services in that year.

However, other major changes to the international system
took place during that period, the first of which was the
ending of the Bretton Woods system of fixed exchange rate
parities in 1971. Starting from an average value of US$2.50
to £1 in 1972 sterling fell to US$1.75/£ by 1977, a fall of
30 per cent, the greatest change occurring in 1975 and
1976. The floating of the exchange rate meant that in one
sense the balance of payments was no longer such an
impediment to economic growth in the UK although a falling
exchange rate would have a substantial impact upon the rate

of price inflation. While the nominal effect of the
exchange rate changes upon prices was much greater than
that of the tariff changes the real exchange rate movements
were not so large compared with the <u>relative</u> movement in EC
and non-EC prices until 1979-80. Thus although one might
expect tariff changes to be partly offset by exchange rate
movements the major fluctuations were due to other causes,
principally domestic wage inflation and the oil crisis. The
change in oil prices contributed £2½ billion to the
deficits of 1974 and 1975, rising to nearer £3½ billion in
1976 (as estimated in Morgan, 1980). It was only the
beginning of substantial North Sea oil production in 1977
which prevented this figure from becoming even larger. By
1980 the contribution to the deficit from this source had
been virtually eliminated (the crude balance on trade in
petroleum and petroleum products was +£273 million,
although there was an associated adverse movement in net
interest, profit and dividend receipts).

While the overall balance of trade improved in 1978 the
increase in exports was mainly due to oil and exports of
manufactures actually fell in volume. This sluggishness in
non-oil exports continued in 1979, while the rise in the
exchange rate by 7 per cent and the consequent rise in
relative export prices was insufficient to offset the 10
per cent rise in the volume of imports. 1980 showed a very
different picture where, despite the continuing rise in
sterling (by 10 per cent in the effective rate) and a rise
in relative exports prices by a similar amount, exports
rose in volume while imports fell by 3 per cent reflecting
in a large measure the 2 per cent fall in GDP in the UK
compared with 1¼ per cent in the rest of OECD. Conclusions
for 1981 must be rather more tenuous as data are not
available for March to September owing to the Civil Service
strike.

The relative position of the UK in 'world' exports of
manufactures helps to put the experience of bilateral trade
with the EC in context. While the UK's share of exports of
the eleven main exporting countries fell steadily through
the 20 years 1955 to 1974 from 19.9 per cent to 8.5 per
cent, since then the share has oscillated and even
recovered slightly (it was 9.7 per cent in 1980). Clearly
if one country's share rises another's must fall. There is
no straightforward pattern in the period since the UK
joined the EC but the main countries showing substantial
decreases in share in the four years 1977-80 are first the
USA and then Japan. In 1980 the UK's share rose despite a
fall in manufacturing output of 15 per cent from its
previous peak and the 10 per cent rise in the sterling

exchange rate and consequent similar rise in relative export unit values of manufactures.

The striking feature of UK trade with the other EC countries since 1972 has been its rate of increase. Imports and exports, while starting with a share of around 30 per cent of their respective totals both increased that share to over 40 per cent by 1980. However, even before 1972 the share of the EC(6) in the UK trade had been increasing, largely at the expense of developing countries, so some increase might have been expected in the subsequent period even had the UK not joined the EC. Imports from the EC(9) already exceeded exports to them in 1972 and this deficit widened during the first two years of accession, thereafter staying in the range £2-2½ billion (representing a decline in real terms) until in 1980 the picture changed. In that year there was a turn round of £3.3 billion (representing a decline in real terms) until 1980 the picture changed. In that year there was a turn of £3.3 billion giving a surplus of £700 million - a shift extraordinarily similar to that in total non-oil visible trade at £3.6 billion to a surplus of £900 million.

As a simple indication of the nature of changes since 1972 Figs. 6.1, 6.2 and 6.3 show how trade between the UK and the EC(6) has progressed since 1972 compared with a continuation of a linear trend in shares estimated over the previous 10 years. (The original data were obtained by Anne Daly who kindly made them available to me, but the updated values and the trends and derived calculations are mine.) Eight major product categories are distinguished and erratic items such as ships, aircraft and precious stones are excluded from the analysis. The first three years after 1972 are plotted and then 1980, thus concentration on the particular 1980 value may be misleading, both because of temporary fluctuations and the sharp change in trade patterns in that year, the general pattern is, however, clear.

It is only in the case of transport products that a linear trend is not a close representation of the data over the period 1963-72 for the share of UK imports coming from the EC (as is explained in Table 6.4). It can be seen from Fig. 6.1 the pattern changes rapidly, even in the first three years after accession. In all cases the share of imports coming from the EC(6) rises, whether the 1963-72 trend was positive or negative, and it is only in the case of transport products that the 1980 share is not higher still and significantly greater than the trend value at the 5 per cent level. The total of this difference in imports between actual and trend values is US$15 billion in 1980. As we noted earlier this total cannot readily be translated into the terms of trade creation and diversion and such

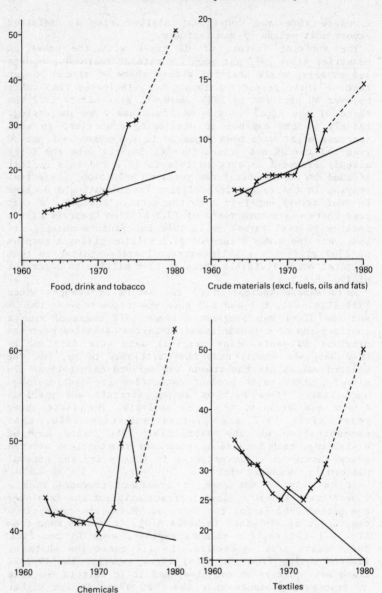

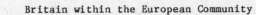

FIGURE 6.1: PERCENTAGE OF UK IMPORTS COMING FROM EC(6)

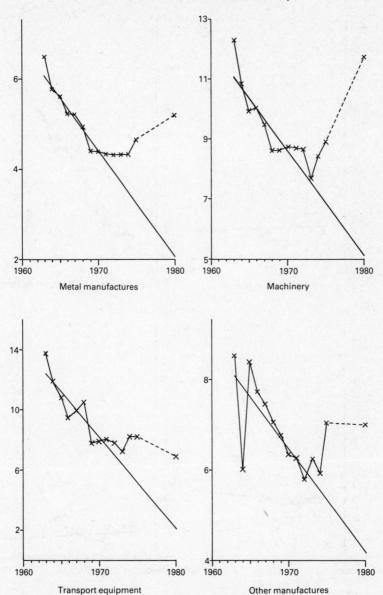

Metal manufactures

Machinery

Transport equipment

Other manufactures

FIGURE 6.1: PERCENTAGE OF UK IMPORTS COMING FROM EC(6)

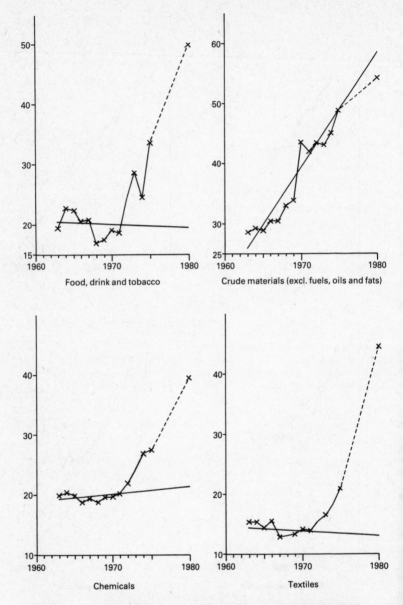

FIGURE 6.2: PERCENTAGE OF EXPORTS IN TOTAL UK EXPORTS

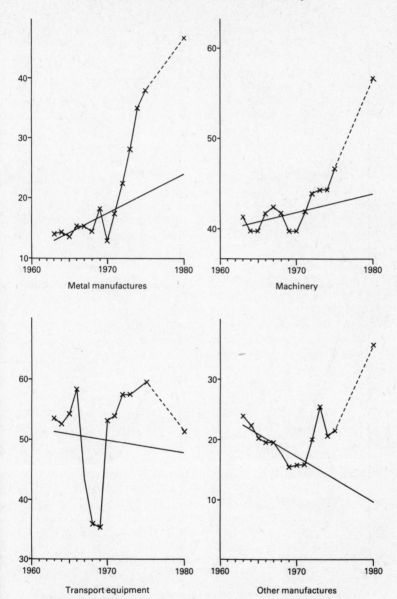

Metal manufactures

Machinery

Transport equipment

Other manufactures

FIGURE 6.2: PERCENTAGE OF EXPORTS IN TOTAL UK EXPORTS

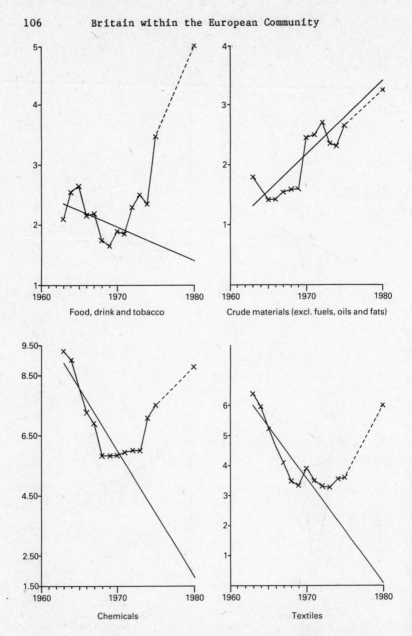

Food, drink and tobacco

Crude materials (excl. fuels, oils and fats)

Chemicals

Textiles

FIGURE 6.3: PERCENTAGE OF EXPORTS IN TOTAL EC(6) IMPORTS

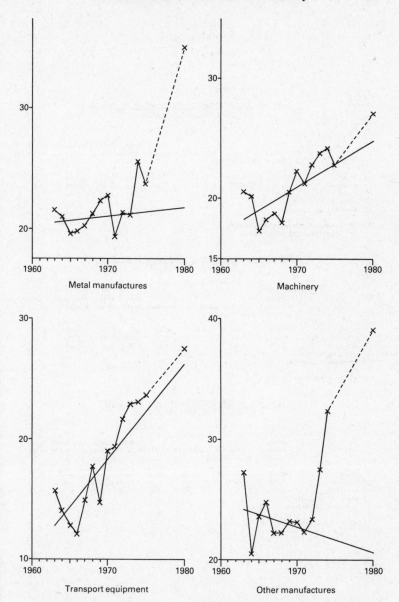

FIGURE 6.3: PERCENTAGE OF EXPORTS IN TOTAL EC(6) IMPORTS

TABLE 6.4: LINEAR TRENDS IN PERCENTAGE OF UK IMPORTS
COMING FROM EC(6), 1963-72

COMMODITY GROUP

	Food, drink & tobacco	Crude Materials(a)	Chemicals	Textiles	Metal manfs.	Mach- inery	Transport equipment	Other manfs.
slope	0.52	0.24	-0.17	-1.09	0.64	0.20	-0.19	-0.76
t value	9.47	5.44	1.39	7.20	2.74	1.28	0.97	3.29
standard error of estimate	0.50	0.40	1.14	1.37	2.12	1.45	8.85	2.10
forecast difference *		*	*	*	*	*		*

(a) excluding fuels, oils and fats
 * significant at 5 per cent

TABLE 6.5: LINEAR TRENDS IN PERCENTAGE OF UK EXPORTS
GOING TO EC(6), 1963-72

COMMODITY GROUP

	Food, drink & tobacco	Crude Materials(a)	Chemicals	Textiles	Metal manfs.	Mach- inery	Transport equipment	Other manfs.
slope	-0.08	1.89	0.13	-0.08	0.07	0.37	0.80	-0.19
t value	0.27	6.62	1.13	0.73	0.52	2.17	3.55	0.97
standard error of estimate	2.65	2.60	1.03	1.01	1.21	1.56	2.05	1.79
forecast difference *			*	*	*			*

NOTES: See Table 6.4.

TABLE 6.6: LINEAR TRENDS IN PERCENTAGE OF EC(6)
IMPORTS COMING FROM UK, 1963-72

COMMODITY GROUP

	Food, drink & tobacco	Crude Materials(a)	Chemicals	Textiles	Metal manfs.	Mach- inery	Transport equipment	Other manfs
slope	-0.05	0.12	-0.42	-0.34	-0.23	-0.35	-0.61	-0.22
t value	1.58	3.17	6.30	6.63	10.49	5.18	6.16	2.64
standard error of estimate	1.47	0.35	0.60	0.47	0.20	0.61	0.90	0.35
forecast difference *			*	*	*	*	*	

NOTES: See Table 6.4.

estimates will not be attempted.

A similar set of calculations can be performed for the share of the UK's exports going to the EC. Here the charts for the eight commodity groups are shown in Fig. 6.2 and the associated information on the regressions in Table 6.5. In this case it is re-assuring that the crude materials category whose relative prices and restrictions were largely unaffected by the enlargement of the EC shows no divergence from its previous trend. The other categories again all showed increases in share relative to trend, however, in the case of machinery and in that of transport equipment these increases are neither substantial, nor significantly different from the previous trend. Export shares showed more variance than import shares over the period 1963-72, making the fitting of linear trends less satisfactory.

It is also possible to look at these same trade flows from the point of view of the EC as an importer. Although the share of UK exports going to the EC may have increased sharply this does not entail that these exports must form an increased share of EC imports. Such a pattern would occur merely if the EC grew faster than other markets and UK shares remained constant in all markets. It is, however, readily apparent from Fig. 6.3 and Table 6.6 that the experience of the EC is the same as that for the UK, with the share of imports from the new partner countries growing rapidly after 1972 in most commodity categories. For the share coming from the UK in particular all categories except crude materials show an increase, although not significantly above the trend over the previous ten years in the case of 'other manufactures' (largely because of the poor fit of the trend).

It is thus clear that the observed changes in trade flows show a broad conformity in the change experienced with that expected on the basis of traditional economic theory. As was argued earlier, it is by no means clear what proportion of these changes should be attributed to the enlargement of the EC rather than to other factors. Nevertheless the changes are on such a large scale and are sufficiently consistent to provide prima facie evidence of a substantial effect on the trading patterns of the UK. Similar general conformity with anticipated changes in trade patterns can be seen by examining trade flows with other countries. Shares tend to move against both the previous EFTA partners, who no longer have a tariff advantage over the EC, and against countries outside both the EC and EFTA (there are of course many individual exceptions), providing part of the basis for the assessment of trade diversion.

If we take UK exports of manufactures as a whole we can
see from Table 6.7 that while the UK's share has risen in
the markets of each of the EC(6) it has fallen in those of
the other two countries, Denmark and the Irish Republic,
which joined at the same time. This is to be expected as
both countries already gave preferential status to imports
from the UK and not to the EC(6). Furthermore the previous
trend in the UK's market share had been downwards in those
two countries. The UK's share also continued to fall in the
US, Canadian and Japanese markets, but while the rate of
decline eased after 1972 in the first two markets,
reflecting a general improvement in the UK's performance
relative to the past, it fell a little faster in the case
of Japan, the majority of the change occurring in the first
two years.

The results are, of course, only indicative and do not
suggest any exact orders of magnitude. Other estimates are
few and far between, Morgan (1980) suggests a figure for
the effect on UK exports of £½ billion in 1976 on the basis
of 1972 trade shares. Our results suggest that if trade had
continued to move in the same pattern as over the 10 years
1963-72 effects of £5-7 billion in 1980 would be by no
means impossible. The estimated effects would be even
larger if the trend shares in the anti-monde were thought
to be smaller, but nearer zero if higher trend values were
expected as they might be in the light of the UK's stronger
performance in third markets in the period after 1972
compared with that in the previous ten years. While such
changes could be divided between increases in total trade
and declines in trade with non-members estimates of trade
creation and trade diversion can only be obtained by
multiplying those changes by the changes in costs involved.
With tariffs on finished manufactures only of the order of
5 per cent on average the total effect on welfare might
only be of the order of £¼ billion, which is very small.
Furthermore, this is the total and not just the static
effect in the framework in which trade diversion and
creation are normally discussed, but it also ignores the
effect of market size in the anti-monde by basing the
analysis on shares alone. Given the small size of welfare
effect on this basis it is not surprising that interest has
tended to concentrate on effects on the rate of growth,
which would dominate it even if they were small in
percentage terms, and also on effects on the balance of
payments and their consequences for macro-economic policy.

TABLE 6.7: UK PERCENTAGE SHARE OF IMPORTS OF MANUFACTURED GOODS INTO VARIOUS MARKETS

	European Community (9)	West Germany	France	Italy	Nether-lands	Belgium/Luxembourg	Denmark	Ireland	Greece	USA	Canada	Japan
1963		8.3	10.1	10.8	9.1	11.4	16.1	63.9	12.7	10.0	9.9	6.8
1964		8.0	9.1	10.4	8.7	10.3	16.3	61.8	12.7	9.2	9.2	7.7
1965		7.0	8.5	9.9	8.3	10.3	15.9	63.4	11.6	9.5	8.3	7.6
1966		6.7	7.7	9.2	7.9	9.6	15.9	64.0	12.3	9.7	7.4	8.6
1967		6.5	7.3	8.2	7.2	9.0	15.7	62.6	11.5	8.3	6.8	7.1
1968		6.1	6.4	7.4	7.1	9.9	14.8	62.5	12.3	7.6	6.2	6.0
1969		5.9	6.1	7.0	7.4	8.7	15.1	60.8	11.2	7.2	6.0	6.3
1970	6.6	5.5	6.2	6.3	7.3	7.2	15.0	61.7	10.3	6.5	5.8	6.0
1971	6.6	5.2	6.1	6.4	7.6	7.8	14.0	58.1	8.9	6.3	5.9	6.6
1972	6.3	4.8	6.4	6.0	6.9	8.1	13.2	58.3	8.6	6.5	5.5	6.2
1973	6.0	4.9	5.8	5.7	6.7	8.3	11.4	56.4	6.7	6.7	4.7	5.4
1974	6.0	5.0	6.2	5.6	7.2	7.6	11.2	53.2	6.4	5.7	4.1	5.0
1975	6.3	5.2	6.6	6.1	7.4	8.0	11.1	55.2	6.5	5.8	4.1	5.7
1976	6.6	5.4	6.7	6.2	8.2	9.0	10.8	52.7	5.9	5.2	3.4	4.4
1977	7.0	5.9	6.9	6.7	8.4	10.4	11.6	52.5	7.0	4.9	3.3	5.1
1978	7.0	6.0	6.7	7.0	8.0	10.8*	10.6	52.0	6.7	4.8	3.5	5.0
1979	7.1 e	6.6	7.0	7.0	8.5	9.5	10.6	51.4	8.1	5.0	3.5	4.3
1980	7.1 e	6.8	6.7	7.2	9.2	9.3 p	9.9	51.6				4.8

e = estimated

* = the 1978 figure comparable to 1979 is 10.1

p = provisional

Source: Monthly Review of External Trade Statistics, 1981 Supplement

THE MOVEMENT OF FACTORS

While it may appear from the previous section that in
general trade flows have moved in the manner which is to be
expected given immobile factors the evidence on the
movement of factors is far more confused. Clearly the same
movements in output could be observed, given their accuracy
of measurement, even if factors had also moved as it is
clear that factor movements are small compared with trade
flow changes. One might also expect that the speed of
adjustment of trade flows was rather faster than that of
factors, particularly labour, especially since the barriers
on factor movements which have been removed may be
relatively small compared with those that remain. However,
even if the barriers to factor movements were to remain
unchanged, changes in factor movemements could be expected
as the result of the changes in trade and activity stemming
from tariff reduction and other aspects of the enlargement
of the EC.

It is probably sensible to consider labour and capital
separately although it is likely that the mobility of
labour has a substantial effect on the mobility of capital.
Immobility of labour can lead to substantial differences in
wage levels among regions and although this may be partly
offset by differing levels of skills, it may mean that a
firm can reduce its total costs by moving production to a
lower wage area. Other costs such as transport and inferior
infrastructure will still ensure the maintenance of the
regional wage differentials.

Turning first to capital, the firm is faced by several
possible decisions for example: (i) it can supply all
foreign markets by exporting to them from its domestic
base, which becomes more attractive when tariffs and other
barriers to trade are removed; (ii) it can set up full
production in foreign countries; (iii) it can site parts of
its productive process in different countries according to
relative cost advantages and hence increase trade not just
in the finished product but in intermediate products; and
(iv) it can participate in the profits from sales and
production in foreign countries by portfolio investment.

In the same way that (i) is made more likely by tariff
reduction, (ii) is made less likely, particularly if there
are economies of scale still to be obtained from domestic
plants. There is likely to be some switching from direct
investment in partner countries to investment in third
countries which are excluded from the EC. However, this
purely static approach like that to trade flows assumes
first that firms concentrate equally on all markets (or

that in aggregate they can be treated as if they do) and that there are no dynamic adjustments which would lead to shifts in capital over and above the simple static framework. Expectations and a longer-run horizon play a more important part in direct investment decisions and hence one might expect to see a rather different pattern from that of trade flows. In the first place, since output lags investment one might expect investment patterns to lead the process of formal changes in the transition to full membership of the EC. Secondly the importance of direct investment by and in North America is such that it cannot be treated purely as part of some general case. The US market is large and relatively homogeneous, hence entry to it represents a source of sales not reproducible in any other single country, indeed some of the propaganda at the time of entry negotiations to the EC likened the enlarged EC market to that of the US.

As is clear from Table 6.8, in the 1960's three quarters of foreign-owned assets in the UK were held by North America. After the enlargement of the EC, US firms would no longer have been faced by tariff disadvantages to supplying the EC from the UK or vice-versa although many other restrictions on trade and foreign ownership of important firms continued. Thus an initial fall is to be expected and the information on investment flows in Table 6.9 suggests that the share of the total investment in the UK by US firms has continued at a lower level. This, however, may reflect merely more investment by non-US firms and not a switch of location for US foreign investment.

Wide yearly fluctuations in the flows in Table 6.9 are to be expected as investment is 'lumpy' and a few important projects can affect the total figures substantially. Nevertheless it appears that there was an increase in UK investment in the EC(10) both in the two years before entry and immediately following, but that investment has settled back to previous proportions since then. Direct investment by other EC countries in the UK appears to show no such surge although there is some increase in the second half of the 1970's i.e. with a lag rather than a lead over the date of entry.

The theoretical bases for this analysis are relatively weak. One might expect there to be equivalent concepts to trade creation and trade diversion, say 'investment creation' and 'investment diversion', although without any welfare connotation, which would have opposite signs to their trade counterparts if the two are substitutes. However, trade and investment have also a large measure of complementarity. According to Panic (1982) a UK Department of Trade enquiry in 1976 revealed that 'about 29 per cent of the exports covered ... went to related enterprises'.

TABLE 6.8: DISTRIBUTION OF UK ASSETS ABROAD
AND FOREIGN ASSETS IN THE UK (AS PERCENTAGE OF TOTAL)

Year	Western Europe	North America	Other Developed	Rest of World	Total (£m)
(a) UK assets					
1962	13.4	23.1	27.1	36.5	3,405.0
1965	15.4	21.8	29.9	32.9	4,210.0
1968	17.6	23.0	30.8	28.5	5,585.3
1971	21.9	20.0	29.8	26.3	6,666.9
1974	27.5	22.0	29.3	21.3	10,117.8
(b) Foreign assets in UK					
1962	20.9	75.9	2.3	0.9	1,429.7
1965	19.9	77.3	1.0	1.8	1,999.9
1968	21.8	75.3	1.8	1.1	2,728.0
1971	23.4	71.2	4.1	1.3	3,817.0
1974	28.1	62.1	4.6	5.2	6,585.3

Source: M. Panic (1982), 'Some longer term effects of short-run adjustment
policies: behaviour of UK direct investment since the 1960's', in
J. Black and J.H. Dunning (eds) International Capital Movements
(London; Macmillan).

TABLE 6.9: DIRECT INVESTMENT BY REGION (% SHARE)

	1970	1971	1972	1973	1974	1975	1976	1977	1978	1979	1980
EC(10)											
In UK	16.8	8.7	10.8	15.3	8.9	15.9	22.0	20.2	24.0	14.9	
By UK	17.2	42.5	33.1	32.3	23.2	14.3	23.2	20.4	21.3	1.2	
(Net £m)	33	248	200	411	289	70	321	117	274	-236	
Other W. Europe											
In UK	5.8	6.0	11.8	8.4	14.1	18.4	9.9	12.9	9.6	14.0	
By UK	6.4	2.1	6.1	6.2	6.3	4.1	9.0	9.8	9.9	3.4	
(Net £m)	14	-13	-3	39	-21	-65	113	13	147	-159	
North America											
In UK	66.1	72.0	61.5	57.5	55.3	45.9	63.0	52.4	65.3	61.3	
By UK	33.9	23.1	21.8	31.5	30.7	29.9	27.6	30.9	40.4	64.6	
(Net £m)	-55	-168	-90	89	11	68	90	-112	263	687	
Other developed											
In UK	10.2	9.1	11.0	2.3	1.4	10.9	0.0	11.7	0.6	3.2	
By UK	20.9	22.3	27.4	17.5	26.0	26.3	19.4	17.7	11.6	9.4	
(Net £m)	77	110	157	267	397	241	419	179	310	203	
Oil exporters											
In UK	0.6	-0.2	0.0	-0.1	12.8	-0.5	-2.3	-1.1	0.8	3.4	
By UK	6.0	3.7	3.3	1.5	2.8	3.5	5.0	9.4	5.7	2.5	
(Net £m)	35	26	24	26	-65	44	125	192	145	7	
Rest of world											
In UK	1.7	4.4	4.9	16.6	7.6	9.4	7.8	3.9	-0.3	3.2	
By UK	15.6	6.4	8.3	10.9	11.1	21.9	15.9	11.8	11.1	18.9	
(Net £m)	79	23	41	55	110	198	278	170	309	468	
Total (£million)											
In UK	363	450	408	734	854	615	799	1,326	1,292	1,818	2,094
By UK	546	676	737	1,621	1,575	1,171	2,145	1,885	2,740	2,788	2,569
(Net £m)	183	226	329	887	721	556	1,346	559	1,448	970	475

Increase in assets of owner shown positive.
Net flows are outward-inward.

Source: Pink Book, 1981.

Thus as set out in possibility (iii) a complex combination of increased investment and trade may be expected according to the detailed production conditions in the various countries involved both inside and outside the EC.

It is not surprising therefore that in the face of this picture of conflicting forces there has been a tendency to develop an eclectic approach to the decision. Dunning (1982) suggests that there are three general areas of perceived gain to firms from direct investment abroad: ownership, internalisation and location. While the first two of these tend to apply rather more to the decision whether to invest abroad as opposed to at home, the third also clearly relates to the decision over which country (or part of which country) to invest in, permitting substitution between different foreign countries as well as between the domestic country and abroad in general. Until we have some clear theory of behaviour we have no means of suggesting what the path of investment would have been without the enlargement of the EC.

The observation that both inward and outward direct investment between the UK and the other western European countries increased rapidly both before and after the UK joined the EC is consistent with Dunning's theory of development of direct investment flows over time. When a country has a low income per head it has only a limited capacity to absorb direct investment. As income per head grows the inflow of capital also rises but somewhere in the range of incomes between that of Singapore and that of New Zealand the net inflow reaches a maximum. This is because beyond some point domestic industrial and financial activity can support an increasing outflow of direct investment thus eventually narrowing the gap between the inflow and the outflow. At some stage of the process of growth in incomes the outflow will tend to exceed the inflow and the country will become a net exporter of direct investment capital. For the EC(9) other than the UK this point was reached in most cases somewhere during the period 1967-75. Clearly structural differences in the organisation of firms and financial markets will affect the level of per capita income at which the changeover from inflow to outflow takes place. Changes like joining the EC could be expected to affect these structures.

The pattern of portfolio investment has been substantially affected by exchange and other controls. In the particular instance of the UK the behaviour since the relaxation of controls in July and their abolition in October 1979, showed the degree to which investors had previously been frustrated in their wishes to diversify their portfolios into foreign assets. While desired foreign holdings were hypothesised by Hughes (1982) to be from around 10 per cent up to even 40 per cent in the case of some unit trusts, this would necessitate about a quarter of the cash flow into portfolios being invested overseas for several years. It is thus clear that investment patterns are severely constrained even between EC member countries by the controls on their movement from many sources. Therefore, discrepancies between predicted changes in patterns upon joining the EC and actual movements could readily be expected both for direct and portfolio investment.

There are clear relations between the movement of labour and the movement of capital. While relatively low wages in one country compared with another may encourage labour to move from the lower wage to the higher wage country to obtain higher incomes, capital will tend to be encouraged to move in the opposite direction to exploit the lower costs. However, income tax rates and employment taxes mean that the benefit to the employee and the labour cost to the employer may not move together. Earned incomes after deductions from a particular job may be higher in real terms in one country while the unit labour cost to the employer is lower (even allowing for differences in deflators between the two groups).

If, however, we isolate the labour movement decision (and initially treat the availability of capital as given) we can consider it in the light of household response to push and pull factors. While the nature of the relative wage incentive and relative employment opportunities may be clear and measurable, the effects of other determinants, such as language, division of the family if only the worker concerned is permitted to move, the availability of housing – which certainly acts as a barrier to internal labour movements in the UK – and similar social considerations are immensely difficult to quantify.

Emerson (1979) produced data on labour movements in the EC(9) for 1976 (and I am grateful to him for discussions of movements since then). The table, shown here as Table 6.10, indicates that behaviour patterns vary quite considerably between countries. Labour movements from the three largest EC countries are all about ½ per cent of the domestic working population or less. Italy had about 3½ per cent working abroad, reflecting perhaps its greater income differential from the other members, and Luxembourg also showed a higher value possibly reflecting its small land area. It is the Irish Republic which stands out. It had the lowest income per head of the nine countries, but the

TABLE: 6.10: FOREIGN EMPLOYEES IN THE EC, 1976

	Nationals working in other member states. (thousands) (1)	Domestic working population (thousands) (2)	(1) as a percentage of (2) (3)
Belgium	68	3,713	1.8
Denmark	7	2,293	0.2
Germany	137	24,556	0.5
France	114	20,836	0.5
Irish Republic	455	1,021	44.6
Italy	694	18,930	3.6
Luxembourg	6	148	4.1
Netherlands	83	4,542	1.8
United Kingdom	61	24,425	0.2
Total EC	1,625	100,568	1.6
Spain	447	12,535	3.5
Greece	239	3,230	7.4
Portugal	569	3,279	17.4
Turkey	587	14,710	4.0
Yugoslavia	458		
Algeria	447		
Morocco	183		
Tunisia	85		
Others	1,392		
Total non-EC	4,407		
Total	6,032		

Source: M. Emerson (1979), 'The European Monetary System in the broader setting of the Community's economic and political development', in P.H. Trezise (ed), The European Monetary System: Its Promise and Prospects (Washington, DC: Brookings Institution).

figure of nearly half as many working in other member countries as in the domestic working population is of course grossly distorted from any general relation by its special relationship with the UK. What it does show is that labour migration can be very large indeed if countries are closely integrated. However, it is also clear from the second half of the table that migration can be very substantial even if countries are not closely integrated as in the case of Portugal. There, despite language barriers, no common frontier with the EC and not having the advantages of membership a number equal to $17\frac{1}{2}$ per cent of the domestic working population were employed in EC countries in 1976.

Since 1976 the pattern has changed very substantially. The high level of unemployment and the lack of demand for labour among the EC countries has meant that the inflow of labour from outside the EC has been reversed and that movements within the EC have also diminished. Thus the overriding importance of the 'pull' factors attracting labour away from the location with the lower remuneration (or higher level of unemployment) is indicated.

Clearly disaggregation is important in the analysis of the movement of factors as it is in the analysis of trade flows, because labour skills are not equally transportable between countries. Not all qualifications are recognised (see El-Agraa and Goodrich, 1980, for example) and despite the absence of restrictions on the ability of nationals of other EC countries to obtain permits to work (given they can overcome the obstacles to obtaining a job abroad in the first place) there are still costs which face the migrant which may not face the indigenous employee – transfer of pension rights, accumulated sickness benefits, etc. Nevertheless some generalisations can be made at the aggregate level.

It appears that there has been no striking movement of factors between EC members and third countries which would not have occurred in the absence of the EC (or its enlargement). General differences in rates of economic growth, unemployment and wage rates have attracted labour movements both within and from outside the EC. However, although movements appear to be largest where the differences are greatest, no detailed comparison with the expectations of economic theory have been possible.

It seems that factor mobility has been relatively limited among the EC countries, even compared with that within individual member states, and that the process of removal of barriers has a long way to go. Even within national boundaries substantial barriers exist to the movement of labour, not least from the pressures of ordinary family life.

PROSPECTS AND FURTHER DEVELOPMENTS

Even allowing for substantial lags in adjustment, most models of behaviour would suggest that the purely static trade effects of the enlargement of the EC from Six to Nine have been exhausted. Further effects are to be expected from the enlargement to Ten but given the size of the trade flows involved they are likely to be small for the UK (although not so for Greece). In any case the estimated direct static welfare effects from integration are generally thought to be small in relation to GNP (up to 1 per cent). More substantial gains from integration are expected to stem from changes in the terms of trade and the dynamic behaviour of the economies involved including the exploitation of economies of scale. In particular, that the change in competitive conditions gives a stimulus to business activity and efficiency resulting in an increase in the rate of economic growth over what it would have been otherwise.

However, it is one thing to state such expectations and quite another to measure what has actually happened in practice. To do so requires the ability to set out what would have happened had the EC Six not been enlarged. Even ignoring the difficulties of deciding what the alternative trading arrangements would have been it is not possible to make a straightforward assessment of what would have happened in those specified other circumstances without having a clear model of macro-economic behaviour in the countries involved. Estimates based on the extrapolation of previous trends augmented by actual behaviour in the post integration period in third countries can only be indicative and may be very seriously biased.

Estimates of the dynamic effects of the formation of the original EC were positive even after allowing for a general increase in growth rates throughout the main industrialised countries. Experience since 1973 has been very different with depressed economies and the oil crisis dominating the changes in international trade flows. Any discussion of positive dynamic effects would therefore have been in terms of the anti-monde getting even worse. In this rather disappointing context emphasis has been placed by some commentators on the adverse movement in the UK balance of trade in the years immediately after accession both in total and with respect to the EC. The deficits coupled with net contributions to the EC Budget, over which there is also acrimonious debate, have helped contribute towards pressures on domestic policy both to deflate the economy to try to reduce the deficit and to permit the depreciation of the rate of exchange entailed by a floating exchange rate with its consequent adverse effect upon domestic price inflation.

This picture has changed radically since 1979 with the eradication of the deficits and the maintenance of a strong exchange rate. Discussions of the future are thus in a different context arguing over whether the past few years are an unusual deviation from trend because of the effects of oil and the relative severity of domestic macro-economic policy, or whether they herald the start of a period under a new structure which will not revert to the difficulties of the earlier years.

Movements in factors, however, present a very different picture. There has clearly been very little adjustment to what one might expect in theory with an integrated market, but the major reason for this is the lack of integration, probably rather more importantly in the case of labour than in the case of capital. Thus unlike trade the scope for movements in the future within the existing EC are substantial. There are many barriers which could be removed. To some extent these represent 'negative' aspects of integration, merely stopping practices which discriminate against other member countries – ownership of capital, for example – but to a much larger extent they require 'positive' moves – deciding upon commonly acceptable qualifications and skills. Such 'positive' actions are much more difficult to achieve and it is thus to be anticipated that trading and production patterns will still tend to reflect national organisation and preferences rather than those of a single Community-wide market. As Hocking (1980) points out, even in a product as international as motor cars producers have still tended to look primarily at their domestic markets when deciding upon their particular products. Clearly producers may widen their horizons in the future but trading patterns are far more on the basis of production firmly embedded in the home market and exported, than aimed directly at the whole EC. Thus there has been a strong development of intra-industry trade and a failure to reap some of the expected benefits from economic integration. In an evolving EC which is slowly reducing the barriers to factor movements and to the creation of a single integrated market, such benefits may still be enjoyed in the future.

Part III
Microeconomic Policies

7 Industrial and Competition Policies: a New Look

Alan Butt Philip

INTRODUCTION

At the end of 1980 Mr. Roy Jenkins, the outgoing President of the Commission, told the world that the EC was 'an agricultural Community with political trimmings'.[1] Such candour is rarely heard from politicians or highly-placed Eurocrats, but Mr. Jenkins spoke the esential truth about the Community, as it now stands, even if some qualification is called for – see chapters 1 and 2. The dominance of the agricultural sector in a self-styled European 'economic community' would seem on the surface to be more appropriate for Western Europe in the mid-eighteenth century rather than at the end of the twentieth century. The hegemony of agriculture in the EC inevitably raises the question as to why, given that its contribution to Community i.e. GNP is only one-fifth that of industry, the industrial interests of the member states have apparently received so little attention both in terms of the Community's budgets and in terms of policy development. The answers to this question belong rather more to the realms of political science and law than to economics. However, it must also be recognised that a very great deal of Community activity is concerned with matters of direct interest to industry – such as the operation of the commercial and competition policies – even if they are not a major charge on the Community's finances. The purpose of this chapter is to trace the development of EC policies in regard to industry and competition in the broadest sense, to review the problems encountered in the framing and implementation of those policies, and to put forward an outline for the future operation and development of industrial and competition policies in the EC.

ORIGINS AND BACKGROUND

It is often difficult for British observers of the EC to appreciate fully the importance of the Treaties of Paris and Rome in determining both what the EC is or is not able

to do in the 1980s, and how Community policy and practice
is applied and interpreted. The importance of these
Treaties as the foundations of Community law has indeed
been increased by the frequent inability of the member
states to agree major follow-up legislation in the
industrial field within the Council of Ministers. The
Treaties themselves define the role of the Commission and
the scope of its legitimate interest, subject only to
review by the European Court of Justice. Commission staff
have often had to search through the small print of the
Treaties to find a way round a political logjam which
prevents a Community initiative from being launched. Two of
the broadest articles of the EEC Treaty from the
Commission's standpoint are Article 100 which empowers the
Council acting unanimously on a proposal from the
Commission to 'issue directives for the approximation of
such provisions laid down by law, regulation or
administrative action in Member States as directly affect
the establishment or functioning of the common market' and
Article 235 which provides for the Commission to submit any
proposals to the Council of Ministers, after consulting the
European Parliament, 'if action by the Community should
prove necessary to attain, in the course of the operation
of the common market, one of the objectives of the
Community and this Treaty has not provided the necessary
powers'. Even with such discretion however the Commission
is constrained by Treaty requirements for unanimity among
the member states. The more specific instruments of
economic law outlined by the Treaties govern the
harmonisation of laws (Arts. 100-102 especially), the
liberalisation of trade and the institution of a
competition policy (Arts. 9-37, 52-66 and 85-94).

Treaty requirements insist upon free competition between
enterprises in the EC within and across member states'
boundaries. Free competition in this respect makes demands
upon individual industrial undertakings and upon
governments. Industrial undertakings must not engage in
practices which infringe the principle of free competition
and which therefore are 'incompatible with the common
market'. Article 85 of the Treaty of Rome outlaws
restrictive agreements, decisions or concerted practices
which prevent, restrict or distort competition between
firms in the Community. Thus market-sharing and price-
fixing are prohibited as are limitations of product or
investment or markets. Article 86 of the Treaty imposes the
same rules of competition on individual industrial
undertakings which enjoy a dominant position within the
'common market' or in a substantial part of it. The rules

of competition in regard to state aids, which is the other
arm of EC competition policy, are to be found in Articles
92 to 94 of the EEC Treaty. These subject each member state
to a monitoring process when government aids to whole
sectors of industry, specified regions within a member
state or individual undertakings are proposed. The full
rigours of free competition may be temporarily suspended if
convincing evidence of industrial restructuring and
employment needs can be provided.

The second dimension is represented by the search for
harmonisation, in Treaty parlance 'the approximation of
laws', which is intended to reduce non-tariff barriers
between member states and thus to give effect to the
operation of principles such as free competition, free
movement of labour and capital, and the right of
individuals or firms to set up in business and to provide
services in each or any member state.

The third dimension concerns the Community's policies
towards trade liberalisation with non-Community countries
both internationally and by means of bilateral agreements.
The Community enjoys substantial powers, delegated by
member states, which may be used to control the flow of
particular goods into the common market. Such powers
whether exercised mandatorily or at the Commission's
discretion evidently can have a major bearing on individual
industrial or agricultural sectors - their profitability,
their capacity to employ people, their investment policies
and hence their long term contribution to the Community's
economy.

The main omission from the EEC Treaty in the economic
field is any specific reference to the preparation or
promotion by the Commission of an industrial policy. This
is a key factor in the failure so far by the EC to develop
an industrial policy. The three dimensions named so far
all form part of the economic law of the Community, but the
fourth dimension - that of industrial policy - lacks such
legal backing. Industrial policy can mean a multitude of
things, whether selective or comprehensive in application,
requiring or avoiding the need for national indicative
planning, and applied to new industries or to restructuring
old industries or to both. The need for a Community
industrial policy has often been argued as an indispensable
adjunct, along with a Community regional policy, to the
effective coordination of economic and monetary policy
between member states, let alone the attainment of economic
monetary union. Yet the fact remains that so far the
Community has been unable to agree even terms of reference
for an industrial policy and its achievements have

accordingly been meagre in this field. Even the agreement
of an industry policy for the Community on an <u>ad hoc</u> basis
has been severely constrained by a continuing ideological
conflict between those countries which favour an
interventionist and directive industrial policy on the part
of the state (such as France) and those countries which
prefer to leave it to market forces to produce changes in
their industrial structure (typically, Germany). The
advocates of the 'unseen hand' approach find it difficult
to establish any meeting of minds with those who adhere to
a 'guiding hand' approach. In summary the 'unseen hand'
advocates have always argued that the creation of a single
market together with a strict competition policy is all
that is needed by way of an industry policy, while 'guiding
hand' supporters typically will only accept the full
rigours of a competition policy and a single market
provided there is some overall framework concerning the
development of industrial structures and investment. This
debate at the European level is largely an acting out of
national traditions concerning industrial policy and
planning issues. The firmest supporters of economic and
monetary union within the Community – Germany and the
Benelux countries – have nevertheless accepted that some
form of industrial policy together with an effective
regional policy were indispensable prerequisites for the
success of this radical step. The Italians especially have
stressed the regional policy aspect. The very limited steps
taken by the Community towards a regional policy coupled
with the complete absence of an agreed industrial policy
indicate all too plainly how distant is the prospect of EMU
long after the original 1980 deadline, proposed at the
Hague Summit in 1969, has passed.

The Commission has not been without ideas in the matter
of industrial policy and an outline of the way the
Commission has had to backtrack on its proposals is
instructive: other authors have however considered such a
development in greater detail.[2] The original Commission
blueprint on industrial policy was presented in March 1970
with the title 'Memorandum on Industrial Policy in the
Community' by Signor Colonna, the then industry
Commissioner.[3] The Colonna Report as this 1970 Memorandum
has come to be known attempted to prove the need for
Community action to some reluctant member states, laying
particular stress on the structural approach of industrial
policy. The main themes of this Report were that many
barriers to trade within the EC remained to be removed so
as to achieve the ideal of a single market; harmonisation
in the fields of company law, taxation and banking were

required to bring about genuinely free movement of capital within the common market; substantial industrial reorganisation was needed to adapt industry to the needs of the common market; technology could righly be promoted at a Community level; the social and regional aspects of industrial development called for Community measures; and the centralisation of trade relations with third countries at the Brussels level also demanded a Community industrial policy to provide part of the framework in which commercial policy decisions could be developed.

No agreement within the Council of Ministers could be reached in regard to the Colonna strategy, but the subject of industrial policy was raised again at the Paris summit in October 1972 and an Action Programme[4] was prepared by the Commission for the Council and published in October 1973. The Commission had by now narrowed down its immediate interest to nine areas for action including such issues as industrial concentration and competition, the promotion of advanced technology, the abolition of technical, legal and fiscal barriers to trade. Rather than suggest a plan for the entire industrial structure of the member states, the Commission now pointed to particular industrial sectors which needed modernisation and restructuring. Once again nothing concrete resulted directly from such proposals. There was not enough agreement within the Council for the Commission to pursue its ideas and once more officials in the Berlaymont had to go back to the drawing-board. They returned in 1976 with some tentative ideas about specific Community programmes to assist 'growth' sectors and 'crisis' sectors in the light of the shocks adminstered to Western economies by inflation, recession and the quadrupled price of oil. In practice, action from Brussels regarding growth sectors (such as computing and data processing, aeronautics and electronics) has been minimal, for the main reason that national governments wish to develop their own approaches in the struggle to regain international competitiveness at least where markets are expanding. It is in the crisis sectors where there appears to have been a greater commitment to Community initiatives and action; especially as the problems of restructuring long-established manufacturing industries came increasingly to be shared by most member states as they intensified through the 1970s and into the 1980s. Intergovernmental cooperation in limited areas of industrial policy has come about hesitatingly within the Community as member states have come to recognise that the Commission can play a useful role on sectoral issues or, at the very least, that

national governments have little to lose by going European
on all their most intractable industrial problems. Even on
such a relatively 'high' politics issue as industry policy
it may nonetheless be possible to achieve a measure of
European integration, if the timing is right.

ACHIEVEMENTS SO FAR

Clearly the early momentum of the Treaties establishing the
European Communities was bound to make some impact on
European industry and the decade following the bringing
into force of the EEC Treaty witnessed unparalleled
economic growth in the member states, especially France and
Germany. Yet the early achievement of the customs union in
the late 1960s also heralded a period of lower economic
growth and greater conjunctural difficulties culminating in
the inflation and the halt to growth induced by the
Smithsonian agreement of 1971 and the oil price rises of
1973-74. It thus becomes rather difficult to chart any
cause/effect relationship between industrial development
and the implementation of the customs union in the
Community together with trade liberalisation measures
affecting principally third countries brought about through
GATT (Kennedy and Tokyo Rounds), through the EC's
'generalised systems of preferences' and its trade
agreements with individual countries or groups of countries
as evidenced by the Mahgreb, Mashreq and Lomé agreements.
Considerable trade liberalisation both between EC member
states and as regards the rest of the world has been
achieved, and the strains felt by the EC's industrial
structures since the mid-1970s are indeed evidence of the
continuing Community commitment to this objective despite
the domestic economic and political difficulties it
engenders. Nevertheless the trade liberalisation policy of
the EC is not absolute and the Community desire to contain
the competitive challenge of the NICs and of large volume
exporters of low technology goods also produced in Europe
as well illustrated by the tougher stance adopted by the EC
in the Multi-Fibre Agreement talks in 1981. But in just
such a case the Commission is able to extract from the more
protectionist member states commitments to restructure
their own declining industries as the price for achieving a
larger measure of protection for the Community as a whole
against third country imports. There is no doubt that
protectionist pressures are now reasserting themselves in
the EC and many claims are being made that even intra-
Community trade is being obstructed by non-tariff trade

barriers. One example from 1982 was the attempt by the
Italian authorities to frustrate British Leyland's sale in
Italy of its new Triumph Acclaim model (produced in
association with the Japanese Honda company) on the grounds
that it had too little EC content. This rather blatant
pretext was soon exposed and withdrawn, but other barriers
remain in place.

The competition policy has had a lop-sided development in
view of many economic authorities in that only parts of the
original policy scheme have been applied with success.
Moreover, generally-speaking, private firms have been
obliged to confirm with the EEC Treaty requirements with
much more success than national governments and state
enterprises. Yet the competition policy is far less rigid
than US antitrust legislation and does allow for exemptions
provided the public interest is not jeopardised.

The Treaty of Rome's definition of competition policy
embraces many aspects of business life in both the public
and private sectors. Price discrimination, price fixing,
resale price maintenance, and the appplication of patents,
licensing agreements and trade marks are all subject to
Community rules.   State aids, dumping, the abuse of
dominant market positions, mergers and quantitative
restrictions on exports and imports are also covered by the
policy. The competition policy is however restricted to
considering anything which affects trade between member
states: thus national measures in theory do not necessarily
come within the ambit of the EC policy, although indirect
as well as direct trade effects may be taken into account.
By the same token, however, actions of firms outside the EC
which bear on trade within the EC do come under the
competition policy. Multinational companies worldwide thus
have reason to take care not to offend against the EC's
competition policy. It is also interesting to note that
private firms may find themselves subject to rules and
procedures which are not reflected in their national
legislation. The EC has granted the Commission in Brussels
substantial delegated executive powers.[5] The Commission has
the right to enter any premises of an industrial or
commercial concern, to demand on the spot oral
explanations, to examine the books and business records of
a firm, and to take copies of the same. The Commission can
also impose fines of up to £560,000 or a sum not exceeding
10 per cent of a firm's annual turnover for breaches of the
policy, subject to the agreement of an Advisory Committee
on Restrictive Practices and Monopolies on which sits an
official of each member state.

British firms have been parties to many declared breaches
of the competition policy. ICI was heavily fined in the
early 1970s for price-fixing agreements with other European
competitors. The Distillers company was told in 1980 that
its differential pricing policy for whisky sold in
different member states was illegal and fined severely.
The British car manufacturers and distributors are now
under pressure to reduce British prices for cars to
continental levels on the same ground of distortion of
competition – a move that could be the death-blow to
British Leyland as a mass car manufacturer. In another
recent case the proposed takeover of the British Sugar
Corporation by S & W Beresford has also been referred to
the EC Commission for clearance under the competition
policy regarding dominant market positions. The policy as
it affects state aids has also had an impact on the UK
where the Regional Employment Premium and not-so-Temporary
Employment Subsidy both fell foul of Community competition
rules. At the same time massive state subsidies to Chrysler
UK Ltd. in 1976 and British Leyland and the British Steel
Corporation from the mid-1970s onwards were all approved by
Brussels. To summarise, the competition policy has begun to
look somewhat ineffective in key areas such as mergers and
state aids – where large-scale support of lame duck
undertakings has been sustained and significant, even if it
has frequently proved unpopular with big business.

The Community, and particularly the Commission, have also
pursued a vigorous approach towards harmonisation
culminating in the General Programme on Harmonisation
launched in 1969 in the belief that a code of EC law was
needed to bring the different member states' legal
frameworks into line so as to create a genuine single
market within the EC. The concept of harmonisation has been
mainly applied against technical barriers to trade but also
in pursuit of free movement of capital and labour and to
secure homegeneity of working hours and conditions (viz. in
the road haulage industry) without which competition might
be distorted. When the 1969 Programme was launched it was
estimated that it would take about 200 principal pieces of
Community legislation over about two years to eliminate the
main tariff barriers. Roughly 130 of these measures have
now been approved by the EC insitutions but a further
thirty are deadlocked in the Council of Ministers. However
even though the Programme itself after enormous delays is
over 75 per cent complete, new barriers to trade have
developed subsequently – for example by national action in
regard to higher standards of public health, environmental
and consumer protection. As many as fifty extra directives

or regulations may be needed to take account of these changes.[6] Meanwhile, many of the most difficult but important proposals for harmonisation (e.g. company law, consumer law and environmental protection) have become stuck in a logjam of national disagreements within the Council of Ministers. A highly 'consumerist' proposal to make manufacturers strictly liable for product defects regardless of fault is one such example: another is the famous Fifth Directive on company law governing company structure, company administration and employee participation. It is interesting to note how, despite strong public commitments to harmonisation made in principle by business leaders in Britain (and elsewhere in the EC), actual harmonisation proposals under discussion so often call for their bitter criticism. Harmonisation, one suspects, is all right so long as others are made to conform to one's own standards, but not on any other terms. Nevertheless important harmonisation measures have been implemented in Britain, for example in regard to disclosures in and presentation of company accounts, the control of dangerous effluents, the supervision of banks, equal pay for women, the declaration of redundancies and the hours worked by drivers of commercial road vehicles.

Trade liberalisation, the competition policy and the Community's drive for harmonisation are not the only areas where EC activities impinge upon the industrial and commercial sectors. The EC's major role in negotiating trade agreements on behalf of all its member states not only has consequence for markets within the Community (where privileged access for LDC products or the application of worldwide agreements like GATT and the Multi-Fibre Agreement are at issue) but can also have a major bearing on potential export markets, especially those with traditional trade links with France and Britain. Occasionally, apparently contradictory policies can be adopted simultaneously such as the Commonwealth Sugar Producers Agreement guaranteeing continued access and favourable prices for cane sugar to the EC at the same time as sugar beet production has been expanded at home under the CAP despite stagnant consumption. The sugar refiners in Britain have thus to some extent been put at loggerheads, with Tate & Lyle (cane refining) competing for EC favours against British Sugar Corporation (beet refining), while both sets of interests have had a joint and very direct interest in the Community's handling of isoglucose, the new cheap starch-based sugar substitute.[7] It is in such complex situations that the fact that the Community is in the business of having an industrial policy (at least in some sectors) becomes clearly evident, even if the words 'industry policy' are excluded from the official nomenclature.

Another important area where the Community has important powers over industry is that covered by the ECSC, which sprang to prominence in 1982 with the outbreak of trade hostilities between the Community and the USA over European steel exports. The Treaty of Paris gives the Commission considerable delegated powers in regard to the monitoring of investment, restructuring and production in the steel industry, together with exceptional powers under Article 58 to set production limits, to impose import levies on non-ECSC steel, and to set minimum prices for steel when 'a state of manifest crisis' exists in the industry.[8] This position was reached in the latter part of 1980 and an agreement between the Commission and a cartel of leading European steelproducts, Eurofer, provided the basis for the Council of Ministers' agreeing to a crisis strategy for the industry which still largely subsists in 1982, although with fewer mandatory controls. Price-fixing, information sharing, and inter-company agreements to limit production which would under normal EC rules offend against every tenet of the competition policy have apparently been legitimised in the name of sorting out the difficulties of a crisis sector.

The structural funds administered through the Community, notably the European Social Fund (ESF) and the European Regional Development Fund (ERDF), also play a part in the industrial development of the member states. They have set down standards for the economic development of poorer regions in structural terms, emphasising particular improvements in infrastructure, and they have sponsored a massive increase in spending on training, retraining and job creation. The full impact of these Funds to date will never be known, for while there is real cause to doubt whether much of the ERDF and ESF monies have been spent 'additionally' (i.e. representing sums of money provided and projects supported solely as a result of EC sponsorship),[9] there has undoubtedly been a considerable cross-fertilisation resulting both from the joint administration of these Funds by officials of the member states and the agreement between governments about regional and social priorities in the Community towards which these Funds are heavily steered.[10] The Treaty of Rome also provides the Community with an important instrument for the coordination of national regional policies in Articles 92 and 93 governing state aids. So far this coordination has resulted only in providing a standard framework against

which national regional aids to industry can be judged,
with a tariff of aid values laid down according to the
severity of each region's problems.[11] Yet the industrial
and competition policy implications of this concern for
economic development in the regions are important. They
indicate once more that the laissez-faire economics of the
EEC Treaty are not inviolable and that government
intervention in the market at the level of the Community
may be sanctioned and indeed orchestrated by the Commission
and the member states.

REASONS FOR FAILURE

There are thus some important conclusions to be drawn from
this survey of what the Community have achieved so far in
the fields of competition and industrial policy. Results
have been obtained in many different ways. The Court of
Justice which interprets the Treaties has, for example,
given the competition policy considerable teeth notably by
bringing subsidiaries clearly into the ambit of the
competition rules, notably through the Continental Can
(1971) and Dyestuffs (1972) cases. The Commission's brief
under the EEC Treaty to represent the Community in world
trade negotiations has given it an important mechanism for
operating an industrial policy for certain key sectors by
the back-door. The accession of new member states in 1973
together with the increased powers and authority of the
European Parliament have both created and strengthened the
Community's concern with regional industrial development.
The failure to agree on industrial policy has not prevented
the Commission from pressing ahead albeit slowly with its
harmonisation programme nor has the Rome Treaty's stout
adherence to free trade within the Community been seriously
compromised.

   Overall the outside observer is nonetheless left with the
impression that the Community's stance on competition and
industrial policy issues is either incoherent or
ineffective. Certainly the Community's inability to agree
an industry policy or to pursue its trade grievances with
Japan with any real commitment must be counted as
significant failures. The reasons for failure are manifold.
The problem of irreconcilably different national policy
traditions in regard to planning and industry policy is a
major obstacle here, as is the fact that member states are
not only economic allies (vis-à-vis third countries) but
industrial competitors within the EC. There are thus
important national interests which frequently favour

national as opposed to Community action, which lead to the creation of new non-tariff barriers to intra-Community trade, which occasion state aids of dubious justification and legality, and which stand in the way of such desirable notions as shared research and development in the highly capitalised high technology industries. The differential treatment as between private sector and public sector undertakings in the context of the competition and state aids policies is also a measure of how hard it is to subsume the interests of national governments into a single Community interest.

Secondly, the inadequate legal framework underpinning Community actions in the industrial and competition policy fields is an important defect. Those areas of policy covered by a clear legal instrument are those which have seen the Community at its most successful. The attack on restrictive practices, the pursuit of the harmonisation programme, the negotiation of trade agreements with third countries, and the coordinated response to the crisis in the steel industry from 1980 are clear examples. But in certain key respects the legal framework breaks down. There is no legal basis for an industrial policy per se, and there are important respects in which a European industrial policy could conflict with the principles of the competition policy. This was made clear in the late 1970s by the EC's inability to agree a full crisis policy response in regard to either the shipbuilding or to the man-made fibre industries. What proved possible for steel, with its own separate Treaty basis, could not surmount the objections of the Directorate-General for competition (DG IV) - one of the more alarming examples in recent years of compartmentalised perspectives within the Commission. There is no way of resolving such conflicts so long as a coherent legal framework and sufficient political agreement within the Council of Ministers do not exist: indeed, the Court of Justice is obliged in the meantime to reassert the principles of free competition if ever they appear to be compromised. In other respects too the legal framework for Community action is deficient. In particular the sections of the Rome Treaty governing state aids and mergers have often proved ineffective. The Commission is naturally most reluctant to do battle in public with a member state which is also one of its political masters in the Council of Ministers. The rise in state aids during the post-1973 recessions has not been seriously challenged and it is highly likely that the Commission would jeopardise its already weak position in relation to the Council of Ministers if it tried to do so: a conspiracy of silence

thus allows state aids to increase with only cosmetic
Commission policing in evidence. On mergers, the
provisions in Article 86 became ineffective as soon as it
was legally established that the act of merger itself had
to be proved responsible for an abuse of a dominant market
position. Pre-emptive prohibitions of proposed mergers are
thus ruled out, and the Community has no power to order a
company after merger to divest itself of any part of its
assets subsequently.[12] The exact legal basis of the
competition policy has in other areas attracted much
criticism from industry, especially in the fields of
industrial property and distribution agreements. Sole
rights to market a product in one EC country negotiated
between manufacturer and producer have for example on
several occasions been ruled illegal by the Court of
Justice. The Commission argues that it must carry out the
law of the Community regardless, which leads to accusations
of legalism. It is indeed the same lack of political
agreement in the Council of Ministers which prevents any
change in the 'legalistic' competition policy rules or
which allows the Commission to develop strongly industrial
policies based upon the catch-all Treaty articles (Arts.
100 and 235). The Commission finds itself trapped both in
terms of the development and implementation of policy, and
in its handling of private sector cases as against the
public sector. The public sector receives less draconian
treatment both on political grounds already explained and
because public sector companies cannot be penalised in the
same way as private sector companies under the competition
policy. Nationalised industries are not fined for abuses as
private companies are: they can only be attacked by
directives or decisions of the Council (a most unlikely
occurrence) or in the Court of Justice under Art. 169.

Thirdly, there is a sense in which many of the
Community's actions in the industrial field lack
legitimacy, and this then becomes an obstacle to further
action or policy development. In one sense, this lack of
legitimacy is just another way of saying that what the
Commission would like to do offends one or more national
governments whether for highly self-interested reasons or
on ideological grounds. There is not much that the
Commission can do in a direct way to circumvent such a
difficulty, but this is not the end of the matter. The
Commission by its own actions can lose the support of
potentially interested parties-cum-partners. In the
operation of the competition policy, for example, the
procedures for the handling of cases adopted by the
Commission frequently fail to live up to the recognised

standards of natural justice. The Commission is
usually both prosecutor, judge and jury in the
interpretation of the competition rules; it is not obliged
to disclose all the evidence it possesses against a company
to that company; nor does it have to give a clear and
precise identification of the conduct which is claimed to
be objectionable. Industrialists all over Europe deeply
resent being subject to such rules and to the long delays
they suffer in securing exemptions from the rules of
competition. [13] The Commission also stands accused of
inadequate fact-finding and economic analysis both in
regard to specific competition policy cases and as regards
harmonisation proposals and industrial affairs. Partly this
is a result of very low staffing levels within the
Commission (contrived by member states) but partly it is a
reflection of the Commission's own weakness in failing to
activate the support of key economic interests for its
policies and in appearing instead to be acting in an
arbitrary and high-handed manner. Because the Commission is
essentially a technocratic body which, in practice, is not
fully accountable either to the Council of Ministers or to
the European Parliament, its concern to establish the
political and moral legitimacy of its actions does not seem
to have been regarded in its highest echelons with anything
like the same concern as the legal legitimacy of its
actions. Given that such legal legitimacy is largely
established by virtue of treaties up to thirty years old,
while the political and moral legitimacy is a matter of
public consent in the Europe of today, the Commission's
standpoint - although understandable in a Community whose
political development has ossified - would appear to be
gravely mistaken.

HOW PROGRESS HAS BEEN ACHIEVED

In most respects the reasons why some policies for industry
have been agreed and implemented are the obverse of those
given as reasons for lack of progress in other directions.
Undoubtedly a legal framework which provides the Commission
with considerable scope for initiative within the
institutions of the Community is of the highest priority.
Where the Community has been at its most effective in
industrial matters there has usually been a strong basis
for its action spelled out in the Treaties. Thus the
Commission's negotiating rights in respect of the common
commercial policy, its strong executive powers regarding
the steel industry and competition principles, and its

clear duty to push for harmonisation under Article 100 of
the EEC Treaty are all evidence of the vital need to
provide a secure legal basis for Community initiatives in
the industrial field. It has proved extremely difficult in
practice to widen the Community's or the Commission's brief
in industrial matters, especially in a Community which can
only proceed on the basis of unanimity among the member
states.   Nothing in the EEC Treaty prevents such an
expansion of its role, particularly given the wide terms
of Article 235 which permits the Community to take the
appropriate measures to attain any of the Community's
objectives where the Treaty has not provided the necessary
powers. But in such cases the unanimity required is rarely
forthcoming; ideological perspectives and national
interests are usually in conflict, and the Commission may
even feel constrained to stretch the powers it knows it has
under Articles 100, 113, 116, 155 or 235 of the EEC Treaty.
The clearest exception to this rule is Regulation 17/62
which provided the Commission with substantial delegated
powers with which to enforce the competition policy. This
accounts in large measure for the effective action that the
Community has taken in regard to the crisis in the textile
and steel industries and for the inability to act over
shipbuilding or motor vehicles.

A satisfactory legal basis for Community action may be a
sine qua non for effective policies but it cannot alone
guarantee them: the failure of Euratom to develop shows all
too clearly what can happen when some national governments
lose interest in projects which they had previously
committed themselves to.   By the same token the acquis
commuanautaire will only hold if it continues on balance to
suit member states to sustain it. Once again nationl
interests play a central and crucial part in the policy
development and implementation in industrial matters within
the Community. The balance of gains over losses has to
continue to remain positive in the eyes of each member
state for the process of mutual trade-offs to occur upon
which are founded all the delicate compromises which
represent Community decisions. In recent years it has most
commonly been a mutual sense of crisis affecting all or
most member states which has paved the way for new policy
development in the economic sphere (e.g. the creation of
the Ortoli facility, the European Monetary System, and the
policies developed towards steel, textiles and
unemployment). A climate of mutual interest in policy
proposals seems to be an important element in forcing
agreement out of a normally reluctant Council of
Ministers.

Such reluctance may need to be overcome not just by clever negotiation and brinkmanship in Brussels but by a painstaking preparation of the ground well in advance among the economic interests which stand to be directly affected by a Commission proposal for a Community policy. The courting of interest groups by the Commission has led to two of the most successful sector policies yet agreed at Community level - the CAP (including structural measures) developed by Commissioner Mansholt in the 1960s and the 'steel crisis policy' developed by Commissioner Davignon since 1979. If the different economic interests within the member states have already become reconciled to a set of proposals emanating from the Commission it becomes so much harder for national governments to turn them down in the Council of Ministers. The Commission can acquire considerable legitimacy for its proposals if it uses the political skills it often possesses but which it has for so long dared not demonstrate.

THE WAY FORWARD

The past experience of the Community concerning industrial and competition policy issues holds important lessons for the future development of policies in these fields. National interests need to be carefully mobilised behind Community policies; an appropriate legal and institutional framework is needed; and the Commission's own legitimacy when intervening must be established not just in the narrow legal sense but politically and morally too. The limitations of working through the Community need to be both understood and partially accepted by those in charge of Community policy. The Community may not always be the appropriate level for international action - the OECD or GATT negotiations may cover the necessary ground better. The political will for new Community industrial policies will normally be in short supply within the Council: it needs to be carefully nurtured by individual member states, such as Britain, as well as by the Commission, if new policies are to be more than still-born. The inadequacies of the Treaties also need to be accepted by the political actors because the overall legal framework of the Community is unlikely to change in the 1980s. Instead particular Treaty provisions can be used and developed to achieve quicker and often efficacious results. For example, if there is one unresolved conflict in the industrial field which above all others has frustrated policy development it is the clash of ideas between the industrial dirigistes and the adherents of an unfettered competition policy. Rewriting the Treaties to correct the present balance within the Community is neither likely nor necessarily conclusive. A better tactic would be for Britain to press for the merger of the industrial and competition Directorates—General of the Commission so that a common line about where the balance of economic advantage lies can be agreed internally case by case.

Some broad lines of agreement on the future direction of the EC's industrial and competition policies does require to be settled urgently in the Council of Ministers. The effective industrial policy of the Community is too heavily weighted in favour of free competition to the point where it prevents both the effective implementation of the competition policy's principles - notably in regard to state aids, as well as agreement on industrial policy objectives. The way forward for Britain and the rest of the Community seems to lie in accepting the <u>de facto</u> Community industry policy, putting it on a sounder footing and giving it a better balance. The Community has already for all practical purposes renounced its ambitions to determine the whole industrial structure of the Community. Instead it has concentrated on sectoral policies, especially those needed by industries in crisis or decline. These are just the industries where protectionist pressures are most keenly felt and where state aids were lavished in the 1970s with marked recklessness. A more interventionist Community stance in favour of positive adjustment in such industries as textiles, shipbuilding, paper and steel is desirable both to develop a humane and effective response to severe economic and political pressures and to protect the practice of free market principles which the Community's competition policy seeks to defend. An explicit Community commitment in favour of positive adjustment policies would do much to stiffen resistance to rising demands for 'protection', from which Britain stands to lose more than most countries because of its high dependence on the export trade.[14] On the external trade relations front the Community is only likely to be able to maximise its bargaining power as a trading bloc if it can agree upon an internal industrial strategy. The clash with the USA over EC steel imports in 1982 only serves to underline the importance of European countries acting together on major world economic and trading issues, and the relative harmony among the EC member states during recent disputes with the USA contrasts starkly with their disunity in trying to secure measures to correct the trade imbalance with Japan. At the time of writing it was too early to know whether the

Community's stand against US duties on EC steel exports would bring results. What is already evident is how little has materialised from EC-Japan trade negotiations over the last decade, owing a great deal to differences of view within the Community as to the seriousness of the Japanese challenge and the appropriate strategy required to counter it. The bargaining power of the EC countries vis-à-vis the USA, Japan and the NICs will have to be maximised if European markets and competitiveness are to be defended. Failure to use the weight of the EC in favour of free trade, and fair trade within the industrialised world, will only reinforce world protectionism and world economic stagnation. Again Britain, with its taste for political cooperation within the Community and its critical need to stem the weakening of its industrial base, has much to gain by giving a lead to other member states on this issue.

Within the EC this measured stance favouring relatively open trading policies worldwide will need to be backed up in two crucial directions. First, the drive to make the Community a single market must be stepped up. Protectionism within the EC is possibly even more dangerous than protectionism in the rest of the world: this is not just a question of imposing sanctions on offending states but also of devising Community legislation (for example in the financial and shipping services sectors which are of great importance to Britain) which will break down non-tariff barriers. Secondly, a considerable expansion of the regional and social policies and funds of the EC will be called for, especially after enlargement, so as to reduce the social and political damage brought about by the need to shift economic resources out of industrial sectors in permanent decline, and to minimise the consequences of the resulting unemployment.

In specific terms a whole series of initiatives from the Commission in pursuit of the above strategy can be envisaged. Clearly sectoral policies for industries in decline will need to continue to develop: candidates here are steel, textiles, footwear, paper and board, shipbuilding and motor vehicles. Then a policy to assist the development of growth sectors such as aerospace, energy industries, telecommunications, computers, electronics, and the telematics could be articulated mainly through Community activities to assist innovation and research and development in industry (viz. energy conservation, exploitation of renewable resources and of high technology). Specific bilateral pooling arrangements for research and development expenditure could also be promoted and sponsored by the Community. A restatement of the aims of the competition policy would certainly be desirable to admit the legitimacy of some planning for industrial sectors, to assist joint ventures, and to stiffen the control over mergers. It is a revealing commentary on the workings of the Community when the Chairman of ICI is moved to suggest that the problems of excess capacity in the EC plastics industry could largely be overcome by a relaxation of the rules on competition rather than by creating a recovery plan based on a Commission-backed plastics cartel.[15] Fairer and speedier procedures for handling the complaints about dumping and the clearances required by the competition policy could also do much to restore the faith of industry in the Commission and the Community's capacity to take effective action. Simultaneously the Commission's challenge to state aids and, in particular, to public sector subsidies, needs to be reviewed and intensified. The suppression of economic 'crimes' in the private sector by the free market hawks in DG IV bears rather an unlovely aspect when public sector offenders are let off with a mild caution. The undeniable political obstacles facing any Commission attempts at even-handed treatment of the public and private sectors can probably only be overcome by a mixture of legal challenges in the Court of Justice and the formation of alliances between the Commission, certain member states and private sector interests across the Community. Another element in the working-out of this industrial strategy ought to be a greater awareness of the needs (and limitations) of small and medium-sized firms. In truth the Commission is showing growing signs that it understands the problem. Certainly the operation of present competition, sectoral, harmonisation, regional and social policies have shown little sympathy for the difficulty that under-staffed and under-capitalised small firms have in handling Community paperwork, applying for Community grants and loans, or complying with well-intentioned but extremely costly regulations.

Harmonisation policy is one area where a major reversal of priorities is called for. Since 1973 the Commission has begun to demand much more evidence of benefits to be gained before endorsing harmonisation proposals. Yet the most important areas for harmonisation – such as common VAT rates and rules, common systems of taxation of companies and of levying social security taxes on employers – are the ones that are usually studiously avoided by the Community. Lack of attentin to this glaring failure to secure a genuine common market that does not discriminate between nationalities may be politically understandable, but it is economic and intellectual lunacy.

Much of the programme that has been outlined here requires clarity of vision form the Berlaymont building and a willingness to make decisions in the Charlemagne building in Brussels: it does not need much finance. If present EC budgetary constraints continue, far more use could be made of the European Investment Bank than hitherto to finance projects and programmes in line with Community policies. Recipients would then dispose of loans rather than grants from the Community. But the widespread take-up of such finance would require some major concessions on interest rates, which would have to be financed mainly from the Community budget, and more reasonable behaviour in regard to covering the currency exchange risks than the present British government will countenance. Lower interest rates for industry are a vital weapon in the drive to keep up investment and innovation in European industries while the world economy is stagnant. A scheme for low interest loans for industry across the Community administered by the EIB could form the basis of a simple, effective and politically saleable industry policy for the Community as a whole. It would certainly be appreciated by British industrialists even though such a policy goes completely against the trend of British policy in recent years.

In conclusion, it can be seen from the above analysis that an incremental approach to industrial policy in the EC is recommended based on existing legal foundations, Community policies and institutions. Success for the Commission and the Community in a series of specific limited actions and initiatives could provide the necessary basis of growing confidence and consent for more far-reaching policies from national governments, economic interests and public opinion generally. The Commission needs to be more open and democratic in style and in accounting for its actions. At the same time it must be more political in building up support across the Community for its specific proposals. There is a great deal of work to be done within the EC before it can be credited with effective industrial and competiton policies. It is work that has to be done if the interests of British and other European people are to be adequately secured and defended worldwide. The tragedy is that the Community has achieved so little relatively-speaking in this direction so far.

NOTES:

1. R. Jenkins, speech reported in <u>The Times</u>, 21 November 1980.

2. Leading sources on the subject of the Community's industrial and competition policies include: Hodges (1977); Jacquemin and de Jong (1977); Swann (1978); and Bayliss (1980).

3. See Commission of the European Communities (1970).

4. See Commission of the European Communities (1973).

5. In particular, powers granted to the Commission under Council Regulation No. 17 of 1962.

6. See The Impact of EEC Legislation on British Business (1981), a staff study published by the Confederation of British Industry.

7. A fuller account will be given in the author's forthcoming book on Pressure Groups in the European Community (Allen and Unwin, 1983).

8. For more details see Butt Philip (1981).

9. The question of additionality has been fully discussed in three reports of the House of Lords Select Committee on the European Communities relating to the ERDF published in 1977 (HL Paper 74), 1981 (HL Paper 93) and 1982 (HL Paper 126).

10. This point is taken up, for example, in the report of the House of Lords Select Committee on the European Communities in regard to the European Social Fund published in 1980 (HL Paper 361).

11. Commission Communications to the Council of 27 June 1973 and 28 November 1973 leading to Commission Decision of 26 February 1975 set out in the Fifth Report on Competition Policy (1976).

12. See Bayliss (1980, p. 128).

13. See The EEC's Anti-Dumping Procedures (1980) — a report published by a working party of the Confederation of British Industry — and the evidence submitted to and the report of the House of Lords Select Committee on the European Communities in regard to Competition Practice (8th Report, Session 1981-82 : HL 91).

14. See the interesting discussion of this theme in Pinder (1982), and also OECD (1979).

15. J. Harvey-Jones quoted in _Financial Times_, 15 July 1982.

8 The True Cost of the CAP

Ali M. El-Agraa

No single topic has raised more interest and discussion in relation to the various facets of the EC than the Common Agricultural Policy (CAP). More specifically, the true cost of the CAP particularly for Britain has been a subject of great concern for the average UK citizen, for farming and consumer organisations within Britain and for nations both inside and outside the EC. Hence the aim of this chapter is to explain and discuss the estimates that have been made regarding the true cost of the CAP especially for the UK and to extend these estimates in order to give them a proper sense of perspective. However, it should be quite obvious that such a discussion will not make any sense without a thorough understanding of the aims, mechanisms and financing of the CAP, hence the first section of this chapter is devoted to a brief discussion of these matters – readers interested in a detailed analysis within a global context should consult El-Agraa (1980a, chapter 7).

OBJECTIVES OF THE CAP

The various schemes for protecting the agricultural sector that were operated by the potential member nations at the time of the formation of the EC made it necessary to subject agriculture to equal treatment in all member states. This was due to the fact that agriculture was a major employer of people with relatively low incomes when compared with the national average (see Tables 8.1 and 1.8) and also because agriculture formed the basis of industrial costs. Equal treatment of coal and steel (which are necessary inputs for industry, hence of the same significance as agriculture) was already under way through the ECSC.

Before stating the objectives of the CAP it is essential to point out that the Treaty of Rome defines agriculture as 'the products of the soil, of stock-farming and of fisheries and products of first-stage processing directly related' to the foregoing (Article 38).

TABLE 8.1: EMPLOYMENT AND GDP ARISING IN THE AGRICULTURAL SECTOR

Member State	Employment in agriculture, forestry and fishing				GDP at factor cost in agriculture, etc. as % of total GDP	
	Number 1959	'000 1976	% of total employment 1959	1976	1959	1976
Belgium	423	128	12a	3	7	3
France	5213	2263	27b	11	12c	5d
Germany	3788	1714	15	7	8	3
Italy	6370	2929	30	15	19	9
Luxembourg	35	9	26a	6	9	4e
Netherlands ·	470	295	11	6	10	5
Community of Six	(16,000)	7338	(24)	10	(11)	(5)
Denmark	–	223	–	9	–	8
Ireland	–	243	–	24	–	18f
United Kingdom	–	660	–	3	–	3
Community of Nine	–	8464	–	8	–	(5)

Notes: (a) 1947;
       (b) 1954;
       (c) 1956;
       (d) at current market prices;
       (e) 1975;
       (f) 1972.

Figures in brackets are rough estimates.

Source: R. Fennell, The Common Agricultural Policy of the European Community p.1 (London: Granada, 1979).

The objectives of the CAP are clearly defined in Article 39 of the Treaty. They are:
1. to increase agricultural productivity by promoting technical progress and by ensuring the rational development of agricultural production and the optimum utilisation of all factors of production, in particular labour;
2. to ensure thereby a fair standard of living for the agricultural community, in particular by increasing the individual earnings of persons engaged in agriculture;
3. to stabilise markets;
4. to provide certainty of supplies;
5. to ensure supplies to consumers at reasonable prices.

The Treaty also specifies that in working out the CAP, and any special methods which this may involve, account shall be taken of:
1. the particular nature of agricultural activity, which results from agriculture's social structure and from structural and natural disparities between the various agricultural regions ;
2. the need to effect the appropriate adjustments by degrees ;
3. the fact that, in the member states, agriculture constitutes a sector closely linked with the economy as a whole.

The Treaty further specifies that in order to attain the objectives set out above a common organisation of agricultural markets shall be formed. This organisation is to take one of the following forms depending on the product concerned:
1. common rules as regards competition ;
2. compulsory co-ordination of the various national marketing organisations; or
3. a European organisation of the market.

Moreover, the common organisation so established :
"may include all measures required to achieve the objectives set out..., in particular price controls, subsidies for the production and distributin of the various products, stock-piling and carry-over systems and common arrangements for stabilisation of imports and exports.

The common organisation shall confine itself to pursuing the objectives set out... and shall exclude any discrimination between producers and consumers within the Community.

Any common policy shall be based on common criteria and uniform methods of calculation."

Finally, in order to enable the common organisation to achieve its objectives, 'one or more agricultural orientation and guarantee funds may be set up'.

The remaining Articles (41-47) deal with some detailed considerations relating to the objectives and the common organisation.

The social issues were discussed and stated in more detail in 1960 after a lengthy discussion of the structural and social aspects of the CAP (see Fennell 1979, p.13):

1. to ensure social protection for agricultural wage-earners and their dependants equivalent to that enjoyed by other categories of workers;
2. to encourage the adaptation of contractual relations within agriculture to accord more with modern conditions;
3. to narrow the gap between agricultural wage earners and those in comparable branches of activity with regard to remuneration, social security and working conditions;
4. to ensure that rural children have the same opportunities for general and vocational education as those elsewhere;
5. to aid young country dwellers wishing to set up as independent farmers or who wish to change to other types of farm work;
6. to ensure that the best conditions for success are available to those leaving agriculture for other employment;
7. to facilitate the retirement on pension of farmers and farm workers at the normal retirement age;
8. to improve rural housing;
9. to improve the social and cultural infrastracture of rural areas.

It can be seen, therefore, that the CAP was not preoccupied simply with the implementation of common prices and market supports; it also included a commitment to encourage the structural improvement of farming, particularly when the former measures did not show much success. Regarding the latter point, the main driving force has been the Mansholt Plan of 1968 (see Fennell, 1979, for later developments). However, the EC budgetary expenditure on the structural aspects now amounts to only 3-4 per cent of total CAP expenditure.

(i) The CAP Price Support Mechanism

Although the CAP machinery varies from one product to another, the basic features for most of the products are more or less similar - for a detailed specification of the

differences see Fennell (1979). The farmers' income support
is guaranteed by regulating the market so as to reach a
price high enough to achieve the objectives stated earlier.
The domestic price is partly maintained by various
protective devices. These prevent cheaper world imports
from influencing the EC domestic price level. But in
addition, certain steps are taken for official support
buying within the EC, so as to eliminate from the market
any actual excess supply that might be stimulated by the
guaranteed price level. These surpluses may be disposed of
in various ways, e.g. they can be destroyed, stored (to be
released at times of shortage), exported, donated to low
income countries (Food Aid Programme) or needy groups
within the EC, or converted into another product which does
not compete directly with the original one (the 'breaking'
of eggs for use as egg powder).

More specifically, the basic features of the system can
be represented by that originally devised for cereals, the
first agricultural product for which a common policy was
established.

A 'target price' is set on an annual basis and is
maintained at a level which the product is expected to
achieve on the market in the area where cereals are in
shortest supply - Duisburg in the Ruhr Valley. The target
price is not a producer price since it includes the costs
of transport to dealers and storers. The target price is
variable, in that it is allowed to increase on a monthly
basis from August to July in order to allow for storage
costs throughout the year.

The 'threshold price' is calculated in such a way that
when transport costs incurred within the EC are added,
cereals collected at Rotterdam should sell at Duisburg at a
price equal to or slightly higher than the target price. An
import levy is imposed to prevent import prices falling
short of the threshold price. The import levy is calculated
on a daily basis and is equal to the margin between the
lowest representative offer price entering the EC on the
day - allowing for transport costs to one major port
(Rotterdam) - and the threshold price. This levy is then
charged on all imports allowed into the EC on that day.

It is quite obvious that as long as the EC is
experiencing excess demand for this product, the market
price is held above the target price by the imposition of
import levies. Moreover, import levies would be
unnecessary if world prices happened to be above the
threshold price since in this case the market price might
exceed the target price.

If target prices result in an excess supply of the product in the EC, the threshold price becomes ineffective in terms of the objective of a constant annual target price and support buying becomes necessary. A 'basic intervention price' is then introduced for this purpose. This is fixed for Duisburg at about 7 or 8 per cent below the target price. Similar prices are then calculated for several locations within the EC on the basis of costs of transport to Duisburg. National intervention agencies are then compelled to buy whatever is offered to them (provided it conforms to standard) of the 'proper' product at the relevant intervention price. The intervention price is therefore a minimum guaranteed price.

Moreover, an export subsidy or restitution is paid to EC exporters. This is determined by the officials and is influenced by several factors (world prices, amount of excess supply, expected trends) and is generally calculated as the difference beteen the EC internal market price and the average world price.

(ii) The Green Money

The various agricultural support prices were previously fixed by the Council in Units of Account and now in terms of the European Currency Unit (ECU) which has the same value as the original Unit of Account. For each member country there is a 'Green Rate' at which the support prices are translated into national prices. The Unit of Account had originally a gold content equal to a US dollar, but in 1973 was linked to the 'joint float' and to the EMS in 1980. This implies that if a member country devalues (revalues) its currency, its farm prices expressed in terms of the national currency rise (fall). It should also be noted that the scope for changing Green currency rates gives the member countries scope for altering internal farm prices independently (but only with the consent of other members and only within certain limits) of price changes determined at the annual reviews for the EC as a whole. In August 1969 the French franc was devalued by 11.11 per cent which obviously disturbed the common farm price arrangements in favour of the French farmers, and the rise in their price level would obviously have stimulated their farm production and aggravated the excess supply problem. Moreover, the devaluation of the Unit of Account would not have improved matters in such a situation, since it would have depressed the price level for the farmer in the rest of the EC, even though it would have nullified the effects of the devaluation of the French franc. Therefore, a more complicated policy was adopted: the French intervention price was reduced by the full amount of the devaluation so as to eliminate the unfair benefit to the French farmer; French imports from and exports to the rest of the EC were to be restored by asking France to give import subsidies and levy duties on her exports to compensate for the effects of the devaluation. The term 'Monetary Compensatory Amounts' (MCAs) was coined to describe this system of border taxes and subsidies. Since then, the MCA system has become general in application and more complicated with the changes in the rates of exchange of the currencies of other EC members. Even though the EC has recently announced its intention to discontinue the MCA system, it seems that it will be with us for some time yet (see Fennell 1979, p.98 for reasons why). It should be added, however, that the currency divergencies are now much smaller than in the hey-day of MCAs.

The reader who is particularly interested in this area of the CAP is advised to read Irving and Fearn (1975), Josling and Harris (1976), Mackel (1978), Hu (1979), and MacLaren (1981). Hu demonstrates that Germany has recently been the main beneficiary of this system.

(iii)Financing the CAP

Intervention, export restitution, storage and the MCA system need to be financed. The finance is supplied by the EC central fund called FEOGA (Fonds Européen d'Orientation et de Garantie Agricole), the European Agricultural Guidance and Guarantee Fund (EAGGF). At the time of inception of the CAP it was expected that the revenues collected from the imposition of extra-area import levies would be sufficient to finance FEOGA but when agreement regarding the financing of the CAP was finally reached, the position was completely different - see Regulation 25/62. FEOGA now takes about 70 per cent of the EC Budget which is financed by contributions from national governments based on a maximum of 1 per cent of the VAT base plus all tariff revenues collected from extra-EC trade industrial tariffs and agricultural levies - see chapter 12.

COMMON MISCONCEPTIONS ABOUT THE CAP

Before considering the true cost of the CAP one needs to mention three common fallacies generally attributed to the CAP. Firstly, it is not true that all agricultural products are price-supported; some are subject to production subsidies (cereals, butter, olive oil and other minor products) and sugar producers are charged a production levy on excess output. Secondly, the actual size of the butter mountains and wine lakes does not at any moment in time, exceed three weeks' EC supply. Finally, the aim of 'security of supplies' is not unimportant; the EC has managed to be self-sufficient at times when there was a global shortage of food supplies.

THE TRUE COST OF THE CAP

A number of studies attempting a calculation of the true cost of the CAP have been published over the past fifteen or twenty years. Space limitations do not allow an adequate consideration of all of them, hence in this section I intend to concentrate on two : those of Godley-Bacon (1979) and Morris (1980). These are selected not only because they are the most recent studies but also because, in my opinion, they are the most serious and most competently carried out of all the studies I have come across.

The theoretical framework for these studies can be explained by using a simple partial-equilibrium diagram. In Figure 8.1 SS and DD are respectively the supply and demand curves for an agricultural product for a member nation of the EC. P_w is the world price with P_wS_w the world supply curve, assumed to be perfectly elastic with the rest of the world being more efficient than the country under consideration. t and t' are two different levels of import levies (tariffs) resulting in two different levels of EC prices for this product - these prices are determined in the manner discussed earlier.

If the import levy happens to be t, this country will produce $0q_2$ domestically, consume $0q_4$ and import the difference (q_2q_4). The welfare dead-weight loss of such a tariff consists of the triangles ACE and BDF [consumers lose $P_wP_w(1+t)DB$, producers gain $P_wP_w(1+t)CA$ and there is a net levy collection of CDFE which is an EC 'own resource']. If the import levy happens to be t' resulting in an EC price of $P_w(1+t')$, there will result an excess supply of q_3q_5 with the welfare dead-weight loss now equal to the sum of the triangles LGB and KHA.

These triangular dead-weight losses include not only the usual net costs to consumers and producers but also the costs of restitution since, as already indicated, not only is any tariff collection an 'own resource' of the EC (if the product is imported from outside the EC) but also the EC has either to buy the excess supply into intervention and therefore incur expenditure in storing it or pay

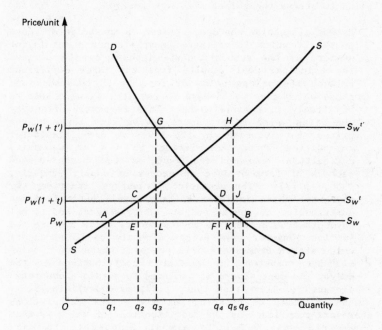

FIGURE 8.1

restitutions of LGHK to sell it at the world price outside
the EC. Of course, if the excess supply has to be disposed
of in the fashion discussed earlier then that also means
expenditure by the EC.

   This simple analysis forms the theoretical basis of the
studies by Godley-Bacon and Morris. Before discussing these
studies it should be pointed out that the analysis makes
clear the elements involved in the calculation of the costs
and benefits: (i) tariff levies or restitution payments;
(ii) storage costs; (iii) MCAs (implicitly in that changes
in the official exchange rates or the Green rates will
imply that these prices are not uniform throughout the EC);
and (iv) the welfare triangular dead-weight losses. These
elements need stressing particularly since most previous

calculations seemed to miss the point that the net budgetary contributions do not take (iv) into account and that is why Godley-Bacon and Morris have gone to great pains to stress the point:

"Recent discussion has concentrated on the budgetary cost to the UK which is neither a complete nor a meaningful measure of the economic costs imposed by the policy. The principal cost results from the large difference between the prices paid for food by UK consumers and those which they would have to pay if they were able to buy freely on a world market. This is partly offset by the gains which UK producers derive from these higher prices, but increased by the taxes on non-agricultural commodities which are levied to finance Community agricultural expenditures such as the purchase and storage of farm produce in excess of supply" (Morris, 1980, p.17). "The 'static' transfers comprise two elements. There is first Britain's well publicised net contribution to the EC Budget. But, second, additional payments from Britain to the Community arise because the British consumer pays prices directly to EC producers which are in excess of world prices; these are foreign exchange transfers no less than contributions to the Budget and must always be included to obtain a complete picture" (Godley-Bacon 1980, p.27, my underlining).

When it comes to carrying out the actual calculations there are complications the most important of which is that the world price, P_W, is almost impossible to know particularly since a 'free trade' world price will be determined by world supply and demand forces. Since the CAP aims at self-sufficiency, i.e. the EC was a net importer of most agricultural products at the time of inception of the EC, it follows that the going market price is definitely an artificial one. The Godley-Bacon study tackles this problem by making an assumption which is clearly exemplified in the case of the UK: in the absence of its EC membership

"the UK would certainly have continued some kind of long-run undertaking to purchase dairy products from New Zealand and sugar from ACP countries at prices well in excess of the present world disposal prices" (Godley-Bacon 1979, p.25). Morris recognises the problem:

"a problem of principle arises because existing world prices reflect existing world flows which are themselves in part the result of the CAP. We therefore need to consider how these flows would change, and what the consequential effect on prices would be, in the absence of the CAP. To do this, it is necessary to consider what

agricultural policies would exist if the CAP did not"
(Morris 1980, p.26).
In spite of this awareness, Morris concludes :
"in many cases a reasonable expectation is that world
prices would not be very different from what they are
now. In the case of cereals, for example, it is likely
that any change in European supplies would eventually be
absorbed by offsetting changes in North American output
with little net effect on prices" (Morris 1980, p.26).
This conclusion is too hard to swallow: why should these
tendencies produce the same price? what about the effect of
supply forces on demand? is it possible to assume <u>automatic</u>
reactions? what does 'eventually' amount to?

Given this general structure, the Godley-Bacon (1979)
study calculates two resource flows implicit in their
analysis: 'net budget receipts' and 'net trade receipts'.
The net budget receipts, which could be positive or
negative, measure the total cash emanating from the CAP
which a country pays into or receives from the EC budget.
Net trade receipts are the costs incurred by countries
which import food from the rest of the EC at prices higher
than they would otherwise have to pay and benefits received
by countries which export food to the rest of the EC at
prices higher than they could obtain on world markets. The
sum of these two items gives the 'net cash receipts and
payments' or the effect on resources due to the CAP. These
calculations are given in the first three columns of Table
8.2.

The Morris (1980) study calculates five flows which can
be seen from Figure 8.1: (i) losses to consumers from
higher prices which are equal to $0q_6$ multiplied by the
relevant tariff rate (t or t'); (ii) losses to consumers
from reduced demand which are equal to DBF or GLB; (iii)
gains to producers from higher prices which are equal to
0_{q3} multiplied by the relevant tariff rate (t or t'):
(iv) additional costs incurred by producers of output which
would not be economic at world prices, i.e., area ACE or
AHK; and (v) the net budgetary contribution to agricultural
support derived from taxes on non-agricultural products
which is equal to expenditure on export restitution, net of
levies, plus expenditure on intervention, storage and
guidance less the value of additions to intervention stocks
(which are valued at world prices - see Morris 1980, p.24).
These are summarised in three columns in Table 8.2.

I have put the calculations of the two studies in one
table simply because both relate to 1978 hence they are
directly comparable. Before making comparisons, however, a
few points need to be explicitly stated : firstly, one

TABLE 8.2: TRUE COST OF THE CAP, 1978 ALTERNATIVE ASSESSMENTS (£m)

	Godley-Bacon's Estimates			Morris' Estimates			
	Net Trade Receipts[1]	Net Budget Receipts	Effect on Resources	Consumer Loss[3]	Producer Gain[4]	Budgetary Contribution[2]	Effect on Resources
Belgium-Luxembourg	-156	+312	+ 156 (4)	- 725	+ 680	- 226	- 259 (5)
Denmark	+289	+329	+ 618 (7)	- 291	+ 713	- 117	+ 324 (8)
Germany	-101	-570	- 671 (2)	-4598	+4035	-1177	-1740 (1)
France	+620	+114	+ 734 (8)	-3167	+3642	- 761	- 286 (4)
Ireland	+221	+254	+ 475 (5)	- 175	+ 408	- 32	+ 201 (6)
Italy	-532	-114	- 646 (3)	-3413	+2257	- 386	-1541 (2)
Netherlands	+441	+190	+ 631 (6)	- 892	+1403	- 305	+ 206 (7)
United Kingdom	-317	-806	-1123 (1)	-1787	+1148	- 731	-1370 (3)

Notes:

1. Net Trade Receipts = the costs incurred by member countries which import food from the rest of the EC at prices higher than they would otherwise have to pay, and the benefits received by countries which export food to the rest of the EC at prices higher than they could obtain in world markets.

2. Budgetary Contribution = the net budgetary contribution to agricultural support derived from taxes on non-agricultural products which is equal to expenditure on restitution, net levies, plus expenditure on intervention, storage and guidance less the value of additions to intervention stocks.

3. Consumer Loss = domestic consumption x difference between domestic and world prices (after allowing for subsidies).

4. Producer Gain = domestic production x difference between domestic and world prices (including Guidance section payments).

Sources: W. Godley and R. Bacon, 'Policies of the EEC', Cambridge Economic Policy Review, vol. 1, no. 5, 1979 and C.N. Morris, 'The Common Agricultural Policy', Fiscal Studies, vol.1, no. 2, 1980.

should expect the Morris calculations to be 'over estimates' since he assumes the 'true' world price to be equal to the going price; secondly one should expect the budgetary contributions for the Morris calculations to be less than those for the Godley-Bacon study since Morris calculates them to be equal to 55.7 per cent not 70 per cent (Morris 1980, p.27); thirdly since the Godley-Bacon study implicitly assumes perfectly inelastic supply and demand curves their calculations will be 'underestimates' since they do not consider the triangular dead-weight welfare losses; and fourthly, given the nature of the EC budget and the EC financing of the CAP one should expect the overall gains and losses to be determined by the degree of self-sufficiency and the difference between the world and EC price levels: a large price differential is detrimental to a country which is less than self-sufficient and is advantageous to one which is more than self-sufficient - see Table 8.3 for self-sufficiency rates and Table 8.4 for agricultural price movements.

Given these considerations it would seem that both studies are on the whole broadly consistent with theoretical expectations, although the Godley-Bacon estimates seem more consistent in terms of their ranking of countries according to the overall costs: UK, Germany and Italy rank in that order in terms of self-sufficiency hence one should expect them to rank more or less accordingly (more or less because of subsidies) in terms of overall

TABLE 8.4 : EC PRICES OF CERTAIN AGRICULTURAL PRODUCTS AS A PERCENTAGE OF WORLD MARKET PRICES, 1977/78.

Barley	206
Beef	196
Butter	388
Milk Powder	494
Oil Seeds	153
Pork	137
Sugar	255
Wheat	216

Source : Yearbook of Agricultural Statistics, 1978.

costs and benefits. However, it seems to me more appropriate to combine the two estimates so that the more realistic budgetary contributions of Morris are added to the Godley-Bacon 'net trade receipts': the result is that

TABLE 8.3: DEGREE OF SELF SUFFICIENCY (%)

	Beef and Veal		Cereals		Eggs		Fresh Fruit		Pork		Poultry Meat		Sugar		Wheat		Overall Ranking In Order of Least Self-Sufficient 1976-1979
	'70	'79	'70	'79	'70	'79	'70	'79	'70	'79	'70	'79	'70	'79	'70	'79	
Belgium/Luxembourg	95	98	41	46	181	141	71	55	164	162	132	90	160	245	41	46	4
Denmark	226	346	91	114	132	104	70	48	506	368	316	222	110	225	112	114	8
W. Germany	90	102	77	91	85	74	60	50	93	89	51	61	92	127	77	91	2
France	107	111	147	172	98	98	98	97	84	85	103	119	132	210	147	172	5
Ireland	523	546	77	94	100	90	27	25	158	144	103	100	107	147	77	94	7
Italy	61	62	70	71	97	96	115	125	83	75	99	99	86	85	70	71	3
Netherlands	124	133	37	30	148	270	82	55	197	225	394	283	102	165	37	30	6
United Kingdom	67	77	59	78	99	100	40	34	62	62	98	100	32	44	45	78	1
EC 9	91	100	84	100	101	101	81	77	101	101	103	105	86	124	85	100	

Source: Eurostat Review, 1970-1979

both the general ranking and magnitude are more consistent
with theoretical expectations [Belgium/Luxembourg – 382(4);
Denmark + 172(7) Germany – 1278(1); France – 141(5);
Ireland + 189(8); Italy – 918(3); Netherlands +136(6); UK
– 1048(2)].

The estimates made in these two studies have been widely
publicised via the media and have been quoted and referred
to quite frequently as the real cost of UK membership of
the EC in terms of the CAP. Indeed, the estimates of
Godley-Bacon and Morris for 1980 (£1.6 and £2.3 billion
respectively) are almost common household statistics!
However, a great deal of caution needs to be exercised with
regard to these particular figures; firstly because the UK
did not become a full member of the EC until 1979/80 – the
period before that was part of the transition; secondly,
the EC did concede the point about the anomalous UK
contributions and the UK is in receipt of refunds to that
effect;   thirdly, as has already been emphasised, the
nature of the EC budget both in terms of revenues and
expenditures and the operations of the CAP make the net
budgetary contributions a fair general guide to the true
cost of the CAP hence a general perspective is needed here;
and finally, the question of the true cost of the CAP for
the UK from its membership of the EC is altogether a
different matter – see below.

The general perspective is provided by Table 8.5 where I
have given the net budgetary contributions for all the
years from 1976 to 1981. It is obvious from this table that
both the Godley-Bacon and Morris estimates for 1980 are
incorrect since the calculations were made on the
assumption that the UK's net contribution for 1980 is
–£1165 million. Also that the true cost of the CAP for the
UK in 1981 is at worst £100 million (double the net
budgetary contribution to allow for the net trade
receipts). This much lower than expected figure is due to
the unusually high world food prices for the year and to a
much more efficient 'management' of the CAP. However it
would be extremely optimistic to expect the 1981 situation
to persist in the future but it would be very pessimistic
to suggest that the true cost of the CAP for Britain would
go back to the 1978 and 1980 levels.

The other question regarding the true cost of the CAP for
the UK which can be attributed to membership of the EC
needs close scrutiny. Let us recall that the UK operated a
deficiency payments system before joining the EC. In terms
of Figure 8.1 this meant that British farmers faced a price
such as $P_w(1+t)$ but British consumers were allowed to
trade at the world price. The dead-weight welfare loss of

TABLE 8.5: GAINERS (+) AND LOSERS (−) FROM THE EC BUDGET (1976-1981) (£m)

	1976	1977	1978	1978 (After full Article 131 refunds)	1979	1980	1981
Belgium-Luxembourg	+222.3	+247.4	+261.2	+252.6	+394	+ 250	+ 351
Denmark	+235.5	+339.7	+411.9	+411.9	+246	+ 174	+ 157
Germany	−630.8	−844.4	−230.3	−281.4	−924	−1177	−1260
France	+ 63.5	− 30.4	− 22.1	− 55.0	− 50	+ 41	+ 102
Ireland	+120.8	+267.0	+352.2	+356.0	+352	+ 372	+ 340
Italy	+130.4	− 43.4	−480.3	− .5	+345	+ 329	+ 215
Netherlands	+183.4	+187.0	+157.2	+146.4	+186	+ 215	+ 81
United Kingdom	−148.0	−408.0	−744.6	−625.8	−549	− 203	− 56

*These figures allow for refunds to Britain of £693m in 1980 and £830m in 1981.
1981 figures are forecasts.
No figures for Greece of equivalent precision for 1981 are yet available.

Source: EC Commission.

the deficiency payment system is triangle ACE. Hence the
true effect of operating the CAP mechanism is to add to the
initial dead-weight loss the consumer dead-weight welfare
loss (triangle BDF) and the tariff revenue CDFE since this
now becomes an EC 'own-resource' if the product is imported
from outside the EC or an additional charge if imported
from another member state. Therefore, the true cost for
Britain from operating the CAP is the size of the triangle
BDF and the rectangle CDFE (if the product is imported from
within the EC) since the UK would have had to incur the
loss of ACE anyway. Moreover, it should have also be stressed
that in the case of the product being imported from outside
the EC, the rectangular loss of CDFE is due to the clumsy
budgetary revenue system, hence a properly reformed EC
budget should take care of that. However, at this stage in
the development of the EC I suggest the sum of BDF and CDFE
to be the true cost to Britain of operating the CAP, but
this is clearly an 'overestimate' since not all UK imports
of agricultural products come from the EC.

   Morris has kindly supplied me with the calculations for
the triangles – see Table 8.6. If one adds £88.85m (size of
BDF) to the budgetary contribution of £731m, this gives a
true (extra) cost of £819.85m. Recall, however, that this
is an overestimate since Morris assumes that world prices
would remain unaltered in the absence of the CAP and
because of the reasoning in the previous paragraph.

REFORM OF THE CAP

It is quite apparent that it would be ideal for the UK if
the EC could be persuaded to change to a deficiency
payments system, although from a purely theoretical
viewpoint a system of direct subsidies to farmers that does
not affect world prices would be most ideal. It would be
naive to expect the EC to adopt either system since there
are so many vested national interests in the present system
– West Germany and the UK being the only countries
adversely affected. However, an EC budget which relied
entirely on a higher percentage of the VAT base and which
allowed agricultural levies to accrue to national
exchequers plus national contributions to pay for
respective national agricultural surpluses coupled with an
alignment of EC agricultural prices to US prices should not
be unacceptable to Britain and it would be quite feasible
to negotiate its adoption by the EC particularly when a
'proper' European Monetary Union is negotiated. Such a
reform would produce a fairer outcome (see Figure 8.2 for

the anomalous position at the moment). It should be added that there will be those who will consider these proposals to be tantamount to abandoning the CAP; that would be a complete misunderstanding of both the nature of the CAP and the argument advanced here.

TABLE 8.6: DEAD-WEIGHT WELFARE LOSSES (£m)

	Consumer Δ	Producer Δ
Belgium/Luxembourg	34.84	24.59
Denmark	14.10	29.95
Germany	227.66	164.62
France	160.91	152.71
Ireland	7.67	15.62
Italy	183.79	91.66
Netherlands	45.41	50.46
United Kingdom	88.85	38.88

Source : Provided, on a personal basis, by
         C.N.Morris.

CONCLUSIONS

With regard to Britain's membership of the EC in the particular context of the CAP one needs to conclude by stressing a few salient points.

Firstly, the CAP has been a success in that it replaced the various agricultural support mechanisms that were operated before the formation of the EC and in this sense the CAP has been an important aspect of the integrative process in the EC.

Secondly, although all concerned would concede the point concerning the undesirability of 'lakes' and 'mountains' if these were looked at in the context of insecure world food supplies and food shortages in low-income countries it would seem that the EC, in aiming at self-sufficiency, is arguably justified.

Thirdly, lest it be forgotten, the CAP was a result of hard bargaining at the time of the formation of the EC and since Britain chose not to participate seriously at that stage it was inevitable that the CAP did not adopt the relatively most efficient mechanism, that of the UK; the CAP mechanism is only a variant of the systems that were

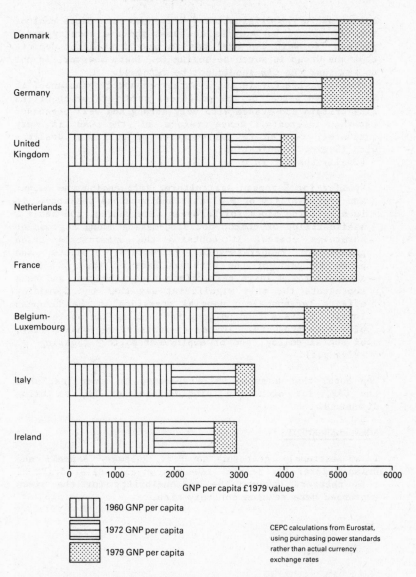

GNP per capita £1979 values

|||| 1960 GNP per capita

≡≡≡ 1972 GNP per capita

⋯ 1979 GNP per capita

CEPC calculations from Eurostat,
using purchasing power standards
rather than actual currency
exchange rates

FIGURE 8.2: REAL GNP PER CAPITA IN THE EC 1960, 1972 & 1979

Source: Cambridge Economic Policy Review, No.5, April, 1979

operating in the Original Six. Hence the true extra cost of the CAP should be seen as the cost which a country which prefers 'to wait and see' has to pay if it later decides that the Group is worth belonging to. That, however, is not to say that the CAP should not be reformed.

Fourthly, the CAP is not a purely economic phenomenon; it is part and parcel of the political structure of countries like Britain and France with very strong and well organised farming interests. Hence reform of the CAP is very intimately related to the question of political dealings with farming organisations.

Finally the CAP is a

"policy for European agriculture, influencing the output and profitability of a diverse and populous industry. It is a building block for European integration, and hence a manifestation of common decision-making among a group of sovereign states. It contains the Community's trade policy for temperate-zone agricultural products, and hence is part of the external face of the [EC]. It accounts for a large part of the common budget, and thus represents the only significant way that the Community effects large-scale financial transfers at the European level. It is a food policy, influencing the whole price of staple products. It has elements of regional policy, of social policy, and of employment policy" (Josling 1979, p.1).

One hopes that a sense of perspective is never lost when the CAP, let alone one single facet of it, is being discussed.

ACKNOWLEDGEMENTS

I am extremely grateful to Drs. Rosemary Fennell and Brian Hillier for helpful comments on an earlier draft of this chapter. However the responsibility for the views expressed here remains entirely mine.

9 The Future of the Common Transport Policy

Kenneth M. Gwilliam

INTRODUCTION

The close equivalence in effect on trade of tariffs and transport costs makes it inevitable that there should be, at the very least, sufficient control and uniformity in the transport policies of the EC member states to prevent them being used as a covert and discriminating way of re-introducing the barriers which the formation of the EC was designed to eliminate. The importance of transport rates in determining the geographical structure of the coal, iron and steel sectors, and their relationships led to their control being an essential and central element in the Treaty of Paris which created the ECSC (see Meade et al, 1962). A pattern for transport policy therefore already existed in the Treaty of Paris when the Treaty of Rome moved the Community forward from a very narrow industrial base to embrace the whole of the economic activities of the member states.

The translation from a policy on the transport of coal, iron and steel to one relating to all goods and passengers could not be a simple one. In several of the member states transport policy had traditionally been used as an instrument of social and distributional policy which they were both to abandon. In the same way that the special features of agriculture were deemed to justify its treatment as a special case outside the general rules of the industry and competition policies, so transport attracted its own chapter in the Treaty of Rome and subsequent efforts to construct a rational and comprehensive Community transport policy. Most crucially it was considered that the economic distortions implicit in the existing organisations of the national transport sectors, and particularly the differences between them, pre-empted any possibility of the immediate introduction of a free competitive market in transport services. Whilst this was stated as the ultimate aim, the path by which this could be achieved was seen to run by way of progressive harmonisation of these conditions and constraints on

167

operation in the national transport market. The strategy of harmonisation before liberalisation, which moulded the early development of common policy initiatives, had a certain air of inevitability.

The way in which the strategy advanced was not inevitable. The Commission — at the behest of the Council of Ministers, of course — in 1961 prepared a blueprint for transport policy, the Schauss Memorandum (see EC Commission, 1961) which might be described as a 'rational comprehensive' approach to policy making. They set out in that document a logical structure for the creation of transport policy from which they were subsequently invited to derive a programme of legislative action. Their structure dealt with the whole range of influences which might be <u>potentially</u> distorting and looked to a programme of legislative interventions which would, on completion, eliminate the distortions. It has been argued elsewhere (see Gwilliam, 1980a) that this was always an impossible objective, given the diversity of the existing transport arrangements and regulations in the member states and the unpracticability of moving immediately to the required end state. To ignore, as the Commission did in its early policy initiatives, the disjunctive effects of upsetting existing, and delicate policy balances in the member states was to court the possibility that the Council of Ministers would not wish to proceed with much of the legislation proposed.

The difficulties of progressing that approach, and particularly the difficulties of developing a comprehensive and effective control over the very fragmented road sector has been discussed elsewhere (see Gwilliam, 1980b) and will only be briefly discussed in the next section. Of most significance for the purpose of this chapter is the fact that these difficulties were recognised and, from 1975 onwards the nature of the policy initiatives have changed, as we shall also briefly explain below.

In looking forward to the future our particular emphasis will be to identify the new challenges to the Community which have arisen since 1975 and to explore the extent to which the current policies and structure of policy making looks appropriate to meet these challenges.

THE POLICY REVIEWED

The Treaty of Rome envisaged the role of transport policy at two levels. Primarily, transport policy was to be so arranged as to contribute in the best possible way to the development of a freer competitive market in all goods and

services. Secondly, it should be aimed at securing a free
market in transport itself. The quandary that faced the
Commission in developing such a policy was that in all the
member states transport had hitherto been extensively used
as an instrument of social policy, and in some had been
consciously used as a discriminating instrument of trade
policy. Structures, regulations and attitudes were all
conditioned to a role for transport seemingly incompatible
with the objectives of the 'common market'.

One of the perennial difficulties about highly regulated
sectors is that the initial objectives of the regulation
ultimately become subservient to the maintenance of the
interests of the chosen instruments. Protection, and the
maintenance of the status quo, too easily dominates the
continued, critical pursuit of the underlying objectives. A
non-discriminatory competitive ethic may be difficult to
reconstruct without wide ranging structural reform; yet
such reform may be unacceptable to the member states
because it would upset intricate and delicate institutional
balances developed over a long period. Given the diversity
of detail in these arrangements between member states the
superimposition of common, but partial, regimes inevitably
generates much opposition.

Confronted by this problem the ultimate aim of the
Commission was the unification of the transport markets of
the member states. To achieve this aim the Commission set
three instrumental objectives, which might also have been
regarded as a phased programme, namely:

1. elimination of obstacles which transport may put in
   the way of the establishment of the 'common market' as
   a whole;
2. integration of transport at the Community level (the
   free movement of services within the Community); and
3. general, and common, reorganisation of national
   transport systems.

Pursuit of the first objective required the elimination
of conscious national discrimination in transport rates,
careful monitoring and control of any general support
tariffs and concerted action to remove physical barriers to
frontier crossing. The necessary actions under this head
were predominantly at government level and it was therefore
reasonable to expect that a commitment to the ends would
ensure successful translation to effective means of
control. Even at this first level of commitment, however,
problems have re-emerged and the Commission has found it
necessary in 1981 to propose a further new regulation to
facilitate the ease of movement of goods across frontiers

within the EC. The need for this has arisen from conscious
maintenance of obstructions to easy cross frontier
movement, particularly on the France/Italy border
reflecting dissatisfaction on the fairness of trading
relationships.

The second objective, or stage of policy, ultimately
requires the complete freedom of establishment and freedom
of international movement of transport within the
Community. The existence of restrictive road haulage
licensing systems in the member states has been the main
barrier here. The development of a Community authorisation
system deals with the problem in principle but the quota of
such licences remains so small that they still only account
for around 5 per cent of the international road freight
movement.

One interpretation of this resistance to the
liberalisation of international movement is that it
represents a fear that the conditions for fair competition
between hauliers of different nationalities do not exist.
Hence the Commission has developed a central concern with
the achievement of harmonisation of the fiscal, technical
and social conditions of operation. All have given
difficulty.

Fiscal harmonisation for road transport has gone as far
as standardising the taxation of fuel in tanks at border
crossings, but the much more significant problems of the
double taxation of road vehicles and fuel taxation
(infrastructure charge) levels have yet to be resolved. For
rail transport there are complex regulations for
normalisation of accounts and attribution of compensation
for public service obligation and co-ordination purposes,
but there is no effective way of ensuring that such
compensation allocations realistically represent the value
of the benefits to which they refer, or to enforce the
pursuit of financial autonomy by the railways after these
appropriate compensatory allowances. Social harmonisation,
consisting of regulations on crew composition, hours and
conditions of work, supported by monitoring procedures (the
tachograph), has received only tardy and grudging
acceptance by some governments, and there are serious
doubts concerning the way in which the regulations are
being implemented. Technical harmonisation in road haulage
has long foundered on the differing national views of the
effect of higher axle loadings and gross vehicle weight on
road and bridge maintenance costs and of the environmental
acceptability of larger dimension vehicles.

The third, and most ambitious objective of the Schauss
Memorandum was the achievement of a common national

transport regulation system throughout the Community. This would have involved common controls on entry (licensing systems), tariff controls, relationship between operators and the state, infrastructure appraisal and charging, and social conditions. Most of these objectives have now been shelved. A mandatory bracket tariff system for international road haulage, introduced in 1968, was replaced in 1975 by a purely advisory reference tariff system. A draft regulation on a common licensing system first submitted to the Council in 1967 was withdrawn in the mid-seventies. Whilst the Community is still committed in principle to the financial autonomy of transport operators, in practice it has been unable to grasp the nettle of railway finances. In infrastructure pricing a good deal of theoretical work has not led to the adoption of any effective regulations or common road charging systems.

Only in infrastructure investment policy does the Commission appear to be maintaining its effort. In 1978 the Council adopted a new procedure of consultation on transport infrastructure programmes, aimed at securing a much more effective co-ordination of national plans. In 1980 the Commission proposed the creation of a special financial instrument for the support of infrastructure investments of Community interest. This proposal has been supported by studies of infrastructure bottlenecks and of the principles on which the Community interest in transport projects might be identified and appraised. But so far there is little sign that a Community transport investment budget is about to emerge.

THE POLICY REVISED

The first enlargement of the EC in 1973 produced, or was associated with, a substantial change of emphasis in the development of the Common Transport Policy. There appear to have been three distinct, but connected aspects of this re-orientation.

Firstly, the Commission appears to have reconsidered its strategy of requiring extensive harmonisation of the conditions of transport operation in the member states as the prerequisite for the ultimate achievement of a free market in transport services. A number of factors contributed to the reappraisal. The new member states were broadly more liberal in their domestic transport policies than the existing members and harmonisation could only be pursued by a rather paradoxical deliberation in these cases. The increased emphasis of the Commission on the

integrity between transport policy and other sector
objectives following the Paris Summit of 1972 provided a
basis on which the new entrants could explain their non-
conformity and defend their domestic arrangements as
essentially consistent with the objectives of that Summit.
Above all, the difficulties of enforcing comprehensive and
consistent implementation of controls over operators in
such a fragmented industry had become very apparent. This
was particularly accentuated by the lack of wholehearted
enforcement by some of the member states.

The policy implications of this mainly related to the
road haulage sector. The intent to secure a common domestic
licensing system throughout the Community was abandoned,
and the intention to extend the mandatory bracket tariff
system from international to all long distance road haulage
was replaced by the provision for a non-mandatory reference
tariff. As a quid pro quo for the more restrictively minded
it was agreed to set up a system of market observation, the
purpose of which would be to give early warning of any
major difficulties that were arising in the national
markets. The Commission now produces quarterly reviews of
the state of the markets.

The same degree of retrenchment of objectives did not
apply to all modes. For railways the Council adopted a
Decision in 1975 aimed at further harmonising their
financial relations with the State. The Council declared
that the railways should be run on commercial principles
with power to set their own tariffs and freedom from
economically unjustifiable political intervention. Public
service obligations on the railways should be precisely
defined and compensation payments related to the costs of
such interventions. Measures were adopted by the Council to
lay down uniform railway costings principles and thereby
secure comparability in railway accounts. Whilst it cannot
be denied that the railway sector is problematical
throughout the Community, it is not at all clear that the
policy initiatives have any substance whatsoever. Even in
such a procedural matter as accounting systems the German
railways are currently moving towards a British style of
contribution accounting just as British Rail are moving
away from it.

The second aspect of the revised approach consisted of an
increased emphasis on infrastructure policy. To some extent
this may simply indicate that the Commission think that
there is more likelihood of obtaining a realistically
enforceable policy where, given the fact that
infrastructure is predominantly provided in the public
domain, the number of control points is limited to the

number of public bodies with that responsibility. But it does also reflect the belief that infrastructure decisions are more strategic than transport operational decisions and as such more appropriate for the attention of a high level strategic authority.

There are two main thrusts in the infrastructure policy – on the planning, management and financing of infrastructure investment and on the pricing of the use of infrastructure.

In 1978 the Council set up a new committee with the function of maintaining continuous consultation on the investment programmes of the member states. This replaced an earlier ad hoc consultation procedure whereby individual projects of Community interest were notified to the Commission by the member states on which other members opinions were subsequently sought. This procedure was widely recognised to be too little and too late for any effective consultation; whether the new procedure is any more effective remains to be seen.

Current activity is directed to remedying two other related defects of infrastructure investment policy. Long term demand forecasting exercises have been undertaken for both freight and passenger traffic on the basis of which a subsequent study has attempted to identify the major bottlenecks in the Community transport infrastructure. It is hoped that this will give the Community policy a much more positive direction than the purely reactive role that it has been able to fulfil so far. The parallel defect has been the absence of any Community financial instrument for transport infrastructure to give some real impetus to Community level initiatives. Initial consultations in this direction received generally negative response even from the UK which might have been expected to be enthusiastic given that proposals for a Channel Tunnel had already resurfaced after the fiasco of 1975. The main weakness of the Commission proposals lay in the absence of any indication of the criteria of Community interest on which Community funds would be allocated. Consequently work has been put in hand to identify such criteria and to demonstrate their applicability in such projects as the Channel Tunnel, the Alpine crossings and the Messina Straits Bridge.

Although activity directed towards the introduction of a common infrastructure pricing regime began even earlier, even less real progress has been made than with investment policy. Theoretical studies in the early sixties resulted in the advocacy of charges both related to marginal social costs and meeting an overall budgetary equilibrium requirement. In 1975 this was supplemented by a study of alternative ways of reconciling the marginalist and budgetary equilibrium objectives. In practical terms, however, very little progress has been made. Even the first step to adjust national taxation systems on commercial vehicles to reflect marginal costs of road use has not been implemented, despite the first proposal of a directive on the matter being now 14 years old.

The third major revision relates to the scope of the policy. The application of the specific transport provisions of the Treaty of Rome to maritime shipping and civil aviation appeared, according to Article 84 of the Treaty, to depend on a specific decision by the Council.

So long as land and inland waterway transport accounted for the bulk of international movement within the Community that situation was perfectly intelligible. The entry of three new members separated by sea from mainland Europe changed matters. In 1974 the European Court of Justice ruled that these two modes could not be exempt from the application of the general rules of the Treaty. In light of this decision it clearly became sensible for the Commission to review the role of these modes in the Community transport sector and to take positive initiatives where approporiate.

These examples all show a degree of responsiveness to the changing nature and situation of the Community which encourages hopes of the development of a relevant and mutually acceptable common policy in the future. But they also show the continuation of a good deal of unrealistic idealism underlying current policy thinking which could still vitiate such modest and sensible developments as are possible. It is to the nature of the new challenges, and the practical requirements of transport policy formulation in response to them that we turn in the rest of this chapter.

THE NATURE OF A COMMON POLICY

There are two quite distinct ways of approaching the formulation of public policy. The first, sometimes referred to as the 'rational comprehensive' approach, starts from the identification of fundamental societal objectives, proceeds through the identification of policies for the achievement of those objectives and culminates in the selection of a set of specific instruments for the implementation of the policies. In this framework policy formulation is a process of very comprehensive co-ordination, involving rational syntheses, relating objectives to instruments.

The second approach, sometimes referred to as 'disjointed incrementalism' starts from the identification of currently perceived problems, proceeds through the identification of specific instruments to attenuate these problems, and culminates in an assessment of the new set of problems which are likely to be produced by the selected measures, or which may arise in any event. What is meant by 'policy' in this framework is more difficult to define. But it may perhaps be identified in terms of the tasks undertaken by the administrative agencies which are essentially the identification of the perceived problems and the analysis of alternative actions to address these problems.

Cynically one might observe a general tendency of organisations to aspire to the first approach but to practise the second. The reason for the gap between aspirations and achievements are partly to be found within the organisation itself and partly in the nature of its environment. Internally, it is rare for any large organisation to be able to achieve either the stable consensus on the nature of its objectives or a sufficiently comprehensive set of instruments necessary for a 'rational comprehensive' policy basis. Externally, the environment in which the organisation operates may itself be changing too rapidly for any comprehensive solutions to be introduced and implemented before the kaleidoscope forms a different pattern. The larger and more heterogeneous these organisations the greater are likely to be these disrupting influences. The multinational governmental organisation is likely to be a polar case of such complexity.

The history of the Common Transport Policy to date, appears as an exemplification of this tendency. The Schauss Memorandum was a blueprint for policy in the 'rational comprehensive' mould, being deduced from an explicit set of Community objectives and generating a comprehensive and interrelated set of specific instrumental acts. The subsequent inability to reconcile this blueprint with the complexities of the transport sectors of the member countries has produced a great deal of trimming − to the ultimate situation of tacitly recognising that it was not feasible to control the details of the operation of such a fragmented sector as road transport in conformity with a rigid blueprint. Despite this, however, there still appears to be a tendency to rational comprehensive aspirations − exemplified in the attempts to introduce a common infrastructure charging system as the basis of securing optimum allocation conditions and in the pursuit of a common basis for appraisal of national railway financial

arrangements. In both of these cases the complexities (and
vested resistance to) a common framework is enormous. It
has never been made very clear how significant the absence
of either is, in practice, as a source of distortion in
resource allocation. The Commission commitment to them is
essentially because they are the keystones to a new
rational comprehensive strategy based on the control over
infrastructure and public enterprises rather than private
enterprises.

It might be the case, of course, that the common policy
had simply been pursued with the wrong instruments (i.e.
control of operations rather than infrastructure) and that
a change of instruments is all that is necesary to
rehabilitate it. Whether or not this is possible in reality
will depend on the degree of consensus on objectives and
cohesion in action that can be obtained internally, and the
nature, direction and pace of the external changes which a
comprehensive Community policy must face. It is to these
contextual issues that we now turn.

NEW MEMBERSHIP

The entry of Spain, Portugal and Greece into the EC will
increase the amount of intra-Community trade, and to some
extent change the patterns of trade. However, given the
fact that over 50 per cent of their exports already go to
other EC countries this will not be a revolutionary change
in either volume or patterns. Nor is it likely that they
will have such fundamental effects on the philosophy of the
Common Transport Policy as was brought about by the
introduction of the greater liberality of the UK in 1973.
But they will inevitably bring some new problems to the
sector policy and produce some new focal points for that
policy.

Firstly, the new members have less well developed land
transport infrastructures and may express demands for
transport infrastructure investment of a different order
from that confronted hitherto. This could significantly
increase the emphasis placed on infrastructure policy, and
in particular the infrastructure budget.

Secondly, because of their peripheral location, they will
generate longer distance inter-Community movements. This
may favour rail or combined road-rail transport and give a
new impetus to the elimination of some residual anomalies
in railway charging structures by the provision of a
genuine system of cost-related through rates for freight
movement.

Thirdly, the Greek interest in shipping may militate in favour of a more competitive approach to shipping policy and particularly strengthen the opposition to allocation systems for shipping, even in trade with developing countries.

Fourthly, the new entrants may change the relationships of the EC with some of the peripheral non-member countries. For example, the entry of Greece will result in a larger proportion of the intra-EC land transport flows being routed through non-member states (Yugoslavia and Switzerland), highlighting the problems of the availability of adequate infrastructure, the charges for the use of that infrastructure and the freedom of movement over it.

Of even greater importance than any of these specific effects may be the fact that the addition of three more countries will increase the difficulty of obtaining agreement on measures of harmonisation. This is likely to move the philosophy of policy formulation further from the original 'rational comprehensive' approach of the Schauss Memorandum and towards the identification of specific, ad hoc, measures of commonly agreed importance.

NEW MODES

The application of the transport provisions of the Treaty of Rome to civil aviation and shipping was made — by Article 84 of the Treaty — to depend on a subsequent Council decision to extend policy interests into these modes. Initially they were not included in the sphere of policy interest. However, in a judgement in 1974 the European Court of Justice decided that neither sector was exempt from the rights and obligations of the Community and that the general rules must apply to them. The member states were thus forced to consider air and sea transport sector policies as subject to, and therefore in the context of, Community rules and hence the incorporation of these sectors within the Community transport policy came under consideration.

(i) Air Transport
Following a draft Council decision on first steps towards joint action in June 1972 (OJC 110, 18-10-72), and a statement of general objectives in October 1975 (Bulletin of the European Communities, Supplement 11/75), Council asked COREPER to identify priority areas for examination. In June 1978 the Council approved a list of such areas and

in July 1979 adopted a memorandum on air transport (Bulletin of the European Communities, Supplement 5/79).

As for the rest of the transport sector it is argued that the general long run objectives shall be consistent with Article 2 of the Treaty - calling for the promotion of a harmonious development of economic activities - but shall also be conditioned by Article 3 - which provides for selected activities to be treated not as ends in themselves but as means towards the achievement of the more general aims of the Treaty.

Three special characteristics of the air transport sector complicating the formulation of a common policy are identified, namely:

1. the importance of safety aspects;
2. the interaction between EC air transport and the rest of the world civil aviation section; and
3. a complex market structure.

The first of these characteristics makes a high degree of control inevitable but has already been provided for outside the common policy. It is thus the resolution of the problems posed by international interactions in a very complex, and initially very controlled, market sector which is the central concern of a common policy.

The context of the problem at the world scale is well known. The international air transport market is supplied by a large number of carriers, some privately owned and operated, but many being the national flag carriers supported financially for strategic and prestige reasons. Landing rights are negotiated bilaterally between countries who are thus able to afford some protection to their national flag carriers and hence minimise the direct financial cost at which the government objectives in air transport are achieved. This has been buttressed by fares agreements arrived at by the airlines through the International Air Transport Association (IATA).

The typical outcome of this system has been the maintenance of high network density, high margins of capacity giving high seat availability, and hence high fares. Competition has been concentrated on quality, also contributing to a high fare outcome. The interests of business travellers in quality of service and availability have dominated those of non-business travellers in prices.

This dominance has been attenuated, for nearly two decades, by the development of inclusive tour and charter services outside the rules applying to scheduled operations. In response to this external competition IATA carriers themselves introduced more flexibility in conditions and began to use price discrimination to protect

the lower end of the market. This process was greatly
accelerated by the deregulation of the US domestic market
by the Carter Administration; and by the renegotiation of
bilateral agreements with foreign goverments. The first of
these was the Bermuda II agreement with the UK, concluded
in July 1977, to be followed by agreements with Israel,
Belgium, Netherlands and West Germany in 1978. The latter
agreements provided for as many airlines as possible on
their routes ('multiple designation'), conditions and
tariffs to be based on those of the country of origin of
traffic ('country of origin rules') and the greatest
possible degree of freedom for operators on tariffs,
frequency and capacity ('the open skies policy'). Although
none of these developments applies directly to domestic
traffic within the EC they inevitably create expectations
of greater liberalisation within a Community theoretically
committed to liberalisation.

In its 1979 Memorandum the Commission discusses a range
of possible measures to improve the EC domestic air system,
which we may categorise into four types:

1. Measures of technical and commercial harmonisation
   These include provisions to stabilise exchange rates
   for tariff construction; to compensate for
   overbooking; to harmonise equipment; to simplify
   formalities; and, most controversially, to improve and
   standardise air traffic control provisions. Although
   these may be difficult in practice to implement they
   do not appear to be difficult in principle.

2. Measures to extend the application of existing rules
   to air transport
   These include the recognition of public service
   obligations of air transport and the corollary
   financial support; the progressive application of
   competition policy to air transport; and the
   application of the principle of the free right of
   establishment within the EC.

3. Measures to extend the services provided
   These include further liberalisation of the inclusive
   tour markets; and provisions for ensuring easier entry
   on new links, particularly between regional centres.

4. Measures to increase flexiblity and reduce fares on
   the main trunk routes
   This is inevitably the most difficult and
   controversial area as it directly confronts the vested

interests of the established national airlines. The
Commission recognises that free access could only be
envisaged in the very long term and separately
specifies a desirable 'long term framework' and a set
of short or medium term action points. The long term
framework would allow new entrants to the market so
long as the new provisions were demonstrated to be
commercially viable, involve significant price
reductions, promise to be stable, were not introduced
at too rapid a pace, and were not matched by existing
operations. In effect this looks rather like a system
of competitive tender for restricted franchises, with
preference given to existing operators. The proposed
short term measures in this direction involved member
states requesting major airlines to introduce more
flexible service types and fare system, including
roundtrip tickets, standby facilities etc., with the
threat that new entrants would be allowed to provide
these facilities if the existing suppliers did not.

Whether this really offers a viable compromise between
the extremes of rigid protection and complete deregulation
remains to be seen. The development of further regional
services may detract from the viability of the main routes
and lead to resistance from governments and the state owned
airlines. A reduced role for the national flag carriers in
a more competitive EC market might weaken their wider
efforts and be equally unacceptable. The failure of Laker
and the apparent financial problems of a number of US major
carriers has cast doubt on the long term stability of the
more competitive regime even in the more favourable
conditions of the USA.

(ii) Shipping
As with air transport, the sea transport interests of the
EC have to be seen in the wider contexts of recent
developments in the world maritime sector. Two are of
particular interst (see EC Commission, 1981i). Firstly,
there is the recently agreed UNCTAD Convention on a Code of
Conduct for Liner Conferences which provides for a 40:40:20
split of carrying of trade between the fleets of the
countries of origin, of destination, and third country
fleets. Secondly, there has been a recent agressive
expansion of the activity of the COMECON countries fleets
which would be admirably placed to take a large share of EC
countries trade if a liberal system prevailed.

The EC quandary is that the UNCTAD Code of Conduct
appears to be both incompatible with the Community

competition policy and contrary to the liberalising
intention of the Common Transport Policy, yet offers a
common protection to EC fleets against COMECON fleets. The
compromise reached has been to apply the UNCTAD rules to
trade with developing countries as a form of aid, but to
apply a free market economy to trade within EC or between
EC and other OECD countries. The developing countries are
now likely to press for the UNCTAD rules to apply also to
bulk cargoes.

A number of spectacular tanker accidents, such as the
wrecking of the Amoco Cadiz off Brittany in 1978, have led
the Council to draw up an 'action programme' to fight oil
pollution and to improve safety. Given the essentially
international nature of the sector this has mostly
consisted of a concerted attempt to secure rectification
and stringent application of appropriate regulations
throughout the world. As much of the implementation effort
takes place in port this has led the Commission to pay
particular attention to ports policy and a programme of
studies of port-problems and needs has now been
implemented.

TECHNOLOGICAL CHANGE AND THE TRANSPORT SECTOR

Throughout the world the transport sector will, during the
next decade or two, have to face two substantial
technological challenges. The first will arise from the
increasing scarcity and rising real cost of the traditional
sources of energy; the second will arise from the
development of microelectronics and its application
particularly in the field of information technology. Our
concern, in both cases, is with the effect that will be
felt on the Common Transport Policy - see Gwilliam and
Allport (1982).

(i) Energy and Transport Policy
The transport sector typically accounts for up to a quarter
of the total energy consumption of the W. European
countries. But, because it is dominantly dependent on oil
(99 per cent of transport energy comes from this source in
the UK), it may take up to one third of the oil consumed.
In the short term it is not easy to substitute any other
primary energy sources. In the long term, as oil supplies
are depleted such substitution must occur.

The likely direction of substitution is first to coal
(either for electricity generation or for synthetic crude
oil) and then to electricity from nuclear or renewable
sources. The timing is uncertain, but the transition to

coal dominance could be as early as the late 1990s. In the process of transition energy in general, and oil in particular, will become more expensive, continuously making obsolescent the infrastructure and rolling stock constructed in eras of low energy prices. This outlook clearly suggests substantial requirements for transport investment in all countries and particular problems, both of cost and security of supplies, for those countries which do not have indiginous coal resources. With the exception of the UK, EC coal reserves are limited.

A particular problem may concern the smoothness of the transition. For the UK, coal production would need to be increased by 60-70 per cent to satisfy existing surface transport demand. The environmental acceptability of the mines and syncrude plants on this scale may, at the very least, slow down the programme. For the EC as a whole it appears essential that either coal or syncrude would have to be imported on a major scale. This raises a host of questions. Given that most of the development and investment in the area of substitute fuels has been undertaken by the oil majors in the USA, will that country (or even other committed friendly nations like Australia) be willing to do more than satisfy their domestic demands given the environmental problems? If not, will the oil majors be prepared to invest in syncrude plants in (less stable) developing countries? Or will coal have to be imported to W. Europe, both substantially increasing the cost of syncrude and imposing the environmental costs in EC countries? Given the very long lead terms in this activity, and the political and environmental problems mentioned, it seems quite possible that serious discontinuities in the growth of transition could occur, quite distinct from any crisis scenario emerging from the politics of the Middle Eastern oil suppliers.

For all of the EC member states this is a problem of mutual concern. It appears to be an area within which a common R & D effort could be fruitful and certainly within which serious consideration of infrastructure investment planning needs to be co-ordinated.

(ii) Information Technology
The convergence of microelectronics, telecommunications and computers into a powerful new technology could have significant effects both on the demand for, and supply of, transport services.

It is already clear that information technology is: producing new communications products (e.g. teleconferencing, videotext, etc); reducing the costs of communications (e.g. through fibre optics and satellite technology); and changing the structure of costs (making costs less dependent on distance and non-dependent on the level of usage of high initial costs, high capacity facilities). Individual life styles, business organisations, and freight distribution will all be affected. But it is not clear in what direction, or to what extent, transport demand will be affected, as there are some markets in which transport and communication appear to be competing and others in which they act as complements.

Possibly the most disturbing consequence, from the point of view of transport policy, would arise from the change in telecommunications cost structure which might further concentrate communications and the complementary transport activity further on the major trunk routes. This could induce changes in location of activities quite contrary to declared regional policies and further aggravate the already difficult problems of maintaining rural accessibility. It is not self evidently optimal for the transport sector and transport budgets to inherit the problems of supporting regional policy objectives against structural change generated in the communications sector.

NEW EXTERNAL RELATIONSHIPS

Hitherto the Common Transport Policy has been essentially inward looking. The exclusion of sea and air transport has meant that the major concerns have been with the internal land transport of the Community, and that external trade patterns have only been of concern to the policy insofar as they determined the port of entry or exit from the Community. Problems of providing efficient links with neighbouring countries have been approached literally on an ad hoc basis (e.g. the exchange of road haulage licences or the international carriage of passengers by coach and bus), or through longstanding multinational conventions (e.g. the International Rhine Convention) agreed with international bodies (e.g. UIC, ECE, UNCTAD, European Civil Aviation Conference, Central Commission for Navigation of the Rhine). For the most part these agreements have concerned the member states of the EC individually, rather than the EC per se, and this has not been seen as a particular weakness. Three significant developments now in process may change this position (EC Commission, 1977).

Firstly, there is the prospect of increasing trade with the COMECON countries. EC purchases of energy from the East (using the gas pipeline now in construction), and possibly of manufactures embodying low wage labour, may provide the finance for reverse flows of higher technology manufactured goods. As the EC has shown, this may well produce pressure on infrastructure which has, since 1945, been oriented in a N/S direction. There may therefore develop a genuine Community interest in the relevant infrastructure which exceeds the direct West German interest in it.

Secondly, there is an increasing problem of transport relationships with the COMECON countries which typically obtain a disproportionate share of the carriage of trade with the West, and have also infiltrated extensively into trades between third countries. This has been achieved partly by the state trading organisations' importing f.o.b. and exporting c.i.f. in order to have the choice of carrier in their own trades, and partly by operating in the free markets, both in road haulage and shipping, at prices which Western European operators claim to be dumping prices. Completion of the Main-Rhine-Danube link would extend this problem in the inland shipping sector. Given their high demand for Western goods and foreign currency such a policy is quite rational. The Commission has already studied the methods and purposes of COMECON policies and the effect that they have had particularly on the EC shipping fleets.

The third development of importance is the entry into the Community of another nation, Greece, for which shipping is a major economic activity. This has heightened the concern about COMECON shipping policies, and has also produced the disparate strain within the Community of its lowest income member being the largest potential loser from acceptance of the UNCTAD 40:40:20 rules in the liner trades, and, a fortiori from their extension beyond the liner trades.

The initial response to these developments is noteworthy. Subsidised competition is viewed as unacceptable, notwithstanding the fact that it may reduce delivered costs for EC consignees. Such a view is tenable if, with high unemployment, the EC transport factors have no other available productive employment; if there are strategic reasons for maintaining the size of the EC fleets; or if maintaining the incomes of EC transport agencies is a particular objective if none of these considerations applies protection against COMECON competition, whether subsidised or not, would not appear to be in the economic interests of the EC as a whole.

In the event, the Community decided to protect against such competition. An additional protocol to the Mannheim Convention has already been adopted which will require authorisations for COMECON fleets to operate on the Rhine.

The Commission also intends to propose new rules for admission to the market to protect both inland waterway and road haulage operators.

These decisions exhibit two interesting characteristics. Firstly, they show that the Community institutions are unwilling to allow foreign access to the freer internal market for transport within the EC if it is deemed to be against EC interests. Secondly, they show a new willingness on the part of the Community to act in concert in its external transport arrangements as well as in the internal market.

THE WAY FORWARD

The medium term future has been characterised as a period of great complexity. The quite exogenous changes in energy availability and information technology introduce substantial uncertainty both about the amount and orientation of the transport which will be required and about the relative efficiency of alternative means of providing for these requirements. Unfortunately the lead times of some of the investments required for some of the possible responses is very long, so that it will not simply suffice to ignore the problems until the effect becomes serious. The same also holds for some of the potential effects of international trade relationships both with COMECON countries and with the developing world. What appears to be called for is a progressive refinement of understanding of the changes that are taking place and their implications for the transport sector, together with some decisiveness in action where the needs become apparent.

Recent internal changes within the Community seem certain to make the achievement of a comprehensive transport policy more difficult. The trend towards transport policy being related to other sectoral objectives, which first really emerged at the Paris Summit of 1972, makes it easier for member states to justify exceptional provisions in the transport sector. Some of the new member countries have distinctly different transport problems from those of the core countries and will quite naturally have different emphases in their policy preferences. Even if they did not, for simple numerical reasons, the harmonisation of 12 existing policy frameworks was likely to be more difficult than that of 9, which was more difficult than that of 6.

Together, this combination of external and internal complexities seems to rule out the possibility that a coherent common transport policy can be arrived at on the basis of a 'rational comprehensive' blueprint from which structural changes in the member states to achieve conformity and harmonisation are derived. If it did not work for the Six in the relatively stable world of the sixties it is unlikely to work for 12 in the less secure world of the eighties.

If agreement could be reached on that conclusion it would be a matter not for pessimism but for optimism. For it would inevitably set the Community approach to transport off on a more modest, but more realistic, basis. The purposes of the Community in this sector would then become those of:

1. identifying commonly perceived problems on which common action could bring relief; and
2. identifying, discussing and hopefully negotiating areas where member states perceived such incompatibility between their objectives, policies or measures that substantially sub-optimal outcomes were occurring.

Although modest in appearance these categories are far from being empty boxes. In the first category fall such issues as transport energy conservation, common external policies to COMECON trading demands, long term research on transport demand and so on. In the second lies the perennial problem of border crossings, through freight transport rates structures, vehicle dimensions and loadings, etc.

The difference between this approach and that adopted hitherto would be that common measures would be derived from, and related to, some measurable perceived mutual benefit. Vive la difference!

10 Energy and the EC

David W. Pearce and Richard Westoby

INTRODUCTION

Strictly speaking, the EC does not have a 'common' energy policy - see Hu (1980). By and large, member countries are free to pursue their own supply and demand control policies on an independent basis.[1] But, as with other resources, the concept of a common policy has been widely advocated as an integral part of the wider meaning of the EC. This chapter takes a preliminary look at <u>one</u> aspect of the early efforts to formulate such a policy, namely the setting of targets for the reduction of dependence on imports of crude or refined oil from countries outside the EC. The basis of this policy is straightforward and is commensurate with policy enunciated in non-EC countries: i.e. increased 'energy independence'. This produces social benefits which, while not quantified in practice, could be approximated by the welfare gains of non-interruption of supplies from monopolistic suppliers such as OPEC - see Weyman-Jones (1981). We attempt to answer the question: how far is the EC likely to succeed in achieving energy independence targets in the next decade?

In concentrating on import targets we ignore, in the main, the other strands on agreed EC policy to date. These are (a) the 'need' to develop nuclear energy, (b) the development of so-called 'new' sources of energy such as geothermal heat, solar energy, combined heat and power, and so on, (c) the development of the indigenous EC coal industry and (d) the extensive reference to energy conservation. However, it will be obvious that the extent to which energy independence is achieved is a function of what we might term 'natural' forces in the development of the economics of the EC which may raise or lower energy consumption per unit of economic activity, and on the other aspects of EC policy listed above. In turn, the success of the policy measure listed above will be determined by factors such as the social and political opposition to nuclear power in a number of EC countries, technological conditions which limit the rate of fuel switching, and the extensive problems of diffusing conservation policies across millions of energy consumers (on the latter problem, see Doyle and Pearce, 1979). In dealing with the central issue of whether a measure of energy independence <u>can</u> be obtained the chapter also ignores the <u>instruments</u> for achieving such an objective. As an example, an EC energy tax which has been widely advocated as the main instrument of a common energy policy (European Parliament, 1980/81).

MEASURING IMPORT DEPENDENCY AND SELF SUFFICIENCY

While concepts of 'import dependency' and the degree of 'self sufficiency' in energy are widely quoted, actual measurement of these concepts is not straightforward. The problem arises from the realities of international trade in energy products particularly from the re-export of imported energy. This latter problem arises specifically with imports of crude oil which are refined in a country and then re-exported to other countries. We can indicate the problem as follows:

The simplest measure of self-sufficiency is the ratio of domestically produced energy (P^d) to aggregate domestic consumption (C^d) of that energy source. Then for the ith fuel we have:-

$$C_i^d = P_i^d - X_i + M_i, \qquad (1)$$

where X and M are, respectively, exports and imports. Then our simple ratio of self sufficiency (ϕ_i) would be:

$$\phi_i = P_i^d / C_i^d.$$

In practice, this ratio is a <u>potential</u> self-sufficiency ratio since some of the domestic production of the ith fuel may be exported. If there were no imports, <u>actual</u> self-sufficiency (ϕ^*) would be measured by:

$$\phi_i^* = (P_i^d - X_i)/C_i^d. \qquad (3)$$

<u>Actual</u> and <u>potential</u> self-sufficiency would diverge according to the level of exports out of domestic production. Moreover, the 'gap' between actual and potential sufficiency may not be closable <u>in practice</u>. An example would be a country producing crude oil of a grade such that only part of that crude is suited as a refinery input in the given country. Or, more realistically, because

of the nature of the oil grade demand profile of the
industrial output of the country. The UK would be an
example. In this context, part of X_i is, as it were,
technologically predetermined, and some is not.   The
'potential' degree of self-sufficiency is thus readily
measured, but its operational meaning becomes unclear.

Note also that the measure of ϕ_i is not constrained to
be less than or equal to unity. Self-evidently, production
can exceed consumption, the balance being exported. The
measure of ϕ^*, however, is constrained to be equal to or
less than unity (ignoring stock changes and the treatment
of marine bunkers). The dominant requirement, however,
should be that any measure of ϕ is not negative. As long as
re-exports do not occur, X_i cannot exceed P_i^d in equation
(3) and this condition is met, as it is with equation (2).

The problem of which measure to use is compounded by any
consideration of imports. If the imports in question are
for direct indigenous consumption then equation (2) or (3)
can be used, and the ratio:

$$Z_i = M_i / C_i^d \qquad (4)$$

becomes the measure of import dependency. The intuitive
appeal of equation (3) now becomes apparent. Because (3)
cannot exceed unity, equation (4) must be equal to unity
minus ϕ^*. No such relationship applies to the use of (4)
with (2).

In practice, however, energy imports, notably crude oil,
are partly used for re-export. This would suggest that
equation (3) be further modified to:

$$\phi^{**} = (P_i^d - X_i^*)/C_i^d, \qquad (5)$$

where X_i^* = net exports. Equation (5) thus becomes a measure
of actual self-sufficiency and if the sign of net exports
is positive (i.e. net exports are deducted from domestic
production) this would be a measure of 'potential' self-
sufficiency if, and only if, the pattern of trade is
technologically determined in the sense discussed above.

Note however that equation (5) must be constrained to
have $X^* > 0$. Otherwise, negative net exports, i.e. net
imports[i], would be added to the numerator and appear as a
contributor to self-sufficiency. The problem now is that
use of equation (5) in a context of comparing countries,
some of whom are net importers, makes the comparison
illicit because different measures of self-sufficiency
would be in operation.

TABLE 10.1: ENERGY BALANCE SHEET FOR THE EC, 1979 (MTOE)

	Indigenous Supply							Exports	Imports				Total	% EUR 9 Consumption
	Hard Coal	Brown Coal	Petroleum Prod. + Crude Oil	Natural Gas	Electrical Energy	Nuclear Heat	Total*		Hard Coal	Crude Oil	Gas	Petroleum Products		
G	61.3	26.1	4.9	15.7	1.5	10.7	120.2	- 27.3	4.8	110.9	31.8	40.3	280.7	28.6
F	11.4	0.8	2.1	6.5	5.8	11.0	37.6	- 19.3	16.3	127.3	15.2	10.5	187.6	19.1
I	-	0.3	1.7	11.1	4.2	0.8	18.1	- 23.6	7.9	114.9	12.6	7.7	137.6	14.0
NL	-	-	1.6	70.8	-	0.9	73.3	- 81.0	3.1	59.4	1.6	19.9	76.3	7.8
B	4.0	-	-	0.0	0.0	2.8	6.8	- 17.3	5.8	34.2	9.7	9.9	49.1	5.0
L	-	-	-	-	0.0	-	0.0	- 0.0	0.2	-	0.5	1.4	2.1	0.2
UK	70.0	-	78.3	32.9	0.4	11.0	192.6	- 56.7	2.6	60.4	7.8	12.2	218.9	22.3
IRL	0.0	0.6	-	0.4	0.1	-	1.1	- 0.2	0.7	2.3	-	4.2	8.1	0.8
DK	-	-	0.4	-	0.0	-	0.4	- 2.7	4.5	8.7	-	9.1	20.0	2.0
TOTAL EUR 9	146.7	27.8	89.0	137.4	12.0	37.2	450.1	-228.1	45.9	518.1	79.2	115.2	980.4	100.0

* including where appropriate, other fuels.

Sources: Energy Statistics Yearbook (Eurostat) and Energy Balances of OECD countries 1975/1979 (IEA)

All this suggests that an 'ideal' measure of self-sufficiency can only be used in certain contexts. In the current chapter we use the 'naive' measure in equation (2). Equation (4) is used as a measure of import dependence where imports are from outside the EC.

EC ENERGY BALANCE, 1979

Table 10.1 shows the EC energy balance in 1979 - i.e. for each country it shows the components of aggregate domestic consumption (indigenous production - exports plus imports). The 'dominant' consumers are Germany, UK, France and Italy, in that order, comprising some 84 per cent of all the energy consumption of the 'Nine' in 1979. Self-sufficiency and import dependence cannot be identified readily from Table 10.1, however, since the export and import data include intra-EC trade.

SELF-SUFFICIENCY

Using the potential self-sufficiency measure (equation 2) gives us Tables 10.2 and 10.3, showing the ratios for 1975 and 1979. Taking the aggregate of all energy sources we see that potential self-sufficiency fell in all the 'Nine' except for the UK whose increased potential self-sufficiency is self-evidently accounted for by North Sea oil and gas. The potential self-sufficiency ratio for the Nine as a whole actually rose from 1975 to 1979 due entirely to the UK's change of energy fortune.

TABLE 10.2: POTENTIAL ENERGY SELF-SUFFIENCY
IN THE 'NINE' 1975(a)

Solids	Oil	Gas	Nuclear	Other Elec.	Agg. Energy
1.113	0.045	0.416	1.000	0.856	0.468
0.564	0.010	0.398	1.000	0.985	0.254
0.123	0.012	0.626	1.000	0.979	0.194
0	0.048	2.187	1.000	0	1.056
0.545	0	0.005	1.000	5.000	0.153
0	0	0	-	0.432	0.040
0.985	0.018	0.976	1.000	0.989	0.558
0.789	0	-	-	1.000	0.244
0	0.009	-	-	0.111	0.008
0.870	0.023	0.937	1.000	0.958	0.424

(a) $\phi_i = P_i^d / C_i^d$

TABLE 10.3: POTENTIAL ENERGY SELF-SUFFIENCY
IN THE 'NINE' 1979(a)

	Solids	Oil	Gas	Nuclear	Other Elec.	Agg. Energy
G						
F						
I	1.161	0.032	0.343	1.000	0.988	0.426
NL	0.435	0.010	0.324	1.000	0.979	0.238
B	0.099	0.017	0.478	1.000	0.959	0.172
L	0	0.038	2.158	1.000	0.000	0.928
IRL	0.383	0	0.003	1.000	4.333	0.135
DK	0	0	0	–	0.083	0.005
B	0.985	0.805	0.815	1.000	1.000	0.874
EUR	0.639	0	1.000	–	1.000	0.195
	0.050	0.027	–	–	0.036	0.032
9	0.830	0.157	0.795	1.000	0.963	0.462

(a) $\phi_i = P_i^d / C_i^d$

The move to self sufficiency has also been aided by
recession. Appendix 1 shows final energy consumption in the
various EC countries since 1970. The growth rates implicit in
these consumption levels are shown in Table 10.4 below.   It
will be seen that the growth in the consumption of energy has
slowed from 1973/4 compared to the average annual rate for
the whole period 1970-1979.

TABLE 10.4: GROWTH RATES IN ANNUAL ENERGY CONSUMPTION,
1970-79 (% p.a.)

	1970-1979	1973-1979	1974-1979
G	2.13	1.27	1.95
F	3.00	1.11	2.06
I	2.72	1.56	1.33
NL	3.90	1.90	2.72
B	2.00	0.90	1.58
L	-1.04	-2.86	-4.59
UK	0.49	-0.01	0.80
IRL	4.37	3.16	4.70
DK	0.04	0.58	2.59
EUR 9	2.04	1.01	1.68

Table 10.5 similarly shows the changes in economic growth. Clearly, had the 1970-1979 trend level of economic growth been sustained, the chances of greater self-sufficiency would have been less.

TABLE 10.5: GROWTH RATES IN REAL GDP, 1970-79 (% p.a.)

	1970-1979	1973-1979	1974-1979
G	2.98	2.44	2.74
F	3.79	2.96	2.90
I	2.85	2.36	2.04
NL	3.17	2.45	2.22
B	3.19	2.25	1.84
L	3.25	0.86	1.03
UK	2.16	1.21	1.73
IRL	3.91	3.52	3.46
DK	2.82	2.14	2.73
EUR 9	2.99	2.28	2.39

IMPORT DEPENDENCE

Appendix 2 provides data on intra-EC oil trade and trade with the rest of the world (ROW). The essentials are summarised in Table 10.6 below.

TABLE 10.6: INTRA- AND EXTRA-EC OIL TRADE, 1975-79

(a) PETROLEUM PRODUCTS (MTOE)

Imports by Exports from		EUR 9 (1)	ROW (2)	WORLD (1)+(2)
EUR 9	75	60.2	50.3	110.5
	77	66.4	56.3	122.7
	79	68.2	52.2	120.0
ROW	75	39.9		
	77	38.5		
	79	45.3		
WORLD	75	100.1		
	77	104.9		
	79	113.5		

(b) CRUDE OIL (MTOE)

Imports by Exports from		EUR 9 (1)	ROW (2)	WORLD (1)+(2)
EUR 9	75 77 79	1.6 9.7 23.1	0.3 6.1 15.7	1.9 15.8 38.8
ROW	75 77 79	477.3 485.1 490.6		
WORLD	75 77 79	478.9 494.8 517.9		

In terms of the actual oil import targets set in June
1979 by the European Council, which aimed at annual import
levels for 1980-1985 of about 470 MTOE (reportedly the 1978
level[2]), Table 10.6(b) illustrates some upward pressure on
imports regardless of the resolutions made. The relevant
entry is ROW's exports to the 'Nine' and it is seen that
this trade grew by about 2.7 per cent from 1975 to 1979.
However, this upward pressure was as low as it was for
reasons largely unconnected with the policy measures which
were meant to bring it about - i.e. expansion of other
energy supplies, and, more important in the short run,
conservation efforts. Table 10.6(b) shows that an increase
of more than 22 MTOE was obtained by intra-EC trade and the
detailed tables (see Appendix 2) indicate that this was
entirely due to North Sea oil, i.e. exports from the UK to
the rest of the EC. The second reason for the contained
upward pressure is not shown by the Table, but derives from
the lower rates of actual GDP growth compared to expected
rates. In short, in so far as the targets were met, they
had little to do with conscious policy efforts on the part
of EC members, especially as it seems fair to treat North
Sea oil as a 'fortuitous' gain for the EC in terms of
reduced imports from the rest of the world.
As indicated earlier, use of a simple oil import figure
could be misleading as a measure of 'dependence' if in fact
the imported crude oil is being used in any significant
quantities for re-export as refined products, or if there

is 'entrepot' trade - e.g. via Rotterdam. In fact, Table
10.6(a) shows EUR 9 exports of refined products to the rest
of the world were fairly constant at some 50 MTOE between
1975 and 1979. It follows that between 1975 and 1979, the
EC actually increased imports of crude oil from the rest of
the world by 13.3 MTOE [Table 10.6(b)], of which only 1.9
MTOE can be said to be 'accounted for' by re-export[3],
leaving 11.4 MTOE growth in imports plus 21.5 MTOE of crude
oil obtained from the UK [Table 10.6(b) and Appendix 2],
making a 'true' growth in oil consumption of 32.9 MTOE,
which is a significant growth in consumption. We conclude
that while the 1979 targets could be said to be being met,
at the start of the policy period (1980 to 1985), this was
only because of indigenous oil from the North Sea and
exogenous factors affecting economic growth.

TABLE 10.7: BREAKDOWN OF EC ENERGY CONSUMPTION, 1979

Total (MTOE) Consumption	Percentage Met from All Supplies					
	Hard Coal	Brown Coal	Oil and Oil Products	Natural Gas	Electrical Energy	Nuclear Heat
281.8	19.0	9.5	50.7	16.1	0.5	3.8
185.3	16.6	0.5	62.0	11.5	3.4	5.9
134.1	7.3	0.3	71.3	17.0	3.5	0.6
67.6	4.9	0.0	45.4	47.9	0.0	1.3
48.5	23.4	0.0	51.7	19.2	-0.2	5.7
3.8	47.0	0.8	33.4	12.3	6.2	-
219.8	34.2	-	42.2	18.4	0.2	5.0
8.4	9.9	10.3	73.7	5.3	0.8	-
20.3	21.4	-	77.2	-	1.4	-
969.7	19.7	3.0	54.2	17.8	1.4	3.8

THE PROSPECT FOR OIL INDEPENDENCE

We have argued so far that any measure of reduced
dependency by EC on non-EC oil imports can be accounted for
by economic recession and the gains to the EC from the
emergence of North Sea oil. The implied measure of
independence has thus been largely a political one in that
the UK has not been regarded as a member of any OPEC-style
grouping that would participate in interruption of supplies

of oil to the EC. If, however, the concern for independence
arises from a desire to reduce the impact of oil <u>price</u>
changes, then North Sea oil cannot be separated out from
the rest of the world oil. Quite simply, North Sea oil
prices are determined on the world market and the prospect
of bilateral deals between the UK and the rest of the EC
for North Sea oil at lower than world prices would seem
remote. In this second sense of independence therefore, the
EC has shown even less progress.

What then are the prospects for oil independence? In May
1980 EC energy ministers set longer term objectives in terms
of EC oil <u>consumption</u> - i.e. regardless of source - aiming
for a reduction of oil consumption as a percentage of
aggregate energy consumption to 40 per cent by 1990. The
picture of fuel shares is shown in Table 10.7. Clearly, the
only country which already meets the objective is Luxembourg,
but this is a diminutive consumer of energy
within the EC (see Table 10.1). Of the four 'dominant'
energy consumers - Germany, Italy, France and the UK - the
UK already converges on the 40 per cent target, Germany
would require a 20 per cent reduction in 1979 oil
consumption over 10 years, France some 35 per cent and
Italy a startling 44 per cent, assuming all other countries
met their objectives. The implications for small energy
consumers such as Denmark and Ireland are also formidable.

In order to gain some insight into what is implied by such
an objective we first make an attempt to estimate energy
demand in 1990. The approach we use is simplistic, but has
proved effective in a separate analysis of the UK - see
Pearce (1982) and Pearce and Westoby (1982). Basically, we
observe that while the much analysed 'energy coefficient'
(the elasticity of energy demand with respect to GDP) reveals
marked instability in the post-1973 period, the simpler
'energy ratio' (energy demand divided by GDP), to which it is
obviously related does not. Indeed, the energy ratio tends to
reveal very stable long term trends over the last century. By
relating the ratio to those factors thought to explain it, it
is possible to obtain a broad estimate of energy demand ten
years hence. Very simply, the forecasting equation would be:

$$\hat{E}_{90} = \hat{r}_{90} \cdot \hat{Y}_{90} \tag{6}$$

where
$$\hat{r}_{90} = \hat{E}_{90}/\hat{Y}_{90} \tag{7}$$

and
$$\hat{Y}_{90} = Y_{79} (1 + g)^{11} \tag{8}$$

where $\qquad$ $\hat{E}_{90}$ = estimated primary energy demand in 1990

$\hat{r}_{90}$ = energy ratio in 1990

$\hat{Y}_{90}$ = estimated EUR 9 GDP in 1990

g = EUR 9 economic growth rate.

Given an estimate of E_{90}, the EC policy target states that no more than 40 per cent of the consumption must come from oil - i.e.

$$\hat{E}_{90}^{OIL} < 0.4 \; \hat{E}_{90}. \qquad (9)$$

From (9), then, it is possible to see what the magnitude of oil consumption, and hence the implied conservation plus non-oil fuel supplies must be.

In this preliminary analysis, no attempt has been made to use a time series of the energy ratio to forecast the 1990 energy demand level <u>directly</u>. Rather we wish to see, first, if our earlier hypothesis that the energy ratio can be explained in terms of (a) the changing structure of GDP, (b) changing fuel mix and (c) changing energy price is sustained. If it is, we can then argue that continuation of certain industrial and energy trends will, in all probability, lead to a continued fall in the energy ratio in the EC. By extrapolation, the energy ratio for 1990 can be obtained from equations (6) to (8), and hence energy demand in 1990. An assumed economic growth rate is required and we set this at 3 per cent real GDP for 1979-1990 on the basis of the experience of the 1970s, inclusive of the oil price 'shock' period. We can then estimate the oil demand consistent with EC objectives as stated in the 1980 Ministerial resolution. The procedure is obviously crude but, we believe, reasonable for a preliminary analysis. The greatest degree of sophistication relates to the checking of the use of the energy ratio for forecasting purposes, even though the regression equation explaining the ratio is not itself used for prediction purposes. That is, we wish to see just how far certain 'natural' trends in the EC economy, notably towards deindustrialisation, will give the EC the context for achieving its oil use objective. Whatever remains to be done <u>after</u> such tendencies are allowed for, reveals the extent to which active policy on conservation and non-oil fuels must be pursued in the EC.

TABLE 10.8: SUMMARY RESULTS OF REGRESSION ANALYSIS WITH Es/GDP AS THE DEPENDENT VARIABLE

Regression	Constant	Coefficient on S.	Coefficient on N.	Coefficient on Es	G	F	I	NL	UK	L	R^2	D.W.
					DUMMY VARIABLES							
(1) Full Model no dummies	-2.434 (-4.376)	0.438 (1.879)	0.067 (1.230)	-1.150 (-6.622)	-	-	-	-	-	-	0.507	0.099
(2) Full Model with intercept dummies	-0.927 (-3.555)	0.452 (3.309)	0.013 (1.396)	-0.543 (-6.621)	-0.115 (-2.363)	-0.308 (-13.768)	-0.258 (9.717)	0.007 (0.282)	0.286 (5.801)	0.631 (17.439)	0.994	1.778
(3) Model without N, with intercept dummies	-0.745 (-3.268)	0.401 (3.015)	-	-0.457 (-8.336)	-0.131 (-2.725)	-0.323 (-16.374)	-0.281 (-13.401)	0.005 (0.202)	0.237 (6.817)	0.662 (23.334)	0.994	1.742
(4) Full Model with co-efficient dummies on S	-0.932 (-2.989)	0.116 (0.350)	-0.014 (-0.669)	-0.424 (-2.913)	0.195 (0.357)	0.236 (0.474)	-0.065 (-0.148)	0.136 (0.235)	0.253 (0.573)	0.308 (0.882)	0.998	2.400
N					0.035 (0.996)	-0.001 (-0.047)	0.033 (1.260)	0.035 (1.129)	-0.002 (-0.071)	0.035 (1.506)		
and Elec. share resp.					-0.010 (-0.055)	0.036 (0.187)	0.197 (1.082)	-0.026 (-0.110)	-0.233 (-1.115)	-0.336 (-2.644)		
(5) Same as (4) except without N	-0.771 (-3.546)	0.417 (1.702)	-	-0.474 (-5.736)	-0.292 (-1.160)	0.298 (1.071)	-0.498 (-1.908)	-0.497 (-1.545)	0.156 (0.619)	-0.057 (-0.252)	0.996	2.322
					0.164 (1.624)	0.010 (0.082)	0.369 (3.116)	0.224 (1.604)	-0.217 (-1.774)	-0.222 (-2.471)		

(t-values in parenthesis)

In order to analyse the relationship between the ratio
and the explanatory variables (a), (b) and (c) above we
develop a model which is specified in the following form:

$$r = \alpha \left[N^{\beta_1} S^{\beta_2} E_s^{\beta_3} \right]$$

where r is the energy ratio measured as gross inland
consumption (MTOE) per unit of GDP at 1975 prices and
purchasing power prices and purchasing power parities (Mrd
PPS). N is the real oil price (a proxy for real energy
price) measured as the average tax paid cost of equity oil
(Arabian Light) adjusted for inflation by the implicit
deflator for EC GDP at market prices (1975 = base). S is a
measure of changes in the structural composition of GDP
such that lower values of S are indicative of
deindustrialisation. In this case S is measured by the
output of manufactured products and building and
construction (gross value added at 1975 market prices) per
unit of GDP at 1975 prices and purchasing power parities.

E_s is a variable providing a measure of changes in the
fuel mix. In fact, as its name suggests, it is the share of
electricity consumption in total final energy consumption
in each EC country. α, $\beta 1$, $\beta 2$, and $\beta 3$ are the
parameters of the model to be estimated.

The estimation procedure used is ordinary least squares
which is first applied to the general model. In effect, the
values of α and β are being constrained to be the same
across different countries. This restriction is released on
the intercept terms only by introducing dummy variables.
The lack of statistical significance of N's coefficient
prompted a re-run of the regression without the oil price
variable. Regressions (2) and (3) in Table 10.8 have the
advantage that they partially deal with the
heteroscedasticity of the error term. Allowing intercept
terms to vary across countries is essentially the
covariance method for estimation with pooled data.

For the sake of completeness the model is estimated (with
and without the oil price variable) allowing the values of
β to vary, but restricting the α's to be equal across
countries. However, as expected, these regressions are of
limited use. The large number of parameters involved given
the limited data base means that it is difficult to obtain
low-variance estimates of the coefficients. In the
circumstances our preferred equation is (3).

In addition to its statistical properties equation (3)

has the merit of being readily translatable into direct
results. Since the N coefficient has been restricted to be
zero, the equation suggests that the direct effect of
changes in energy prices on the energy ratio in the short
run is minimal. It should be noted that energy prices may
well be very important via their indirect effects on the
energy ratio through their influence on fuel shares in the
energy market, and the structural composition of GDP,
particularly in the long run.

The coefficient of the equation tells us that a 1 per
cent <u>fall</u> in the electricity share is likely to result in a
0.457 <u>rise</u> in the energy ratio for countries in the EC. A 1
per cent fall in S, on the other hand, will result in a
0.401 per cent fall in the energy ratio.

Our assumption now is that, since changes in fuel mix and
the move towards service economies appear to be reasonably
good explanatory variables of the enegy-GDP ratio, and
since the movements in this ratio over time have been
downwards and stable, indicating greater 'efficiency' of
energy use per unit output, it is reasonable to extrapolate
the EC's energy ratio forward in time. That is, we expect
the factors explaining the past changes in the ratio to
continue being relevant in the 1980s. If anything, we would
expect longer term analysis to show the individual
importance of the real price of energy (as was the case in
our work on the UK).

Accordingly, we extrapolate the ratio using a simple
linear equation:

$$r = 0.835 - 0.0098T$$
$$(89.062)\ (-5.557)$$

with R^2 = 0.768, DW = 1.222 (inconclusive at 5 per cent
level). This would suggest a ratio for 1990 of 0.639 and
for 1985 of 0.688. Given our assumption about the growth of
EUR 9 GDP, it follows that we can obtain GDP for 1990 and
this is given by:

$$Y_{90} = 1266.1.(1.03)^{11} = 1752.6$$

Hence energy demand in 1990 would be given by:

$$r_{90}.Y_{90} = 111.9.9\ \text{MTOE}.$$

In turn, if the aim is to supply no more than 40 per cent
of this total from oil products, oil consumption cannot
exceed (0.4) (1119.9) = 448 MTOE.

Thus, by use of the energy ratio, by argument that the ratio is a stable declining function of time, and by taking a 'reasonable' economic growth rate for the EC for the 1980s, we suggest that the 1990 'independence' target can be translated into an absolute objective of not consuming more than, say, 450 MTOE.

Now oil consumption in 1979 in EUR 9 was some 530 MTOE, so that an effective reduction of 15 per cent in absolute consumption of oil is required over 10 years in the context of a moderate but sustained economic growth.

The final problem, then, is to decide whether such an objective is feasible given the kinds of policies which are regarded as integral to EC energy policy in so far as it is clearly formulated. The 'test' we propose is slightly unorthodox in that it does not rest on disaggregated estimates of what the indigenous supply industries can achieve, or rates at which boiler capacity can be converted to dual firing to allow the substitution of imported or indigenous steam coal for oil, and so on. Instead, we look at the professional judgement of one oil company, Shell, that has long been engaged in scenario analysis of oil trends in the world and individual countries. The procedures used are sophisticated but not widely disseminated, in terms of methodology anyway – see Choufoer (1982). We regard them as reliable assessments on the basis of past experience and use of the results for the UK in other work (Pearce et al, 1980).

The Shell analysis relevant to our own interest does not extend beyond 1985, but it still provides a good check on the feasibility of our estimated EC oil consumption target of 450 MTOE. Figure 10.1 shows the Shell scenario for all OECD Europe countries in terms of the ratio of oil consumption to GDP. The two reactive measures considered in the scenario are 'belt tightening' – i.e. further efforts to conserve energy through insulation, reduction of waste energy and so on – and 'further investment' which reflects the potential for the expanded supply in non-oil industries. The lowest point shown for 1985 suggest an oil/GDP ratio of some 55 per cent of its 1972 level: that is, what we would regard as the maximum feasible reduction in the ratio by 1985. Note that the range is wide and that the upper limit on feasibility is perhaps 75 per cent of the 1972 oil/GDP ratio.

We know that for the EC the oil/GDP ratio for 1972 was 0.492. The minimum feasible ratio for 1985 on Shell's analysis is thus:

$$(0.492) \ (0.55) = 0.271$$

and the upper end of the range is probably:

$$(0.492) \ (0.75) = 0.369.$$

We also project 1985 EC GDP to be 1512 thousand million PPS[4] which would mean that Shell's range for <u>feasible</u> oil consumption, i.e. given conservation and investment measures, is:

$$(0.271) \ (1512) \ \text{to} \ (0.369) \ (1512) = 410\text{--}558 \ \text{MTOE}$$

To relate this to our own suggested 'targets' for the EC if it is to meet its 1980 resolution goals we need to know the <u>path</u> that might be taken in achieving the objective. If, for simplicity, we assume that the reduction in oil consumption as a percentage of all energy consumption proceeds at a constant rate, the oil/energy ratio would be about 46.5 per cent in 1985. To see what the target means for 1985 in absolute terms, then, we require:

$$r_{85} \cdot Y_{85} \cdot O/E_{85} = (0.688) \ (1511.8) \ (0.465)$$

$$= 484 \ \text{MTOE}$$

The previous analysis suggests that to be 'on target' for its 1990 objective, EC would have to be consuming no more than 484 MTOE in 1985, and, of course, it must be assured that there are no diminishing returns to efforts for reduced oil dependence. Now, the 484 MTOE fits neatly into the suggested EC feasible range implied by Shell's analysis. The Shell analysis has been adapted for EC but using feasibility assumptions for OECD Europe. We see no reason to adjust for the inclusion of non EC countries in OECD Europe. However, a possible upwards adjustment may be in order (i.e. reduced feasibility). This is to some extent borne out by a comparison of what Shell believe the energy-GDP ratio will be for OECD in 1985 compared to our own estimates. Shell's data implies a ratio of 0.615, whereas our own extrapolations suggest 0.688. Arguably, by dividing these two ratios, we can secure a crude adjustment for what we would thus regard as an element of optimism in the Shell data. The adjustment factor would be $0.688/0.615 = 1.12$. This could then be applied to the Shell feasibility range, changing it to a range of 461–625 MTOE. If adjustments of this kind are even approximately correct, we now see that the 1985 'target' of 484 million tonnes is still within the

FIGURE 10.1: SHELL SCENARIO FOR OECD EUROPE

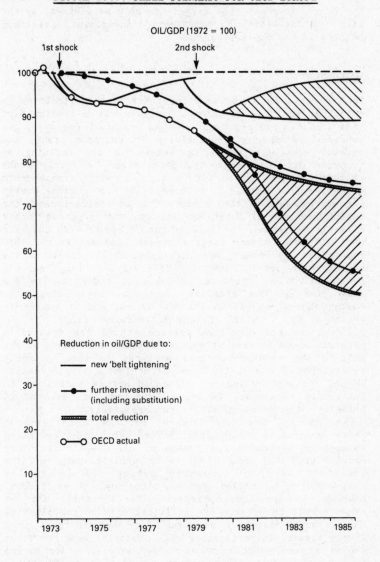

OIL/GDP (1972 = 100)

1st shock 2nd shock

Reduction in oil/GDP due to:

——— new 'belt tightening'

—●— further investment (including substitution)

▓▓▓ total reduction

○—○ OECD actual

range, but is perhaps perilously close to the lower end of
the range. In short, the target can only be achieved by the
kind of substantial conservation/investment programme
posited in the Shell scenario.

CONCLUSION

We have observed throughout that there are difficulties in
defining 'energy independence' targets for a trading bloc
that includes one major oil and gas producer, one major gas
producer, a country specialising in entrepôt trade, and
several countries which specialise in the refining of
imported oil for re-export. Nonetheless, a fairly clear
picture emerges. In so far as the EC energy independence
objectives can be held to be consistent with current energy
consumption levels, they achieve this objective through the
fortuitous gain of North Sea oil and the exogenous factor
of world recession. Analysis of the decade to 1990 suggests
that oil independence targets of the kind set in the 1980
resolution can be met, but that substantial efforts on the
conservation front and in diversifying into non-oil
technologies are required. We suggest these results are
indicative of the fragility of even fairly simplistic
energy objectives within the EC. If so, and if energy is
accepted as a vital policy-determining factor in EC
politics in the next two decades, there are formidable
problems ahead for any attempt to formulate a common energy
policy. The obverse of this argument is that an early
recognition of the difficulties of achieving simple 'goals'
on oil consumption and imports could act as a catalyst to
integrative measures. We leave it to the students of EC
politics to gauge which effect is more likely.
     What then is the 'way forward' for the EC in terms of
energy policy? We would gauge that market forces, operating
through an increased real price of oil despite temporary
'gluts' in 1981 and 1982, will achieve many of the
immediate aims of Community policy. In so far as
intervention is called for to 'top up' those forces,
however, we are less optimistic. The Community has not
shown itself to possess the political will to grapple with
the major adjustments required for the redirection of
energy trends. In particular, the Community, like any other
energy consuming nation needs to pay more attention to the
fact that energy policy cannot be pursued as if it is
something different to economic policy in all its
complexity. We argue that we have shown this already simply
by demonstrating the forceful relationship between the

structure of GDP and energy consumption. By concentrating on energy conservation and fuel switches the Community is engaging in a wholly understandable but short term policy. In the long term, the way forward lies in a much bigger 'push' into oil substitution policies, in the matching of the heat content of supplies to end-uses, and in technological change to develop high value added, low energy techniques of production. In this the Community faces the same problems as many countries the world over. Its particular problem is that it must achieve this objective with a quasi-federal structure of government and a probable sustained level of mutual suspicion between energy abundant and energy dependent members. In this sense, the future for energy policy is predominantly determined by political will and not be economic and technical forces.

ACKNOWLEDGEMENT

We wish to acknowledge the generous support of the Leverhulme Trust for financial support for the project giving rise to this chapter.

NOTES:

1. For a description of individual EC country energy policies, see International Energy Agency (1980).
2. See Central Statistical Office (1981). There are difficulties in making different sources of statistics comparable given: (a) different definitions of 'crude oil'; (b) allowances for stock changes (including stockpiling); (c) bunkers; and (d) errors in the recorded statistics in different sources.
3. Obviously, one cannot trace 'barrels of oil' so that the 're-exports' could equally well have been exports of refined indigenous UK crude oil.
4. PPS = Purchasing Power Standard. In 1975, £1 = 2.15 PPS.

APPENDIX 1: TABLE 1

DATA: TOTAL FINAL ENERGY CONSUMPTION (MTOE)

	1970	1970	1972	1973	1974	1975	1976	1977	1978	1979
G	177.30	178.18	188.00	202.82	194.54	181.69	190.90	190.65	199.34	211.81
F	115.98	119.76	126.65	140.40	136.46	129.78	135.31	135.88	143.97	155.68
I	90.69	94.51	99.56	105.78	104.96	100.21	105.70	103.02	104.46	109.81
NL	37.82	39.19	46.21	49.73	49.11	48.30	53.73	52.44	56.70	61.79
B	32.64	32.28	34.99	36.99	36.03	33.24	35.21	34.89	36.73	38.49
L	3.82	3.76	3.86	4.10	4.60	3.58	3.61	3.44	3.77	3.58
UK	146.31	143.76	146.39	154.44	147.82	139.81	143.53	146.72	147.62	153.60
IRL	5.14	5.64	5.49	5.51	5.88	5.31	5.43	5.82	5.89	6.71
DK	15.71	15.25	15.63	15.92	13.85	14.29	15.68	16.01	16.18	16.51
EUR 9	625.39	632.29	666.70	715.62	693.17	656.21	689.09	688.88	714.65	757.98

Source: Energy Balances of OECD Countries, 1975/1979 (IEA)

APPENDIX 2: TABLE 1

CRUDE OIL 1975 (000 tonnes)

(EXPORTS TO)

EXPORTS	G	F	I	NL	B-L	UK	IRL	DK	EUR 9	Rest of World	World
G	·	·	·	14	·	·	·	·	14	·	14
F	·	·	·	·	·	·	·	·	·	·	·
I	·	·	·	·	·	·	·	·	·	·	·
NL	55	·	154	·	219	349	·	·	777	·	777
B-L	·	·	·	·	·	·	·	22	22	60	82
UK	40	·	·	276	·	·	485	·	801	252	1053
IRL	·	·	·	·	·	·	·	·	·	·	·
DK	·	·	·	·	·	·	·	·	·	·	·
EUR 9	95	·	154	290	219	349	485	22	1614	312	1926
Rest of World	91023	106081	95859	54246	29293	90412	2417	7915	477246		

Source for Appendix 2:   OECD, Statistics of Foreign Trade and Energy; Eurostat, Statistics Yearbook

APPENDIX 2: TABLE 2

1977 CRUDE OIL (000 tonnes)
(EXPORTS TO)

EXPORTS FROM	G	F	I	NL	B-L	UK	IRL	DK	EUR 9	Rest of World	World
G	·	·	·	·	·	·	·	·	·	·	·
F	207	·	·	·	·	·	·	·	207	·	207
I	·	·	·	·	·	·	·	·	·	·	·
NL	·	·	·	·	·	·	·	1	1	·	1
B-L	·	·	·	·	·	·	·	·	·	·	·
UK	2645	1651	·	3571	119	·	478	968	9432	5854	15286
IRL	·	·	·	·	·	112	·	·	112	·	112
DK	·	·	·	1	·	·	·	·	1	215	216
EUR 9	2852	1651	·	3572	119	112	478	969	9753	6069	15822
Rest of World	95302	115732	105368	56063	35418	68735	2206	6301	485125		

APPENDIX 2: TABLE 3

1979 CRUDE OIL (000 tonnes)
(EXPORTS TO)

	G	F	I	NL	B-L	UK	IRL	DK	EUR 9	Rest of World	World
G	.	.	.	.	.	.	.	.	.	.	.
F	.	.	.	.	.	.	.	.	.	.	.
I	.	.	.	.	.	.	.	.	.	.	.
NL	2	.	.	.	13	.	.	.	15	.	15
B-L	.	.	.	.	.	.	.	.	.	.	.
UK	9775	2660	.	6974	268	.	373	3019	23069	15722	38791
IRL	.	.	.	.	.	.	.	.	.	.	.
DK	.	.	.	.	.	.	.	.	.	.	.
EUR 9	9777	2660	.	6974	281	.	373	3019	23084	15722	38806
Rest of World	98310	124281	114004	54678	33141	58351	2219	5664	490648		

(EXPORTS FROM)

APPENDIX 2: TABLE 4

1975 PETROLEUM PRODUCTS (000 tonnes)
(EXPORTS TO)

	G	F	I	NL	B-L	UK	IRL	DK	EUR 9	Rest of World	World
G	.	1021	86	615	378	428	.	565	3093	5139	8232
F	2883	.	979	553	725	972	.	163	6275	4280	10555
I	1264	910	.	2360	175	1116	.	234	6059	12373	18432
NL	15478	718	822	.	3472	4701	44	2375	27610	15248	42858
B-L	2408	380	370	1701	.	1592	10	1193	7654	5896	13550
UK	632	147	251	2661	313	.	2497	2181	8682	5278	13960
IRL	.	.	.	10	.	470	.	.	480	4	484
DK	112	.	.	63	.	218	.	.	393	2059	2452
EUR 9	22777	3176	2508	7963	5063	9497	2551	6711	60246	50277	110523
Rest of World	14431	4742	6468	1490	4867	3288	444	4135	39865		
World	37208	7918	8976	9453	9930	12785	2995	10846	100110		

(EXPORTS FROM)

APPENDIX 2: TABLE 5

1977 PETROLEUM PRODUCTS (000 tonnes)
(EXPORTS TO)

	G	F	I	NL	B-L	UK	IRL	DK	EUR 9	Rest of World	World
G	·	975	87	798	411	514	·	499	3284	5218	8502
F	3274	·	1700	971	593	896	185	353	7972	5901	13873
I	660	1935	·	1677	197	1737	41	349	6596	14940	21536
NL	17017	542	604	·	3770	4031	83	2369	28416	17001	45417
B-L	3868	362	230	1794	·	3475	81	1520	11330	5452	16782
UK	1069	576	206	1477	436	·	2613	2062	8439	6186	14625
IRL	·	·	·	·	·	4	·	·	4	·	4
DK	27	·	115	55	1	174	·	·	372	1562	1934
EUR 9	25915	4390	2942	6772	5408	10831	3003	7152	66413	56260	122673
Rest of World	15005	3815	6270	2576	3884	2219	557	4146	38472		
World	40920	8205	9212	9348	9292	13050	3560	11298	104885		

APPENDIX 2: TABLE 6

1979 PETROLEUM PRODUCTS (000 tonnes)
(EXPORTS TO)

	G	F	I	NL	B-L	UK	IRL	DK	EUR 9	Rest of World	World
G	.	989	57	618	486	418	.	189	2757	4663	7420
F	2676	.	976	1851	835	1268	301	510	8417	7726	16143
I	316	1897	.	5208	300	1230	82	47	9080	15179	24259
NL	16249	817	133	.	4599	4236	91	2378	28503	14569	43072
B-L	3631	349	155	2423	.	1713	54	616	8941	5012	13953
UK	1068	907	125	2306	815	.	2865	1673	9759	3174	12933
IRL	28	3	11	1	.	93	.	.	136	12	148
DK	32	61	.	152	21	354	.	.	620	1841	2461
EUR 9	24000	5023	1457	12559	7056	9312	3393	5413	68213	52176	120335
Rest of World	15978	5385	6024	6473	3979	2723	759	3981	45303		
World	39978	10408	7481	19032	11035	12035	4152	9394	113515		

(EXPORTS FROM)

11 The Impact of Social Policy in the United Kingdom

Doreen Collins

The argument for the integration of Western Europe through the creation of the three communities, ECSC, EEC and Euratom, did not depend for its essentials upon the need for a strong social policy at supra-national level. The analysis was far more concerned with broad political and economic issues whose positive effect upon social well-being, although very significant in a general sense, would be mainly indirect. Whilst it is impossible to under-rate the importance of achieving a stable political environment and of encouraging the growth of resources as a contribution to social welfare, in large part the construction of the Community left the specific use of such larger resources under the control of member governments.

Nevertheless, certain questions of a social nature became subject to commitments although these were themselves of varying degrees. Issues seen to be related to the immediate task of Community building were identified and appropriate provision made, but it was also fully recognised that little was known about specific national social obligations on a comparative basis and less about the effect such obligations would have on the building of the new unit, so considerable emphasis was laid on the need for consultation, investigation and research, on the functions of the Community institutions to ensure that such activities were undertaken and on the Community right to take subsequent action should it be required.

A positive influence came from the experience of the ECSC which had taught certain valuable lessons about the role of an international organisation in the field of social policy. Pioneering efforts had been made in the investigation of social questions whilst direct measures to improve housing, health and safety standards at work had begun. The executive had learnt of the need to work with local bodies, unions and employers, not just central governments, and to begin to relate social activity to

213

broader issues such as regional development. Its provision of cash benefits to individual workers in the coal and steel industries where the labour force was being run down or retrained had helped to establish the public acceptability of the new organisation and encouraged states to develop schemes which would be eligible for ECSC grant aid. In this way the grants had a stimulatory effect on member state action. In total, therefore, the social experience of the ECSC had been a positive one upon which the new institutions would be anxious to build to establish a competence of wider applicability.

SOCIAL POLICY IN THE TREATY OF ROME

Despite the hesitancy in the original Treaties concerning the role of social policy it has shown a considerable growth since the early years. This suggests that, in certain areas at any rate, a useful function can be performed by the EC. Before discussing the present scope of social policy, however, it will probably be helpful to summarise the provisions of the Treaty of Rome which form the base upon which policy is still primarily built.

One of the major aims of the EC is defined as the constant improvement of the living and working conditions of the population and this objective is taken up again as the major theme of the section of the Treaty entitled social policy. It is done by stating the agreement of member states upon the need for such a development and not by giving the EC, qua EC, an obligation to take its own action to ensure that progress occurs. This is a critical distinction for it implies that any new social policy initiative on the part of the EC must be fought for de novo and cannot be subsumed under the general rubric of a redistributive policy. The discussions of recent years on the 'anti-poverty programme' make clear that this is still the case. Thus, from the start, member states jealously guarded their position as the main fountain head of social progress whilst cautiously recognising that the processes of the 'common market' and the evolution of legislative acts by the EC would no doubt influence national social policies towards a future harmonious development. Since, however, it was recognised that very little was actually known about the provisions in force in the member states and even less about their possible impact upon the process of European integration, it was arranged that the Commission should have the responsibility to promote close collaboration between members in the social field. Whilst nothing was said formally about the purpose of such collaboration, it appears to have been generally understood that it was a necessary preliminary to decision as to whether existing provision did in fact impede the operation of the 'common market' and thus to the extent to which Community legislation would be necessary to control this effect.[1]

This caution on the part of member states was observed at the time of signature in 1957 and, subsequently, the same defensive attitude was expressed in Britain when the issue of accession required domestic discussion. Fears of an attack on the British welfare state were quietened with the statement that whilst we might find an obligation to change certain detailed rules we would be left free, as was each member state, to determine our own arrangements in the provision of social security benefits and health care. All that was asked of us was to engage in close collaboration over social matters which might lead to the harmonisation of policy as improvements spread through the population. "We shall expect to join in that upward harmonisation but there will be no obligation upon us to change" and we will never be forced to take a decision against our national interest.[2] Although over the years there have been many discussions about a policy of harmonisation and the equalisation of social standards it now seems generally accepted that any formal policy is inappropriate in view of differences in national priorities, GDP, living standards and patterns of life so that the principle remains as a general context within which joint discussions, studies and reasearch may be carried on and specific obligations on certain matters, such as industrial health, may be undertaken when the need for them arises.

Very considerable concern had been expressed at the time of discussion of the new Treaty over the incidence of social charges and of equal pay legislation on the competitive position of firms and this accounted for the insertion of particular provisions into the Treaty. A definite obligation to ensure and maintain the principle of equal pay for equal work was undertaken and members agreed to try to maintain their existing arrangements for holidays with pay. A general report on social developments was to be drawn up by the Commission each year supplemented by reports on particular issues as the need was felt. The possibility of asking the Commission to undertake other tasks to implement common measures was allowed for. All these provisions suggest a heavy emphasis on finding out more about social questions and their impact on integration and the assumption of general powers under which future action might be taken should it prove necessary rather than the blueprint for a formal social policy at supra-national level.

A most important obligation was undertaken in the Treaty of Rome to secure the free movement of workers within the Community and to ensure that there should be no discrimination based on nationality regarding wages and conditions of work. It thus became necessary to ensure that there were no such barriers to: workers accepting offers; looking for work; living in a new country; and remaining permanently if they so wished. It was recognised that such a policy would require effective collaboration between employment services not just to circulate a knowledge of job opportunities and available workers but to systematise such information in ways to make it usable throughout the Community. The growth of social security schemes on a national basis can also act as a deterrent to movement and the better they are the more likely it is that people will be reluctant to move. Thus arrangements were made to maintain entitlement to benefit by aggregating eligibility periods spent in any part of the EC, ensuring benefits are paid anywhere and maintaining cover for dependants.

A similar principle of free movement, although with different rules and methods of applicability, was applied to self-employed people and to the supply of services across national frontiers. Whilst this principle has been applied relatively easily to business activity it has required considerable negotiation where professional services are involved because of the varying protective rules surrounding the provision of such services and the educational patterns which lie behind them. Thus services are only gradually being liberalised but both medical and legal services have established arrangements.[3]

Whilst the physical movement of workers into the towns from the countryside and from areas of unemployment was a striking feature of the European economy at the time of the formation of the EC and subsequently, occupational mobility is also a characteristic of working life and the EC set up the European Social Fund (ESF) to assist with both tasks. This represents the major grant-aiding facility that the EC possesses in the social field (see below). The belief in the need for the qualitative improvement of the labour force led to a statement of the need to establish general principles for a common policy on vocational training but in practice this has proved less necessary than originally thought so that attention is concentrated today on an outline agreement and on research and study programmes rather than on fundamental changes in national training schemes. Similarly, a specific arrangement to encourage the exchange of young workers has never developed on the scale that was originally envisaged. It has been overtaken

with the growth of tourism and student exchanges, but a
modest programme continues.

These represented the main social policy outlines of the
Treaty. It should be appreciated that the free movement of
labour policy, together with the commitments that flow from
it, was not classified as social policy at all but seen as
a necessary ingredient of a 'common market'. Taking the
Treaty as a whole, however, it can be seen that social
policy concentrated on employment matters and, together
with certain specific formal undertakings, relied very
heavily on long term co-operation and agreement so that
states would move steadily in the same direction in the
pursuit of their own social policies. Although the Treaty
was criticised from time to time for its weakness in social
policy, in fact considerable developments occurred which
prepared the way for new initiatives which were noticeable
during the 1970s. The reasons for a new upsurge of interest
in the social policy role of the EC need to be considered
for it coincided with the period of the debate on, and the
fact of, British entry into the EC.

THE SUBSEQUENT DEVELOPMENT OF SOCIAL POLICY

The boom years of the 1960s brought with them a rapid
development of social expenditure by national governments.
The changes in health care systems, social security
structures and educational facilities which had been
ushered in by post-war reforms and which were aimed at
extending coverage comprehensively over the population were
now beginning to bear fruit. Improvements in medical
technology, rising demand for health care, greater
comprehensiveness of old age pensions and child benefits,
more young people entering higher and further education all
required rapid expansion of provision and suggested that
demand in such areas was infinite. The realisation that,
unchecked, the demand for social welfare would outrun the
capacity generated by economic growth brought such issues
into the highest councils of the EC as it tried to consider
the future of its economy. The introduction of medium term
economic policy programming in 1967 marked, therefore, an
important stage in the recognition of social policy
concerns by the EC by posing the need for quantitive
assessments of future expenditures and by recognising its
significance in the growth of public expenditure. In turn,
the programme influenced the adoption of a similar approach
in the social field, namely the construction by the
Commission of the European Social Budget. It is unfortunate

that the exercise acquired such a misleading name for it is not an account of EC social spending as one might expect. It is a statement of spending through social security and health care systems by member states over a five year period. It therefore provides much valuable information of a comparative nature on coverage and trends as well as providing an assessment of resources likely to be required. The collation of such material makes it easier to identify common trends, different priorities and coverage gaps so that it serves as a basis for discussing further social policy development but it has to be remembered that the exercise is not fully comprehensive and far more staff resources would be necessary if it were to extend into other fields of social expenditure such as social housing, educational systems, employment conditions, environmental protection and the use of taxation systems as a social instrument. Nevertheless it contributes to the knowledge necessary for the harmonisation goal. Despite the increase in social spending of the time, the unevenness of growth proved to be one of its more notable characteristics. The second half of the 1960s marked the re-discovery of poverty within affluence as certain groups appeared not to benefit from increased standards of living.   Far from being peculiar to one country the phenomenon appeared generally, although the particular groups who were forced into the margin of the affluent society were not necessarily the same in each country.[4] The elderly did form a common group because of their growing number and the general lack of buoyancy in pension levels, but large families, single-parent families, migrants and the handicapped were further examples of groups whose living standards tended to be relatively depressed. The cumulative decline of facilities and services in the inner cities as the better-off moved into the suburbs, the lack of social integration of migrants and their families, the sense of increasing social division as the arbitrary nature of improvements was realised, all contributed to a re-assessment of the role of social policy in modern society.   Concepts of fairness, equality and social justice came to be applied to the discussions in such varied fields as incomes, access to health care and to educational facilities. It merged into larger questions subsumed in the phrase 'the quality of life' which began to incorporate aspects of environmental welfare as well. Thus the inter-relationship of social policy, in the narrower sense of social welfare benefits, with the broader social goals of the Community and its economic health became increasingly self-evident. As the Commission began to discuss the development of the EC for the 1970s it proved not immune to these broader questions[5], whilst the politicians meeting in Paris in October 1972 also showed their sensitivity to the changing mood.

The Summit meeting, the first to be attended by the UK as a member of the EC, laid considerable stress on the Community's social role and can therefore be accounted the moment from which a new impetus in social policy can be dated. The heads of government announced that social policy was of equal importance to the EC as the goal for economic and monetary union, referred to the willingness to adopt concrete measures with corresponding resources and referred particularly to the importance of reforming the ESF.[6] This statement led to the formulation of the Social Action Programme (SAP)[7], accepted by the Council of Ministers in 1974, which has formed the starting point for subsequent moves in the various fields of social policy through developing and firming up the work which had begun earlier and, it was hoped, would give social policy a greater importance and more attention in Community activities.

THE EXECUTION OF SOCIAL POLICY

The interest in employment remains as the core of the Community's social policy as the major objectives of the SAP demonstrate. These are the attainment of full and better employment, the improvement of living and working conditions so as to make possible their harmonization while the improvement is being maintained and increased involvement of management and labour in the economic and social decisions of the Community and of workers in their firms. Since the work of the EC is now very wide, certain areas of work have been singled out here for discussion, drawing attention to the impact of such activity in the UK.

(i) Health and Safety at Work

A major area of EC interest has always lain in this important field. A special effort was made from 1951 in relation to the coal and steel industries where an obligation to encourage research into safety matters exists. Safety and Health Committees exist for both industries. Similarly the Euratom Treaty contains an obligation to ensure the protection of workers and basic standards concerning the emission of ionising radiation have been established. The prevention of occupational accidents and diseases is one of the many fields of co-operation specified under the Treaty of Rome and in 1978 a new programme of work was adopted. An example of the effect

is the 1980 Directive on the protection of workers from
exposure to chemical, physical and biological agents.[8]
Directives also exist on safety signs at work. It is of
course true that such activities are also conducted on a
national scale but an extra stimulus comes from working co-
operatively in such matters. It is signficant that a Times
Report of a policy paper prepared by Congress House staff
for trade union leaders quoted it as saying "On the other
hand EEC legislation has sometimes been beneficial,for
example in helping to achieve high health and safety
standards."[9]

The concern for health and safety is now being extended
further. An example is the contribution to a healthier
environment deriving from the EC Directive on the purity of
water supplies, a matter which in many instances cannot be
controlled by one state alone.[10]

(ii) Working Conditions

A general framework to protect the interests of workers in
an economy affected by the growth of multi-national
companies, take-over bids and bankruptcies rests on three
directives. The need to approximate national laws over mass
dismissals by insisting upon consultation, notification to
the employment authority and to safeguard employees' rights
when businesses are transferred or become insolvent have
all been recognised.[11]

Through such legislative acts, of which only examples
have been given, the EC undoubtedly plays a part in
establishing a framework within which material action to
improve living and working conditions may be pursued.

(iii)Employment Aids

The most obvious impact on working life made by the EC is
through its grant-aiding facilities provided by the ESF and
the ECSC.

The creation of the EC led to the establishment of a fund
to aid schemes for labour retraining and resettlement. It
is unfortunate that the name of the fund still gives rise
to misunderstanding in the UK where it is often assumed
that the fund has general grant aiding capacity in the
social welfare field whereas it is primarily geared to
employment questions, although there are a few exceptions.
It is better, therefore, to think of it as a European
Employment Training Fund. After a number of years in which
the ESF was used to support schemes of labour mobility as
workers moved from agriculture into industrial employment,
the Fund was reformed in order to provide it with a
function more related to the changing employment situation
and in which the EC itself would have greater influence on
the nature of schemes to be supported. A Council decision

in 1971[12] established two broad categories of function. The first relates to the effect of large scale changes in the economy and of the development of the Community itself on employment opportunities and the second to the need to assist states' own employment policies aimed at helping in regional development, in responding to technical changes and in aiding the handicapped to obtain open employment. The first category (usually known as Art 4 interventions) is based on specific decisions by the Council of Ministers to support schemes for particular groups of workers. These include persons leaving agriculture and textiles, women, migrant workers and young people. The second (Art 5 interventions) is particularised by the categories mentioned above but an agreement ensures that at least half the ESF Budget is spent in the regions under Act 5. In recent years, the choice of applications under all headings has led to a situation in which about 80 per cent of ESF money is directed to schemes situated in the regions.[13]

Whilst the ESF has been increasing in real terms in recent years it has by no means kept pace with demand or with the rapid growth in unemployment rates. Applications in 1980 exceeded resources by nearly 60 per cent[14] and were particularly heavy in some of the smaller categories such as schemes for women and migrant workers. The commitment allocation for the Fund in 1981 was 963m ECU (Approx. £500m) but this is only about 4.8 per cent of the total Community Budget.[15] It was agreed at the Summit meeting in November 1981 that the ESF should be significantly increased[16] but this depends upon agreement being reached to curtail agricultural expenditure for there is no sign that member states are willing to increase the resources available to the EC at the present time. It must be expected, therefore, that competition for awards will remain keen and that the impact they have on employment will be limited.

Although the Commission is to some extent in touch with actual schemes it is not in a position to administer grants directly and it relies heavily upon member governments to perform this function, to advise it on applications, to ensure the necessary publicity and to act as a clearing house for applications and most grants. This causes a degree of frustration, delay and difficulty particularly for non-governmental organisations who are often particularly vulnerable to uncertainties about grant-aid but who find themselves dealing with bureaucratic hierarchies which can find it difficult to respond quickly. This dependence also enables member governments to exercise considerable influence on the destination of grants.

However, a feature of the ESF is that it has resisted the imposition of national quotas for grant aid. In theory, at least, grants can be allocated according to priority criteria, although in practice there is clearly some consideration to national destination, as table 11.1 demonstrates. (The special column for 1977-8 should be disregarded from this point of view in that it related to adjustments required by the introduction of a new European monetary unit.)

TABLE 11.1 : ASSISTANCE BY COUNTRY[17](%)

	'73	'74	'75	'76	'77/'78	'77	'78	'79	'80
Belgium	3.9	2.6	2.2	1.8	0.7	1.5	2.0	2.1	2.9
Denmark	2.8	4.7	2.4	2.4	0.2	2.3	2.5	1.9	1.9
Germany	10.9	10.9	11.2	10.2	5.9	9.6	10.1	6.8	10.6
France	17.7	19.6	19.8	17.5	18.6	20.4	15.2	17.4	19.2
Ireland	5.4	6.6	6.1	7.2	7.3	7.6	7.8	7.5	7.9
Italy	24.0	28.4	27.7	33.3	57.5	19.5	41.0	36.3	32.3
Luxembourg	0.1	0.1	0.1	0.1	0.1	–	–	0.1	0.1
Netherlands	3.7	2.6	2.9	2.9	–	2.0	1.7	2.5	1.8
United Kingdom	31.5	24.5	29.6	24.4	9.7	37.1	19.7	25.4	23.3

The reform of the ESF is now (1982) being discussed in Brussels and the major issue appears to be whether grants should be increasingly diverted to schemes designed to keep people in work and to job creation projects of various kinds rather than be used primarily for retraining. Priority is already given, where possible, to training in cases where there is a specific job awaiting the trainee but this is not always practical. In the case of the Manpower Services Commission (MSC) schemes of open-ended training have always been carried out in the hope of improving the general skill level in an area and developing the pool of applicants rather than a more tailor-made

approach on an individual basis and there are good reasons
for this policy. However, the Commission wishes to avoid
being placed in a position in which it is grant-aiding
projects whose trainees have no realistic prospect of
obtaining work. The question now is the extent to which
grant aid should be tied to schemes specifically designed
to ensure openings which the market itself is not
providing. There are already some possibilities open to the
ESF under its existing rules which could be promoted more
actively quite apart from any new policy initiatives. These
include aid for workers over 50 years of age for the first
6 months of vocational retraining and aid to supplement the
wage paid to a newly employed worker, again for 6 months,
where work is provided in the regions.[18] In December 1978,
the Council also agreed to support work experience and job
creation schemes for young people under 25 years old.[19]
Obviously there are precedents here for further development
of supportive activity but it must be remembered that,
until such time as the ESF obtains a significant injection
of resources, this would inevitably be at the expense of
other worthwhile schemes.

The main shape of the Budget for the ESF is determined by
the Commission when it forms the Preliminary Draft Budget
and this is its opportunity to indicate its view of
relative priorities among the various tasks. However the
budget is subsequently submitted to a long drawn out
political process, notably the battle between the
Parliament and the Council of Ministers, in the course of
which the ESF budget may undergo considerable change. The
final allocations for the Fund thus represent the
equilibrium obtained between these various political
forces.

It will be seen (Tables 11.2 and 11.3) how important the
support of young people and of regional schemes has become
at the present time and this policy was reinforced at the
Summit meeting of November 1981. It was agreed that special
attention must be given at present to young people in, or
seeking, their first job and that, when more efficient and
reformed, the ESF should be steered towards the most needy
zones, particularly those facing a decline of traditional
manufacturing industries.[21] These priorities are obviously
useful to the UK, which is currently concentrating
considerable effort in these fields and also looks to the
EC for financial support in return for her general budget
contributions. This latter aim is ensured in that most
schemes in these two categories are run in the UK by the
MSC so that the allocations are a direct advantage to
government accounts. Since the UK cannot expect to receive

TABLE 11.2 : ESF BUDGET COMMITMENTS, 1980[20] (MILLION ECU)

1.   Art. 4.

      Agriculture)
)   35.06
      Textiles   )

      Young people – training   281.12

      Young people – employment   111.65

      Handicapped persons   0.08

      Migrant workers   38.03

      Women workers   21.14
                            ————
                            487.08

2.   Art. 5.

      Regions   )
)   454.61
      Groups of Firms   )
)
      Technical Progress)

      Handicapped Persons   77.18
                            ————
                            531.79

3.   Pilot Schemes and Studies   3.05
                            ————

                         1,021.92

favourable treatment under all ESF headings without absorbing what would appear to be a disproportionate amount of the whole, the situation of individual firms or voluntary organisations interested in particular and more specialised schemes may well be made less eligible.

TABLE 11.3 : GRANTS TO UK, BY CATEGORY, APPROVED IN 1980[22]

	million ECU	% of each allocation
Agriculture	-	-
Textiles	2.12	11.5
Young people - Training	85.95	30.3
Young people - Employment	37.69	34.7
Handicapped	-	-
Migrants	2.14	5.7
Women	0.12	0.6
Regions	89.02	21.0
Groups of Firms	0.97	26.6
Technical progress	1.24	5.4
Handicapped	16.64	21.6
Pilots	0.61	20.6

The UK would be likely to continue to do well if the ESF were enlarged at the expense of agricultural expenditure in the EC Budget but against this it must be remembered that the enlargement of the EC is likely to lead to heavy demands on the ESF. Employment training schemes in Greece require considerable development and the whole of Greece has been temporarily designated as a special region under the ESF where higher rates of grant aid apply. Other entrants would no doubt require similarly favourable treatment so it should not be assumed too readily that the UK will necessarily benefit significantly from any new developments.

Related types of expenditure are channelled through the ECSC for work specifically in these industries and here the

UK is at present the major recipient (see Table 11.4) because of the severe rundown in the steel industry. In addition to redeployment grants to cover retraining and mobility allowances, two temporary measures were introduced in 1981 to help finance early retirement and short time working schemes, for which an extra 50m ECU were set aside − Table 11.4 shows the 1981 allocations.

THE WOMEN'S POLICY

Brief reference has already been made to the insertion of the equal pay for equal work as an issue of social costs but because the question appeared to have little relevance to competitive costs in the early years of the 'common market' not much attention was paid to the matter. During the 1970s, however, the Community became a great deal more active in this area and this can, once again, be seen as a response to social change and the new concerns of the public at large. The rapid increase in the number of women in the labour force, including married women, together with relatively high marriage, divorce and re-marriage rates showed that many women experienced practical disadvantages which social policy could at least help to overcome. Less favourable employment outlets and promotion prospects, social security rights which had not changed to accommodate new living patterns, inadequate child care facilities, greater difficulty in obtaining certain types of job training all helped to keep women in a less favoured position and concentrated in less well paid work than that available to men. Thus it was realised that an equal pay policy was unlikely to be beneficial unless it formed part of a wider policy to improve employment opportunities and to these pressures the Commission was responsive. In 1975 an Irish application to postpone the implementation of Art 119 was refused and the same year the Court of Justice made a significant pronouncement to the effect that this article of the Treaty had social as well as economic aims.   It thought that in the former regard the principle had a part to play in the wider goal of improving living and working conditions. Energetic action on the part of the Commission led to several Directives being accepted. In 1975 equal pay acquired a wider definition, introducing the concept of equal pay for work of equal value, and providing a closer framework within which member states may act. Legislation incompatible with the Treaty must be repealed, collective agreements which do not recognise the principle are unenforceable, information about the right to equal pay

TABLE 11.4 : ECSC AIDS, 1981[23]

) On-going Aids

untry	Coal		Steel		Totals	
	ECUs	Workers	ECUs	Workers	ECUs	Workers
lgium	–	–	2,444,250	2,354	2,444,250	2,354
Germany	–	–	16,543,500	10,783	16,543,500	10,783
ance	4,866,250	1,059	–	–	4,866,250	1,059
aly	–	–	916,250	987	916,250	987
xembourg	–	–	280,750	193	280,750	193
therlands	–	–	1,750,000	700	1,750,000	700
ited ngdom	8,986,000	2,426	88,199,750	29,258	97,185,750	31,684
TALS	13,852,250	3,485	110,134,500	44,275	123,986,750	47,760

) 1981 Addition ECUs		(c) Allocations for 1981 (%) Tables (a) and (b)	
Belgium	4,753,014	Belgium	4.2
W. Germany	811,494	W. Germany	10.1
France	21,388,559	France	15.2
Italy	2,115,674	Italy	1.7
Luxembourg	289,818	Luxembourg	0.3
United Kingdom	19,272,885	Netherlands	1.0
	48,631,444	United Kingdom	67.5
			100

must be provided and a formal claims procedure
established.[24] The following year a directive on the equal
treatment of men and women in regard to employment,
vocational training and working conditions was accepted[25]
and in 1979 a third directive was passed on the progressive
implementation of equality of treatment for men and women
over matters of social security.[26] This provided a period
for the adjustment of rules concerning contributions and
entitlement to benefit under social security schemes
although it has postponed consideration of differential
retirement ages. In 1977 an 'intervention' was opened for
women under the ESF whilst the previous year the Ministers
of Education had made special mention of the problems
facing girls in their resolution on the preparation of
young people for working life.[27]

The establishment of true equality will clearly take a
very long time and is much affected by social attitudes and
habits of both men and women. A new promotional programme
was agreed by the Commission in December 1981 designed to
encourage action in pursuit of the goal of equal treatment
in the member states. It is based upon two policy goals,
namely the introduction of specific measures to strengthen
individual rights and overcoming the many non-legal
obstacles to the employment of women.[28]

Some concrete results are now beginning to be felt in the
UK in that a number of cases concerning policy have found
their way to the European Court of Justice which has thus
been able to give its view on the scope and meaning of Art
119 of the Treaty of Rome. The application of the equal pay
policy of the UK, is thereby affected.[29] The Court has
reiterated that Art 119 must be given direct effect whilst
its policy is designed to interpret the meaning of the
article and subsequent directives in a liberal rather than
a narrow sense. Secondly, the Commission considers that the
Equal Pay Act 1970 is inadequate to fulfil the higher
requirements of Community legislation as laid down in the
Directive. Thirdly the Commission has recently asked the
Court of Justice to consider whether the terms of the Sex
Discrimination Act 1975 and the Sex Discrimination
Northern Ireland) Order 1976 are sufficiently widely drawn
to meet the requirements of the directive on equal
treatment having found the British government unresponsive
to its 'reasoned opinions'.[30]

LABOUR MOBILITY

The free movement of labour policy has not perhaps impinged

so directly on the UK in that the main movement of workers
into Britain during the 1960s and 1970s has been from
outside the Community. Certain minor adjustments have been
made in British social security regulations in order to
meet the policy of maintaining social security rights for
EC nationals. Perhaps more interesting, however, is the
fact that Britain has been a major contender in moves to
improve the EC social security regulations by removing some
of their limitations so that they accord better with the
more liberal approach characteristic of her universal
schemes. An example is the recent extension of certain
benefits (including medical aid and a range of cash
benefits) to the self-employed on moving and this becomes
operative in July 1982.[31] This will clearly fit the British
approach to social insurance rather better than the
original exclusions which arose from the concept of social
insurance as a feature of employee status which formed the
basis of the original regulations. Non-employed persons
(other than family dependants) still remain outside the
arrangements despite British efforts, but this area of
social policy is an example of circumstances where Britain
can help to improve standards for the EC generally rather
than one where British policy has to be adjusted to meet EC
requirements.

Since the EC is not in a position to insist upon a
comprehensive policy towards migrant workers which would
cover matters of social integration and apply to migrants
from outside the Community, it must rely upon persuasion
when it wishes to see action undertaken and upon the
willingness of member governments to commit themselves to
joint action. The 'action programme for migrants ' of
1976[32] deserves to be better known as a statement of the
position of the EC, making clear the extent to which member
states are prepared to commit themselves to joint action
and thus, conversely, the areas where policy remains in
national control. The Council resolution of 9 February
1976[33] made clear that states were prepared to consult on
policies relating to migrants from countries outside the
EC, to encourage steps to ensure the equal treatment of
such migrants, legally within the EC, with others and to
strengthen inter-state co-operation against illegal
immigration, but there was no question of a Community
policy towards such migration being established. As far as
Community nationals were concerned, states accepted that
more employment at home in order to prevent the necessity
for migration was a desirable long-term policy but agreed

that, in the meantime, in relation to existing migrants and
those who might move in the future, far more needed to be
done in order to ensure effective equality of treatment,
improved procedures for the moving process and better
social integration.

These principles suggested a new drive to improve the
collaboration between employment services, steps to assist
social integration abroad when migrants returned home,
special attention to such matters as vocational training,
access to housing, social services, medical and social
care, the schooling of migrants' children, wider
informational facilities and the promotion of better
understanding on the part of the general public.

The migrant programme has led to a Directive on the
education of migrant children passed in 1977.[34] Concern had
been growing with the relatively high educational failure
rate leading in turn to considerable disadvantage when
young people came to look for jobs. Whilst the reasons for
this are manifold, the particular problems presented to
children not competent in the language of instruction and
conscious of living in an alien social environment were
readily identifiable and a major theme of the Directive is
to ensure proper attention to these matters.   More
controversially for the UK, it also contains provision for
some teaching to be carried out in the mother tongue and
for instruction in the indigeneous culture, reflecting the
situation in other EC states where migration policy has
assumed the character of short-term residence rather than
permanent settlement. Whilst it may be argued that a
broader range of linguistic and cultural instruction in
British schools is in any case desirable to express her
multi-racial nature, this is a broader question than that
of the Directive whose legality is confined to facilities
for EC nationals.

The movement of Community nationals has led to debate on
wider issues and notably the question of whether they
should be excluded from voting rights, particularly at
local elections, since they are directly affected by
policies on housing, social services and education which
are often determined at local level. The EC would like to
see such rights extended, as the UK already does for
Commonwealth and Irish citizens but which is not normal
practice within the context of the EC rules on the free
movement of labour.

CONCLUSION

In general, therefore, social policy involves a two-way
process for the UK. Britain shares in the discussion
of social policy issues, which extend over a wide field not
limited by treaty obligations and which is a continuous
process. Out of this may come a gradual change of attitude
on the part of officials, employers, trade union and
organisation leaders which will ultimately affect
procedures at home. It also leads, as occasion demands, to
specific EC legislation which the UK helps to formulate, as
in the case of the Directives which have been mentioned. As
these come to be operated it may indeed appear that UK
practice does not conform to EC standards and requires
amendment, but it must be remembered that the same process
is going on elsewhere as all states are similarly imposing
upon themselves a process of improvement. There are
occasions, too, when the UK can act as an example to other
members for the development of social policy. In addition
the UK gains from the grant-aiding procedures. The grants
are small in amount compared to the size of her problems
but her favourable treatment relative to other member
states (which is shown in the ESF tables) suggests that her
partners have been responsive to the reality of these
difficulties. In the areas where EC and UK social policy
overlap, membership seems to have been of positive
advantage rather than otherwise but the EC has not yet
developed sufficiently to have a fully comprehensive view
of social policy. The substance of the common interest may
well change over the years reflecting the movement of EC
interests but such broad changes take place slowly and the
past indicates that they occur when states have themselves
recognised the need for further development and are not
imposed 'out of the blue' by an alien body.

NOTES:

1. See discussion in Holloway (1981).

2. K.Joseph (Secretary of State for Social Services)
    22 Oct. 1971. <u>Hansard</u> 1970-1, Vo. 823. Cols. 1113-
    1115.

3. Dir. 75/362/EEC. OJ, L167, 30.6.75 (doctors). Dir.
    77/249/EEC. OJ, L78, 26.3.77 (lawyers).

4. As examples see Abel Smith and Townsend (1965) and
    Lenoir (1974).

5. See EC Commission (1971).

6. See especially point 6 of the final communiqué, the full text of which is published in R.Pryce (1973).

7. See EC Commission (1974).

8. Dir. 80/1107/EEC. OJ, L327, 3.12.80.

9. Times. 10.12.81.

10. Dir. 75/440/EEC. OJ, L194,25.7.75.

11. Dir. 75/129/EC. OJ, L48, 22.2.75.
    Dir. 77/187/EEC. OJ, L61, 5.3.77.
    Dir. 80/987/EEC. OJ, L283, 28.10.80.

12. Decision 71/66/EEC as amended by Decision 77/801/EEC. OJ L28, 4.2.71 and OJ, L337, 27.12.77.

13. House of Lords, Session 1979–80 (361). Select Committee on the European Communities. The European Social Fund, Q. 357.

14. COM (81) 343 final. 9th Report on the Activities of the European Social Fund, p.9.

15. See 15th General Report on the Activities of the European Communities in 1981. pp. 42–3. There will have been some additional carry over monies to make the actual budget rather larger.

16. Agence Europe. No. 3262. 3.12.81.

17. 9th ESF Report. op.cit., p.69.

18. Council Regulation (EEC) No. 23 96/71 amended by Regulation (EEC) No. 2893/77. OJ, L337, 27.12.77.

19. Council Regulation (EEC) No. 3039/78. OJ, L.361, 23.12.78.

20. 9th ESF Report. op. cit., p. 56.

21. Agence Europe. No. 3259. 28.11.81.

22. 9th ESF Report op. cit., p. 67.

23. 15th General Report, op.cit., pp. 123-4.

24. Dir. 75/117/EEC. OJ, L45, 19.2.75.

25. Dir. 76/207/EEC. OJ, L39, 14.2.76.

26. Dir. 79/7/EEC. OJ, L6, 10.1.79.

27. The resolution referred to pilot projects and studies
     to help evaluate and develop national policies in
     various directions which included specific action to
     ensure equal educational opportunities for girls. OJ,
     C308, 30.12.76.

28. Agence Europe. No. 3267. 10.12.81.

29. e.g. Case 129/79 Macarthys Ltd. v. Smith (1980) 2 CMLR
     205. Case 69/80 Worringham & Humphreys v. Lloyds Bank
     (1981) 2 CMLR 1. Case 96/80 Jenkins v. Kingsgate
     (Clothing Productions) Ltd. (1981) 2 CMLR 24. Case
     12/81 Garland v. British Rail Engineering Ltd.

30. Agence Europe. No. 3323. 5.3.82.

31. Regulation 1390/3. OJ, L143, 29.5.81.

32. See EC Commission (1976).

33. ibid.

34. Dir. 77/486/EEC. OJ, L199, 6.8.77.

Part IV
Macroeconomic Policies

12 EC Fiscal Policy

Ali M. El-Agraa

INTRODUCTION

Very widely interpreted, fiscal policy comprises a whole
corpus of 'public finance' issues: the relative size of the
public sector, taxation and expenditure, and the allocation
of public sector responsibilities between different tiers
of government (Prest, 1979). Hence fiscal policy is
concerned with a far wider area than that commonly
associated with it, namely, the aggregate management of the
economy in terms of controlling inflation and employment
levels.

Experts in the field of public finance (Musgrave and
Musgrave, 1976, rightly stress that 'public finance' is a
misleading term, since the subject also deals with 'real'
problems) have identified a number of problems associated
with these fiscal policy issues. For instance, the relative
size of the public sector raises questions regarding the
definition and measurement of government revenue and
expenditure (Prest, 1972), and the attempts at
understanding and explaining revenue and expenditure have
produced more than one theoretical model (Musgrave and
Musgrave, 1976; and Peacock and Wiseman, 1967). The
division of public sector responsibilities raises the
delicate question of which fiscal aspects should be dealt
with at the central government level and which aspects
should be tackled at the local level. Finally, the area of
taxation and expenditure criteria has resulted in general
agreement about the basic criteria of allocation (the
process by which the utilisation of resources is split
between private and social goods and by which the 'basket'
of social goods is chosen), equity (the use of the budget
for achieving a fair distribution), stabilisation (the use
of the budget as an instrument for achieving and
maintaining a 'reasonable' level of employment, prices and
economic growth and for achieving equilibrium and stability
in the balance of payments), and administration (the
practical possibilities of implementing a particular tax
system and the cost to the society of operating such a

system). However, a number of very tricky problems are involved in a consideration of these criteria. In discussing the efficiency of resource allocation, the choice between work and leisure, for example, or between private and public goods, is an important and controversial one. With regard to the equity of distribution, there is the problem of what is meant by equity: is it personal, class or regional equity? In a discussion of the stabilisation of the economy, there exists the perennial problem of controlling unemployment and inflation and the trade-off between them. A consideration of administration must take into account the problem of efficiency versus practicality. Finally, there is the obvious conflict between the four criteria in that the achievement of one aim is usually at the expense of another; for example, what is most efficient in terms of collection may prove less (or more) equitable than what is considered to be socially desirable.

The above relates to a discussion of the problems of fiscal policy in very broad national terms. When considering the EC fiscal policy, there are certain elements of the international dimension that need spelling out and there are also some inter-regional (intra-EC) elements that have to be introduced.

Very briefly, internationally, it has always been recognised that taxes (and equivalent instruments) have similar effects to tariffs on the international flow of goods and services - non-tariff distortions of international trade (Baldwin, 1971). Other elements have also been recognised as operating similar distortions on the international flow of factors of production (Bhagwati, 1969; Johnson 1965; Johnson and Krauss 1973).

In the particular context of the EC, it should be remembered that its formation, at least from the economic viewpoint, was meant to facilitate the free and unimpeded flow of goods, services and factors (and the other elements discussed in Chapters 1 and 2) between the member nations. Since tariffs are not the only distorting factor in this respect, the proper establishment of intra-EC free trade necessitates the removal of all non-tariff distortions that have an equivalent effect. Hence, the removal of tariffs may give the impression of establishing free trade inside the EC, but this is by no means automatically guaranteed, since the existence of sales taxes, excise duties, corporation taxes, income taxes, etc. may impede this freedom. The moral is that not only tariffs, but all equivalent distortions, must be eliminated or harmonised.

At this juncture it should be pointed out that there are

at least two basic elements to fiscal policy : the
instruments available to the government for fiscal policy
purposes (i.e. the total tax structure) and the overall
impact of the joint manoeuvring of the instruments (i.e.
the role played by the budget). The aim of this chapter is
to discuss, briefly, the progress made by the EC with
regard to tax harmonisation and to explain the nature of
the EC Budget, concluding with a section on the future role
of EC fiscal policy - the reader interested in a more
detailed discussion of the first two aspects should consult
El-Agraa (1980a, chapters 11 and 12).

TAX HARMONISATION IN THE EC

Before assessing the progress made by the EC in the field
of tax harmonisation one should specify what precisely is
meant by the term. In earlier years, tax harmonisation was
defined as tax coordination (Dosser, 1973). Ideally, in a
fully integrated EC, it could be defined as the identical
unification of both base and rates, given the same tax
system and assuming that everything else is also unified.
Prest (1979, p.76) rightly argues that 'coordination' is
tantamount to a low-level meaning of tax harmonisation,
since it could be 'interpreted to be some process of
consultation between member countries or, possibly, loose
agreements between them to levy tax on a similar sort of
base or at similar sorts of rates'. Hence it is not
surprising that tax harmonisation has, in practice, come to
mean a compromise between the low level of coordination
(the EC is more than a low level of integration - see
chapters 1 and 2) and the ideal level of standardisation
(the EC is nowhere near its ultimate objective of complete
political unity).
    It should be added that Article 99 of the Treaty of Rome
specifically calls for the harmonisation of indirect taxes,
mainly turnover taxes and excise duties. Harmonisation here
was seen as vital, particularly since the removal of
tariffs would leave taxes as the main source of intra-EC
trade distortion. However, given the preoccupation of the
EC with the process of unification, the Treaty seems to put
very little stress on the harmonisation of its initial tax
diversity (see El-Agraa, 1980a, pp. 208-11). Moreover, the
Treaty is rather vague about what it means by
'harmonisation': for example, in Article 100 it does not
specify more than that laws 'should be approximated' with
regard to direct taxation. Hence, the whole development of
tax harmonisation has been influenced by the work of

'special' Committees, informal discussions, etc. This, however, should not be interpreted as a criticism of those who drafted the Treaty. On the contrary, given the very complex nature of the subject and its closeness to the question of political unification, it would have been short-sighted to have done otherwise.

This being the general background, it is now appropriate to describe the progress made by the EC with respect to tax harmonisation. In the area of indirect taxation most of the developments have been in terms of VAT — which the EC adopted as its turnover tax following the recommendations of the Neumark Committee (1963), which was in turn based on the Tinbergen Study (1953) — since it was realised that the removal of intra-EC tariffs left taxes on traded goods as the main impediment to the establishment of complete free trade inside the EC. Between 1967 and 1977, six Directives were issued with the aim of achieving conformity between the different practices of the member countries. These related, apart from the adoption of VAT as the EC sales tax, to three major considerations : the inclusion of the retail stage in the coverage of VAT; the use of VAT levies for the EC central budget (see below); and the achievement of greater uniformity in VAT structure.

Having adopted the VAT system and having accepted a unified method of calculating it, the EC has also acceded to the 'destination principle' which is consistent with free intra-EC trade. It has been agreed by all member states that the coverage of VAT should be the same and should include the retail stage, that crude raw materials, bought-in elements and similar components are to be deductible from the tax computation, and that investment stock and inventories should be given similar treatment by all member nations. There is agreement about the general principle of VAT exemptions, but the precise nature of these seems to vary from one member country to another, thus giving rise to the problems concerning the tax base — see El-Agraa and Brown in El-Agraa (1980a).

On the other hand, this similarity of principles is, in practice, contradicted by a number of differences. The tax coverage differs from one member country to another, since most seem to have different kinds, as well as different levels, of exemptions. For example, the UK applies zero-rating for foodstuffs, gas and electricity (zero-rating is different from exemptions, since zero-rating means not only tax exemption from the process, but also the receipt of rebates on taxes paid at the preceding stage). There is a wide difference in rate structure.

With respect to corporation tax, the Neumark Report of

1963 recommended a Split-Rate system, the van den Tempel Report of 1970 preferred the adoption of the Separate or 'classical' system and the Draft Directive of 1975 went for the Imputation system. Moreover, the method of tax harmonisation which is accepted is not the ideal one of a single EC Corporation tax and a single tax pattern, but rather a unified EC Corporation tax accompanied by freedom of tax patterns. Hence, all systems have been entertained at some time or another and all that can be categorically stated is that the EC has, at this stage, limited its choice to the Separate and Imputation systems.

As far as excise duties are concerned, progress has been rather slow and this can be partially attributed to the large extent of the differences between the rates on the commodities under consideration in the different member countries. This is a partial explanation however, because these taxes are important for government revenue purposes and it would be naive to suggest that rate uniformity can be achieved without giving consideration to the political implications of such a move.

The greatest progress has been achieved in tobacco, where a new harmonised system was adopted in January 1978. The essential elements of this system are the abolition of any duties on raw tobacco leaf and the adoption of a new sales tax at the manufacturing level, combined with a specific tax per cigarette and VAT. Prest (1979) argues that the overall effect of this will be to push up the relative prices of the cheaper brands of cigarettes.

It has been suggested (Prest, 1979) that the harmonisation of tax rates here is misguided, since the destination principle automatically guarantees fair competition. This is a misleading criticism, however, since the harmonisation of the tax structure should be seen in the context of the drive in the EC for monetary integration and political unification, processes which become increasingly difficult without tax harmonisation.

Some progress has been achieved with regard to Stamp Duties. Harmonisation here is necessary for promoting the freedom of intra-EC capital flows. The 1976 Draft Directive recommended a compromise between the systems existing in the member countries. This recommendation has been accepted, with the proviso that time will be allowed for adjustment to the new system.

Nothing has been attempted in the area of personal income taxation and very slight progress has been achieved in social security payments, unemployment benefits, etc. These are discussed in some detail in chapter 11.

In concluding this section, it must be emphasised that

the lack of fundamental progress in EC tax harmonisation should not come as a surprise. There are three basic reasons for this. First, lest it be forgotten, the EC stands for the harmonised integration of some of the oldest countries in the world, with very diverse and extremely complicated economic systems, and this diversity and complexity is increasing with the enlargement (and potential enlargement) of the EC. Secondly, tax harmonisation is intimately connected with the role played by the government in controlling the economy and since this role depends on a complicated package of taxes, it should be apparent that the separate harmonising of the different components of the package is extremely difficult and probably also misguided. Finally, and more importantly, tax harmonisation, or at least the complex and sensitive elements within it, is very closely linked with the question of monetary integration and political unification – see chapter 13. It would therefore be naive to expect substantial progress in tax harmonisation, without similar progress in these other fields.

EC GENERAL BUDGET

The general EC Budget provides for two broad types of expenditure. Firstly, there are the administrative expenses (staff salaries, information, etc.) of the institutions of the EC: the Commission, the Council, the European Parliament, the Court of Justice, the ECSC, the ESF and the ERDF (see chapters 1, 2, 11 and 13); and secondly, the operational expenditures of the Commission such as FEOGA intervention and guidance expenses, ERDF support grants, 'Food Aid', etc. The EC Budget also provides for a miscellaneous collection of 'minor' expenditures.

In 1982, the EC General Budget amounted to about 22 billion ECUs which is roughly equivalent to £15 billion at current rates (see Table 12.1). Of this total, 62 per cent (the smallest percentage ever) was expenditure on the 'guarantee' section of FEOGA (see chapter 8 for more detail). Hence, the total size of the EC Budget is of the same order of magnitude as that of a large UK department such as Health and Social Security or Education and Science. Incidentally, note that the suggestion that the EC has a large bureaucracy is incorrect since only about 6 per cent of the EC Budget is expenditure on 'administration'.

The EC Budget expenditure is divided into two categories: (i) compulsory; and (ii) non-compulsory. The former is the expenditure emanating essentially from commitments in the

TABLE 12.1 : GENERAL BUDGET OF THE EC, 1973-83

YEAR	TOTAL (ECUm)	FEOGA - Guarantee (%)
1973	4641	77.4
1974	5037	67.3
1975	6214	69.6
1976	7993	71.8
1977	8483	76.8
1978	12363	70.2
1979	13716	69.3
1980	16233	73.0
1981	18438	65.9
1982	21984	62.1
1983	21901	64.2

Sources : Bulletin of The European Communities, no. 5, vol.15, 1982 and Fifteenth Report of The Activities of The European Communities in 1981.

Treaties (such as FEOGA price support and certain types of foreign aid to third countries) while the latter arises from the operational areas of the EC Budget (such as some of the expenditures of the ERDF and the ESF). Hence, compulsory expenditures have a priority claim which is why the EC Budget is necessarily 'functional', i.e. the EC has been endowed with revenues "to discharge certain specific functions arising from the well-defined activities it was required to undertake either in the original Treaty or as subsequently agreed by the Council" (Rybczynski, 1981).

Turning to the financing side, the EC Budget revenues come from gross contributions termed 'own resources', i.e. EC independent revenues : member nations pay to the EC what actually belongs to it (Godley, 1980, p.72) - the principle of 'own resources' was adopted after the Council Decision of April 21, 1970; it was to replace in 1980 the previous system which was entirely based on national contributions. There are three basic categories of 'own resources' : (i) agricultural and sugar levies; (ii) customs duties, i.e proceeds from industrial tariffs; and (iii) up to 1 per cent of the common VAT base yield - see Table 12.2. If more than 1 per cent of the VAT base yield is required further legislation ratified by all the member nations would become necessary.

Table 12.3 gives gross contributions, gross receipts and 'net' receipts broken down by member nation. It should be clear from the table that the UK and Germany provide the largest share of gross contributions with regard to all three categories of EC Budget revenue; the levies and tariffs categories are easily explained in terms of the two countries' large extra-EC trade. The table also shows Germany and the UK to have been practically the only net losers with regard to 'net' receipts; this has been the main reason for the UK budgetary battles with the EC particularly since the UK has been the second largest net loser when its position in the league of GDP has been third from bottom - see Figure 12.1. This anomaly arises simply because a large percentage of the EC Budget expenditures falls on agriculture when the 'size' of the agricultural sector is not strictly related to GDP (Denmark with a large agricultural sector has the highest per capita income) and VAT contributions, which are to a large extent related to GDP, form only just over half of the total EC Budget revenues.

Finally, although the EC Budget is meant to be balanced, it is not strictly true that gross contributions and expenditures sum to zero; there has been "a small but significant increase in cash balances held by the Community which exercises a small deflationary effect on the system as a whole" (Godley, 1980, p.76).

THE EC BUDGET TRANSFERS

If the EC Budget is to be regarded as the 'embryo centre of a federal system', its small size relative to EC GDP (less that 1 per cent) means that it is at a very early stage in its development. However, because the EC Budget expenditures are dominated by agriculture, it does play a significant role in the transfer of resources between member nations, hence the British EC Budget quarrels. Discussion of this aspect has been very disappointing indeed; it concentrates on the CAP when a 'proper' evaluation of the extent of transfers should include similar treatment of industrial products. For example, if a member nation ceases to import a manufactured product from outside the EC and replaces it by imports from a partner nation, that country will contribute less to the EC Budget revenues (reduced proceeds from industrial tariffs) but since this act is one of trade diversion, it will pay more per unit of that product. This element of transfer of resources must be included in any proper evaluation - to simply allege that, on balance, this element is 'mutually advantageous' to all the member nations (Cambridge Economic

TABLE 12.2 : REVENUES OF THE EC BUDGET, 1982 and 1983

Revenue	1982 ECUm	1982 %	1983 ECUm	1983 %	Change %
Agricultural Levies	1899.1	8.6	1558.5	7.1	−17.93
Sugar and Isoglucose Levies	786.0	3.6	1013.2	4.6	+28.91
Customs Duties	6939.0	31.6	7574.5	34.6	+ 9.16
VAT	11998.3	54.6	11384.5	52.0	− 5.12
Financial Contributions	197.5	0.9	180.4	0.8	− 8.67
Miscellaneous Revenue	164.5	0.7	190.5	0.9	+15.81
TOTAL	21984.4	100.0	21901.6	100.0	− 0.38

Source : Bulletin of the European Communities, no.5, vol. 15, 1982.

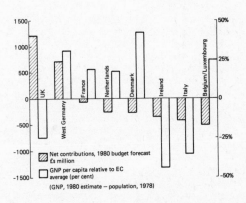

FIGURE 12.1: NET CONTRIBUTIONS TO THE EC BUDGET AND GNP PER CAPITA

TABLE 12.3: EC GENERAL BUDGET - NATIONAL RECEIPTS AND PAYMENTS

	Gross Contributions, 1980 (% Share)	Gross Contributions by Source, 1980 (%)			Gross Receipts, 1980 (% Share)	Net Receipts (£m)		
		Agricultural Levies	Industrial Tariffs	VAT		1979	1980	1981
Belgium/Luxembourg	6.1	11	7	5	11.9	+394	+250	+351
Denmark	2.4	2	2	3	4.4	+246	+174	+157
France	20.0	13	15	24	20.0	- 50	+ 41	+102
Germany	30.1	20	30	31	23.5	-924	-1177	-1260
Ireland	0.9	0.5	1	1	3.8	+352	+372	+340
Italy	11.5	20.5	9	14	16.8	+345	+329	+215
Netherlands	8.4	15	9	6	10.5	+186	+215	+ 81
United Kingdom	20.5	19	27	16	8.7	-549	-203*	- 56*

*These figures allow for refunds to the UK in 1980 and 1981 - see Notes to Table 8.

Sources : Wallace, W. (1980) and EC Commission, various publications.

<u>Policy Review</u>, no. 5, April 1979), hence it is appropriate to ignore it, is to by-pass the intricate issues raised in chapter 6. Therefore, this subject will not be pursued here since the true cost of the CAP is discussed in chapter 8 and the impact of EC formation and enlargement on industrial and other products is covered in chapter 6.

EC BUDGET AND FISCAL POWERS

The interesting question that should be asked is : can the EC Budget be made to perform proper fiscal policy functions? At the moment the EC Budget does very little in this respect (due to its small size) and what it does is essentially regressive (VAT excludes investment which amounts to a <u>high</u> percentage of GDP for countries with <u>high</u> GDP) and anomalous particularly for countries like the UK. However, the MacDougall Report (1977) considered the possibilities for an enlarged EC Budget to promote a move towards closer EC 'economic and monetary union'. The Report asserts that the "role of public finance (essentially, of the national budget) in this connection is a very considerable one ... it generally tends to diminish differences of income and welfare not only between richer and poorer people, but ... between states or regions with different average income levels, and it may be claimed that this is, on balance, a factor tending to promote and preserve the economic union in question" (Brown, 1980, p.228; Brown was a member of the group). The Report also saw the need for a built-in mechanism of net transfers from those countries doing well at a particular moment in time to those doing badly as an 'insurance against economic misfortune' that may be a characteristic of membership of an economic and monetary union.

When the members of the MacDougall Study Group examined evidence from eight countries and federations, they realised that an EC Budget which was to carry out such functions would seem to require about 10 per cent of EC total public expenditure, i.e. at least 4-5 per cent of EC GDP. On closer examination it was noted that while public expenditure of about 45 per cent of GDP went with about 40 per cent reduction in interregional inequalities, the 'net' transfer from richer to poorer regions was nearly the difference between payments to and receipts from the central government - about 2-5 per cent of GDP. Hence, if the extension of the EC functions 'involved not giving rather more to the poor than to the rich, but giving to the poor <u>only</u>', a significant degree of equalisation could be

achieved with a smaller budget than that originally
envisaged by the Study Group. Indeed, some members of the
Group felt that an EC Budget which handled about 10 per
cent of EC GDP (including Defence expenditure, see chapter
15) or 6-7 per cent (excluding Defence), with an
appropriate 'progressive' tax-base and a concentration of
its non-defence expenditure on grants or benefits directed
towards poorer regions would be able to carry out the
specified functions.

When it came to making actual recommendations, the Group
realised that even that modest percentage is not feasible
at this juncture. They therefore recommended an EC Budget
of about 2-2½ per cent of EC GDP, i.e. a trebling of its
present size (0.8 per cent of GDP). This was to be achieved
by transferring to the EC Budget "most of the external aid
undertaken by its members, a partial takeover of
unemployment benefits and vocational training, and various
forms of grant to weaker member states and regions" (Brown,
1980, p.230). Although the proposals amounted to the EC
taking over national expenditures rather than adding to
them, the Group realised that an increase in total public
expenditure of less than 1 per cent of GDP might be
required. They suggested a further tranche of VAT as a
possible source of finance but recommended in addition a
progressive tax-base (i.e. personal income tax).

CONCLUSION

It should be apparent from the discussion in the previous
section that a proper analysis of the future prospects for
the EC Budget cannot be confined to its present structure.
The EC Budget must not only be seen in its proper context
of 'public finance' but also in the wider context of the
ultimate objectives of the EC (see chapters 1 and 2). Given
its present structure and the present stage reached in the
EC integrative process, an equitable Budget, in the absence
of forthcoming proper reform of the CAP, must aim at
increasing the 'non-compulsory' expenditures (regional,
social and industrial aspects including employment
generation). This would require new legislation to increase
the VAT base yield contribution beyond the legal 1 per
cent, which is broadly consistent with 'equity' even though
VAT is regressive.

In terms of the ultimate objectives of the EC, the
analysis in the MacDougall Report, as opposed to its actual
recommendations, is most appropriate - the actual
recommendations are, arguably, consistent with a 'step in

the right direction'. If EMU is to become a reality, albeit
in the distant future, a common Central EC Bank which
possesses the common pool of foreign exchange reserves and
is responsible for the coordination of the monetary
policies of the member nations must necessarily influence
and in turn be influenced by, fiscal policy (see El-Agraa
1980a). For instance, a fiscal decision regarding regional
distribution in any particular area would have clear
guideline implications for EC Central Bank operations:
where money is raised or contracted would have to be
consistent with the regional distributional target. Since
in a fully-fledged monetary and economic union fiscal
policy is essentially about the 'regional problem', it is
important to conduct research into the borrowing powers of
the EC Central Bank as well as the implications of its
'open market operations' in terms of the overall regional
'equalisation' targets.

Let me conclude this chapter by speculating about ways in
which this problem can be approached. Looking at it in
purely economic terms and asking how one would organise an
EC Budget from first principles, the answer would be : free
movement of goods, services and factors of production,
central control of public finance (uniform progressive
taxation except in so far as special variations are
introduced on regional policy grounds - congestion taxes,
etc.), expenditure in accordance with criteria of personal
needs for public goods, for example, education, retraining,
environmental services. This is, of course, a long view and
some would argue that it is so long that its value at
compound discount is rather low.

Looking at the problem solely in terms of existing
political constraints is not likely to be helpful either,
since such an approach envisages neither the long term
objective nor the path to be taken to it.

There is an awkward middle ground which corresponds to
the reality of most federations and unitary states (with
local government authorities). Local (and federal state)
governments do not want to be mere agents of the central
government, providing the amounts of public goods that are
prescribed by central policy; they want some revenue
sources which they can vary themselves, even if they do
rely mainly on central government grants. The division of
the fisc therefore becomes an issue of paramount
importance; this is partly inconsistent with free movement
and possibly also with optimum progressiveness, but it has
to exist so long as there are local, as opposed to either
individual or central, allegiances. It all stems from the
fact that people are by nature imperfectly mobile (see El-

Agraa, 1980).

What then is the moral? Discussing the correctness or otherwise of the EC Budget is both meaningless and futile without knowing what is expected of it. Its main objectives should be the promotion and enhancement of a specified integrative aim or process. Let that be defined quite clearly before an appropriate EC Budget is devised.

13 EC Monetary Arrangements: Britain's Strategy

David T. Llewellyn

The EC has not been short of plans for formal monetary integration. In the second half of the 1960s, a series of proposals (notably the Barre and Schiller plans[1]) were made with a view to inducing a greater degree of monetary integration between members. The Werner Report was an attempt at reconciling fundamentally conflicting approaches to monetary integration particularly over the issue of whether a fixed exchange rate mechanism was to be the spur to policy co-ordination, or the culmination of a general process of convergence – see El-Agraa (1980a). In December 1969 the EC Heads of State agreed to establish full Economic and Monetary Union (EMU) by 1980.

With the benefit of hindsight, the early plans for monetary integration were formulated and decided upon at a time when the Bretton Woods system was being subject to insurmountable pressures and the regime of fixed exchange rates was coming to an end. While European governments and monetary authorities had become increasingly disenchanted with many features of the operation of the Bretton Woods system (especially the role of the dollar and the USA) this was not the predominant motive for monetary integration in the EC in the late 1960s. The ambition to secure greater monetary independence from the USA was real enough and held more by some members than others. But, unlike a decade later when the European Monetary System (EMS) was instituted in 1979, the main impetus was internal. After the establishment of the Customs Union and Common Agricultural Policy, formal moves towards monetary integration were viewed as the obvious next stage in the broader political ambitions of the EC. The driving force was internally rather than externally generated.

To set current monetary arrangements in perspective, and to demonstrate how far removed the EC is from EMU, present arrangements may be set against the characteristics of EMU as defined in the Werner Report: (i) Community currencies would be freely convertible and parities irrevocably fixed; preferably, national currencies would be replaced by a Community currency; (ii) monetary and credit policy would

251

be centralised; (iii) there would be a centralised Community monetary policy vis à vis the rest of the world; (iv) members would unify policies on capital markets; (v) the main components of budget policy would be decided at Community level; and (vi) a Community central banking system would determine monetary conditions. In effect, balance of payments positions between members would become irrelevant (just as they are within existing monetary unions based upon nation states) and, again as within existing nation states, regional transfers would occur automatically through a substantially enlarged Community budget. Thus while intra-balance of payments positions would be irrelevant, an uncompetitive region (country) within the union would experience regional unemployment rather than, as now, a balance of payments deficit. With irrevocably fixed exchange rates this common symptom of an uncompetitive real wage could not, by definition, be alleviated by an exchange rate adjustment. This means that some other method has to be introduced to deal with it.

While the 1970s began with an air of unrealistic optimism for European monetary integration following the Grand Design of the Werner Report, little if any progress was made over the decade in formal European monetary arrangements. Very little materialised along the lines outlined in Werner and, far from establishing full monetary union as envisaged for 1980, the decade during which gradual moves were to be made towards this goal ended in some respects with less monetary co-ordination and certainty than at the beginning. Although various formal exchange rate arrangements were instituted in Europe (Snake-in-the-Tunnel, Joint Float, 'Mini-Snake' and the EMS) together with associated short and medium term credit facilities, in general less progress has been made in the monetary area in the EC than in many other major aspects. In addition to revealing the general disparity of economic performance between members, the economic conditions of the 1970s demonstrated that the political commitment towards formal monetary integration and its implications were weak.

The objective of this chapter is threefold: (1) to review the aspirations and achievements of formal monetary integration in the EC; (2) to consider the case for an exchange rate rather than a monetary target for the UK in the context of the EMS; and (3) to consider what further initiatives might be appropriate given the degree of economic and financial integration that has taken place. The discussion is set throughout in the context of the constraints imposed upon policy autonomy by economic and financial integration.

THE EMS

The latest in a long line of EC exchange rate mechanisms is the EMS. While Mr. Roy Jenkins (1978) had earlier attempted to revive interest in EC Monetary Union this did not feature in the ambitions of politicians and central bankers when devising the EMS. It was purely a reflection of disturbances in the foreign exchange markets. No serious consideration was given to the wider issue of EMU at the end of the 1970s. It was not claimed at the time of its inception that it was a formal move in the direction of EMU; it was a less ambitious but more realistic initiative at trying to secure more immediate exchange rate stability within Europe.

According to official statements at the time, several factors in the world economy and financial system prompted this move: (i) a general disillusionment with the operation of floating exchange rates; (ii) the long standing European concern at the hegemony of the US dollar in the international monetary system, and (iii) a rather imprecise view that a co-ordinated policy approach by European governments would be a more effective means of improving the general performance of the European economies and of reducing unemployment and inflation in particular. But above all else it was the substantial pressure on the US dollar in the exchange markets that was the dominant factor. When the dollar came under pressure it was largely into the Deutschmark that speculative funds flowed. The predominant motive was to mitigate the disruptive effects on intra-EC exchange rates that resulted from this pressure. The objective of Germany in particular was to spread the pressure that was usually directed at the Deutschmark at the time of weakness of the US dollar (see Oppenheimer, 1981). This is related, however, to the more general and long standing objective of EC countries of securing a higher degree of monetary independence from the US without having to accept the implications of floating exchange rates between themselves. The broad objective of the EMS was to create a 'zone of monetary stability' in Europe.

EMS EXPERIENCE [2]

Circumstances were particularly favourable at the time the

EMS was established in 1979. The US dollar was comparatively stable in the early months of the scheme partly associated with a more interventionist strategy in the foreign exchange market by the FED. It is also significant and helpful that the Deutschmark was untypically comparatively weak at various times in the period 1979-1981 associated with Germany's substantial current account deficit. This had the effect of reducing potential pressure on cross rates within the EMS. In this respect it is interesting to note that the realignment of central rates in September 1979 and the devaluation of the Lira in March 1981 occurred when the Deutschmark was strong. The balance of payments position of France (with a potentially weak currency) was also strong in 1979. This had the effect of reducing potential pressure on cross rates within the EMS. The scheme was also begun after several central rates were already adjusted to likely inflation differentials, and in addition Italy operates with a wider margin of fluctuation around central rates (6 per cent compared with the standard 2¼ per cent).

But the success of the arrangement in the period 1979-82 was due also to the flexibility of its operation. Interest rate policy had been used (sometimes on a co-ordinated basis) to maintain currencies within the allowable margin of fluctuation. Above all, changes in central rates (which have to be mutually agreed by participants) had not been delayed and had been executed with comparative ease although in February 1982 there was considerable resistance to the desire of the Belgian monetary authorities to secure a 12 per cent devaluation. In the event, they secured only 8½ per cent. Potential strains within the system did emerge in the period 1979-82 but, as originally envisaged, they met with a flexible reponse. Intervention in the foreign exchange market was substantial, interest rates were adjusted to ease potential pressure and a series of small alignments of central rates was made.

While in essence a fixed exchange rate arrangement, the EMS proved in the period 1979 to 1982 to be an effective and workable compromise between floating exchange rates and rigidly fixed rates. As the adjustment to central rates frequently occurred without inducing any immediate change in nominal rates (the band being moved around currently prevailing nominal exchange rates), the disadvantages of freely floating rates were removed without the problem of securing substantial speculative profits that was a feature of the fixed rate system of the 1960s and early 1970s. Providing small adjustments are made to central rates without simultaneously causing nominal rates to move, exchange rate adjustments can be made without inducing substantial speculative capital movements associated with the 'one-way-option' inherent in the Bretton Woods regime. In effect, the EMS has been operated along the lines of a 'Crawling Peg' system, and has to date been operated considerably more flexibly than the fixed exchange rate regime in the Bretton Woods system.

In a comprehensive review of the early working of the EMS, Davies (1982) reports that the scheme has had the effect of reducing exchange rate fluctuations between member currencies. To that extent the central objective of creating a 'zone of monetary stability' was achieved at least in the period 1979-82. Davies reports that standard deviations and average changes of intra-EMS cross rates dropped by statistically significant amounts between the Snake and EMS periods. The study also notes that this was not fortuitous in that it was not the result of a general improvement in currency stability between the two periods. In particular: (i) volatility calculations for non-EMS cross rates increased after March 1979, (ii) intra-EMS volatility was about half that of similar cross rates outside the EMS, and (iii) the group of EMS currencies was not any more stable relative to outside currencies (such as sterling and the dollar). It cannot, therefore, be said that the EMS has contributed to greater stability in world currency markets overall. This partly reflects a failure to develop a concerted and co-ordinated policy with respect to outside currencies, notably the US dollar. This in turn is associated with the reversion to a 'Benign Neglect' stance of the FED in the Reagan administration.

Of more serious concern is the conclusion that the EMS has not promoted convergence in domestic economic performances of members as inflation and monetary trends have, if anything, tended to diverge, certainly compared with the period of the 'Snake'. This implies that over the period 1979-82 the high inflation members suffered a significant loss of competitiveness which eroded the favourable competitive positions which existed at the time the system was initiated. Thus, notwithstanding the adjustments made to central rates, there have been significant changes in real exchange rates which are likely to create problems in the future. Unless greater convergence is secured there are potential problems ahead.

EXCHANGE RATE vs MONETARY TARGETS

Most plans for formal monetary integration in the EC

involve some form of fixed exchange rate arrangement with
varying degrees of operational flexibility. But this was
contrary to the trend of the 1970s. One reason for the move
towards a regime of floating exchange rates in the early
1970s was the greater priority given to control of the
domestic money supply by governments in many industrial
countries. Given the degree of international financial
integration this was considered to be incompatible with
obligations to intervene in the foreign exchange market
which usually, though not invariably, has a domestic
monetary counterpart. The related objective of securing
monetary independence of the USA was also a powerful
factor. The commitment of several governments to specific
money supply targets also made precise obligations for
foreign exchange market intervention problematic. One of
the most rigid forms of a monetary target was adopted in
the UK in 1979 with an announced commitment to reduce over
a four year period the rate of growth of a specific
monetary aggregate (sterling M3). This medium term
financial strategy (MTFS) if fully implemented would have
constrained intervention in money and foreign exchange
markets designed to secure any interest rate or exchange
rate objectives.

A rigid and precise exchange rate target implies domestic
monetary policy being subordinated to the requirements of
maintaining the exchange rate within a specified range. It
also implies a degree of consistency of monetary policy
with that of currencies against which the target is set.
While the conflict between an exchange rate and a monetary
target may be less powerful than traditionally presented,
there is a general requirement with a monetary target to
accept the exchange rate implications, and with an exchange
rate target the domestic money supply becomes largely
endogenous. The force of the conflict depends, however, on
the rigidity of the chosen target.

Given the experience of monetary targets, and the
operation of monetary policy generally in the UK in the
latter part of the 1970s, the case for adopting an exchange
rate target can now be considered with less scepticism. The
case is made for less rigidity generally with formal
targets than has been implied in the UK, but also for the
adoption of an exchange rate target in the context of UK
membership of the EMS. The general case for membership of
the EMS may be summarised as follows:

1. The EMS is a viable exchange rate system and its
   operation to date (though strains are emerging)
   indicates that it is a workable compromise between

freely floating exchange rates and rigidly fixed rates which would be clearly non-viable in the current economic and financial environment.

2. The experience of floating exchange rates indicates that they have not operated as beneficially as some analysts predicted. The case for membership of the EMS is both positive but also negative with respect to the operation of floating exchange rates.

3. The apparent loss of sovereignty and policy autonomy implied by a more defined obligation to support the exchange rate in the foreign exchange market is probably less than traditionally postulated for four reasons. Firstly, there is doubt about the effectiveness of exchange rate adjustments to either influence real magnitudes in the economy or adjust the balance of payments. Secondly, the conflict between monetary and exchange rate targets is less acute than traditional monetary analysis suggests, particularly in the short run, and there is scepticism about the role of strategies for precise monetary control. Thirdly, the experience of floating rates indicates that the alleged policy autonomy in general, and with monetary policy in particular, is in practice less than theoretical models tend to indicate. Fourthly, if monetary policy is unable to affect the long run values of real magnitudes in the economy, the supposed ability of a government under floating rates to decide upon its own monetary policy confers only the ability to determine nominal magnitudes in the economy. While this might be viewed as of value in the short run, its longer run significance can be questioned. The limited loss of effective sovereignty implied by surrendering policy control over the exchange rate and the domestic money supply is discussed further in Llewellyn (1982a).

4. If monetary control is desired in order to achieve an inflation objective, objections to the EMS (which, for the UK, would imply an exchange rate target against the Deutschmark) must be based upon the constraints imposed by the requirements of having UK monetary policy consistent with that of Germany. But in general Germany's inflation and monetary performance has been superior to that of the UK. If the objective of monetary policy is the control of inflation, the discipline imposed by German monetary policy would, in most circumstances, probably prove to be beneficial.

While the EMS is in essence a fixed exchange rate mechanism, the allowable margin of fluctuation is not insignificant, and it has operated flexibly with respect to adjustments to central rates. It is not as constraining with respect to monetary policy as a rigid exchange rate target, and has in practice been operated almost as a 'Crawling Peg' arrangement which seeks to secure whatever advantages are available from exchange rate adjustments without the disadvantages of freely floating exchange rates.

The establishment of any intermediate target decomposes the policy process into two relationships: (1) between policy instruments and the intermediate target and, (2) between the target and the ultimate policy objective. The general case for establishing targets is threefold: (i) they may influence behaviour, (e.g. the establishment of a monetary target might induce more moderate wage claims), (ii) they can give an early indication of the movement of the goal variable (e.g. rate of inflation) and as such be a guide to policy adjustments, and (iii) they may be regarded as a 'discipline' on all agents in the economy including the government and monetary authorities.

But there are also problems with the establishment of targets. Firstly, to the extent that the two key relationships (between instrument and target and between target and objective) are variable and unpredictable, serious policy errors can arise. Secondly, the efficiency of particular targets in yielding information about conditions in the economy can frequently be distorted. This was particularly significant in the UK in the period 1979-81 when the efficiency of money supply data was seriously impaired following the distortions associated with the 'Corset' and the abolition of exchange control. Thirdly, there is a practical danger that, given the commitment made to it, the target in effect becomes the objective almost irrespective of its effect upon the ultimate goal variable. It is also apparent that, for the same reason, policy can be adjusted so as to produce cosmetic effects upon the target without influencing the ultimate policy objective. The alternative to target-orientated policy strategies is to focus upon the ultimate objective and to adjust policy instruments to them. There is the technical option to "derive preferred time paths for policy instruments from the best feasible time paths of the ultimate target variable in a single, integrated decision" (Bryant, 1980)[3].

On the basis of this, the most appropriate conclusion is that, while targets may have a useful role, policy should not be aimed exclusively at any <u>single</u> target, and that no target should be adhered to rigidly.

(i)   Critique of Monetary Targets

Several governments adopted money supply targets during the 1970s with varying degrees of flexibility. Paradoxically, given the poor record of achievement in 1980 and 1981, the most extreme version was the MTFS in the UK though this was effectively abandoned in the 1982 budget. The basic rationale of monetary targets in the UK has been: (1) to supposedly establish credibility to the government's anti-inflation strategy, (2) the government originally believed that monetary targets would have a beneficial effect on inflation expectations and so induce more moderate wage claims and settlements, and (3) the concept of an 'elastic' money supply (through which the government passively 'finances' potentially inflationary wage claims) was considered to be inherently inflation biased.

But the record in the UK has not been encouraging. Money supply targets have not been an effective mechanism for inducing changes in labour market behaviour (see Llewellyn, 1982b) and the chosen target (£M3) has been an inefficient indicator. Sterling M3 is an arbitrary statistic which is difficult to justify on theoretical grounds.

The evidence also suggests that the demand for money functions are not sufficiently stable or predictable to warrant exclusive, or even predominant, reference to a money supply target. Above all, at the technical level £M_3 has been particularly difficult to control and in the first two years of the MTFS it rose by 48 per cent against a maximum target of 24 per cent. There are several reasons for this difficulty (see Llewellyn, 1982b) but central to the problem is the role of interest rates in the process of monetary control. Firstly, the demand for credit seems not to be very sensitive to interest rate movements. Secondly, high interest rates designed to secure monetary control adds substantially to the PSBR. Thirdly, high interest rates induce a high proportion of corporate funding to be made through the banking system (which adds to the money supply) rather than through, for instance, the debenture market which doesn't. Fourthly, through the effect on the exchange rate, it causes an unwarranted directional effect from monetary policy. Overall, the record of focussing upon a monetary target in the UK has not been good and neither has it in many other countries (Foot, 1981). A similar conclusion, particularly with respect to the rigidity of monetary targets, was given by the Bank for International Settlements in its 1980/81 <u>Annual Report</u>:

"there is no denying that governments were less well advised in relying chiefly, if not exclusively, on monetary policy to combat inflation. In the majority of cases this was not a deliberate choice, but was dictated by the practical difficulty of implementing other policies simultaneously - ie fiscal policy, incomes policy, measures to promote competition and to eliminate rigidities in both price and income formation and the optimum allocation of the factors of production. However, whether by choice or by force of circumstances, the overwhelming reliance placed on monetary policy in the fight against inflation is creating increasingly serious problems". (p.164)

The general role of monetary policy in moderating inflation may also be questioned on the basis of an analysis of the nature of 'causes' of inflation (Llewellyn, 1982b).

(ii) The Weakness of Floating Rates
A second strand in the argument in favour of EMS membership is associated with the negative aspects of the experience of floating exchange rates. Several advantages have traditionally been claimed for free floating: (i) the money supply becomes exclusively domestically determined and hence easier to control, (ii) floating rates enhance the power of monetary policy, (iii) while each country is forced to absorb its own inflation, the domestic economy is similarly insulated from disturbances originating in other countries, though this is critically determined by the nature of the disturbance (Bryant, 1980), and (iv) policy can be framed with purely domestic objectives in mind. But with experience, each of these alleged advantages has increasingly come to be challenged.

Overall, floating rates have not worked as efficiently as many analysts predicted. Exchange rates have frequently been volatile (though it might be contended that this in turn is due predominantly to monetary policy instability), and there is substantial evidence of short run overshooting of longer run equilibrium values. There is a dearth of speculators prepared to take a longer term view on equilibrium exchange rates, which in itself introduces unwarranted volatility which can have adverse economic and trading effects. It is also apparent that in practice floating rates have not conferred a high degree of policy independence. They have not enabled governments to pursue domestic objectives exclusively while ignoring external considerations (Maynard, 1978). Neither is it reasonable to suppose that floating rates could totally insulate economies from external disturbances (Bryant, 1980).

In addition to these general considerations, there is increasing doubt about the power of adjustments to nominal exchange rates to significantly influence real variables in the economy or provide an effective balance of payments adjustment mechanism. In particular: (i) changes in nominal rates have an uncertain (and small in the long run) effect upon real exchange rates because of the offsetting effect on domestic wages and prices (see, for instance, Ball, Burns, and Laury, 1977, and Robinson, Webb and Townsend, 1979), and (ii) any net changes in real exchange rates seem not to have powerful effects upon the balance of payments.

Part of the observed volatility of floating exchange rates is associated with the short run dominance of exchange markets by transactions in financial assets. This is to be expected given that markets in financial assets are well organised, information is disseminated and absorbed quickly, speculative gains can be made quickly and in general transactions costs are low. It also means that expectations have a powerful impact on exchange rates. But this tends to further accentuate volatility, not because speculators are irrational or perverse, but because they respond quickly (short run) to 'news' that may have its final impact only in the long run. Thus, while a rise in the money supply may have its effect on prices over say one year, and trade may respond only slowly to changes in real exchange rates, so called 'rational' speculators tend to discount the potential exchange rate effect immediately. The combination of lagged price effects and an immediate exchange rate response to a monetary contraction implies that monetary policy to moderate inflation operates largely through the effect on the real exchange rate. While this may accelerate the convergence on the targeted rate of inflation, it also has the effect of: (i) concentrating the real short run effect of monetary policy on the traded sector of the economy, and (ii) raising the cost of monetary contraction in terms of the magnitude of the (short run) unemployment effect (Artis and Currie, 1981). The former is undesirable as it is likely to cause unwarranted disturbances to wage differentials between traded and other sectors. To the extent that the unemployment effect of monetary contraction is concentrated, its impact on aggregate wage demands is also likely to be less powerful. If 'news' is erratic (especially monetary trends) so too will be speculators' expectations and hence exchange rates, even though the 'news' per se may, in the absence of speculation, have effects only in the long run.

The difference in time lags in financial and goods markets is one factor accounting for overshooting. The influence of temporary 'shocks' is a second factor which can be further accentuated by phases of extrapolative expectations. A third factor in overshooting is the risk premium required for equilibrating speculation.

The predominant motive in establishing the EMS was to avoid 'unnecessary' fluctuation in exchange rates. Given the way the scheme can be operated this objective can be secured without impeding required exchange rate adjustments. Irrevocably fixed exchange rates, or even a Bretton Woods scheme, would be inappropriate in the current world economic environment. The rationale for the EMS is a compromise between an unworkable regime of fixed exchange rates and the limitations of freely floating exchange rates.

(iii) An Exchange Rate Target

Central bank intervention in the foreign exchange market may be designed either to minimise the degree of fluctuation in the exchange rate or alternatively to maintain a specific exchange rate target. Most central banks (including, at times, the FED) undertake the former and 'rules' or 'guidelines' have been proposed by various analysts (International Monetary Fund, 1974; Ethier and Bloomfield, 1975; Artus and Crokett, 1978; and Mikesell and Goldstein, 1975). In the case of a target, the volume and direction of intervention is determined by the previously established target, and the flexibility of that target together with the tolerated margin of fluctuation. The case for 'smoothing' intervention is almost universally accepted. The establishment of a specific target is more controversial.

Arrangements such as the EMS in effect view the exchange rate as both a target (in the short run) but also an instrument though its frequent use as an instrument detracts from its value as a target. As a target it is a guide to the conduct of monetary policy, and dependent upon its credibility, a factor for wage bargainers to incorporate. Its use as an instrument is twofold: (i) to offset policy 'errors' (restore the value of the

real exchange rate) and, (ii) to secure a required change
in the real exchange rate due to autonomous pressures such
as differential shifts in productivity and trade patterns,
and structural phenomena such as the discovery of a
valuable resource such as North Sea oil. These are
'autonomous' in that they are not directly attributable to
policy. Vaubel (1978) observed a clear requirement for
changes in real exchange rates in the EC which were
sometimes quite substantial (as much as 3.5 per cent per
annum). For this reason if there is to be any 'rule' for
periodically adjusting exchange rate targets (whether it be
by reference to a formula or by discretion) it should not
be by reference to a 'purchasing-power-parity' requirement.
There may, therefore, be a requirement for changes in real
exchange rates as well as for changes in nominal exchange
rates to offset domestically induced changes in
competitiveness. In principle stable nominal rates could be
achieved even with a requirement for changes in real
exchange rates, but this would require domestic inflation
differentials to be determined by the required change in
real exchange rates. In practice this would be difficult to
maintain and hence any exchange rate arrangement, including
the EMS, must incorporate a mechanism for adjusting nominal
rates. One of the problems of a rigid exchange rate target
is that it precludes adjustments to nominal rates to secure
required changes in real exchange rates.

With this dual function ('managed fixing' as described in
Bryant, 1981), neither the exchange rate nor external
reserves are fixed in the long run, as both are adjusted in
relation to objectives and the nature of disturbances. It
is in this sense that, while the case is here made for an
exchange rate target, there is no presumption of total
rigidity. Totally fixed exchange rates (and hence by
extension EMU) is not a feasible immediate proposition.

The proposal is that sterling should be incorporated in
the EMS with the exchange rate used both as a target and a
periodic instrument. The case for its use as a target, as
opposed to a monetary aggregate target, is based upon its
perception by decision makers and particularly wage
bargainers. The credibility of monetary targets has already
been considered. With respect to the exchange rate the
threat of a devaluation (and its impact on prices and hence
real wages) would be more likely to be credible. Exchange
rate adjustments, when they are made, have an immediate and
direct effect upon prices and real wages. Secondly, while
the exchange rate is not adjusted the appeal of employers
to a loss of competitiveness (in terms of foreign currency
prices or profits) associated with wage demands in excess

of productivity is also likely to be more credible.
Thirdly, an exchange rate target is technically easier to
achieve, through intervention and interest rate policy than
is any definition of the money supply.

The role of the exchange rate as an instrument has been
indicated. But its credibility as a target would be lost
if: (i) the full extent of monetary policy errors were
allowed for in exchange rate adjustments and, (ii) if
adjustments were made frequently and whenever an upper or
lower band of fluctuation was reached. An exchange rate
adjustment has a useful role in adjusting to single policy
errors providing the error is not continuous. If the error
is continuous there may still be a role for exchange rate
adjustments if such changes are technically easier to
execute than removing the policy bias. Thus, it may for
technical reasons be difficult to secure a target for the
money supply but easy for the immediate external effect of
relative inflation to be offset by exchange rate
adjustments. But in this case the exchange rate has no
value as a target or disciplinary factor, except to the
extent that it more quickly demonstrates the futility of
attempting to secure real wage increases independent of
productivity through money wage adjustments. The case for
an EMS-type arrangement in this event is solely to avoid
volatile movements in the exchange rate. The strong
presumption, therefore, is that some policy adjustment must
be made to correct policy errors.

An argument against any exchange rate target is that
monetary control is severely constrained because of the
domestic monetary counterpart of foreign exchange market
intervention. This may be true while intervention is taking
place (though this too can be questioned). But one of the
objects of the target is to frame monetary policy with a
view to maintaining the exchange rate without permanent
intervention. This is sustainable if the collective
monetary policy of the group of countries in the exchange
rate system is acceptable. Short run changes in the money
supply have little economic significance which means that,
until foreign exchange market intervention becomes
continuous, the monetary problem is limited. If
intervention became continuous there would need to be
either an internal policy adjustment or an adjustment to
the exchange rate target.

In practice, monetary control with fixed exchange rates
is not totally constrained (Llewellyn, 1980), because of a
series of insulating mechanisms (forward exchange rate
adjustments, switches by banks between domestic and
external sources of high powered money, etc.) and because,

in the short run, the monetary effects of foreign exchange
market intervention can be _sterilised_. Sterilisation,
however, works against balance of payments adjustment and
can induce dynamic instability if simultaneously attempted
by several countries (De Grauwe, 1973). It is also
technically possible for a central bank to influence the
spot rate by intervening in both the forward and spot
markets without there being any net external effect upon
the domestic money supply. Thygesen (1981a) notes that
there is no evidence to date that the EMS has made it more
difficult to meet monetary targets.

It is not apparent that any current members of the EMS
are concerned about the lack of monetary control through
membership, and several countries (notably Germany and
Switzerland) have been able to combine elements of an
exchange rate and monetary target. Policy towards the
monetary target itself may be constrained by tolerance
limits set for the exchange rate. Both Germany and
Switzerland have at times adopted a monetary policy which
takes into account the behaviour of the exchange rate.
Faced with conflicts between adherence to monetary targets
and their effect upon the real exchange rate, both Germany
(1978/79) and Switzerland (1978) compromised on the
monetary target. The Swiss National Bank temporarily
abandoned its monetary target in favour of an explicit
exchange rate target. Overall, the strict dichotomy between
an exchange rate and monetary target is less precise in
practice than traditional theoretical models assume. At a
more general level, the analyses of Artis (1981) and Artis
and Currie (1981) indicate that an exchange rate target is
probably superior to a monetary target on the basis of
minimising the variance of prices around an established
target.

Adherence to an exchange rate target would not in
practice represent a radical change in policy for the UK.
Strict adherence to the MTFS should have implied no
exchange rate target. But in practice, the MTFS targets
were breached largely because of their interest rate and
exchange rate implications (Llewellyn, 1982b). Towards the
end of the second year of the MTFS increasing emphasis was
being given to the exchange rate and the level of interest
rates. In the March 1982 Budget there was a radical change
in the overall strategy of UK monetary policy. The change
centred upon: (i) the effective abandoning of the MTFS;
(ii) the replacement of the target for a single money
supply concept by a weaker target for a wide range of
liquidity aggregates, and (iii) the effective switch from
'money supply' as the target of policy to interest rates
and the exchange rate. Even before that time the Bank of

England (1982) had stated: "The exchange rate is both an indicator of monetary policy and one of the channels by which the effects of policy are transmitted to the economy...the behaviour of the exchange rate is therefore a consideration which must be given due weight in implementing monetary policy". The background to the change was the continued overshooting of the declared monetary targets in the first two years of the MTFS. This in turn was largely due to an unwillingness to accept the exchange rate and interest rate consequences rather than any technical inability to control the growth of monetary aggregates.

FUTURE STRATEGY

One exchange rate strategy for the UK would be membership of the EMS with a view also to influencing its operation along the following lines:
1. Adopt a 'Crawling Peg' mechanism for changes in central rates which would not imply discontinuous nominal rates.
2. Members should move in the direction of devising mechanisms to make explicit co-ordination of monetary policy consistent with minimal changes in central rates. This would need to be approached initially on an experimental basis. At the very least institutional mechanisms are required to highlight the mutual monetary policy implications of the EMS.
3. Ideally there would be more progress in developing, preferably with the co-operation of the USA, a concerted and consistent intervention policy with respect to non-member currencies. This would be particularly significant for the UK given that around 30 per cent of its trade is denominated in US dollars. This might also imply an element of monetary policy co-ordination with the US though this would appear ambitious under current conditions.
4. In order to reinforce the target role of the exchange rate the short term and medium term credit facilities could be extended and developed. Use could be made conditional upon mutually agreed monetary policy adjustments though of a less comprehensive nature than IMF conditionality provisions. Any mutually agreed exchange rate system necessarily has implications for consistent monetary policies and a degree of collective decision making, implying an element of 'pooled sovereignty', could be accepted as the means

towards making the exchange rate scheme effective.
5. While the 'Crawling Peg' mechanism would be used both
   to compensate for non-policy induced changes in the
   real exchange rate and for policy errors, the latter
   should be circumscribed in order to maintain some
   target role for the exchange rate. It could, for
   instance, imply that only 50 per cent of the
   calculated required change in the real exchange rate
   due to differential inflation would be incorporated
   into central rate adjustments. This would necessitate
   use of credit facilities to support the exchange
   rate.

The EMS can legitimately be viewed as little more than an
exchange rate mechanism, with monetary policy implications.
It would be unrealistic to view it as any initial stage in
a process towards full economic and monetary union.

The viability of the EMS would be enhanced if member
central banks developed a concerted and co-ordinated policy
with respect to intervention against the US dollar. Sharp
movements against the dollar present a potentially
difficult external environment for three reasons. Firstly,
a general climate of exchange market uncertainty can affect
intra-EC exchange rates. Secondly, they have a strong
potential to create tensions within the EMS itself as not
all member currencies have an equal status in speculative
flows. Movements out of the dollar frequently have a
counterpart in movements into the Deutschmark rather than
all member currencies. When the DM has been strong against
the dollar it has frequently been moved towards the upper
end of its EMS band and to the bottom end when the US
dollar has been strong. In fact, much of the pressure that
developed in the 'Snake' arrangement was associated with
speculative movements involving the US dollar. A third
problem is that, without a co-ordinated approach, there is
a danger of inconsistent intervention against the US
dollar.

Continuous external interventions would be problematic
without a degree of monetary policy co-ordination with the
USA. This was found at times in the Bretton Woods regime.
De Grauwe (1973), for instance, suggests that the Bretton
Woods system was made non-viable partly because of
inconsistent monetary policies. Co-ordinated intervention
as between members would also be less problematic if it was
also co-ordinated with the Federal Reserve. Over the 1970s,
the predominant strategy of the US authorities was one of
'Benign Neglect' with monetary and fiscal policy framed on
the basis of domestic targets, and the exchange rate
allowed to reflect foreign exchange market trends (Midland

Bank, 1979). For much of the 1970s the FED reserved foreign exchange market intervention for periods when exchange markets were manifestly 'disorderly'. For this reason, until 1977 the US dollar/Deutschmark rate was only lightly managed and only at times of 'disorderly' markets. The attitude of the US authorites changed, however, towards the end of 1977 when the US dollar came under sharp pressure. There was massive intervention in support of the US dollar in the final quarter of 1977 and the first three months of 1978 when the Bundesbank and FED intervened to an amount of over DM17 billion. Again, towards the end of the year as pressure continued similar intervention amounted to DM16 billion in two and a half months. The strategy of 'Benign Neglect' clearly changed after 1977 and towards the end of 1978 the FED announced a support package of $30 billion. But early in 1981 the new Reagan administration reverted to a 'Benign Neglect' posture. The Federal Reserve Bank of New York (1981) notes: "In mid-April the Treasury announced that, after study and consultation with officials of the Federal Reserve, the US authorities had adopted a minimal intervention approach".

This 'Benign Neglect' approach produced tension between US and European governments particularly in 1981. One of the features of international money markets in 1981 was the influence that monetary conditions in the USA had on interest rates in Europe. This became a major issue of dispute between European and American governments and came to be highlighted by European governments for several reasons. Firstly, American interest rates were high in real terms and were thought to be a major impediment to economic recovery both in the USA and in Europe. Secondly, the techniques of monetary control in the USA were such as to also induce more interest rate volatility in America which, given the Administration's 'Benign Neglect' policy over the exchange rate, induced corresponding exchange rate instability in Europe. Thirdly, there was concern in Europe that the very large Federal deficit, coupled with the monetary policy stance of the FED, meant that interest rates could stay high and volatile for some time.

EMS AND POLICY COORDINATION

For the EMS to remain viable, even with a 'Crawling Peg' mechanism for adjustments to central rates, there is a requirement for a higher degree of economic convergence, particularly with respect to rates of inflation. The divergent trends between EMS members was probably masked in

the first two years by fortuitous factors maintaining the
viability of the scheme. It is unlikely that market
mechanisms left alone will produce this within the required
period. More explicit policy co-ordination will almost
certainly be necessary to ensure durability of the scheme.
EC monetary and exchange rate policy has a structure of coordination through the Monetary Committee and the Committee
of Governors of Central Banks which meets monthly to
discuss and monitor developments within the EMS and current
issues of monetary policy.

In the final analysis any durable fixed exchange rate
arrangement requires compatible monetary trends, though the
problems of <u>ex ante</u> co-ordination are substantial. Firstly,
there would inevitably be protracted negotiations over the
standard to aim at resulting from a conflict of interest,
at least in the short run, between high and low inflation
centres. Secondly, the technical problem of calculating
for each member the rate of growth of the money supply that
is compatible with a fixed exchange rate would also be
formidable. In addition, the experience of monetary targets
suggests that, even if consistent money supply targets can
be agreed, there would remain difficult problems in
attaining them. Effective coordination also requires a
recognition that coordination is a less costly and more
certain method of securing targets which in turn
presupposes the absence of attempts to impose national
targets on unwilling partners. As is implied in Meade's
analysis (1951), if national targets are not consistent and
each country <u>believes</u> it is powerful enough to impose its
will, <u>ex ante</u> coordination is unlikely to be adopted.
Conflict can also arise over the distribution between
countries of the net policy changes required.

CONCLUSION

The original aim of full economic and monetary union is not
a feasible proposition <u>under current conditions</u>. It need
not be a significant issue for debate. Given the present
degree of economic and financial integration, which
constrains policy autonomy, the real costs, and true loss
of effective sovereignty implied by membership of such a
union, are probably not substantial (Llewellyn, 1982a).
Governments traditionally tend to overestimate their
autonomy and whatever residual national autonomy that does
remain is prized. But this does not detract from the case
for more formal monetary arrangements within the EC.

The case for the EMS is based upon: (i) the general

advantages of fixed exchange rates, (ii) scepticism about the power of exchange rate changes to adjust real wage differentials and the balance of payments, and (iii) the limited extent to which independent monetary policy affects the level of employment. But in the final analysis, the scheme, to be successful, must be based on acceptance by member governments of these propositions. This in turn requires that member governments pursue policies to produce consistent rates of inflation. Above all, it requires some mechanism to ensure that the monetary policies of member governments are compatible and conducive to exchange rate stability. It is unfortunate that much of the official discussion when establishing the EMS tended to concentrate on the technical issue of 'grids' vs. 'baskets' etc. rather than upon the more fundamental issue of how the required degree of convergence and policy compatibility is to be secured. The durability of the scheme will be determined, in no small part, by the willingness of high inflation countries to accept the short run employment costs of the necessary monetary adjustment. In this respect, past experience does not engender optimism with governments implicitly tending to value the short run costs more highly than longer run benefits of adequate monetary control policies. This will require a substantial political commitment to the scheme. No amount of eloquent political rhetoric about the virtues of 'zones of monetary stability' will substitute for what is ultimately required, namely a mechanism for ensuring that economic policies in general, and monetary policies in particular, are sufficiently compatible to remove the temptation to use the exchange rate mechanism as a regular instrument of policy.

NOTES

1.   See Presley, J.R. and Coffey, P. (1971) for a discussion of these plans and for a more detailed historical account see Hellman (1977).

2.   The mechanics and technical detail of the EMS are well described by the Bundesbank (1979) and the BIS (1979). Broader aspects are discussed in, for instance, Thygesen (1981b), Llewellyn (1982a), van Ypersele (1979), De Grauwe and Peeters (1979) de Vries (1980), IMF (1979), MacMahon (1979); Thygesen (1979). A good review of its operation is given by Mesera, (1981).

3.   Bryant (1980) contains detailed theoretical analysis and simulations of the stability conditions of alternative targets.

14 The Assignment of Regional Policy Powers within the EC

Harvey W. Armstrong

INTRODUCTION

The EC regional policy which has emerged since 1973 has been the subject of considerable controversy, much of which has concentrated upon the weaknesses of the policy as currently constituted (e.g. Van Doorn, 1975; Armstrong, 1978; MacLennan, 1979; Nevin, 1980) or on the manner in which it has been achieved (Talbot, 1978; Hull, 1979). Since EC regional policy has been changing over time, criticisms can be quite justifiably deflected on the grounds that it is unfair to attack a policy in its formative stages and which has some distance to go before reaching full strength.

A more fundamental issue than the existing assignment of regional policy powers to the EC is whether there is some optimal assignment and if so, what it is. This is a complex and controversial issue. Indeed, it will be argued later that there is no such thing as an optimal assignment since the particular regional policy powers suitable for the EC depend upon the degree of integration achieved and upon what other economic policy powers are eventually lodged with the EC. The optimal assignment will therefore change over time as the EC itself changes.

The following section examines the existing assignment of regional policy powers to the EC and member states.[1] Developments in regional policy since 1973 will also be discussed. The final section is much more speculative, and considers the criteria which can be used to justify EC involvement in regional policy. In the light of the issues examined in the final section conclusions will be drawn for appropriate changes to EC regional policy with specific reference to the UK. It will be argued that in certain important aspects EC regional policy falls short of what could be regarded as an 'absolute minimum', whilst in other ways the basic minimum has been already exceeded.

271

THE EXISTING ASSIGNMENT OF REGIONAL POLICY POWERS

Taking a broad view of what constitutes 'regional policy',
there are a number of policy options which are available.
It is unlikely that they would be all in use at any one
time. Of the policies set out in table 14.1 (based on
Armstrong and Taylor, 1978, p.163) regional policy has
traditionally been regarded as comprising measures designed
to reallocate capital in favour of assisted areas (options
1 to 5) and measures to reallocate labour (options 6 to 9).
In the UK capital reallocation policies, such as Regional
Development Grants, have predominated.

It is now widely accepted that many fiscal tax and
expenditure policies (options 12 and 13) can be used to
combat regional problems even though they are not
specifically regional policies. The work of Short (1978,
1981) and the MacDougall Report (1977) has shown that tax
and expenditure policies have substantial regional effects
which could, in many cases, be harnessed for regional
policy purposes. This already occurs in a rather haphazard
manner in the UK (e.g. defence spending, transport
infrastructure) and systematically in the EC though
regional impact assessment (RIA) procedures designed to
analyse and influence the regional effects of all major EC
policies.

In principle monetary policy (option 10) too could be
given a regional bias (e.g. easier credit in depressed
regions), though this is rare. Trade controls and tariffs
(option 11) could also be designed to assist particular
regions (Dauphin, 1978).

Finally, there is a third group of options which come
into their own in multi-jurisdictional systems such as the
EC (options 14-16). Policies are required to coordinate
same-level jurisdictions (option 14); that is, to
coordinate the policies of the different member states.
Policies are required to coordinate different-level
jurisdictions (option 15); that is, to coordinate EC
policies with member state policies. Finally, policies are
required to coordinate specifically regional policies with
other policies having a regional impact (option 16). This
latter form of coordination applies equally to a member
state and to the Community.

There has been no attempt to assign to the Community the
whole of the regional development function, all 16 policy
options of table 14.1. Three distinct types of assignment
have occurred. Firstly, some policy options have remained
solely assigned to member states. For example,
disincentives on investment such as Industrial Development

TABLE 14.1 : A CLASSIFICATION OF REGIONAL POLICY OPTIONS

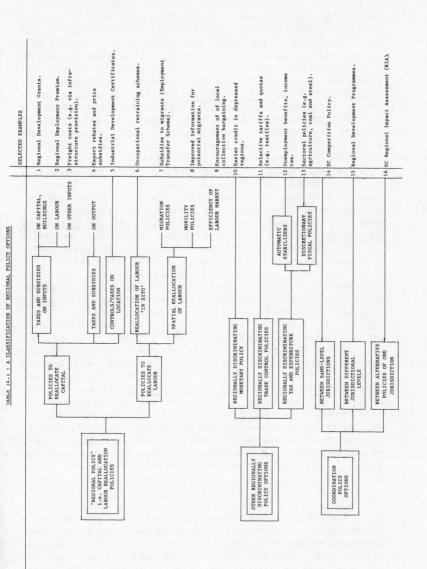

SELECTED EXAMPLES

1 Regional Development Grants.

2 Regional Employment Premium.

3 Freight costs (e.g. via infrastructure provision).

4 Export rebates and price
   subsidies.

5 Industrial Development Certificates.

6 Occupational retraining schemes.

7 Subsidies to migrants (Employment
   Transfer Scheme).

8 Improved information for
   potential migrants.

9 Encouragement of of local
   collective bargaining.

10 Easier credit in depressed
   regions.

11 Selective tariffs and quotas
   (e.g. textiles).

12 Unemployment benefits, income
   tax.

13 Sectoral policies (e.g.
   agriculture, coal and steel).

14 EC Competition Policy.

15 Regional Development Programmes.

16 EC Regional Impact Assessment (RIA).

Certificates (IDC), and labour subsidies like the Regional Employment Premium (REP (until 1977)) have remained member state functions. Secondly, one or two policy options have been assigned solely to the Community, for example, the EC has been instrumental in developing a number of coordination policies. Thirdly, and this has been the most common situation, joint authority in the provision of policy options has developed; these being situations where both the Community and the UK government operate a policy option. Most of the 'traditional' regional policy options fall into this category, particularly investment incentives, labour retraining and migration subsidies.

Breton and Scott (1978) identify a number of methods by which assignment and re-assignment of functions occurs in federal systems. Since effective power is held by member states through the Council of Ministers, EC regional policy has been assigned powers by a process of delegation of authority. In most cases the member states have delegated to the EC authority to participate in regional policy options, such as investment subsidies, which they themselves were previously operating and which they have continued to operate as part of their own regional policies. In one or two cases the EC was allowed to occupy a policy. The coordination policies were simply occupied by the EC. In principle member states could have bilaterally or multilaterally coordinated their regional policies, but in practice they did not. The EC was therefore able to take over a policy option not effectively being exercised by anyone. Occasionally too the EC has been allowed to take powers by changing jurisdictional boundaries. In 1979, for example, a 'non-quota' section of the European Regional Development Fund (ERDF) was established. For this section the jurisdictional boundaries of the ERDF were effectively widened because whereas 'quota' section expenditures must be made within the boundaries of member state assisted areas, 'non-quota' expenditures can be made anywhere in the EC.

(i) ERDF
In terms of the subsidies offered, the ERDF is in a situation of joint authority with member states, who have continued to operate their own regional policies much as before. The financial resources of member state regional policies greatly exceed those of the ERDF. Moreover, member states have restrained the discretion the EC has over four main aspects of the ERDF operations:

1.   the manner in which projects are chosen and

assisted;
2.   its financial size;
3.   the geographical distribution of its expenditures; and
4.   the types of policy option exercised.

In the manner in which projects are chosen and assisted two extreme alternatives can be envisaged. A 'minimum involvement' ERDF would be where the Fund was used merely as a vehicle to transfer resources for regional policy purposes from more prosperous to less prosperous member states. Member states would be left with complete discretion over the allocation of those resources. A 'maximum involvement' ERDF would give the EC complete discretion in choosing what the Fund is to assist and the way in which assistance is given. The present ERDF is somewhere between these two extremes in that the EC does have powers to receive, assess and choose projects to assist, but only within a framework of detailed regulations concerning the manner in which assistance is given. There are quite precise constraints on the minimum size of projects, on associated job creation and maintenance, on the types of project assisted (see also Commission, 1981a), on the maximum grant per project, and on the need for reciprocal member state subsidies on any ERDF-assisted project (Commission, 1975b, 1981b).   Applications and payments are also channelled through member states governments.
Recent proposals (Commission, 1981c) would lead to more EC discretion for "the Commissions' regional activities will be cast in a new mould, evolving from tasks mainly to do with bookkeeping and checking conformity with the Regulation, towards defining policy, promotion, planning, and providing technical assistance; from the functions of a financing body to those more clearly identified with a development agency" (Commission, 1981d). EC discretion would, under these proposals, be increased in three main ways:
Firstly, the 'non-quota' section of the ERDF would increase from 5 to 20 per cent of the total. This section, so-called because it need not be allocated among member states in pre-set national proportions, is designed to be linked with other EC policies or to help regions suffering particularly serious structural problems. 'Non-quota' expenditure, compared with 'quota' expenditure is much more at the discretion of the EC in terms of the eligible areas, the detailed manner in which aid is given, the size of the ERDF contribution and in the types of subsidies given (see,

for example, Commission, Official Journal L271 of 15/10/1980). 'Non-quota' expenditure is distinctive in that it is given through special multi-annual programmes rather than on a project-by-project basis. It is proposed that in future the Commission, rather than the Council of Ministers of member states, be given the power to authorise 'non-quota' assistance.

Secondly, it is proposed that 'quota' assistance too, over a three-year transition period, should move from the current project-by-project method to a system of multi-annual programme contracts with member states. As with the 'non-quota' programmes there would be greater EC discretion in the manner in which assistance is given. Only very large (over 40 million ECU[2]) projects would be separately financed.

Thirdly, integrated development operations of the type pioneered in Naples and Belfast (Commission, 1981c) would be extended. These are closely coordinated 'packages' of EC, member state and local authority initiatives focussed on specific small-area problems.

The gross financial size of the ERDF has been closely controlled by the member states, and also by the predominance of the CAP expenditure in the EC Budget; in 1981, agriculture took 61.9% of all EC appropriations for commitment - see chapter 8. The ERDF, meanwhile, took only 7.7 per cent of appropriations for commitment and 4.1 per cent of appropriations for payment (Commission, 1982a). Resources allocated to the ERDF have consistently fallen short of Commission requests.

As a result, ERDF expenditures have remained small relative to member state regional policy expenditures. In 1977, for example, grants from the ERDF[3] were 610 million EUA[4] whilst the combined member state subsidies[5] totalled 3,500 million EUA (Deacon, 1982, p.55). ERDF allocations to the UK for 1975-82 (first allocation) have totalled £859.83 million, £197 million of which were made in 1981. This compares with GB expenditure on regional policy of £701 million in 1976/77 alone (Marquand, 1980).

The financial impact of the ERDF is further reduced if member states choose to substitute ERDF expenditures for their own regional policy expenditures, something which is widely regarded as having been on a substantial scale. An obvious direct method of trying to ensure 'additionality' would be to make total ERDF expenditures in a member state depend upon the member state's own total regional policy expenditures rather than the present system of predetermined national 'quotas' from the ERDF. At present it is only at the level of individual projects that member state and ERDF subsidies are linked.

Instead of direct methods the EC has used indirect methods to try to prevent substitution of ERDF expenditures. Simple persuasion has been tried. The EC has also used improved information flows and better planning procedures such as the Regional Development Programmes (RDPs - see below) to get member states to commit themselves and subsequently justify their regional policy expenditures. The 1981 proposals (Commission 1981c) have maintained this approach. In addition, closer involvement with both member states and regional authorities through 'non-quota' special programmes, 'quota' programme contracts, integrated development operations and the like would give the EC a better chance of checking and putting pressure on member states. Payments to ERDF recipients direct, rather than through member states, are also proposed. However, it is hard to see how these various indirect methods will completely prevent a determined member state from substituting ERDF expenditures for its own.

EC discretion in the geographical distribution of ERDF expenditures is constrained in two ways. Firstly (table 14.2), 95 per cent of ERDF expenditures are made on the basis of national 'quotas' set by the Council of Ministers. This limits the discretion of the EC over the national distribution of ERDF expenditures (see table 14.3). Secondly, whilst the EC has greater control of the regional distribution of ERDF expenditures, this control is not total. 'Quota' section assistance is available only in the assisted areas as designated by the member states. Of course, within these assisted areas the EC can use its discretion to concentrate ERDF expenditures. Table 14.4 shows the distribution of ERDF expenditures by region in the UK.

The small 'non-quota' section introduced in 1979 gives the EC greater freedom over the national distribution (since it is not allocated by national 'quota') and over the regional distribution (since it need not be confined to member state assisted areas). Under the 1981 proposals member states assisted areas will still form the basis for ERDF 'quota' assistance, but not all would be eligible. Only those with high unemployment rates and low GDP per capita would be eligible and the EC would decide the GDP per capita and unemployment rate thresholds.

Finally, the types of policy option available to the ERDF are limited basically to grants and interest rebates on EC loans for investment in infrastructure, industrial, handicraft or service projects. Member states operate far

TABLE 14.2: GEOGRAPHICAL DISTRIBUTION OF EUROPEAN REGIONAL
DEVELOPMENT FUND

	Distribution by Member State	Distribution by Region
(a) 1973 Proposals[1]	No national 'quotas' for Fund expenditures.	Areas delimited by Commission[2] using multiple indicators. Assisted areas must be eligible for member state regional aids, have GDP per head less than EC average, and be either dependent on agriculture, declining industries or suffering structural under-employment.
(b) 1975 Regulation[3]	100% of Fund resources to be allocated on a 'quota' basis. Belgium 1.5% Denmark 1.3% France 15.0% Ireland 6.0% Italy 40.0% Lux'bourg 0.1% N'lands 1.7% Germany 6.4% U.Kingdom 28.0% Ireland also to receive £2.5m (1975-78) from all others except Italy.	Those areas also eligible for member state regional aids. Requirement to direct assistance to national priority areas.
(c) 1977 Proposals[4]	Separate 'quota' and 'non-quota' sections. For 1978 a 'quota' section of 87% of the total was proposed. To be allocated nationally using the quotas set out under 1975 regulation (above). 1978 'non-quota' section of 13% of the total proposed.	(a) 'Quota' section: as 1975 Regulation (above). (b) 'Non-quota' section: at the discretion of the EC and may be in areas other than those defined for 'quota' assistance.

TABLE 14.2 (contd/...)

	Distribution by Member State	Distribution by Region
(d) 1979 Regulation[5]	Separate 'quota' and 'non-quota' sections established. National quotas:	As 1977 proposals (above).

	1978-80	1981
Belgium	1.39%	1.11%
Denmark	1.20%	1.06%
France	16.86%	13.64%
Ireland	6.46%	5.94%
Italy	39.39%	35.49%
Luxembourg	0.09%	0.07%
N'lands	1.58%	1.24%
Germany	6.00%	4.65%
U.Kingdom	27.03%	23.80%
Greece	-	13.00%

'Quota' section to comprise 95% of all allocations. 'Non-quota' section to comprise 5% of all allocations.

	Distribution by Member State	Distribution by Region
(e) 1981 Proposals[6]	No 'quota' system ("poor man's quota"): **France:** Overseas depts. 2.47% **Denmark:** Greenland 1.30% **Ireland:** all regions 7.31% **Italy:** Mezzogiorno 43.67% **U. Kingdom:** assisted areas 29.28% of N.Ireland; Scotland;Wales; N.N.W. **Greece:** all except 15.97% Athens and Thessalonika 'Quota' section: 80% 'Non-quota' section: 20% of total.	(a) 'Quota' section: using boundaries as designated by member states but some member states given zero quotas while in the rest eligible regions designated by Commission on the basis of low GDP per capita and high long-term unemployment rates. (b) 'Non-quota' section: as before.

Notes:
1. EC Commission (1973a).
2. EC Commission Proposal for a Council Regulation on the List of Regions and Areas referred to in Regulation (EC) Establishing Regional Development Fund, COM(73),1751. Brussels 1973.
3. EC Commission (1975b).
4. EC Commission (1977a).
5. EC Commission (1981b).
6. EC Commission (1981c).
7. Separate assisted regions are delimited for mountain and hill farming area subsidies.

TABLE 14.3 : ERDF GRANTS BY MEMBER STATE, 1975-81

Member State	Assistance Approved 1975-1981	1981	Payments Made 1981
Belgium	53.75	2.67	9.17
Denmark	66.66	19.35	10.69
Germany	336.67	56.46	36.19
Greece	250.22	250.22	122.00
France	784.11	157.18	62.16
Ireland	336.47	105.72	79.32
Italy	2,119.56	700.80	210.16
Luxembourg	5.00	1.59	0.96
Netherlands	82.93	12.43	5.66
United Kingdom	1,257.77	361.51	255.10

Notes: 1. Figures are in million European Currency Units (ECU).
2. At 29/12/81 1 ECU = £0.569012.

Source: Commission (1982a).

TABLE 14.4 : ERDF ALLOCATIONS : BY UK REGION, 1975-82

(Figures are in £ million)

Region	Industry,Tourism	Infrastructure	Mountain Region Infrastructure	Total
North	75.46	118.14	-	193.60
North West	67.13	52.07	-	119.20
Yorkshire/ Humberside	5.41	42.14	-	47.62
East Midlands	1.42	7.12	-	8.54
South West	3.10	17.86	-	20.95
Scotland	52.91	149.54	10.92	213.38
Wales	39.95	98.00	-	137.98
N. Ireland	49.18	67.19	1.81	118.19
West Midlands	-	0.35	-	0.35
TOTAL	294.56	552.42	12.73	859.83

Note : Figures include only the first allocation of grants for 1982.

Source : EC Commission, Press Release ISEC/15/82.

more incentives (Commission, 1979a) and disincentives
(Commission, 1981e). New types of subsidies were
introduced through the 'non-quota' section after 1979 and
similar extensions are proposed for 'quota' expenditures
(Commission, 1981c). These involve subsidies for such
costs as management consultancy, tourist promotion,
innovation dissemination and implementation, and easier
capital market access. They are aimed particularly at
indigenous small and medium sized firms in the regions.

(ii) Other Community Financial Instruments
The European Investment Bank (EIB) raises resources largely
by borrowing on national and international capital markets,
and makes loans either direct to individual investment
projects or indirectly to smaller projects through 'global'
loans to financial intermediaries. It also guarantees loans
made by other financial institutions.

Regional development loans are only part of the EIB's
activities, which also includes loans of common interest to
several member states (e.g. in energy or transport
infrastrucure - see chapter 9), and loans for the
modernisation, conversion and creation of enterprises. EIB
also operates on behalf of the EC in non-member states.
Between 1958 and 1980, 72 per cent of all EIB loans within
the EC were for regional development (table 14.5). In 1981
two thirds of the 3,361.3 million ECU of EIB loans within
the EC were for regional development. Between 1973 and
1980 the UK received 27.5 per cent of EIB loans.

The New Community Borrowing and Lending Instrument (NCI),
created in 1978 (Commission, 1978a) and administered
through EIB has increased the resources available for
regional development loans. It is designed to assist
economic integration, and energy and infrastructure
projects, especially in depressed regions. A recent
extension envisages the NCI being used particularly for
oil-replacement, regional infrastructure and small and
medium-sized project loans (Commission COM(81) 790 of
9/12/81).

EIB loans are a genuine form of regional assistance. They
are often at attractive rates because of the non-profit
making nature of the EIB and its ability to borrow at
favourable rates. In addition a range of EIB loans are
eligible for interest rebates: from the ERDF; from the EC
on exceptional loans to Italy and Greece following
earthquakes (Commission, Official Journal, OJ L37 of
10/2/81 and L367 of 23/12/81); and from the EC on loans to
Italy and Ireland under a European Monetary System
arrangement (Commission, Official Journal, OJ L200 of

TABLE 14.5 : REGIONAL DEVELOPMENT OPERATIONS OF EIB, 1958-80

(Figures are in millions of Units of Account[1])

Objective	From EIB Own Resources	From NCI[2] Resources	Total	%
(A) Regional Development				
Belgium	90.0	–	90.0	0.8
Denmark	152.4	–	152.4	1.4
Germany	372.6	–	372.6	3.5
France	1,436.1	–	1,436.1	13.5
Ireland	925.4	128.4	1,053.8	9.9
Italy	4,776.5	143.6	4,920.1	46.1
Luxembourg	4.0	–	4.0	–
Netherlands	70.5	–	70.5	0.7
United Kingdom	2,539.4	25.9	2,565.3	24.1
TOTAL	10,366.9	297.9	10,664.8	100.0
(B) Modernisation and Conversion of Undertakings	274.7	–	274.7	
(C) Projects of Common Interest	5,670.8	232.8	5,903.6	
TOTAL[3]	14,407.7	474.6	14,882.3	

Notes: 1. During fourth quarter 1980 1u.a = £0.585871.
          2. New Community Instrument.
          3. (A) + (B) + (C) exceed the grand total because some projects
              can be justified simultaneously under more than one objective.

Source: European Investment Bank (1981), pp. 28-29.

8/8/79). Finally, a system of exchange risk cover has been provided by the UK on EIB (and ECSC) loans (European Community, 8/9, 1980. pp. 6-9).

The ECSC also has a substantial regional impact because of the particular industries it assists. As table 14.6 shows, its loans are largely for investment projects in the two industries themselves. In addition, 'conversion' loans are made to other industries to create jobs as coal and steel industry employment falls. Interest rebates are offered on loans and 'global' as well as direct loans are given.   Between 1975 and 1980 projects assisted by 'conversion' loans may have led to 49,087 new jobs, or about 37 per cent of coal and steel jobs lost (Commission COM(81) 717 final of 25/11/81). As with EIB loans, ECSC loans are often on quite attractive terms.

TABLE 14.6 : ECSC LOANS PAID OUT, 1954-81

(Figures are in million ECU)

Country	Industrial Investment (iron-ore, coal, steel, power stations)	Industrial Conversion	Workers Housing	Research etc	Total
Benelux	525.3	94.1	60.2	10.7	690.3
Denmark	55.5	–	1.4	–	56.9
Germany	1846.8	231.5	150.7	10.8	2239.8
Greece	–	–	–	–	–
France	1318.4	293.7	40.0	1.0	1653.1
Ireland	29.4	1.6	0.6	–	31.6
Italy	1239.2	72.4	32.5	11.6	1355.7
United Kingdom	2035.2	320.4	12.5	15.1	2383.2
TOTAL	7049.8	1013.7	297.9	49.2	8410.6

Source: Commission   of   the   European   Communities, Fifteenth   General   Report   of Activities of the European Communities in 1981, Brussels, 1982.

The ECSC also finances a number of labour reallocation policies - 'readaptation' aids to assist retraining, resettle workers and maintain the income of coal and steel workers.

FEOGA (or EAGGF) operations are important because many depressed regions are heavily dependent on agriculture and because of the predominance of EAGGF expenditures in the EC Budget. Guarantee Section expenditures in support of agricultural prices dominate EAGGF and have tended to particularly benefit the already prosperous milk, sugar and cereals producing regions of northern Europe (Commission, 1981f). The Guidance Section, designed to assist restructuring of the industry, has fallen from 15 per cent of EAGGF expenditure in 1964 to around 5 per cent now - see chapter 8. Guidance Section assistance has been given in a wide variety of ways: assistance to agricultural investment projects; subsidies for withdrawal from agriculture and land consolidation; training; direct aids to specific types of farming etc. In recent years attempts have been made to change the regional impact of both sections (Commission, 1982b), including particular measures for disadvantaged regions such as the mountain and hill farming areas and for the Mediterranean regions and Ireland (Commission, 1978b). Integrated programmes for specific areas and encompassing other EC aid as well as EAGGF have also been introduced (Commission, 1982b).

Finally, there is the European Social Fund (ESF) which supports a number of labour reallocation policies - vocational training, retraining and resettlement policies especially - see chapter 11. A range of groups are supported (women, handicapped, the young, those in agriculture and textiles) and there is a deliberate and increasing bias towards schemes in high unemployment regions and in industries undergoing rapid change. Specifically 'regional' assistance alone comprised 395 million ECU of the 963 million ECU appropriations for commitment in 1981. The UK receives about a quarter of all ESF aid.

(iii) Coordination Policies
Table 14.7 gives a broad classification of the range of possible coordination policies. The EC has become involved in all four categories, but particularly in coordination between its own regional and other policies (category 2), between member state regional policies (category 3A) and between EC and member state regional policies (category 4A).

From the start the EC has tried to coordinate its ERDF operations with those of other EC policies. From 1977 a regional impact assessment (RIA) procedure was introduced to systematically examine the regional effects of major EC policies. RIA is designed to either modify a policy before it is introduced; change a policy already in existence; or to allow remedial measures to be planned if changes cannot be made (especially using the 'non-quota' resources of ERDF).

Collecting, improving and analysing data on regional problems and policies has been a necessary pre-requisite to coordinating EC and member state policies. Information flows from member states have been improved. The Regional Policy Committee (RPC) established in 1975 studies and reports on a whole range of regional issues (as well as assessing large ERDF infrastructure project applications). The central role is allocated to the Regional Development Programmes (RDPs). These are meant to be specific documents submitted and updated by member states and designed to guide ERDF expenditures and allow coordination of EC and member state policies. The RPC was given the task of devising a standard format and assessing each programme as it was submitted. The initial set of programmes proved rather disappointing as planning documents (Commmission, 1979b).

Subsquent developments have been both 'upstream' and 'downstream' of the RDPs. On the 'upstream' side the Commission (with the RPC) has begun to produce biannual periodic reports on EC regional development (Commission 1981h), which form the basis of a set of regional policy priorities and guidelines (Commission, 1981d). Under the 1981 proposals the periodic reports will be every 2½ years and each alternate one will be timed to coincide with the examination of EC medium-term economic programmes (Commission, 1981c). On the 'downstream' side the 'non-quota' special programmes, the integrated development operations, the proposed 'quota' programme contracts, and the specific transfrontier programmes now being encouraged (Commission 1981g) all represent close cooperation with member states and, significantly, with regional and local authorities.

EC competition policy has also been involved in the coordination effort, principally in coordinating member state regional aids, but also regional and sectoral aids (Deacon, 1982, p.56,61) – see chapter 7. Competition policy coordination is exercised through a detailed system of controls (Commission, 1971b, 1976a, 1978c). The main features of the controls are a system of 'ceilings' on permissable regional subsidy per project, the 'ceilings' being higher in particularly depressed regions; a set of 'specificity' requirements (e.g. subsidies must not cover the whole country, must be in clearly defined areas etc); and restraints on the use of operating subsidies as distinct from initial investment subsidies.

TABLE 14.7 : CLASSIFICATION OF TYPES OF REGIONAL POLICY COORDINATION

		UNITED KINGDOM		OTHER MEMBER STATES		EUROPEAN COMMUNITY	
		Regional Policy	Other Policies With Regional Impacts	Regional Policy	Other Policies With Regional Impacts	Regional Policy	Other Policies With Regional Impacts
UNITED KINGDOM	Regional Policy		1	3A	3B	4A	4B
	Other Policies with Regional Impacts			3B	3B	4B	4B
OTHER MEMBER STATES	Regional Policy				1	4A	4B
	Other Policies with Regional Impact					4B	4B
EUROPEAN COMMUNITY	Regional Policy						2
	Other Policies with Regional Impacts						

CATEGORY 1   Coordination by a member state between its regional policy and its other policies.

CATEGORY 2   Coordination by the EC between its regional policy and its other policies.

CATEGORY 3   Coordination between member states:

3A   Between their regional policies alone.

3B   Between their other policies and between regional policies and their other policies.

CATEGORY 4   Coordination between member states and the EC:

4A   Between their regional policies alone.

4B   Between their other policies and between regional policy and their other policies.

CRITERIA FOR EC INVOLVEMENT IN REGIONAL POLICY

Forte (1977) has argued that "the study of ... assignment
in public expenditure theory has been mostly developed with
reference to the supply of public goods in the narrow
sense. However, it can, and should, fruitfully be extended
... to the entire spectrum of public functions" (p.324).
Elaborating Forte's list of criteria (pp.359-360) it is
possible to develop some generalisations concerning the
optimal assignment of regional policy powers to the EC.
Three groups of assignment criteria are suggested (table
14.8) - economic spillovers; operating efficiency of
regional policy; and non-economic spillovers.

(i) Economic spillover effects
One of the main reasons for national governments to take
for themselves regional policy powers is the spillover of
economic benefits of regional development from the assisted
regions across the whole nation. By similar logic if it
could be shown that assisted area development generates
benefits which reach out not only across the other regions
of the same member state but also across other member
states of the EC, then there would be a case for EC
involvement in regional policy[6].
A number of types of economic equity and efficiency
spillovers are said to exist.[7] Equity gains are widely
regarded as a major justification for regional policy.
Traditionally equity has been regarded, for a variety of
reasons, as a top-level function (Musgrave and Musgrave,
1973; Oates, 1972). This would seem to support a strong EC
regional policy. One major reason is the public good
characteristics of redistribution (Thurow, 1971). People
throughout the EC can be regarded as deriving utility from
the knowledge that residents of UK assisted areas are made
better off. That is, the benefit area of regional policy
exceeds the jurisdictional boundaries of both the region
itself and the member state of which it is part.
There may be several reasons for these equity spillover
gains to other EC residents. In part it may be pure
altruism. Alternatively it may be a fear of the social
effects of poverty. Finally, rising incomes in assisted
areas may yield external benefits through better education
and health from which the whole EC would benefit (Pauly,
1973).
Whilst equity spillovers do constitute a case for an EC
regional policy, what is less obvious is just how much EC
involvement is justified. One convincing point of view is
that redistribution is a local public good (Pauly, 1973),

TABLE 14.8 : CRITERIA FOR EC INVOLVEMENT IN REGIONAL POLICY

Criterion	UK GOVERNMENT PARTICIPATION	EC PARTICIPATION	DOMINANT JURISDICTION	FAVOURED BY FURTHER INTEGRATION
(1) ECONOMIC SPILLOVER EFFECTS				
a) Equity Spillovers	✓	✓	UK	EC?
b) Efficiency Spillovers	✓	✓	UK	EC
(2) OPERATING EFFICIENCY OF REGIONAL POLICY				
a) Financial Resources	✓	✓	EC?	EC
b) Uniformity and Coordination		✓	EC	EC
c) Invisibility and Economies of Scale	✓		UK	Unchanged
d) Innovation and Competition	✓		UK	Unchanged
e) Democratic Control	✓		UK	EC?
f) Ease of Evaluation	Polar Case*	Polar Case*	Polar Case*	Polar Case*
(3) NONECONOMIC SPILLOVERS	✓	✓	UK	EC?

*Polar case. Evaluation would be easier if either the UK or the EC dominated any given policy instrument. Situations of joint authority in policy are hardest to evaluate.

utility spillover benefits diminishing with distance from
the assisted region. A resident of London, for example,
would be most concerned with low-income Londoners, rather
less concerned with low-income residents of Scotland, and
even less concerned with low-income residents of southern
Italy. An opinion poll in 123 EC regions recently showed
that "European citizens are prepared ... to help the less
prosperous regions, but ... people feel more solidarity
with the regions of their own countries than with regions
in other Community countries" (Bulletin of the European
Communities, Volume 14, No. 7/8, 1981, p.38). The more
redistribution is a local rather than an EC-wide public
good, the greater will be the extent to which equity
spillovers are confined within member state boundaries, and
the smaller will be the scale of EC participation
justified. It is possible that in an integrating EC equity
spillovers will increase over time justifying a greater EC
involvement in the future.

Efficiency spillovers are also alleged to flow from
regional policy, [8] particularly during periods of low
unemployment. Once again, to the extent that these extend
across the member state there is a case for national
involvement in regional policy and to the extent they reach
out to other member states there is a case for EC
involvement. Two main efficiency spillover arguments exist
- that regional policy increases the utilisation of
resources and that regional policy improves the allocation
of resources.

Regional policy has the potential to increase the
utilisation of resources by bringing into employment the
pockets of unemployment which persist in depressed regions
even when there is high aggregate demand. This is a
spillover benefit because all regions will benefit from the
resulting once-for-all increase in output. By similar logic
the unequal incidence of unemployed resources in the EC
means that a EC regional policy may lead to a higher EC
level of output from which all member states would benefit.

Once again it is not clear just how much EC participation
in regional policy is justified. The extent to which other
member states benefit from greater resource utilisation in
UK assisted areas is an empirical question which has not
been explored. There has been some discussion of the
mechanisms by which UK non-assisted areas benefit from
increased UK assisted area output (Moore and Rhodes, 1975).
Two types of spillover benefit are indicated.

Firstly, reduced unemployment and increased assisted area
incomes generate a number of fiscal effects for the
national exchequer. On the one hand there is the actual

financial cost of operating the regional policy, but on the other hand increased economic activity in assisted areas generates greater tax revenues, reduces benefits payments, and creates a variety of other beneficial clawback effects. These clawback benefits can be very substantial (Needleman and Scott, 1964). Indeed, Moore and Rhodes (1975) have argued that under certain assumptions the fiscal benefits can outweight the fiscal costs of regional policy. In such a case, tax-payers in non-assisted areas would, paradoxically, actually gain from regional policy. Whether such a 'fiscal spillover' exists in the UK is an extremely controversial issue and depends upon the crucial assumption made by Moore and Rhodes (1975) that the successful diversion of economic activity to areas of higher unemployment would allow the government to operate a more expansionary macroeconomic policy with lower tax burdens in all regions. The chances of a similar 'fiscal spillover' effect operating <u>between member states</u> is even less likely than it occurring within the UK because it is the member states and not the EC which control the fiscal policy instruments which generate the spillover. Any tax or expenditure benefits of UK assisted area improvement will, under present financial arrangements, accrue to UK taxpayers and not across the EC.

Secondly, during periods of high aggregate demand, by channelling demand into areas where unemployed resources exist, it ought to be possible to run the whole economy at a higher level of output for any given inflation or balance of payments constraint. All regions should benefit from a higher <u>sustainable</u> level of demand. In principle this argument should also apply at the EC level. It has not, however, ever been demonstrated empirically to be a substantial effect even at the national level and is obviously of little relevance during periods of low aggregate demand as currently characterise the EC. In any event, decisions concerning sustainable aggregate demand are a matter for member states at present, and reduced regional imbalances in the UK are hardly likely to encourage other member states to expand their economies.

Utilisation of resource spillovers do not therefore seem a strong justification for EC participation in regional policy. In a much more integrated EC with fewer tax and expenditure powers in the hands of the member states, and during periods of high aggregate demand, the resource utilisation case would be stronger.

<u>Allocation of resources</u> benefits are also occasionally alleged to flow from a successful regional policy, by reducing pressures on major urban centres and by relieving

congestion and other urban externalities. This has never
been a strong argument. The diseconomies involved are
extremely localised and are more a target for urban policy
than for regional policy (Cameron, 1974).

Taken together, the various economic spillover arguments
used so effectively in the past to justify the
establishment of regional policies by member state
governments do not represent a very strong case, at
present, for a powerful EC regional policy. There is,
however, one further economic spillover argument which has
been much more forcefully put by supporters of the EC. A
stronger EC regional policy, it is alleged, "is not only
desirable: it is now one of the conditions of continuing
European economic integration" (Commission, 1977a). This is
a special case of the economic spillover justification for
an EC regional policy. Realising the benefits of further
economic and monetary integration, which would be enjoyed
right across the EC, can only occur if there is a powerful
regional policy designed to mitigate regional imbalances
arising from further integration.   Regional policy is
therefore seen as a means to an end rather than something
beneficial in its own right (Forte, 1977).

This argument is ingenious and commands wide support.
There is little doubt that economic and monetary union
would cause major additional regional problems in the EC.
Member states would find it more difficult to protect the
competitiveness of their economies and their depressed
regions, and greater factor mobility and freer trade would
cause profound structural change in the EC regions
(Armstrong, 1978; McCrone, 1971). The integration argument
must, however, be kept in perspective. It is not the case
that full economic and monetary union would imply that EC
regional policy should replace member states regional
policies or even that it should necessarily be the dominant
partner. Just because the EC may cause further regional
problems does not mean that it is EC regional policy alone
which is best placed to solve them. Equally, however the
magnitude of the regional problems arising from economic
and monetary union would be likely to be such that
individual member states would also be unable to tackle
them alone.

In addition, the economic and monetary union argument for
EC regional policy presupposes that further integration is
worthwhile. EC regional policy is seen as being necessary
if further integration is to be negotiated, and further
integration is used to justify an EC regional policy in
order to tackle the resulting new regional problems.   This
line of reasoning rests on the fundamental presumption that

further economic and monetary integration would bring such substantial benefits that an EC regional policy would be a small price to pay. Not all would agree with this presumption.

(ii) Operating Efficiency of Regional Policy
(a)   Financial resource transfers

Since regional problems are not equally shared among the member states and since future developments are unlikely to lead to a 'fairer' share of regional problems, by channelling financial resources to less prosperous member states, EC regional policy can ensure adequate funding where it is most needed. There is enormous potential here for improving the overall efficiency of the regional policy effort.

Regional problems are very unequally distributed amongst member states. Most central regions are relatively prosperous and most peripheral regions are depressed (Holland, 1976a, 1976b; Commission, 1977b). Some member states (Ireland, Greece, Italy, UK) are virtually depressed regions in their own right.

Nor is the economic integration likely to lead to a more equal share of regional problems among member states. Improved capital and labour mobility coupled with more favourable market access in central regions (McCrone, 1971; Clark et al, 1969) is likely to favour 'core' areas of the EC. Moreover, there is no reason to expect each member state to share equally in the costs or benefits of integration, as earlier chapters have demonstrated. New and distinct types of regional problem will emerge (Hansen, 1977).

Existing ERDF transfers are too small to properly exploit the potential gains from improving regional policy funding in less prosperous member states. In addition, they are overshadowed by the complex regional effects of EC revenue-raising (custom duties, agricultural levies, value-added tax - see chapter 12) and expenditure policies dominated by agriculture policy spending. The small scale of transfers between member states for regional policy purposes is the major failure of EC regional policy.

Over the longer-run the need for financial transfers could develop an additional importance. A member state with major regional problems may find its fiscal base so weak that high tax burdens develop. In a highly integrated EC problems of taxpayer mobility in response to tax burdens could occur. The loss of firms and households would weaken the fiscal base further. Taxpayer mobility will, however, never be the problem at EC level that it is at the urban

level. Labour mobility between member states faces many
restrictions and firm's location decisions depend on many
variables apart from taxation.

(b) Uniformity and coordination

The EC is the obvious forum for organising coordination
policies to improve the efficiency of the overall regional
policy effort. There is a distinction between coordination
to prevent policies from contradicting one another and
coordination to exploit an opportunity for greater regional
policy efficiency. Examples of the former are competition
policy 'ceilings' to prevent member states from using
regional incentives to competitively bid for mobile
capital; and attempts to change the existing regional
impact of the CAP. Examples of the latter are transfrontier
programmes and projects of common interest to several
member states.

The case for EC involvement in coordination is clear cut.
The priorities for future action, in diminishing order of
importance, are the need to coordinate the CAP much more
with regional policy; the need to improve the coordination
of member state and EC non-regional policies with regional
policy and, possibly, a more coherent coordination of
disincentive schemes (though opinions are divided on the
latter - Commission, 1981e).

Two coordination issues are more controversial and
deserve more consideration. The first concerns the degree
to which it is necessary for the EC to become involved in
the details of how the policies are implemented 'on the
ground' in order to improve coordination with member
states. Initially the EC confined itself to providing a
broad planning framework (through RDPs, periodic reports,
etc.) and to providing an analytical role in which
situations likely to benefit from coordination could be
identified. More recently there has been closer
involvement through schemes like the integrated development
operations.

The second issue concerns the case for very strong types
of coordination; that is, uniformity for a policy. The
competition policy 'ceilings' and restrictions on policy
types represent some degree of imposed uniformity. It is
not perfect uniformity: the 'ceilings' are not
simultaneously 'floors' and are also allowed to vary
depending upon how severe the regional problems are. There
is a trade-off between the advantages of a degree of
uniformity (e.g. to prevent competitive bidding for mobile
investment) and the advantages of giving member states as
much discretion as possible in selecting and operating

their own regional policies (see below).

(c) Indivisibilities and economies of scale

Indivisibilities and economies of scale are sometimes used to justify central government provision of public goods. Since regional policy involves no physical act of production this is not an important criterion.

Presumably a single (EC) regional policy would be less costly to administer than ten separate member state regional policies. Administrative costs of regional policy are, however, trivial by comparison with the subsidies disbursed.   Moreover, it would surely be illogical to concentrate in Brussels all employment associated with administering regional policy when creating regional employment opportunities is a major objective.

Above all it is important to distinguish between control and execution of a policy. Wherever final regional policy control powers are assigned, the actual execution activities ought surely to be decentralised as far as is possible.

(d) Innovation and competiton

These considerations strongly favour member state and regional authority control of regional policy. Competition is important for morale and encourages innovation. More importantly the EC simply cannot expect to match member states and regions in their understanding of their own particular regional problems.

(e) Democratic control

This too favours member state and regional participation in regional policy.

(f) Ease of Evaluation

This is not a trivial criterion. Effective evaluation is vital to the development of new types of regional policy and the improvement of existing types. The existing situation of joint authority makes it very difficult to disentangle the effects of EC and member state regional policies. Evaluation would be easiest if a particular regional policy instrument was wholly assigned either to the member states or to the EC, but not to both. Fairly standard, easily quantified policies would also be preferred. This obviously conflicts with some of the other criteria.

(iii) Noneconomic spillovers

Regional policy may yield benefits to the whole EC of a

political or social nature. Reduced regional disparities
are often alleged to be necessary for greater political
cooperation. Some regions may have political or strategic
value (e.g. W.German border regions). Preservation of local
languages and cultures may also be considered valuable. As
with economic spillovers many of these non-economic
spillovers no doubt diminish with distance from the region
concerned, implying the need for a EC regional policy less
powerful than member state regional policies.

CONCLUSION

The various assignment criteria discussed in the third
section reveal just how complex and controversial the case
for a EC regional policy is. The criteria themselves
frequently conflict. On the one hand the criteria of
indivisibility and economies of scale, innovation and
competition, and democratic control all favour the
decentralised control of regional policy with only a weak
EC involvement. On the other hand the various spillover
criteria, together with the financial transfer and
coordination criteria would all favour some degree of EC
control of regional policy. On balance, and certainly for
the foreseeable future, some form of joint authority is
suggested, with member state regional policies playing the
major role and EC regional policy the minor role.
    Just how minor a role the EC should play is another
matter. The most convincing arguments for an EC regional
policy given the present degree of integration of the EC
are firstly, the potential that exists for the EC to
improve the funding of regional policies in less prosperous
member states such as the UK; and secondly, the potential
for EC-led coordination of the regional policy effort. An
'absolute minimum' EC regional policy would therefore
comprise two parts. Firstly, a financial mechanism to
transfer resources from member states with a small
proportion of EC problem regions (such as France and
Germany) to those with a high proportion (such as the UK).
Secondly, a set of coordination policies.
    Current transfers to the UK through the existing
financial mechanism (ERDF) fall well short of the minimum
justifiable and are rendered even less effective by member
states substituting ERDF expenditures for their own, and by
the relatively unplanned regional impacts of other EC
revenue and expenditure policies, especially the CAP. These
three issues (the size of ERDF; member state substitution
of ERDF expenditures; and the regional impact of various EC

revenue and expenditure policies) are the key to the future
of the EC regional policy. There has been some limited
progress on all three which has helped to change the EC
regional policy so that it is more suited to UK
requirements. The progress has been strictly limited
however. The size of the ERDF remains small; member state
substitution of ERDF expenditure has not been eliminated;
and the regional impact of the dominant CAP expenditures
still leaves a lot to be desired. Attempts to tackle the
problem of financial transfers have been very <u>ad hoc</u> (e.g.
through one-off schemes such as the supplementary measures
granted to the UK under the 1980 budget compromise -
Commission, <u>Official Journal</u> OJ L284 of 29/10/80 and OJ L96
of 8/4/81). The recent proposals for changing the ERDF
(Commission, 1981c) are complex and far-reaching but are
largely concerned with issues other than this central issue
of the size of the financial transfer.

Whilst falling short of the 'absolute minimum' in terms
of financial transfers, the ERDF exceeds the 'absolute
minimum' in other aspects of its operation. The ERDF is not
simply a financial instrument. It's resources are not
unconditionally transferred to member states. There is
already a fair degree of EC involvement in the manner in
which ERDF assistance is implemented. The recent proposals
envisage a large increase in direct ERDF involvement.

As has already been noted, there is a clear case for EC
participation in coordination policies and there is scope
for quite a lot more progress, in particular in
coordinating regional polices with other policies of member
states and the EC itself.

From a UK viewpoint future development of the ERDF would
preferably be concerned with the size of financial
resources available to it. Changes in the ways in which the
EC is involved in disbursing assistance are interesting but
of much less importance. They also run the risk of
interfering in member states discretion over their own
regional policy, something which may conflict with several
of the criteria examined in the final section.

Finally, there is a case for gradually increasing EC
involvement in regional policy if further economic
integration occurs, but member states regional policies
will necessarily continue to have the major role to play in
the future.

ACKNOWLEDGEMENTS

The author is grateful for constructive comments and advice

from Jim Taylor of the University of Lancaster and
Edward Nevin at the University College of Swansea. Any
omissions and errors, of course, are entirely my own
responsibility.

NOTES

1.   The question of assigning economic development powers
to sub-national governments is not considered. Regional and
local jurisdictions have only weak economic development
powers in the UK, the member state of particular interest.
That is not to say that regional and local jurisdictions
should be weak. Indeed the emergence of ad hoc development
organisations such as the Scottish and Welsh Development
Agencies suggests that they have a role. Such agencies are
not democratically elected but can still be regarded as
jurisdictions, defined as "any institution to which a
function has been assigned or to which one could be
assigned" (Breton and Scott, 1978, p.347). In addition, the
chapter will not consider the merits of assigning functions
within the EC itself among the various funds, directorates
and institutions which comprise the EC. This too is a very
interesting issue of some importance. The division of
functions, for example, between competition policy and
regional policy directorates (Commission, 1979a) and
between the ERDF and ESF are assignment questions of major
importance to the effectiveness of the EC regional policy
effort, but are beyond the scope of this chapter.

2.   At 29 December 1981 1 European Currency Unit (ECU) =
£0.569012.

3.   Including ECSC aid.

4.   European Unit of Account (EUA), like the ECU, is
defined in terms of a 'basket' of currencies and its value
fluctuates with exchange rates; it pre-dates ECU.

5.   Deacon (1982) notes that these figures underestimate
member state subsidies in several ways (e.g. infrastructure
grants are included in ERDF figures but not member state
figures; grant elements only were estimated, such as
interest rebates on loan; and some member state aids were
ignored).

6.   Note that this justification would be valid
irrespective of the causes of the regional problems.

Economic spillovers suggest that, assuming they are substantial, the EC would be justified in involving itself not only in tackling those regional problems for which it bears responsibility, but also in tackling regional problems which already existed or which would have developed irrespective of the EC. This was the view taken in 1977 Guidelines (Commission, 1977a) and in the creation of 'quota' (to assist member states) and 'non-quota' (specific EC measures) sections of the ERDF in 1979 (Commission, 1981b).

7.   All of these justifications have their critics. Opponents of the equity spillover argument for example have claimed that regional policy is an inefficient method of redistributing income compared with, say, progressive taxation or interpersonal transfers. Others (e.g. West, 1973) argue that there may be a conflict between 'place prosperity' and 'people prosperity' if regional policy makes rich persons in poor regions better off.

8.   Critics would argue that the efficiency spillovers are negative not positive where regional policies cause an inefficient location of firms.

15 EC Defence Policy

Keith Hartley

DOES EUROPE NEED A DEFENCE POLICY?

Although defence is outside of the EC's remit, it has an
indirect involvement, reflected in three areas. First, the
EC nations form a European sub-set of NATO, reflected in
Eurogroup and the Independent European Programme Group
(IEPG).[1] Second, the EC is developing industrial and
technology policies, both of which involve weapons
industries (e.g. aerospace, communications, electronics,
nuclear power, shipbuilding, vehicles – see EC Commission,
1978). Third, the EC is likely to distort resource
allocation and trade flows between members if it promotes
free trade and competition in civil goods and services to
the exclusion of weapons markets. Inevitably, questions
arise as to whether the EC needs a defence policy embracing
the development and production of weapons and the provision
of collective security. In other words, is it possible for
the EC to improve the efficiency of Europe's contribution
to NATO's defence output (i.e. peace, security,
protection)? Much depends on whether there are unexploited,
but worthwhile, opportunities for improving the operation
of European weapons and defence markets.

Certainly, this is a subject area which has seen
considerable controversy amongst European nations. An
extended peace in Europe has created pressures for reduced
defence spending which has conflicted with the opposing
demands for larger military budgets to meet the apparently
ever-increasing threat from the Warsaw Pact. Debates have
arisen about nuclear weapons, the siting of cruise
missiles, disarmament, burden-sharing in the Alliance,
standardisation and the need to protect European
independence. Within the UK, there has been a continuing
debate about the optimal size of the defence budget,
whether Britain should concentrate on Europe or retain a
world-wide capability, the need for a domestic weapons
industry, and the costs of an independent nuclear deterrent
in terms of the sacrifices of conventional weapons
(Hartley, 1981l; Hartley and McLean, 1981). In general,

299

these debates reflect the classic choice problem
confronting all nations, namely, how much to spend on
defence and how to allocate budgets between manpower and
weapons, nuclear and conventional forces, between each of
the armed services, and the geographical distribution of
the forces. Economists are fond of analysing such issues in
terms of market failure and the possibilities of achieving
an optimal outcome through national and international
government intervention (e.g. alliances). But such an
approach neglects the possibilities of government failure,
reflecting the self-interested behaviour of agents in each
nation's political market. This raises the general question
of whether economic analysis offers any guidelines for a
European defence policy and how any such guidelines are
likely to be affected by the national and international
political markets in which public choices are made. A
starting point has to be a consideration of the economic
characteristics of defence and alliances.

THE ECONOMICS OF DEFENCE AND ALLIANCES

Defence is the result of combining resource inputs,
particularly manpower and weapons, to provide an output in
the form of peace, protection and security for a nation's
citizens. There are three distinctive characteristics.
First, in most NATO nations, military manpower is partly
conscripted, with only the UK and the USA relying on all -
volunteer force recruited in competition with civilian
jobs. Second, increased defence spending and advances in
weapons technology by a potential enemy reduce the
protection provided by a defending nation's existing
military budget. This contrasts with other government civil
expenditure, such as education and health, where more
public spending by a foreign nation on those goods does not
reduce the output of our schools and hospitals (Peacock,
1972). Third, defence is a public good in that its
provision for one citizen does not exclude the protection
of others (e.g. air defence of the UK). In this situation,
people have an incentive to conceal their true valuation of
protection, thereby 'free riding': hence, with large
numbers of citizens, governments usually have to intervene
to finance defence through national taxation. Similarly, a
small group of nations might benefit from collective
defence arrangements. NATO is a classic example of a
military alliance, where the continued voluntary
participation suggests that each nation believes that
membership is worthwhile.

NATO provides a public good in the form of collective defence and deterrence: an attack on one member is regarded as an attack on all. Economic models predict that the larger nations in an alliance will devote a larger proportion of their national output to defence than smaller countries (Olson and Zeckhauser 1966). Also, the more defence a nation's allies provide, the less that nation will spend on defence. Inevitably, the incentives and opportunities for 'free riding' in an alliance create controversy over the sharing of defence burdens; free riding constitutes a threat to the continued existence of an alliance. Smaller countries may conceal their 'true' valuations of the benefits of combined defence if they believe that larger nations' defence efforts will provide them with uncovenanted benefits. Here, it has to be remembered that NATO is a <u>voluntary</u> club of independent states and not a supranational organisation with independent budgetary and allocative powers. NATO cannot act as a dictator selecting the 'optimal' size of the defence budget for the Alliance, determining military tasks and weapons manufacture on the basis of each nation's comparative advantage, and allocating financial burdens to members, including compensation. Instead, defence choices in NATO are made by each national government, with variations in their policy aims, in the valuation of military and civil goods, in attitudes to risk and uncertainty and in established interest groups. Indeed, in so far as there is some uncertainty about the Alliance response to an armed attack, members are likely to make their own 'insurance' arrangements. They have an incentive to maintain a balanced range of national forces (i.e. army, navy and air force), to retain an independent strategic nuclear deterrent, and to support a domestic weapons industry. National independence means that each member will aim to maximise private benefits from the NATO club through free riding and adopting force structures and weapons which will contribute to national welfare rather than to collective security. As a result, agreements between members to increase military spending (e.g. by 3% p.a.) without reference to the composition of this expenditure are likely to be sub-optimal from the Alliance viewpoint (Sandler, 1977). For example, nations will differ in their 'willingness to pay' for a domestic weapons industry, especially since procurement policy tends to embrace objectives other than protection. Usually, jobs, exports, import-saving and the acquisition of advanced technology are amongst the 'goods' being acquired. Once such wider policy aims are part of the purchased 'product', it becomes increasingly difficult to assess the efficiency of procurement choices. Further modifications to the simple economic model of alliances arise from the existence of political markets.

European members of NATO have different constitutional arrangements for making public choices. With defence, voters are usually unable to express their preferences on specific issues due to the general nature of elections and legal constraints on the provision of information. As a result, governments will have discretion in interpreting the 'national interest', subject to advice and influence from bureaucracies and interest groups. In this context, UK defence choices are influenced by the Ministry of Defence and the Armed Forces seeking to protect and increase military budgets, supported by weapons contractors and scientists offering to protect British jobs, advance national technology and avoid 'undue dependence' on foreigners. Further support for UK defence spending will come from NATO and other Allies aiming to shift the burdens of military expenditure (e.g. by arguing that the UK's contribution to European defence is a vital and indispensable part of the Alliance). The EC and its members might also seek to persuade the UK to become involved in collaborative ventures for new weapons projects, the aim being to create European industries (e.g. aerospace – see Hartley, 1981). Opposition to military spending will come from the social welfare departments such as Education and Health, together with the Foreign Office favouring diplomacy and the Treasury concerned about controlling expenditure on high technology domestic weapons projects. Opposition is also likely from UK and European peace movements (e.g. CND), together with trade unions seeking larger government expenditure on the social services. Thus, given the variety of agents in the national and international political bargaining market, the resulting level and composition of NATO defence spending is unlikely to approach the 'optimal' collective outcome indicated by applying orthodox economic criteria (see Table 15.1). Various indicators have been used to influence the defence policies of European NATO members. References are made to the 'threat' from the Warsaw Pact, relative defence burdens and to the opportunities for cost savings from weapons standardisation.

EUROPE'S DEFENCE EFFORT

Within NATO, burden-sharing has been a continuing source of

TABLE 15.1 : EUROPE'S DEFENCE EFFORT, 1980

Nation	Total defence expenditure (US $ millions 1980 prices)	Defence as a percentage of GDP (%)	Defence Expenditure per capita (US $ 1980 prices)	Expenditure on defence equipment (US $ millions, 1980 prices)	Armed forces (military personnel) (000s)	Armed forces (military & civil) as percentage of total labour force (%)	Population (000s)	Area (square miles)	GDP (US $ millions 1979 prices)
Belgium	4,000	3.3	405	576	106	2.8	9,876	11,761	114,117
Denmark	1,600	2.4	311	292.8	33	1.6	5,134	16,629	65,674
France	26,200	4.1	487	3,877.6 (e)	575	3.1	53,665	211,208	580,333
Germany	26,700	3.3	437	3,951.6	490	2.5	61,034	95,976	768,540
Greece	2,100	5.6	218	394.8	186	6.2	9,517	50,944	38,124
Italy	8,700	2.4	153	1,522.5	500	2.4	57,110	116,304	337,863
Luxembourg	49	1.2	135	0.9	1	0.8	364	998	4,170
Netherlands	5,200	3.1	372	936	107	2.7	14,069	15,770	156,996
Norway	1,700	2.9	409	328.1	40	2.6	4,083	125,182	48,473
Portugal	800	3.6	83	48.8	88	2.3	9,971	35,553	21,517
Turkey	2,100	4.3	47	98.7	717	4.3	45,227	301,382	71,006
UK	26,300	5.1	470	6,627.6	330	2.2	55,952	94,227	401,064
NATO Europe	105,449	3.7	323	18,655.4	3175	2.8	326,002	1,075,954	2,608,877
NATO EC	100,449	4.1	378	18,179.8	2330	2.5	266,721	614,008	2,467,881
USA	140,500	5.6	632	28,521.5	2075	2.9	222,327	3,615,122	2,301,529

Notes:

1. France is a member of NATO without belonging to the integrated military structure. The relevant figures are indicative only and the equipment expenditure was estimated using German equipment data.

2. NATO EC data for total armed forces as a percentage of labour force is a median.

3. The data were not obtained from a single source: hence some small inconsistencies between aggregate and shares. Total defence expenditure and military spending per capita were estimated from Cmnd 8212, 1981, and the remaining figures were obtained from NATO 1981(b).

controversy, not only between Europe and the USA, but also among European members. Table 15.1 shows some of the main indicators of Europe's defence effort. Europe as a whole has a higher aggregate GDP and a larger population than the USA, but it spends less on defence measured in terms of total outlays, per capita expenditure, shares in GDP and equipment spending (i.e. Europe's effort is 51%-75% of the US figures): hence the American claim that it bears an 'unfair' share of the Alliance defence effort. Similarly, within Europe, the UK has often argued that its military contribution, as measured by shares of national output, should be brought more into line with that of its major European Allies, namely France and Germany. Inevitably, disputes arise about equitable sharing arrangements and the choice of an appropriate indicator of burdens. For example, in 1980, the UK was ranked second or third (and not first) in NATO Europe using most of the indicators shown in Table 15.1, with a much lower ranking for military manpower.

The economic theory of alliances predicts a positive association between the share of defence in total output and the size of a country's national income. Previous studies have found substantial support for this hypothesis (Kennedy, 1979). However, for 1980, the rank correlation coefficient between defence shares and national income was $R = 0.303$ for NATO; $R = 0.259$ for the European members of NATO; and $R = 0.383$ for the EC group of NATO countries, none of which were statistically significant. This lack of support for the positive model of alliances reflects the relatively high defence burdens of the smaller countries such as Greece and Turkey (a potential conflict situation) and the relatively low burden of some of the larger nations such as Canada, Germany and Italy (see Table 15.1). Predictably, references to defence burdens involve normative issues, with each member of the Alliance selecting an appropriate indicator showing that it is bearing its 'fair' share, or more. In principle, various burden-sharing criteria are available, including equality, payments related to benefits or the ability to pay (cf. progressive income taxes). Table 15.2 shows two examples for the EC. Each nation's share of defence in GDP might be related to its share of the Community's GDP or to the NATO cost-sharing formula. Alternatively, to maintain the 1980 level of Community military spending, each member of the EC might contribute the EC average share of defence, namely, 4.1 per cent (see Table 15.1). Or, some progressivity might be introduced by exempting poorer members such as Greece and Italy, with the remaining EC states each bearing a higher defence burden equivalent to 4.8% of GDP. Or, in

TABLE 15.2 : EC BURDEN SHARING CRITERIA, 1980

Country	Defence expenditure as proportion of EC defence (%)	National output as proportion of EC GDP (%)	National contributions assuming NATO cost sharing formula applied to EC (%)
Belgium	3.9	4.6	7.2
Denmark	1.6	2.7	4.8
France	25.9	23.5	19.8
Germany	26.5	31.1	34.3
Greece	2.1	1.6	1.1
Italy	8.6	13.7	10.3
Luxembourg	0.04	0.2	0.2
Netherlands	5.2	6.4	6.6
United Kingdom	26.1	16.3	15.7

Notes: 1. EC NATO only, excluding Eire.

2. NATO operates a cost-sharing formula for financing its common infrastructure. The contributions of the EC members have been extracted and rounded to 100% - i.e. assuming that the EC members would contribute to the NATO common infrastructure: (NATO, 1981(a) p.192, Table V).

addition to exempting Greece and Italy, a set of rising tax
bands could be introduced, with the UK contributing the
current average rate of 4.1% (i.e. D/GDP) and the richer
members of the Community paying higher rates. Although the
various criteria are illustrative rather than
comprehensive, they tend to offer similar conclusions,
particularly from a UK perspective. Generally, the
criteria indicate a rise in the defence burdens of most EC
members and a substantial reduction in Britain's
contribution. How might the EC contribute to re-arranging
burdens and 'improving' the efficiency of the European
defence effort, either as part of the Atlantic Alliance or
as the basis for protecting an independent Europe?

A ROLE FOR THE EC?

Positive theories of alliance predict that the members have
an incentive to cease providing the collective good before
the socially desirable output for the group has been
provided (since marginal costs for one nation exceed the
marginal benefits to that country - see Olson and
Zeckhauser, 1966). However, the model recognises that
worthwhile increases in the output of the collective good
can be achieved by substituting a union for an alliance. In
this way, the various parts of the union can be required to
contribute the amounts needed by their common interests. At
the EC level, the analysis implies that a European
political union is a means of achieving the optimal amount
of European defence. Ideally, the result would be each EC
member specialising in providing military forces and
producing weapons on the basis of its comparative
advantage.

In the absence of a complete political, economic,
monetary and defence union, the EC might contribute to
debates about burden-sharing by including military
expenditure in the assessment of each member's contribution
to the Community Budget. In other words, why not allow the
EC to treat defence forces and weapons industries in the
same way as agriculture? Here, the EC has a potential
comparative advantage in providing an existing organisation
which would minimise transactions costs between members who
have already accepted a degree of interdependence (i.e. via
international treaty). Also, the EC provides the obvious
basis for creating a European 'common market' in weapons
production and trade and, as a single entity, it would have
an advantage in bargaining with the USA within the context
of NATO. By including defence in negotiations about the

Community Budget, it is hoped that nations which are reluctant to contribute their 'fair' share to European defence would find themselves subject to other economic pressures involving their national interests (e.g. farm prices). Moreover, if EC members accepted specialisation by comparative advantage in their military forces and/or weapons industries, the Community Budget would provide an obvious mechanism for internationally-agreed financial transfers to compensate the potential losers (e.g. to re-allocate manpower from defence to civil goods). Attractive though such solutions appear, they are likely to be distorted by the unpredictable international bargaining process. The uncertainty of outcome partly results from the diversity of agents in each nation's political market, with national negotiators subject to pressure from voters, bureaucracies and interest groups. In addition, bargaining within a military alliance might be constrained by the desire to avoid exits! Nonetheless, it is not difficult to imagine the bargaining environment if the EC were to become involved in defence policy.

Controversy is inevitable as EC members are likely to differ on the 'proper' objectives of the Community's defence policy (e.g. independence from the USA; NATO membership; and the mix of nuclear and conventional forces). Debates might arise over the optimal level and composition of military expenditure for each EC member, and there are obvious criticisms of using normative criteria based on target shares of defence in GDP. Nations differ in their combinations of military and internal police forces, in their allocation of forces to European and NATO defence, and in the use of cheap conscripts. Moreover, it might be claimed that non-defence expenditures contribute to European integration and protection, such as overseas aid, diplomacy and collaborative projects (e.g. Concorde; European Space Agency). Governments might also be reluctant to sacrifice one of their supreme indicators of sovereignty, namely national defence. They are likely to vary in their willingness to pay for defence and might insist upon relating expenditure to the military budgets not of their allies, but to those of their potential enemies. Furthermore, emphasis on defence shares and expenditure are misleading since they measure inputs and not the output of defence: hence, they ignore the efficiency of each nation's military effort. And, whilst specialisation of forces within the EC is attractive on efficiency grounds, nations might not accept their allocated specialisations (assuming that a central allocative agency could be created). After all, each nation's political market contains bureaucracies and established interest groups whose income-earning prospects would probably be affected adversely by specialisation. Without a central defence decision-making agency to represent Community <u>collective</u> security, the EC's efforts to re-distribute military burdens would be unlikely to change the incentives for each member to select the combination of expenditure and forces which maximises its <u>national</u> benefits. Indeed, in the absence of a political union, it is likely that the EC members are exploiting and appropriating most of the worthwhile gains from voluntary collective action through their membership of a larger and specialist military alliance, namely NATO with (Eurogroup and the IEPG representing European interests).

THE UK'S CONTRIBUTION TO EUROPEAN DEFENCE

When negotiating contributions to the EC budget, the UK has every incentive to emphasise its European defence effort, as reflected in its independent nuclear deterrent, its allocation of conventional forces to the land and air defence of continental Europe and maritime forces for the protection of the Atlantic. Table 15.3 provides some orders of magnitude and shows the long-run trend towards a greater share of the UK's defence budget being allocated to European theatre ground forces, namely BAOR, and the corresponding reduction in its worldwide role as reflected in other army combat forces. In 1981-82, estimated UK expenditure on BAOR and the air units located in Germany was about £4,000m (including an allowance for overheads and support), or over 30% of the defence budget, excluding Britain's commitment of maritime forces to the NATO defence of the Atlantic.   Furthermore, the UK maintains a substantial independent defence R & D programme which could be offered as a potential contribution to creating an EC R & D effort capable of competing with the USA. From a UK perspective, there are attractions in offering to exchange its contribution to the defence of Europe for favourable treatment elsewhere in the EC budgetary arrangements (i.e. via an international treaty commitment to European defence). In addition, <u>within defence</u>, basic principles of substitution suggest that a given output can be maintained by different combinations of weapons, manpower and force structures. On this basis, the UK could offer to substitute nuclear for its conventional forces, as well as substituting air force units located in Germany and its Atlantic naval units for BAOR.

TABLE 15.3 : FUNCTIONAL ANALYSIS OF UK DEFENCE EXPENDITURE

Programmes		1966-67		1981-82	
		£m	%	£m	%
1.	Nuclear Strategic Forces	105	4.8	269	2.2
2.	Navy General Purpose Combat Forces	309	14.2	1663	13.5
3.	European Theatre Ground Forces:	264	12.1	1881	15.3
	(a) BOAR and Berlin	(169)	(7.9)	(1329)	(10.8)
	(b) Home Forces	(91)	(4.2)	(552)	(4.5)
4.	Other Army Combat Forces	121	5.5	44	0.003
5.	Air Force General Purpose Combat Forces	229	10.5)	2240)	18.2
6.	Air Mobility	135	6.2)	)	
7.	Reserve and Auxiliary Formations	37	1.7	253	2.1
8.	Research and Development	275	12.6	1676	13.6
9.	Training	188	8.6	1097	8.9
10.	Production and Repair Facilities in UK	153	7.0	814	6.6
11.	War and Contingency Stocks	38	1.7	326	2.6
12.	Other Support Functions	301	13.8	2081	16.9
13.	Miscellaneous Expenditure and Receipts	-38		-70	
14.	Special Materials	55	2.5		
	TOTAL	2172	100.0	12274	100.0

Notes: 1. Figures in brackets are sub-totals.

           2. The 1981-82 budget consisted of 12 programmes only - i.e. air
               mobility and special materials programmes were abolished.

Sources: Cmnd. 8212, 1981.

A EUROPEAN COMMON MARKET IN WEAPONS: THEORY AND REALITY

The EC is often criticised for 'wasteful duplication' of its weapons industries, with member countries purchasing defence equipment from their national suppliers. The result is a diversity of weapons operated by the European members of NATO, with each nation purchasing relatively small quantities. This lack of standardisation has implications for the size of defence budgets and Community industrial policy. One study estimated that within NATO, 'wasteful duplication' amongst the Europeans amounted to the whole of the European R & D expenditure plus 25% of its procurement outlays, giving a total development and production 'waste' of $4.4 billions (1975 US prices - see Callaghan, 1975, p.37). In addition, rising weapons costs mean that a given defence budget purchases smaller quantities of equipment. For example, the production cost of a strike aircraft exceeds £10m per unit (e.g. Tornado, 1981 prices) and, in real terms, it is probably four times as costly as its predecessor. Within each nation, the result is rising R & D costs per unit and fewer opportunities for scale economies in production: hence, government support for a small scale domestic weapons industry, typical of most European nations, is costly.   Table 15.1 shows that the equipment expenditure of each European nation is considerably below that of the USA, although a combined EC procurement agency would greatly reduce the scale differential. Nor would the potential benefits of an EC involvement in weapons policy be confined to defence. Weapons industries are amongst the technological leaders; they manufacture civil products (e.g. aerospace, electronics, nuclear power, tele-communications) and they are substantial employers. In other words, EC efforts to develop a common industrial and technology policy cannot ignore the defence industries (Layton, 1969; Klepsch, 1978). How might the EC improve the efficiency of its weapns industries and markets?

EC weapons industries are often far from competitive. They are usually characterised by monopolies, some of which are state-owned, together with government-created barriers to entry and exit, as well as the regulation of prices and profits: such market structures have considerable potential for inefficiency (Hartley and Watt, 1981). But weapons differ from civil products in that they are purchased by national governments rather than by large numbers of consumers. In other words, if European weapons markets are failing to work properly, this is likely to be the result of government policy and reflects a preferred outcome (i.e. policy could be changed). For example, an EC government

could promote weapons standardisation by purchasing another
member's equipment! Standard economic models would suggest
that the EC could improve the operation of its weapons
markets through policies designed to promote competition
and free trade between members, the aim being the creation
of a common market in defence equipment (as well as in
civil goods and services). To achieve this, the EC could
reduce entry barriers by requiring member states to allow
firms from partner countries to bid for defence contracts
on the same terms as national suppliers. Each nation would
have to circulate proposals for new weapons contracts to
other members, allowing all EC firms to submit competitive
bids.   The resulting market solution would be improved
efficiency in satisfying different national weapons
preferences, with successful firms expanding and operating
at a larger scale.   Evidence from the UK and the USA
suggests that the introduction of competitive bidding might
lead to cost savings of some 10% - 20% for a given output;
and such savings represent substantial magnitudes for major
projects such as the Tornado programme costing over
£10,000m at 1982 prices (Forsyth, 1980; Millward, 1981;
Savas, 1980). Also, a competitive solution would contribute
to weapons standardisation by allowing rival firms to
submit alternative bids showing the cost penalties of
national product differentiation. A nation would then
possess alternative cost yardsticks to assess whether its
specific national (differentiated) weapons requirements are
worthwhile.

Critics of the market approach claim that it would not
achieve the 'socially desirable' amount of weapons
standardisation (whatever this might mean - see Hartley,
1981b). It is argued that the development of an EC common
market in defence goods also requires the creation of a
Community procurement agency designed to eliminate
'wasteful duplication' and purchase large quantities of
each type of weapon on behalf of member governments. By
harmonising different national weapons requirements (not a
costless process), such a centralised procurement agency
would provide a volume of business for creating a European
defence industry able to operate at a large scale and so
compete with the USA. Indeed, it has been argued that the
creation of a single European procurement agency and a more
competitive European industry are necessary conditions for
the formation of a NATO free trade area in weapons (hence
promoting trade creation rather than trade diversion). But
this seems a strange argument since a NATO free trade area
can be created by eliminating tariffs and other state-
imposed barriers to international trade. Also, proposals

for an EC procurement agency imply a degree of political
union which is only likely to be attained in the long run!
Moreover, fascinating though it can be to apply standard
economic models of competition to European defence
industries, actual EC policy choices will be made in
political markets dominated by politicians, bureaucrats and
interest groups. The worry is that in such markets, any EC
policy towards defence industries will be a 'managed'
solution based on equity rather than efficiency criteria:
each partner will demand a fair share of the work. Indeed,
advocates of weapons standardisation aim to create 'healthy
and controlled competition', which would eliminate
'needless' duplication whilst achieving rationalisation,
specialisation, fairness and equity in all procurements
(Cornell, 1980, p.19).

Political markets have considerable potential for
distorting resource allocation. Within the EC, national
bureaucracies and domestic weapons contractors can combine
to persuade vote-sensitive governments that a competitive
procurement policy and a NATO free trade area in weapons
mean losing jobs, technology and 'valuable' foreign
exchange, as well as becoming 'too dependent' on foreigners
(e.g. USA). If complete independence is too costly,
political markets are likely to favour collaborative
arrangements with the international sharing of development
and/or production work. EC nations have been extensively
involved in collaborative programmes, ranging from such
joint ventures as the 3-nation Tornado strike aircraft to
the 4-nation European co-production programme for the
acquisition of the American F16 aircraft. Evidence from
these programmes indicates the cost penalties which
European nations are willing to pay to obtain the jobs,
technology and other benefits from undertaking some defence
work domestically. There are also a set of established
interest groups (e.g. Panavia, Euromissile, Airbus
Industrie) which cannot be ignored in formulating any EC
policy.

EUROPEAN EXPERIENCE WITH COLLABORATIVE WEAPONS PROJECTS

Joint projects represent one form of international
collaboration in which Europe has a comparative advantage.
Examples include the UK-French Concorde, Jaguar and
helicopter projects; the UK-German-Italian Tornado; and the
French-German Alpha Jet trainer. Joint ventures are
voluntary associations or clubs with 2 or more nations
sharing both R & D and production work. If, say 2

countries, each requiring 200 units of an aircraft, agreed to equal sharing, each partner would halve its R & D outlays and the doubling of output would reduce unit production costs by about 10%.[2] In this way, club membership enables a small group of nations to purchase a set of benefits which each would be unwilling to finance independently (e.g. weapons, technology, jobs). However, the diversity of benefits and end outputs associated with club membership provides opportunities for discretionary behaviour by politicians, bureaucrats and firms, as well as increasing the difficulties of any independent economic evaluation of joint projects. For example, it has been suggested that UK involvement in such joint projects as Concorde and Tornado was part of the 'entrance fee' to the EC as well as in investment in the creation of a European aerospace industry (Heath, 1979). Indeed, a study of European and US firms found that one of the major benefits claimed for joint projects is that they are much more difficult to cancel (Hartley, 1983)! Nor does it follow that joint projects will result in the cost savings indicated by the ideal case. There are substantial transactions costs in negotiating, monitoring and administering joint ventures; in addition, each partner might require modifications so raising development costs and reducing the production economies from a long-run of one type; partners will also demand their 'fair' share of each sector of new technology and production work. Consequently, development and production work on joint ventures will tend to be allocated on the basis of equity rather than comparative advantage (resulting in a collaboration premium or X-inefficiency). Interesting questions arise as to the magnitude of such inefficiencies, how far they are incorporated into a government's choice set and whether joint ventures are regarded as worthwhile.

In an interview study, European aerospace firms were unanimous that joint ventures involved higher R & D costs compared with a national project.[3] But, opinions differed on the magnitude of the collaboration premium. The estimated extra costs ranged from 'very little' to over 70%, with a median of 30%; although it was suggested that the collaboration premium continues to fall with experience (Hartley, 1982 and 1983). A substantial number of firms interviewed also believed that joint projects take longer to develop than a national programme, with estimates in the region of an extra 20% to more than 3 years. Delays result from the need to harmonise different operational requirements and to reach agreement between 2-3 nations and their associated companies. Beliefs about delays on joint

ventures can be further tested by comparing development
times on collaborative and national projects. An example is
shown in Table 15.4, which compares the 3-nation Tornado
with similar US aircraft and average development times.
Such comparisons are illustrative since there are the
inevitable difficulties of identifying equivalent projects,
holding constant other relevant variables (e.g. development
costs, urgency), and obtaining accurate data on the dates
of start and in-service. Even so, Tornado required
considerably longer than the average development time for
UK aircraft and it took twice as long to develop as the US
F111 and F15 aircraft. The TSR-2 is shown as an example of
a similar project which was developed by newly-formed
airframe and engine companies: hence, it is an example of
the problems associated with collaboration between <u>domestic</u>
firms.

An alternative form of collaboration embraces the
international sharing of production work through some form
of licensed or co-production, industrial collaboration or
offset arrangement. These involve the domestic manufacture
of another nation's weapons, either wholly or in part. An
example was the original General Dynamics F16 European co-
production contract with its 10%-40%-15% sharing
arrangement on an initial 998 aircraft programme.
Originally, the USA ordered 650 aircraft and the European
consortium of Belgium, Denmark, the Netherlands and Norway
ordered a further 348 units. The European consortium was
allocated manufacturing work on 10% of the initial US
order, plus 40% of their own order and 15% of export sales
to other countries (exports were estimated at 500 units).
In general, work sharing arrangements result in higher
costs than if the weapon had been purchased 'off-the-shelf'
from the main manufacturer. Interview evidence based on US
firms suggested that the typical cost penalties for any
form of shared production work are in the range of an extra
10% to 50%, with the lower bound estimate applying to
advanced economies and the higher figure to under-developed
nations. For the F16, it has been estimated that Europe
will pay at least an extra 20%-25% for their co-production
programme compared with purchasing directly from the USA.
Further costs result from the time required to transfer
technology to the licensed or co-producer. Typically, such
transfers require some 2-2½ years, although there can be
considerable variation depending on the nature of the
transfer and the experience of the recipients (e.g. it
might be a simple transfer and interpretation of drawings
compared with establishing an independent local production
facility). In return for such extra costs, the licensed

TABLE 15.4 : DEVELOPMENT TIMES

Project	Development Times:		
	Start to first Flight	First flight to service	TOTAL
Tornado	6yrs 1m.	5yrs 11m.	12yrs
TSR-2	5yrs 8m.	cancelled	
Average for UK military aircraft (1955–69)	4yrs 10m.	3yrs 6m.	8yrs 4m.
USA			
F1-11	2yrs 1m.	2yrs 5m.	4yrs 6m.
F15	3yrs 7m.	2yrs 4m.	5yrs 11m.
Average for US military aircraft (1955–69)	3yrs 7m.	2yrs 8m.	6yrs 3m.

Source: Elstub, 1969.

or co-producer claims to benefit through some saving on R & D outlays compared with an independent national venture and additional gains in the form of extra jobs and technology, particularly manufacturing technology (e.g. experience of working with new materials, precision machining and new management techniques – see Hartley, 1983, chp. 7). In the case of the F16 co-production programme, the European consortium presumably believed that the extra costs were worthwhile.

CONCLUSION: POLICY PROPOSALS

From a European perspective, the F16 co-production programme illustrates the diversity of preferences and

policy solutions amongst EC members. Clearly, the
consortium states preferred a US aircraft and its
associated co-production benefits for their domestic
weapons industries to purchasing a European aircraft or
involvement in a joint European venture. (e.g. 'conflicts
of interest' between the weapons industries of the
consortium and those of the major EC armaments producers).
This has implications for the development of any EC policy
towards weapons industries. Sovereign states will seek to
satisfy their defence preferences either independently or
through some form of voluntarily-agreed and mutually-
advantageous association with nations of their choice.
Accepting that preferences for weapons can differ, it might
be appropriate for the EC to aim at creating a 'common
market' in weapons through promoting an exchange of
information and removing the major entry barriers.
Certainly, there are considerable opportunities for
introducing competition into EC weapons markets. Nor would
such a proposal preclude a group of members voluntarily
forming a purchasing consortium to secure a more favourable
transaction either from EC suppliers or from the USA. Of
course, the creation of a competitive European weapons
market would involve structural adjustments and a reallocation of resources, especially manpower. Here, there
could be a further role for the EC through the use of the
Community Budget to compensate the potential losers from
any changes.

NOTES:

1.   Eurogroup consists of the European member governments
      within NATO and it seeks to co-ordinate and improve
      the effectiveness of the European contribution to the

      Alliance. The IEPG, which includes France, is the
      forum for promoting equipment co-operation among
      European allies.

2.   Assuming a 90% unit production cost curve for each
      doubling in cumulative output -i.e. derived from an
      80% labour learning curve (Hartley, 1983).

3.   Replies were based on 17 respondents.

Conclusion

16 Has Membership of the EC been a Disaster for Britain

Ali M. El-Agraa

The main emphasis in this book has been on Britain's role within the EC and most particularly on the way forward : the EC is seen as a dynamic institution capable of adapting itself to incorporate elements which would be beneficial to the UK without imposing undue constraints on her partners. Those who consider such an approach either over-optimistic or unjustifiable will no doubt prefer an analysis of the present state of affairs. Obviously, such an approach is not neglected here since a proper appreciation of the way forward depends on understanding the EC policies within a status quo context.

The analysis of EC policies as they stand at present indicates both costs and benefits for the UK from her membership of the EC. In spite of this there are a number of practising politicians as well as economists (although the majority are not true specialists in the field of international economic integration) who claim that Britain's membership of the EC has been an unmitigated disaster. The purpose of this concluding chapter is to bring together some directly relevant information with the aim of throwing light on this particular issue. Before doing so, however it should be stated that the claim could be based on economic, social and/or political grounds. Some political objections are that a united states of Western Europe is neither desirable nor necessary for promoting world stability, nor will it promote the socialist ideal desired by a certain faction of the British Labour Party. These are of course not mutually exclusive; indeed they could be mutually supporting. However, as no solid theoretical argument has been advanced in support of such contentions (there are theories in support of the contrary view), there is no justification for wasting valuable space discussing them. Moreover, it should be clear that world stability has not been promoted by only two or three dominant nations and that membership of the EC has not undermined the Italian Communist Party nor has it stopped France from electing a socialist government.

A further basis for objection on political grounds could

be the undesirable loss of sovereignty implied by EC
membership. This could be confronted directly : if by loss
of sovereignty is meant that 'all decisions will be made in
Brussels' as some senior British politicians have publicly
stated, it should be clear that such an assertion is either
based on ignorance of the facts (the EC decision-making
process allows for consultation with individual
governments, particularly those directly involved, in all
major decisions - see El-Agraa 1980a chapter 2 and Fennell
1979, chapter 3) or is deliberately made to mislead for
reasons that may be related to the social aspects discussed
below. If by loss of sovereignty is meant that Britain will
no longer be able to act independently in major decisions
such as exchange-rate policies, monetary control, defence,
etc. that would be an equally uninformed opinion since no
such absolute independence exists : member nations of the
OECD work very closely together in economic terms; the
Western Alliance dominates Western politics as well as
defence (NATO).

A final political objection is based on the allegation
that membership of the EC is making Britain 'go
continental'. If by this is meant that we have become more
continental and less international a thorough analysis
would be needed to demonstrate the validity of such an
interpretation particularly since a strong and united EC
can bring great weight to bear on decisions affecting the
world via EC external trade and political relations.

On the social basis it is argued that membership of the
EC makes us lose our insularity, an interpretation which
seems to suggest that all British citizens are naive
patriotic bigots.

Those being some possible political and social bases for
the statement that EC membership has been an unmitigated
disaster for Britain, it would seem sensible to concentrate
on the economic aspects.

THE ECONOMIC FACTS

Now, consider the economic facts:

(i) Table 16.1 gives the rate of growth of real income
between 1955 and 1978 for all members of the EC except for
Greece which is excluded from the major part of this
section since it joined the EC in 1981 and is still in the
transitional stage.   The table shows that during the
periods 1955-73 and 1973-81 the UK experienced the
slowest rate of growth of real income when compared with

either the rest of the individual members of the EC or the average for the whole of the EC Nine. However, of particular significance is the fact that the UK and Ireland are the only two countries within the EC to have had a <u>below average rate of fall</u> between the two periods.

(ii) Table 16.2 provides information on inflation between 1960 and 1979. The table clearly demonstrates that there has been an increase in the rate of inflation in all the specified members of the OECD. Indeed, rising inflation has been a world-wide phenomenon - see World Bank (1981, pp.134-35). However, the rate of change in Britain's inflation between 1960-70 and 1970-79 is below only that of Greece and Italy; it is also more than 4 times that of West Germany and more than twice that of the USA. Figure 16.1 gives a vivid indication of this within the EC context.

(iii) Information on monetary expansion in the EC Nine (both M_1 and 'real') during the period 1976-80 is given in Figure 16.2. The figure portrays the severe nature of the restrictive monetary policy which is being pursued by the UK. Indeed, monetary control in Britain is shown to be more strict than that of any of her eight EC partners - see figure 16.2(b). This information is confirmed in figure 16.3 which shows the high UK interest rates and their high rate of increase.

(iv) Table 16.3 gives recorded unemployment as a percentage of labour force for the EC Nine for 1973, 1979 and 1981 with projections for 1985. The picture that clearly emerges is that Britain's performance in 1973 and 1979 coincided with the average for the EC as a whole. However, that average performance had gone completely out of line by 1981 and is expected to deteriorate even further by 1985. The table also shows that higher unemployment has been a general phenomenon - indeed, it has been a global one. However, the UK seems to be significantly worse off in this respect than any of her EC partners.

(v) Table 16.4 gives the growth rates for output, employment and productivity in the EC as a whole for the periods 1955-65, 1965-73 and 1973-81. The table also provides the equivalent rates for 'manufacturing' and 'market services'. Although this table does not relate specifically to individual nations, it provides a general perspective since it clearly shows that output, employment and productivity <u>all</u> declined between the two latter periods for the 'whole' economy, 'manufacturing' and 'market services'.

(vi) Table 16.5 gives the growth rates for government and private expenditures between 1973 and 1981. While for the whole EC, government expenditure on 'goods and services' and on 'transfers' and 'privately financed expenditure' all increased respectively by 2.5, 4.7 and 0.3, the equivalent rates for the UK were respectively 0.6, 4.9 and minus 1.4. This shows that the UK was completely out of line in both government expenditure on 'goods and services' and 'privately-financed' expenditures.

(vii) Table 16.6 gives information comparing the UK with the EC as a whole in terms of : (i) net balances as a percentage of total income; (ii) growth rates of exports of 'manufactures', changes in the ratio of 'manufactured imports' to real income and changes in total real income; and (iii) ratio of 'manufactured exports' to 'manufactured imports'. A glance at the two columns headed 1965–73 and 1973–81 and a comparison with the average figures for the EC as a whole (given in brackets) clearly indicates that : the UK has become better off as a result of North Sea oil (an unfavourable oil balance turned favourable); the UK's current balance has swung from a deficit to a surplus; and the UK is faring relatively worse in terms of 'manufactures' and exports of 'manufactures'.

The information in this table should be supplemented by that given in the statistical appendix to chapter 1 (Tables 1.8 and 1.9) and Table 6.3. These clearly show that the UK's trade with the EC has increased by about a third since joining the EC, that UK exports of manufactures to the EC have shown a constant trend and that since 1980 the trade balance has been positive with both the EC and the rest of the world.

(viii) Finally, Table 16.7 gives changes in government deficits and net external borrowing for the EC between 1973 and 1981. The table shows that over this period the UK was the only member of the EC to reduce government deficit with the consequence of reduced borrowing or increased lending, i.e. the increased savings shown in column 1 and the falling government deficit shown in column 2 led to reduced government borrowing or increased lending.

INTERPRETATION OF THE FACTS

The economic facts clearly show that the slow rate of

growth of real income in the UK is a deep-seated problem and there is a voluminous literature supporting this interpretation - see, _inter alia_ Kaldor (1966) and Brown (1977 and 1979). In spite of this, the relative rate of decline has _slowed down_ since Britain joined the EC. Hence, if any inference can be made on this count alone, it must point to a favourable effect on the UK of EC membership.

This inference is reinforced if two other facts are taken into consideration : the stringent monetary control policies and the reductions in government deficits. These policies have coincided (with a lag!) with exceptionally high unemployment levels and rates of increase as well as lower productivity rates. Hence, irrespective of any positions taken by trade unions regarding wage and salary bargaining, it would seem that less stringent policies would have slackened the rate of fall in the rate of growth of real income even further. Of course, it is possible to argue that these policies have resulted in a slower rate of inflation even though inflation is still very high. Hence both 'Keynesians' and 'monetarists' have their joy and there is no need for dogmatic views on either side.

When added to this interpretation is the fact of Britain's increased trade with the EC, running at a surplus since 1980, at a time of severe world recession triggered off by the upheavals of the early 1970's, it becomes even more apparent that EC membership has been quite beneficial for the UK. Without that extra share of trade there would have resulted an 'appropriate' fall in UK output and employment since these extra exports could not have been sold in the rest of the world, particularly when the UK's overall share of the world market has declined.

Of course, there will be those who claim that all these benefits are due to North Sea oil. Such claims are simply nonsensical : countries export what they possess and others do not, and/or what they are good at producing, and/or what others simply have a taste for; and countries import what they have not and others have, and/or what they are not good at producing, and/or what foreign goods they have a taste for. It is fine to analyse the balance of payments by categories of commodities and factors but in the end the balance is an 'overall' one and has to be seen as such. Those who prefer to concentrate on certain categories will have to justify the implied lack of interrelationship : North Sea oil is good to have but if it can be obtained only at a very high cost (higher oil prices) that is tantamount to higher industrial costs particularly in times of lower productivity, hence leading to a worsening in the country's 'international competitive' position in

manufactures. In short, North Sea oil is a 'blessing' which
has price inflationary (world economy deflation)
consequences given the world circumstances that made its
extraction possible (unprecedentedly high prices), hence
the declining trend in UK exports of manufactures to the
rest of the world should not come as a surprise. Given
this, the constant, if not rising, trend in UK exports of
manufactures to the EC must necessarily reflect a benefit
for the UK from her EC membership.

COSTS AND BENEFITS

In order to evaluate the costs and benefits for the UK from
her membership of the EC one has to add the cost of the CAP
and receipts from the European Regional Development Fund
(ERDF). Given the qualifications stated in chapter 8, it
could be argued that the true cost of the CAP for the
period 1974–1981 was about £4000m. Over the period 1975–81,
receipts from the ERDF amounted to just under £800m. These
two elements together amount to a net loss of about
£3,200m. Against this loss one has to add the benefits of
increased trade with the EC. These cannot be expressed in
pounds unless some drastic assumptions are made – see
chapter 6. However, if one divides £3,200m. by the number
of years between 1974 and 1981 this results in £400m. per
annum, a figure just slightly more than half the 1980 trade
surplus with the EC. It is therefore either a very bold
analyst or a prejudiced and uninformed person who would
claim that these figures add up to a negative number of
pounds, i.e. losses for the UK due to her membership of the
EC, given the status quo.

CONCLUSIONS

Lest it be forgotten, it should be added that the
discussion in this chapter has not taken into consideration
any feasible reform of the CAP and the EC Budget. Nor has
account been taken of EC effects on factor movements and
foreign investments : the former has been insignificant and
is very difficult to quantify and the latter depends on
investors' motives (e.g. the Japanese investing in the UK
to gain access to the EC implying that if the UK were
outside the EC they would invest in other member nations).
    The basic economic facts given in this chapter clearly
show that Britain's economic problems are deep-seated and
that membership of the EC has helped to ease the situation.

Given this, it is implicit that some sort of 'international co-operation' is helpful for Britain and if this help persists it may, in the long term, assist in solving the real problem. However, this 'international cooperation' cannot be promoted outside the EC since if the UK were to leave the EC not only would she have to face the common external tariff in the context of a declining world market share but also forego the potential bargaining position with the outside world that a strong and united EC has. Moreover, the suggestion that the UK should rejoin EFTA to take advantage of the EC-EFTA free trade agreement in 'manufactures' is a nonsense since the EC is certainly not going to continue the arrangement when the UK leaves — recall that EFTA creation was instigated by the UK with the main object of counteracting any 'harmful effects of EC formation'. Hence those who conclude on the basis of these facts that the 'rationale for continued participation in the Community's common market has to be called in question' (Cambridge Economic Policy Review, vol. 7, no. 2, December 1981, p.45) have a lot to answer for. Also, those who claim that Britain's membership of the EC has been an unmitigated disaster will have to 'uncover' their hidden motives for saying so.

TABLE 16.1 : GROWTH OF REAL INCOME

	1955-73 (1)	1973-8 (2)	CHANGE (2) - (1)
Belgium	4.2	0.7	-3.5
Denmark	4.8	0.4	-4.4
France	5.4	1.9	-3.5
West Germany	5.1	1.7	-3.4
Ireland	4.2	1.6	-2.6
Italy	5.2	1.6	-3.6
Netherlands	4.7	1.1	-3.6
United Kingdom	3.0	0.2	-2.8
EC 9	4.6	1.3	-3.3

Source: Cambridge Economic Policy Review,
        vol. 7, no. 2, December, 1981.

TABLE 16.2 : AVERAGE ANNUAL RATE OF INFLATION (%)

	1960-70 (1)	1970-79 (2)	CHANGE (2) - (1)
Belgium*	3.6	8.1	+ 4.5
Denmark	5.5	9.8	+ 4.3
France	4.2	9.6	+ 5.4
West Germany	3.2	5.3	+ 2.1
Greece	3.2	14.1	+10.9
Ireland	5.2	14.6	+ 9.4
Italy	4.4	15.6	+11.2
Luxembourg*	3.6	8.1	+ 4.5
Netherlands	5.4	8.3	+ 2.9
United Kingdom	4.1	13.9	+ 9.8
Portugal	3.0	16.1	+13.1
Spain	8.2	15.9	+ 7.7
Canada	3.1	9.1	+ 6.0
Japan	4.9	8.2	+ 3.3
USA	2.8	6.9	+ 4.1

*   Belgium and Luxembourg are counted together as BLEU.
Source: World Development Report 1981, World Bank, Oxford University Press.

TABLE 16.3:   RECORDED UNEMPLOYMENT IN THE EC

(% OF LABOUR FORCE)

	1973	1979	1981	1985
Belgium	3	8	11	14(0.62)
Denmark	1	5	9	12(0.32)
France	2	6	8	12(2.29)
West Germany	1	3	5	7(1.78)
Ireland	6	8	11	15(0.18)
Italy	5	7	8	12(2.88)
Netherlands	2	4	8	12(0.64)
United Kingdom	2	5	10	16(4.09)
EC 9	2	5	8	12

Figures in brackets are in millions.

Source: Cambridge Economic Policy Review, vol. 7, no. 2, December, 1981.

TABLE 16.4 : GROWTH IN OUTPUT, EMPLOYMENT AND

PRODUCTIVITY IN THE EC (GROWTH RATES, % P.A.)

	1955-65 (1)	1965-73 (2)	1973-81 (3)	CHANGE (3)-(2)
Whole Economy				
Output	4.7	4.6	1.7	-2.9
Employment	0.6	0.2	-0.2	-0.4
Output per head	4.1	4.4	1.8	-2.6
Manufacturing				
Output	6.0	5.5	0.6	-4.9
Employment	1.0	0.0	-1.8	-1.8
Output per head	4.9	5.6	2.5	-3.1
Market Services				
Output	4.7	4.8	2.6	-2.2
Employment	1.5	1.3	1.1	-0.2
Output per head	3.2	3.5	1.5	-2.0

Source: Cambridge Economic Policy Review, vol. 7, no. 2, December, 1981.

TABLE 16.5 : GROWTH OF GOVERNMENT AND PRIVATE EXPENDITURE

(GROWTH RATES, % P.A.)

	Government Expenditure on Goods and Services	Government Expenditure on Transfers	Privately-financed Expenditure
Belgium	3.9	4.8	0.2
Denmark	3.6	6.0	- 2.3
France	3.3	5.5	0.5
West Germany	2.9	4.5	1.3
Ireland	4.0	4.7	2.0
Italy	3.2	3.1	0.8
Netherlands	2.3	5.9	0.1
United Kingdom	0.6	4.9	- 1.4
EC 9	2.5	4.7	0.3

Source: Cambridge Economic Policy Review, vol. 7, no. 2, December, 1981.

TABLE 16.6 : CHANGES IN THE BALANCE OF PAYMENTS OF UK
RELATING TO EC COUNTRIES, 1965 - 73

Changes in Net Balances as % of Total Income	1965 - 73	1973 - 81
Food and Raw Materials	+1.4 (+1.1)	+2.9 (+1.4)
Fuels	-0.5 (-0.4)	+2.7 (-2.9)
Manufactures	-3.8 (-0.4)	-1.1 (+0.5)
Services and Transfers	+1.3 (-0.5)	-1.4 (-0.4)
Current Balance	-1.6 (-0.2)	+3.1 (-1.4)

Growth rates, % p.a.		
Exports of Manufactures	4.9 (7.5)	1.6 (4.3)
Ratios of Manufactured Imports to Income	8.5 (4.5)	2.7 (3.3)
Total Real Income	2.9 (4.4)	0.2 (1.3)

	1965	1973
Ratio of Manufactured Exports to Manufactured Imports (%)	190 (144)	116 (128)

* Figures in brackets relate to the EC average.
Source: Cambridge Economic Policy Review, vol. 7, no. 2, December, 1981.

TABLE 16.7:   CHANGES IN GOVERNMENT DEFICITS AND

NET EXTERNAL BORROWING, 1973-81 *
(CHANGES IN NET BORROWING AS A PERCENTAGE OF TOTAL INCOME)

	Deterioration in Personal and Business Financial Balances	Increase in Government Deficit	Increase in Net External Borrowing
Belgium	2.9	6.6	9.5
Denmark	- 10.1	11.3	1.2
France	- 1.7	2.8	1.1
West Germany	- 1.6	5.0	3.4
Ireland	3.6	6.3	9.6
Italy	0.3	0.0	0.3
Netherlands	1.0	5.5	6.5
United Kingdom	- 2.0	- 1.0	- 3.0
EC 9 Average	- 1.3	2.7	1.4

* Positive figures indicate increased borrowing or reduced
  lending. A minus sign indicates a fall in borrowing or
  a rise in lending.
Source : Cambridge Economic Policy Review, vol. 7, no. 2, December, 1981.

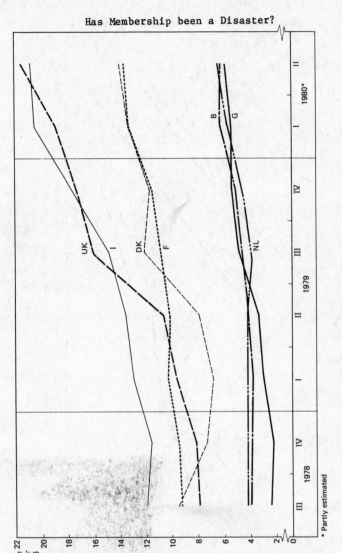

FIGURE 16.1 : INFLATION RATES IN EC COUNTRIES (Consumer
Prices, % change of previous year, quarterly averages)

Source : International Financial Statistics
         (Jan 1980) p.45; (Oct 1980) p.45.

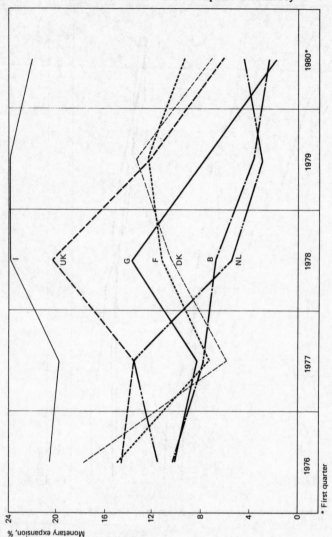

FIGURE 16.2(a) : MONETARY EXPANSION IN EC COUNTRIES (M$_1$)
(Change against previous year)

Source : International Financial Statistics
           (Aug 1980) pp.44-5

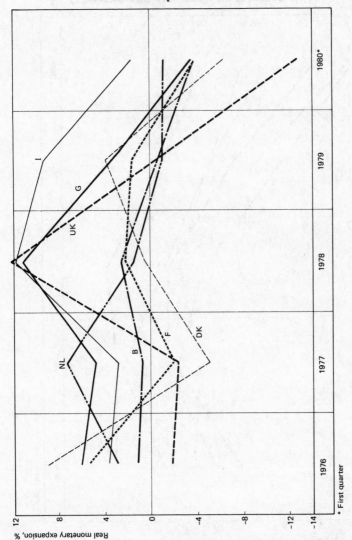

FIGURE 16.2(b) : REAL MONETARY EXPANSION IN EC COUNTRIES
(change against previous year)

Source : International Financial Statistics
(Aug 1980) pp.44-5

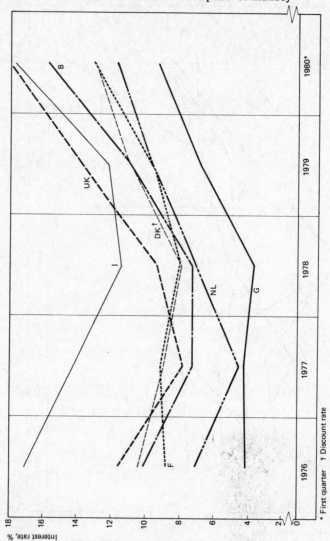

FIGURE 16.3(a) : MONETARY MARKET RATES IN EC COUNTRIES
(three months)

Source : International Financial Statistics
(Aug 1980) p.45; Weltwirtschaft, No. 1 (1980)
Table 5.

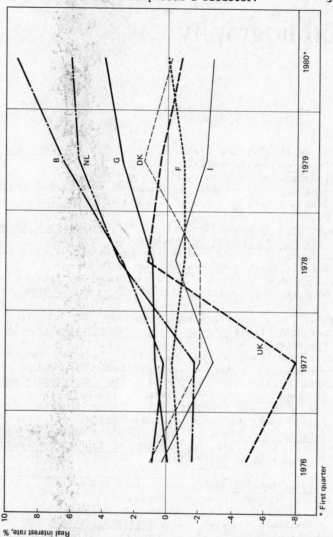

FIGURE 16.3(b) : REAL INTEREST RATES IN EC COUNTRIES (three
months money market rates minus rate of
consumer price increase; year over year

Source : International Financial Statistics
(Aug 1980) p.45; Weltwirtschaft, no. 1 (1980)
Table 5.

Bibliography

Abel Smith, B., and Townsend, P. (1965) The Poor and the Poorest (London: Bell).

All Saints Day Manifesto (1975) The Economist.

Armington, P.S. (1969) 'A theory of demand for products distinguished by place of production', IMF Staff Papers, March.

Armstrong, H., and Taylor, J. (1978) Regional Economic Policy and Its Analysis (Oxford:Philip Allan).

Armstrong, H. (1978) 'Community regional policy: a survey and critique', Regional Studies, vol. 12, no. 5.

Arndt, S.W. (1968) 'On discriminatory versus non-preferential tariff policies', Economic Journal, vol. 78.

Artis, M.J. (1981) 'From monetary to exchange rate targets', Banca Nazionale del Lavoro Quarterly Bulletin, September.

Artis, M.J., and Currie, D.A. (1981) 'Monetary targets and the exchange rate: a case for conditional targets', in W.A. Eltis, and P.J.N. Sinclair, The Money Supply and the Exchange Rate (Oxford University Press).

Artus, J.R., and Crockett, A.D. (1978) 'Floating exchange rates and the need for surveillance', Essays in International Trade (London: Allen and Unwin).

Balassa, B. (1962) The Theory of Economic Integration (London: Allen and Unwin).

Baldwin, R.E. (1971) Non-Tariff Distortions of International Trade (London: Allen and Unwin).

Ball, R.J., Burns, T., and Laury, J.S.E. (1977) 'The role of exchange rate changes in balance of payments adjustments – the UK case', Economic Journal, vol. 87.

Bank of International Settlements (1979) Annual Report 1978, Basle.

Bank of England (1982) Quarterly Bulletin, March.

Bayliss, B.T. (1980) 'Competition and industrial policy', chapter 6 of A.M. El-Agraa (ed.), The Economics of the European Community (Oxford: Philip Allan).

Begg, I., Cripps, F., and Ward, T. (1981) 'The European Community problems and prospects', Cambridge Economic

Policy Review, vol. 7, no. 2.

Berglas, E. (1979) 'Preferential trading theory – the commodity case', Journal of Political Economy, vol. 81.

Beveridge, W. (1940) Peace by Federation?, Federal Tract No. 1. (London: Federal Union).

Bhagwati, J.N. (1969) Trade, Tariffs and Growth (London: Weidenfeld and Nicholson).

Bhagwati, J.N. (1971) 'Customs unions and welfare improvement', Economic Journal, vol. 81.

Black, J., and Dunning, J.H. (eds) (12982) International Capital Movements (London: Macmillan).

Breton, A., and Scott, A. (1978) 'The assignment problem in federal structures', in M. S. Feldstein, and R.P. Inman (eds), The Economics of Public Services (London: Macmillan).

Brown, A.J. (1977) 'What is wrong with the British economy?', The University of Leeds review, vol. 20.

Brown, A.J. (1979) 'Inflation and the British sickness', Economic Journal, vol. 89.

Brown, A.J. (1980a) 'The transfer of resources', Chapter 7 of W. Wallace (ed.), Britain in Europe (London: Heinemann).

Brown, A.J. (1980b) 'Fiscal policy: II the Budget', Chapter 12 of A. M. El-Agraa (ed.), The Economics of the European Community (Oxford: Philip Allan).

Bryant, R.C. (1980) Money and Monetary Policy in Interdependent Nations (Washington, DC: The Brookings Institution).

Bundesbank (1979) Monthly Review, March.

Butt Philip, A. (1981) 'The harmonisation of industrial policy and practices', in C. Cosgrove Twitchett (ed.), Harmonisation in the EEC (London: Macmillan).

Callaghan, T. A. Jr. (1975) US-European Economic Cooperation in Military and Civil Technology, Centre for Strategic and International Studies (Georgetown University Press).

Cameron, G.C. (1974) 'Regional economic policy in the United Kingdom', in N. M. Hansen (ed.), Public Policy and Regional Economic Development (London: Saxon House).

Camps, M. (1964) Britain and the European Community 1955-63 (Oxford University Press).

Central Statistical Office (1981) Britain in the European Community, Reference Pamphlet 137 (London: HMSO).

Choufoer, J.H. (1982) 'Future of the European Energy Economy', address to the Conference of European Petroleum and Gas, Amsterdam.

Clark, C., Wilson, F., and Bradley, J. (1969) 'Industrial location and economic potential in Western Europe',

Regional Studies, vol. 3, no. 2.

Cmnd. 8212 (1981) _Statement on the Defence Estimates_, vol.1 (London: HMSO).

Coffey, P. (1979) _Economic Policies of the Common Market_ (London: Macmillan).

Cohen, B.J. (1981) 'The European Monetary System', _Essays in International Finance_, no. 142 (Princeton University).

Collier, P. (1979) 'The welfare effects of customs union: an anatomy', _Economic Journal_, vol. 89.

Collins, C.D.E. (1980) 'Social policy', Chapter 15 of A.M.El-Agraa (ed.), _The Economics of the European Community_ (Oxford: Philip Allan).

Commission of the European Communities (1961) _Memorandum on the General Lines of a Common Transport Policy_, Brussels.

Commission of the European Communities (1970a) 'Report to the Council and the Commission on the realisation by stages of economic and monetary union in the Community', _Bulletin of the European Communities_, Supplement, no. 11 (The Werner Report).

Commission of the European Communities (1970b) _Industrial Policy in the Community : Memorandum from the Commission to the Council_, Brussels.

Commission of the European Communities (1971a) 'Preliminary guidelines for a social policy', _Bulletin of the European Communities_, Supplement 2/71.

Commission of the European Communities (1971b) 'General regional aid systems', _Official Journal_, OJ C111 of 4.11.1971, Brussels.

Commission of the European Communities (1973a) 'Proposals for a Community regional policy', _Official Journal_, OJ C68 of 16.10.1973; and OJ C106 of 6.12.1973, Brussels.

Commission of the European Communities (1973b) _Programme of Action in the Field of Technological and Industrial Policy_, SEC(73)3824 final, Brussels, October.

Commission of the European Communities (1974) 'Social Action Programme', _Bulletin of the European Communities_, Supplement 2/74.

Commission of the European Communities (1975a) 'Report and proposal decision on a programme of action for the European aeronautical sector', _Bulletin of the European Communities_, Supplement 11/75.

Commission of the European Communities (1975b) 'Council Regulation (EEC) 724/75 of 18 March 1975 establishing a European Regional Development Fund', _Official Journal_, OJ L73 of 21.3.1975, Brussels.

Commission of the European Communities (1975c) _Report of_

the Study Group 'Economic and Monetary Union 1980', Brussels, March (The Marjolin Report).

Commission of the European Communities (1976a) Fifth Report on Competition - EEC, Brussels.

Commission of the European Communities (1976b) 'Action Programme in favour of migrant workers and their families', Bulletin of the European Communities, Supplement 3/76.

Commission of the European Communities (1977a) Guidelines for Community Regional Policy, COM(77)195 final, Brussels.

Commission of the European Communities (1977b) 'Regional concentration in the countries of the European Community', Regional Policy Series No. 4, Brussels.

Commission of the European Communities (1977c) Report of the Study Group on the Role of Public Finance in European Integration, 2 vols., Brussels, April (The MacDougall Report).

Commission of the European Communities (1978a) 'Council Decision of 16.10.1978 empowering the Commission to contract loans for the purpose of promoting investment in the Community', Official Journal, OJ L298 of 25.10.1978, Brussels.

Commission of the European Communities (1978b) Twelfth General Report of the Activities of the European Communities in 1978, Brussels.

Commission of the European Communities (1978c) 'Regional aid systems', Official Journal, OJ C31 of 3.2.1979, Brussels.

Commission of the European Communities (1978d) Report on Some Structural Aspects of Growth, Brussels.

Commission of the European Communities (1979a) 'Regional incentives in the European Community', Regional Policy Series No. 15, Brussels.

Commission of the European Communities (1979b) 'The Regional Development Programmes', Regional Policy Series No.17, Brussels.

Commission of the European Communities (1979c) 'Air Transport - a Community Approach', Bulletin of the European Communities, Supplement 5/79.

Commission of the European Communities (1980) La Suisse et la Communauté, Brussels.

Commission of the European Communities (1981a) Communication to the Council on the Categories of Infrastructure to which the ERDF may Contribute in the Various Regions aided by the Fund, COM(81)38 final, Brussels.

Commission of the European Communities (1981b) Principal

Regulations and Decisions of the Council of the European
Communities on Regional Policy, Luxembourg.

Commission of the European Communities (1981c) 'Proposal
for a Council Regulation amending Regulation (EEC) 724/75
establishing a European Regional Development Fund',
Official Journal, OJ C336 of 23.12.1981, Brussels.

Commission of the European Communities (1981d) New Regional
Policy Guidelines and Priorities, COM(81)152 final,
Brussels.

Commission of the European Communities (1981e)
'Deglomeration policies in the European Community — a
comparative study, Regional Policy Series No. 18,
Brussels.

Commission of the European Communities (1981f) 'Study of
the regional impact of the Common Agricultural Policy',
Regional Policy Series No. 21, Brussels.

Commission of the European Communities (1981g) 'Commission
recommendation of 9.10.1981 on transfrontier coordination
for regional development', Official Journal, OJ L321 of
10.11.81.

Commission of the European Communities (1981h) The Regions
of Europe : First Periodic Report on the Social and
Economic Situation in the Regions of the Community,
Luxembourg.

Commission of the European Communities (1981i) 'The
European Community's Transport Policy', Periodical 2/1981
(Brussels : EC Documentation).

Commission of the European Communities (1982a) Fifteenth
General Report of the Activities of the European
Communities in 1981, Brussels.

Commission of the European Communities (1982b) The
Agricultural Situation in the Community — 1981 Report,
Brussels.

Cooper, C.A., and Massell, B. F. (1965a) 'A new look at
customs union theory', Economic Journal, vol. 75.

Cooper, C.A., and Massell, B. F. (1965b) 'Towards a general
theory of customs unions in developing countries',
Journal of Political Economy, vol. 73.

Corden, W.M. (1972a) 'Economies of scale and customs union
theory', Journal of Political Economy, vol. 80.

Corden, W.M. (1972b) 'Monetary Integration', Essays in
International Finance, no. 93 (Princeton University).

Cornell, A.H. (1980) 'Collaboration in weapons and
equipment', NATO Review, October.

Cosgrove Twitchett, C. (ed.) (1981) Harmonisation in the
EEC (London: Macmillan).

Currey, W.B. (1939) The Case for Federal Union
(Harmondsworth: Penguin).

Dauphin, R. (1978) The Impact of Free Trade in Canada
(Ottawa : Economic Council of Canada).

Davies, G. (1982) 'The EMS : its achievements and
failures', Special Analysis (London: Simon and Coates).

Deacon, D. (1982) 'Competition policy in the Common Market:
its links with regional policy', Regional Studies vol.
16, no. 1.

De Grauwe, P. (1973) Monetary Interdependence and
International Monetary Reform (Westmead: Saxon House).

De Grauwe, P., and Peeters, T. (1979) 'The EMS, Europe and
the Dollar', The Banker, April.

de Vries, T. (1980) 'On the meaning and future of the EMS',
Essays in International Finance, no. 138 (Princeton
University).

Dixit, A. (1975) 'Welfare effects of tax and price
changes', Journal of Public Economics, vol. 4.

Dosser, D. (1973) British Taxation and the Common Market
(London: Knight).

Doyle, G. and Pearce, D.W. (1979) 'Incentive problems in
implementing low energy conservation scenarios in the
UK', Energy Policy, December.

Dunning, J.H., (1982) 'Explaining the internal direct
investment position of countries : towards a dynamic or
developmental approach', in J. Black and J.H. Dunning
(eds) International Capital Movements (London:
Macmillan).

Economic and Social Committee of the European Communities
(1977) EEC's Transport Problems with East European
Countries (Brussels: EC Commission).

Eeckhout, J-C. (1975) 'Towards a common European industrial
policy', Irish Banking Review, December.

El-Agraa, A.M. (1979a) 'Common markets in developing
countries', in J. K. Bowers (ed.), Inflation, Development
and Inegration : Essays in Honour of A. J. Brown (Leeds
University Press).

El-Agraa, A.M. (1979b) 'On tariff bargaining', Bulletin of
Economic Research, vol. 31.

El-Agraa, A.M. (ed.) (1980a) The Economics of the European
Community (Oxford: Philip Allan).

El-Agraa, A.M. (1980b) 'Fiscal policy : I tax
harmonisation', Chapter 11 of A.M.El-Agraa (ed.), The
Economics of the European Community (Oxford: Philip
Allan).

El-Agraa, A.M., and Goodrich P. S. (1980) 'Factor mobility
with specific reference to the accounting profession',
Chapter 16 of A. M. El-Agraa (ed.), The Economics of the
European Community (Oxford : Philip Allan).

El-Agraa A.M. (1981) 'Tariff bargaining: a correction',

Bulletin of Economic Research, vol. 33.

El-Agraa A.M. and Jones, A.J. (1981) *The Theory of Customs Unions* (Oxford: Philip Allan).

El-Agraa, A.M.(1982a) 'Professor Godley's proposition: a theoretical appraisal, *Leeds Discussion Papers*, no. 105.

El-Agraa, A.M.(1982b) 'Professor Godley's proposition: a macroeconomic appraisal', *Leeds Discussion Papers*, no. 113.

El-Agraa, A.M. (ed.) (1982c) *International Economic Integration* (London: Macmillan).

El-Agraa, A.M. (1982d) 'Comments On Rybczynski', in M. T. Sumner, and G. Zis (eds), *European Monetary Union* (London: Macmillan).

Elstub, St.J. (1969) *Productivity of the National Aircraft Effort* (London: HMSO).

Emerson, M. (1979) 'The European Monetary System in the broader setting of the Community's economic and political development', in P. H. Trezsie (ed.), *The European Monetary System : Its Promise and Prospects* (Washington, DC: Brookings Institution).

Ethier, W., and Bloomfield, A.J. (1975) 'Managing the managed float', *Essays in International Finance*, no. 122 (Princeton University).

European Investment Bank (1981) *Annual Report 1980*, Luxembourg.

European Parliament (1980) *European Taxation 1980/81* (Luxembourg: Energy Commissions).

Eurostat (1980) *Review 1970-1979* (Brussels: EC Commission).

Federal Reserve Bank of New York (1981) *Quarterly Review*, summer.

Fennell, R. (1980) *The Common Agricultural Policy of the European Community* (London : Granada).

Foot, M.D. (1981) 'Monetary targets; nature and record in the major economies', in B. Griffiths and G. Wood, *Monetary Targets* (London: Macmillan).

Forsyth, M. (1980) *Reservicing Britain* (London: Adam Smith Institute).

Forte, F. (1977) 'Principles for the assignment of public economic functions in a setting of multi-layer government', in Commission of the European Communities, *Report of the Study Group on the Role of Public Finance in European Integration*, vol. II (The MacDougall Report), Brussels.

Gehrels, F. (1956-7) 'Customs unions from a single country viewpoint', *Review of Economic Studies*, vol. 24.

George, K.D., and Joll, C. (eds) (1975) *Competition Policy in the United Kingdom and the European Economic Community*

(Cambridge University Press).

Godley, W., and Bacon, R. (1979) 'Policies of the EEC', Cambridge Economic Policy Review, vol. 1, no. 5.

Godley, W. (1980a) 'Britain and Europe', Cambridge Economic Policy Review, vol. 6., no. 1.

Godley, W. (1980b) 'The United Kingdom and the Community Budget', Chapter 4 of W. Wallace (ed.), Britain in Europe (London: Heinemann).

Godley, W. (1981) 'Interview with Wynne Godley', Marxism Today, July.

Gremmen, H., Pelkmans, J., and Mayes, D.G. (1981) 'The empirical measurement of static customs union effects', mimeograph, University of Tilburg, Netherlands.

Gwilliam, K.M. (1980a) 'Realism and the common transport policy of the EEC', in J.B. Polak, and J.B. van der Kemp (eds), Changes in the Field of Transport Studies (The Hague: Martinus Nijhoff).

Gwilliam, K.M. (1980b) 'The Common Transport Policy', Chapter 8 of A.M.El-Agraa (ed.), The Economics of the European Community (Oxford: Philip Allan).

Gwilliam, K.M., and Allport R.J. (1982) 'A medium term transport research strategy for the EEC - Part 1: context and issues', Transport Review, no. 3.

Haas, E.B. (1958 and 1968) The Uniting of Europe (London: Stevens and Sons).

Haas, E.B. (1967) 'The uniting of Europe and the uniting of Latin America', Journal of Common Market Studies, vol. 5.

Hansen, N.M. (1977) 'Border regions : a critique of spatial theory and a European case study', Annals of Regional Science, vol. X1, no. 1.

Hartley, K. (1981a) 'The aerospace industry : problems and policies', in H.W. de Jong (ed.), The Structure of European Industry (The Hague: Martinus Nijhoff).

Hartley, K. (1981b) 'The political economy of NATO defence procurement policies', in M. Edmonds (ed.), International Arms Procurement (New York : Pergamon Press).

Hartley, K. (1982) 'Defence and advanced technology', in D. Dosser, D. Gowland, and K. Hartley (eds), The Collaboration of Nations (Oxford: Martin Robertson).

Hartley, K. (1983) NATO Arms Cooperation : A Study in Economics and Politics (London: Allen and Unwin).

Hartley, K., and McLean, P. (1981) 'UK defence expenditure', Public Finance, vol. 36, no. 2.

Hartley, K., and Watt, P. (1981) 'Profits, regulation and the UK aerospace industry', Journal of Industrial Economics, vol. 29, June.

Heath, B.O. (1979) 'MRCA Tornado : achievement by international collaboration', Aeronautical Journal,

September.

Hellman, R. (1977) Gold, the Dollar and the European Currency Systems (New York: Praeger).

Hocking, R.D. (1980) 'Trade in motor cars between the major European producers', Economic Journal, vol. 90.

Hodges, M. (1977) 'Industrial policy : a directorate general in search of a role', in H. Wallace, W. Wallace and C. Webb (eds), Policy-Making in the European Communities (London: Wiley).

Holland, S. (1976a) The Regional Problem (London : Macmillan).

Holland, S. (1976b) Capital versus the Regions (London: Macmillan).

Holland, S. (1980) UnCommon Market : Capital, Class and Power in the European Community (London: Macmillan).

Holloway, J. (1981) Social Policy Harmonisation in the European Community (London: Gower).

Hu, Yao-Su (1979) 'German agricultural power : the impact on France and Britain', The World Today, vol. 35.

Hu, Yao-Su (1980) 'Energy Policy', Chapter 14 of A.M.El-Agraa (ed.), The Economics of the European Community (Oxford: Philip Allan).

Hughes, M. (1982) 'The consequences of the removal of exchange controls on portfolios and the flow of funds in the UK', Chapter 9 of D. C. Corner, and D. G. Mayes (eds), Modern Portfolio Theory and Financial Institutions (London: Macmillan).

Hull, C. (1979) 'The implications of direct elections for European Community regional policy', Journal of Common Market Studies, vol. 17, no. 4.

Ingram, J.C. (1973) 'The case for European monetary integration', Essays in International Finance, no. 98 (Princeton University).

International Monetary Fund (1974) Guidelines for Floating Exchange Rates (Washington: IMF).

International Monetary Fund (1979) 'The EMS', IMF Survey, Supplement.

International Energy Agency (1980) Energy Policies and Programmes of IEA Countries, 1979 Review (Paris: OECD).

Irving, R.W., and Fearne, H.A. (1975) Green Money and the Common Agricultural Policy (Ashford Kent: Centre for European Agricultural Studies, Wye College).

Jacquemin, A.P., and de Jong, H.W. (1977) European Industrial Organisation (London: Macmillan).

Jenkins, R. (1978) 'European Monetary Union', Lloyds Bank Review, January.

Jennings, W.I. (1940) A Federation for Western Europe (Cambridge University Press).

Johnson, H.G. (1965a) 'Optimal trade intervention in the presence of domestic distortions', in R.E. Baldwin et al. (eds), Trade, Growth and the Balance of Payments (Amsterdam: North-Holland).

Johnson, H.G. (1965b) 'An economic theory of protectionism, tariff bargaining and the formation of customs unions', Journal of Political Economy, vol. 73.

Johnson, H.G., and Krauss, M.B. (1973) 'Border taxes, border tax adjustments, comparative advantage and the balance of payments', in M. B. Krauss (ed.), The Economics of Integration (London: Allen and Unwin).

Johnson, H.G. (1974) 'Trade diverting customs unions : a comment', Economic Journal, vol. 81.

Jones, A.J. (1979) 'The theory of economic integration', in J.K.Bowers (ed.), Inflation, Development and Integration : Essays in Honour of A.J.Brown (Leeds University Press).

Jones, A.J. (1982) 'A macroeconomic framework for customs union theory', Leeds Discussion Papers, no. 112.

Josling, T, and Haris, W. (1976) 'Europe's Green Money', The Three Banks Review, March.

Josling, T. (1979) 'Agricultural Policy', Chapter 1 of P. Coffey (ed.), Economic Policies of the Common Market (London: Macmillan).

Kaldor, N. (1966) Causes of the Slow Rate of Economic Growth of the United Kingdom (Cambridge University Press).

Kennedy, G. (1979) Burden Sharing in NATO (London: Duckworth).

Klepsch, E. (1978) Report on European Armaments Procurement Cooperation, Working Document (Luxembourg: European Parliament).

Krause, L.B. (1968) European Economic Integration and the United States (Washington, D.C.: Brookings Institution).

Krauss, M.B. (1972) 'Recent developments in customs union theory:. an interpretative survey', Journal of Economic Literature, vol. 10.

Laury, J.S.E., Lewis, G.R., and Ormerod, P.A.(1978) Properties of macroeconomic models of the UK economy: a comparative study', National Institute Economic Review, no. 83..

Layton, C. (1969) European Advanced Technology (London: Allen and Unwin).

Lenior, R. (1974) Les Exclus : un Français sur Dix (Paris : Editions du Seuil).

Lindberg, L.N. (1963) The Political Dynamics of European Economic Integration (Stanford University Press).

Lindberg, L.N., and Scheingold, S.A. (1970) Europe's Would-

Be Policy Patterns of Change in the European Community (New Jersey: Prentice-Hall).

Lipgens, W. (1968) Europa-Föderationspläne der Widerstandsbewegungen 1940–45 (Munich: R. Oldenbourg Verlag for the Forschungsinstitut der Deutschen Gesellschaft für Auswärtige Politik).

Lipgens, W. (1982) A History of European Integration Vol. 1 1945–47: The Formation of the European Unity Movement (Oxford: The Clarendon Press).

Lipsey, R.G. (1957) 'The theory of customs unions, trade diversion and welfare', Economica, vol. 24.

Lipsey, R.G. (1960) 'The theory of customs unions: a general survey', Economic Journal, vol. 70.

Llewellyn, D.T. (1980) International Financial Integration: the Limits of Sovereignty (London: Macmillan

Llewellyn, D.T. (1982a) 'European monetary arrangements and the international monetary system', in M.T.Sumner, and G. Zis (eds), European Monetary Union (London: Macmillan).

Llewellyn, D.T. (1982b), Chapter 1 of D.T. Llewellyn, et al., Framework in UK Monetary Policy (London: Heinemann).

Lord Lothian (1939) The Ending of Armageddon (London : Federal Union). Reprinted in P. Ransome (ed.) (1943), Studies in Federal Planning (London: Macmillan).

MacDougall Report (1977), see Commission of the European Communities (1977c).

Machlup, F. (1977) A History of Thought on Economic Integration (London: Macmillan).

Mackay, R. W. G. (1940) Federal Europe (London: Michael Joseph).

Mackel, G. (1978) 'Green Money and the Common Agricultural Policy', National Westminster Bank Review, February.

MacLaren, D. (1981) 'Agricultural trade and the MCAs : a spatial equilibrium analysis', Journal of Agricultural Economics, vol. 32, no. 1.

MacLennan, M. C. (1979) 'Regional policy in a European framework', in D. MacLennan, and J. B. Parr, Regional Policy : Past Experience and New Directions (Oxford: Martin Robertson).

MacMahon, C. (1979) 'The long run implications of the EMS', in P. H. Trezise (ed.), The European Monetary System : Its Promise and Prospects (Washington, DC: The Brookings Institution).

Mansholt, S. (1969) Le Plan Mansholt (Brussels: EC Commission).

Marjolin Report (1975), see Commission of the European Communities (1975c).

Marquand, J. (1980) 'Measuring the effects and costs of

regional incentives', Government Economic Service Working Paper No. 32 (London: Department of Industry).

Maximova, M. (1971) Osnovnye Problemy Imperialisticheskoy Integratsii (Moscow: Mysl).

Mayes, D.G. (1976) 'The estimation of the effects of trading areas on trade', mimeograph, University of Exeter.

Mayes, D.G. (1978) 'The effects of economic integration on trade', Journal of Common Market Studies, vol. 17, no. 1.

Mayes, D.G. (1981) Applications of Econometrics (Englewood Cliffs: Prentice-Hall).

Mayes, D.G. (1982) 'The problems of the quantitative estimation of integration effects', in A.M. El-Agraa (ed.), International Economic Integration (London: Macmillan).

Maynard, G. (1978) 'Monetary interdependence and floating exchange rates', in G. Maynard, et al., Monetary Policies in Open Economies (Tilburg: SUERF).

McCrone, G. (1971) 'Regional policy in the European Community', in G. R. Denton (ed.), Economic Integration in Europe (London: Weidenfeld and Nicholson).

McLachlan, D.L., and Swann, D. (1967) Competition Policy in the European Community (Oxford University Press).

McMillan, J., and McCann, E. (1981) 'Welfare effects in customs unions', Economic Journal, vol. 91.

Meade, J.E. (1951) The Balance of Payments (Oxford University Press).

Meade, J.E., Liesner, H.H., and Wells, S.J. (1962) Case Studies in European Economic Union : the Mechanics of Integration (Oxford University Press).

Mesera, R.S. (1981) 'The first two years of the EMS: the exchange rate experience', Banca Nazionale del Lavoro Quarterly Review, September.

Midland Bank (1979) 'The dollar: an end to Benign Neglect?', Midland Bank Review, autumn.

Mikesell, R.F., and Goldstein, H.N. (1975) 'Rules for a floating rate regime', Essays in International Finance, no. 109 (Princeton University).

Millward, R. (1981) 'The performance of public and private ownership', in E. Roll (ed.), The Mixed Economy (London: Macmillan).

Monnet, J. (1955) Les Etats-Unis d'Europe ont Commencé (Paris: Robert Laffont).

Moore, B., and Rhodes, J. (1975) 'The economic and Exchequer implications of British regional economic policy', in J. Vaizey (ed.), Economic Sovereignty and Regional Policy, (London: Gill and Macmillan).

Morgan, A.D. (1980) 'The balance of payments and British

membership of the European Community', Chapter 3 of W. Wallace (ed.), Britain in Europe (London: Heinemann).

Morris, C.N. (1980a) 'The Common Agricultural Policy', Fiscal Studies, vol. 1, no. 2.

Morris, C.N. (1980b) 'The Common Agricultural Policy : sources and methods', Institute of Fiscal Studies Working Paper, No. 6.

Morris, C.N., and Dilnot, A.W. (1981) 'The distributional effects of the Common Agricultural Policy', Institute of Fiscal Studies Working Paper, no. 28.

Mundell, R.A. (1964) 'Tariff preferences and the terms of trade', Manchester School, vol. 32.

Musgrave, R.A., and P.B. (1976) Public Finance in Theory and Practice (New York: McGraw-Hill).

NATO (1981a) Facts and Figures, Information Service (Brussels).

NATO (1981b) Financial and Economic Data Relating to NATO Defence, Press Release (Brussels).

Needleman, L., and Scott, B. (1964) 'Regional problems and the location of industry policy on Britain', Urban Studies, no.12.

Neumark, F. (1963) Report of the Fiscal and Financial Committee (Brussels: EC Commission).

Nevin, E.T. (1980) 'Regional policy', Chapter 13 of A. M. El-Agraa (ed.), The Economics of The European Community (Oxford: Philip Allan).

Oates, W.E. (1972) Fiscal Federalism (London: Harcourt Brace).

OECD (1979) The Case of Positive Adjustment Policies : A Compendium of OECD Documents 1978/79 (Paris: OECD).

Olsen,M., and Zeckhauser, R. (1966) An Economic Theory of Alliances (Chicago: Rand McNally).

Oppenheimer, P.M. (1981) 'The economics of the EMS', in J. R. Sargent (ed.), Europe and the Dollar in World-Wide Disequilibrium (Netherlands: Sijthoff and Noordhoff).

Page, S.A.B. (1979) 'The management of international trade', National Institute Discussion Papers, No. 29.

Panić, M. (1982) 'Some longer term effects of short-run adjustment policies : behaviours of UK direct investment since the 1960s', in J. Black, and J.H. Dunning (eds), International Capital Movements (London: Macmillan).

Pauly, M.V. (1973) 'Income redistribution as a local public good', Journal of Public Economics, vol.2.

Peacock, A.T., and Wiseman, J. (1967) The Growth of Public Expenditure in the UK (London: Allen and Unwin).

Peacock, A.T. (1972) The Public Finance of Inter-Allied Defence Provision : Essays in honour of Antonio de Vito de Marco (Bari: Cacucci Editore).

Pearce, D.W., et al (1980) Low Energy Scenarios for the
United Kingdom : their Social, Economic, Political and
Environmental Implications, Report to the Energy
Technology Support Unit (London: Department of Energy).

Pearce, D.W. (1982) 'Conservation and UK energy strategy',
paper delivered to Joint Institution of Nuclear Engineers
and the British Nuclear Energy Society, Glasgow.

Pearce, D.W., and Westoby, R. (1982) 'Energy trends in the
United Kingdom: a fresh look', mimeograph, University of
Aberdeen, Department of Political Economy.

Petith, H.C. (1977) 'European integration and the terms of
trade', Economic Journal, vol. 87.

Pinder, J. (1982) 'Industrial Policy in Britain and the
European Community', Policy Studies, vol. 2, part 4,
April.

Prais, S.J. (1982) Productivity and Industrial Structure
(Cambridge University Press).

Presley, J.R., and Coffey, P. (1974) European Monetary
Integration (London : Macmillan).

Prest, A.R. (1972) 'Government revenue, the national income
and all that', in R.M.Bird, and J.G. Read, Modern Fiscal
Issues (Toronto University Press).

Prest, A.R. (1975) Public Finance in Theory and Practice
(London: Weidenfeld and Nicholson).

Prest, A.R. (1979) 'Fiscal Policy', Chapter 4 of P. Coffey
(ed.), Economic Policies of the Common Market
(London: Macmillan).

Pryce, R. (1962) The Political Future of the European
Community (London: Marshbank).

Riezman, R. (1979) 'A 3X3 model of customs unions', Journal
of International Economics, vol. 9.

Robbins, L. (1939) The Economic Causes of War (London:
Jonathan Cape).

Robbins, L. (1940) 'Economic aspects of federation', in
M. Chaning-Pearce (ed.), Federal Union (London:
Jonathan Cape). Reprinted in P. Ransome (ed.) (1943),
Studies in Federal Planning (London: Macmillan).

Robinson, P.W., Webb, T.R., and Townsend, M.A. (1979) 'The
influence of exchange rate changes on prices: a study of
18 industrial countries', Economica, February.

Rybczynski, T. (1982) 'Fiscal Policy under EMU', in
M.T. Sumner, and G. Zis (eds.), European Monetary Union
(London: Macmillan).

Sandler, T. (1977) 'Impurity of defence: an application to
the economics of Alliances', Kyklos, vol.30.

Savas, E.S. (1980) 'Comparative costs of public and private
enterprise in municipal services', in W. Baumol (ed.),
Public and Private Enterprise in a Mixed Economy (London:

Macmillan).

Scitovsky, T. (1958) Economic Theory and Western European Integration (London: Allen and Unwin).

Shanks, M. (1977) European Social Policy, Today and Tomorrow (Oxford: Pergamon Press).

Short, J. (1978) 'The regional distribution of public expenditure in Great Britain, 1969/70–1973/74', Regional Studies, vol. 12, no. 5.

Short, J. (1981) 'Public Expenditure and Taxation in the UK Regions (London: Gower).

Sumner, M.T., and Zis, G. (eds) (1982) European Monetary Union (London: Macmillan).

Swann, D. (1978) The Economics of the Common Market (London: Penguin).

Talbot, R.B. (1978) 'The European Community's regional fund', Progress in Planning, vol. 8, no. 3.

Thirlwall, A.P. (1979) 'The balance of payments constraint as an explanation of international growth rate differences', Banca Nazionale del Lavoro Quarterly Review, vol. 128.

Thirlwall, A.P. (1980) 'The Harrod trade multiplier and the importance of Export-Led growth', paper presented to the IMF in September.

Thirlwall, A.P. (1982) 'De-industrialisation in the United Kingdom', Lloyds Bank Review, no. 144, April.

Thirlwall, A.P., and Dixon, R.J. (1979) 'A model of Export-Led growth with a balance of payments constraint', in J. K. Bowers (ed.), Inflation, Development and Integration: Essays in Honour of A. J. Brown (University of Leeds Press).

Thurow, L.C. (1971) 'The income distribution as a public good', Quarterly Journal of Economics, vol. 85.

Thygesen, N. (1979) 'EMS : precursors, first steps and policy options', in R. Triffin (ed.), The EMS : the Emerging European Monetary System (Brussels: National Bank of Belgium).

Thygesen, N. (1981a) 'Are monetary policies and performance converging?', Banca Nazionale del Lavoro Quarterly Review, September.

Thygesen, N. (1981b) 'The EMS : an approximate implementation of the Crawling Peg?', in J. Williamson (ed.), Exchange Rate Rules (London: Macmillan).

Tinbergen, J. (1953) Report on Problems Raised by the Different Turnover Tax Systems Applied within the Common Market (The Tinbergen Report) (Brussels: European Coal and Steel Community).

Tinbergen, J. (1954) International Economic Integration (Amsterdam: Elsevier).

Trezise, P.H. (ed.) (1979) The European Monetary System :
Promise and Prospects (Washington, DC : The Brookings
Institution).
Van Doorn, J. (1975) 'European regional policy : an
evaluation of recent developments', Journal of Common
Market Studies, vol. 13, no. 3.
Van Ypersele, J. (1979) 'Operating principles and
procedures of the European Monetary System', in P. H.
Trezise (ed.), The European Monetary System : Promise and
Prospects (Washington, DC: The Brookings Institution).
Vaubel, R. (1978) Strategies for Currency Unification
(Tübingen: J. C. B. Mohr/Paul Siebeck).
Verdoorn, P.J., and Schwartz, A.N.R. (1972) 'Two
alternative estimates of the effects of EEC and EFTA on
the pattern of trade', European Economic Review, vol. 3.
Viner, J. (1950) The Customs Union Issue (New York:
Carnegie Endowment for International Peace).
Wallace, H., Wallace, W., and Webb, C. (eds) (1977) Policy-
Making in the European Communities (London: Wiley).
Webb, C. (1977) 'Variations on a theoretical theme', in
H. Wallace, W. Wallace, and C. Webb (eds), Policy-Making
in The European Communities (London: Wiley).
Wenban-Smith, G.C. (1981) 'A study of the movement of
productivity in individual industries in the United
Kingdom 1968-79', National Institute Economic Review, no.
3.
Werner Report (1970), see Commission of the European
Communities (1970a).
West, E.G. (1973) ' "Pure" versus "Operational" economics
in regional policy', in G. Hallet (ed.), Regional Policy
for Ever? (London: Institute of Economic Affairs).
Weyman-Jones, T. (1981) 'Energy independence', paper
presented to the Conference of the Association of
University Teachers of Economics, University of
Loughborough.
Whalley, J. (1979) 'Uniform domestic tax rates, trade
distortions and economic integration', Journal of Public
Economics, vol. 11.
Wheare, K.C. (1941) What Federal Government Is, Federal
Tract No. 4 (London : Macmillan). Reprinted in P.
Ransome (ed.) (1943), Studies in Federal Planning
(London: Macmillan).
Wilson, J.H. (1940) 'Economic aspects of Federalism', in
Federal Union Research Institute, First Annual Report
1939-40 (London), mimeographed, obtainable in the
British Library and Chatham House Library.
Wooten, B. (1941) Socialism and Federation; Federal Tract
No. 6 (London: Macmillan). Reprinted in P. Ransome (ed.)

(1943), <u>Studies in Federal Planning</u> (London: Macmillan).

World Bank (1981) <u>World Development Report</u> (Oxford University Press).

Yuill, D., and Allen, K. (1982) <u>European Regional Incentives - 1981</u>, Centre for the Study of Public Policy (University of Strathclyde Press).

Author Index

351

Subject Index